ELVIS DIED FOR SOMEBODY'S SINS BUT NOT MINE

A Lifetime's Collected Writing

BY MICK FARREN

with illustrations by Michael Robinson

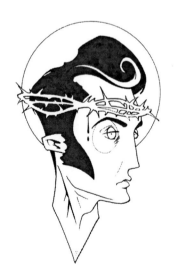

A HEADPRESS BOOK

ELVIS DIED FOR SOMEBODY'S SINS BUT NOT MINE

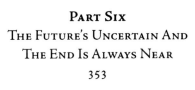

CONTENTS

Foreword

BY CHARLES SHAAR MURRAY

"… and then the greasy 'oodlums arrived!"

MICK FARREN IS A MAN OF MANY PARTS, AN IMPRESSIVE number of which are still working despite the natural wear-and-tear incurred by decades of research and recreation. First and foremost amongst these are brain and fingers, and this book is evidence of the excellent use he's made of those particular bits from 1967 (the so-called 'Summer Of Love') right up to the more-or-less present day.

At various points along that timeline highway from Young Punk to Grand Old Man Of The Counterculture, he's been—often simultaneously—a critic, commentator, novelist, journalist, polemicist, political activist, lyricist, rock performer, screenwriter, poet, memoirist, raconteur, life and soul of many parties and a member in better than good standing of the Most Honorable Association Of Cultural Infidels.

Or—to misquote an old Kris Kristofferson song memorably recorded by one of Mick's primo heroes, Johnny Cash—he's a poet, he's a prophet, he's a preacher and a pilgrim and a problem when he's stoned, he's a walking contradiction, partly truth and partly fiction…

And he's also—as you can discover for yourself by randomly opening this book at virtually any page—very sharp, very funny, very perceptive and possessed of a highly distinctive prose style: simultaneously hardboiled and self-deprecating. And it all comes from a POV as unique as said prose, which is: a rockin' way of knowledge. Farren is of the generation which encountered rock'n'roll when it was brand new, when white kids just hitting—or, to be more precise, getting hit by—puberty encountered something which had never previously existed in the world of American white-picket-fence conformity and English net-curtain-land suburbia. Something which was marketed as entertainment but which manifested, no matter how spuriously, as liberation. Hence the famous line, often heard during drug-fuelled downtime chitchat around the *NME* offices during Farren's now-celebrated seventies tenure there, about how everything was *boring*... "and then the greasy 'oodlums arrived!" Said greasy 'oodlum invasion was spearheaded by Elvis Presley—hence this book's title—rapidly followed by the likes of Little Richard, Jerry Lee Lewis, Chuck Berry, Gene Vincent, Eddie Cochran and many more. They transformed lives—where would John Lennon, Paul McCartney, Lord Keef Richards, Jimmy Page ad-bleedin'-infinitum have been without them?—but for Micky they kicked down not one wall but many, providing a point of entry into whole worlds of art, culture, literature and politics. As I said: a rockin' way of knowledge, of which he turned out to be both its Carlos Castaneda and its Don Juan. Just how rich and varied those worlds turned out to be can be gauged by the extraordinary breadth of scope covered by the present collection; just how deceptively rigorous the intellectual processes involved turned out to be can be likewise gauged by the consistency of worldview displayed in a collection of pieces addressing so many different topics and written over such an intimidating span of time.

I'm not going to recount Micky's life story: he's already done it himself, and quite brilliantly, in an autobiography entitled *Give The Anarchist A Cigarette*, and it comes very highly recommended indeed. All I'll tell you is this: Micky managed to attain a ranking position at the London forefront of High Hippie whilst having no truck whatsoever with the whimsy of Flower Power: no bells around *his* neck, mate! He favored mirrorshades, studded belts, motorcycle jackets and cowboy boots, all topped off with a spectacularly broken nose and one of the half-dozen best whiteboy 'fros in the known universe: part biker, part urban guerilla. He absolutely looked like a rock star, though whether he sounded like one is highly debatable: he fronted The Deviants, a band so heroically unlistenable (by 1967 standards, anyway) that their music made no sense whatsoever until the arrival of punk almost a decade later.

Within these pages you'll meet—via the occasional interviews—the likes of Frank Zappa, Johnny Cash, Chuck Berry and Gore Vidal, and steam open correspondence between the author and Pete Townshend. And, much more importantly, you're about to go one-on-one with a world-class raconteur. Micky once described his Doc40 blog in terms which apply at least as appropriately not only to the present collection but to any significant period of time spent in the actual real-life face-to-face presence of its author as his "Own Cosy Leather-Jacket Gin Joint, 24-Hour Global House Party And Medicine Show, offering sharp conversation, bad ideas, cheap stimulation, dirty concepts and links to revolution…"

Sounds like a good time to me. If this kind of mess-around seems like your cup of meat, then prepare your relaxant of choice, kick back and dig in. The greasy 'oodlums are at your door.

Charles Shaar Murray
London
February 2012

Preface

BY FELIX DENNIS

I'VE KNOW MICK FARREN FOR LONGER THAN YOU HAVE been alive, unless you are of our generation—or even older. I have fought the law with him, lectured him, listened to him, mocked him, shouted at him, shared barricades, women and whiskey with him, commissioned him, published him, laughed and cried with him, played poker with him in smoke-filled Soho rooms while the sun rose over defunct chimney pots and have called him long-distance in the wee-wee hours when there was nobody else I dared call who would understand why I needed to call anyone.

If I had to describe him in six words, they would be: talent, style, idiot savant, outlaw, friend. Not necessarily always in that order, but often enough to bet your next-to-last last dime on; unless you were in serious trouble, in which case the order could be relied upon to reverse itself swiftly. To the world at large he has played many roles: doorman, editor, journalist, rock star, rabble rouser, critic and commentator, charlatan, jester, impresario, gunslinging cross-dresser, icon, author, songwriter, poet and—perhaps strangest of all—the Godfather of Punk.

Of Farren's writing, I have nothing to say. It speaks for itself and has done for decades. I have lost count of the hours I have spent immersed in his fictional worlds. The range of his non-fictional subjects is remarkable, of course, and much of it was written to make money; but as Dr. Johnson once remarked: "no man but a blockhead ever wrote, except for money." Certainly, much of what Mick has written over the years in plays, columns, dialogues and poetry never earned him a cent. All the same, these select remnants have survived the test of time in fine fettle. As Jenny Fabian put it when reviewing *Give The Anarchist A Cigarette*, I found myself "laughing all the way to the memory bank' as I gulped down the originals and the wry commentary in the margins.

I will leave you with a short anecdote. We are in downtown Manhattan more than a quarter of a century ago and Mick is living in a small house near a river tunnel with his long-suffering second wife, Betsy. They have invited me and my aged mother (who is visiting New York during the Christmas holidays) over for a Boxing Day drink.

When we arrive, I find that Mick has laid out his entire robot collection over the living room floor. After my mother has been introduced and shepherded to a chair with an enormous gin martini in her hands, Mick begins the complex task of starting-up each robot. Pandemonium erupts as scores of androids begin their noisy mechanical march across rugs and floorboards while our hero solemnly intones rubbish from Chairman Mao's *Little Red Book*. The lights have been dimmed and torches are being waved in drunken circles as each robot crashes into whatever barrier it encounters. Eventually, only a single demented robot is left spinning in a crippled circle, its rocket booster flashing feebly.

The lights are switched back on. "Superb!" my mother cries. "Let us rescue them and do it all over again—but this time beginning on the top of the stairs!"

Mick raises an eyebrow. "Hmmm. Like mother, like son. We should have been introduced a long time ago, Dorothy!" So it is, that a ninety-three-year old lady who lives in leafy Warwickshire, still asks her son on a regular basis: "And how is that nice friend of yours? The one with the robots? Such an *intelligent* young man—and very talented, too."

I am told that the Danish sage, Søren Kierkegaard, is the author of one of my favorite maxims: "Life can only be understood backwards; but it must be lived forwards." That may be so, but it took Mick Farren to prove it to be true—to me, at least. Not as a philosophical construct, but as a glorious life's work.

Felix Dennis
Dorsington, Warwickshire
March 2012

Introduction

GHOST DANCER

THE ARMED ASSHOLE ENTERS THE WESTERN MOVIE barroom in his black hat and sinister gloves. Drinking bad whiskey, and lacking a better idea of fun, he fires bullets into the rough wood floor, close to the feet of an unarmed innocent bystander. His instruction is simple. "Dance." Faced with the choice of dancing or being shot in the foot, the innocent bystander dances, but—if he is not quite as innocent as the bully assumes—he will use all of his cunning to choreograph a performance that will confuse and ultimately confound the asshole in the black hat. Either that, or the innocent bystander will continue dancing until black hat runs out of ammunition. The other part of the trick is to learn to enjoy the dance, because the assholes have endless supplies of ammunition.

On July 16, 1945, in approximately the same geography as many Western movies, on White Sands Proving Ground, a flat stretch of empty desert some thirty-five miles southeast of Socorro New Mexico, human beings kindled one tiny piece of a sun right on the surface of Earth. The name of the exercise was Trinity, and it was a culminating recklessness from a species not noted for its caution. The small group of scientists and soldiers who watched, close up in the trenches, wore black protective goggles. To look the atom-flash in the eye was to be blinded.

Earlier in the process that led to Trinity, the possibility had been discussed that the atomic explosion might set the planet's atmosphere on fire, but the risk, it had been decided, was worth taking. These scientists who built and lit the fuse on the unearthly vaporizing flash called their work an "implosion-design plutonium bomb," and we have all seen the films. We are familiar with the images of the searing flash, the mesmerizing fireball, the hurricane of searing heat, and the final mushroom cloud towering into the desert sky. Most of us have heard the legend of how Robert Oppenheimer, as he gazed on the terrible bloom of his creation, was initially triumphant—"It works!"—but then reflectively quoted the Vedas. "I am become death, the destroyer of worlds."

The implosion-design plutonium bomb was planned as the ultimate weapon. At the inception of the Manhattan Project, that made Trinity possible, the intention was to obtain a nuclear bomb before the Germans, and force a conclusion of World War II. Then the Red Army took Berlin, Hitler shot himself, and Nazism collapsed. Instead of being shelved, Trinity assumed a life of its own. The White Sands test went ahead and, three weeks later, two Japanese cities were incinerated. In Hiroshima, a small child looked up and saw a lone silver airplane, high and tiny in the blue morning sky, and then, just seconds later, a burning biblical hell became reality and was visited on the city. Three days later, the same absolute destruction was repeated in Nagasaki. Human beings had the technology of their annihilation.

A century before Trinity, the land that became the historic test site was regularly traveled and hunted by the Navajo, Ute, Hopi and Pueblo. These Native Americans were not only from another century, but from another epoch. Their tribal cultures moved in nomadic patterns across plains and mountains, forests and deserts, in harmony rather than attempting to master or control their environment. These Indians had not invented the wheel, and their grasp of metalworking was rudimentary, but their spiritual belief system was deep and multidimensional. They lacked the European emphasis on the individual, or the motivation to ownership. The Native Americans didn't share the Europeans' need to build machines and invent industrial systems, or the near-viral European imperative to expand their territory. A hundred years before Trinity, however, it was already too late for their way of life. These supposedly advanced Europeans were firmly settled on the Eastern Seaboard and rapidly spreading west. The Indians must have seen, even during their first encounters, that these invaders were up to no good.

Maybe the Cherokee didn't instantly guess that mules and covered wagons would be followed by railroads and Gatling guns, but it must have been obvious—if only by the way the cowboys pissed in the creek—that, left unchecked, they would spread disease, destroy habitats, break food chains, and generally remake the mountains and prairies, all in the name of white, European, alcoholic capitalism with its materialism, mineral rights, and myopia. A society without any concept of private property was going to have problems with the rapaciousness of a people who would elevate greed (for want of a better word) to the status of a virtue, and eventually detonate atomic devices. As more and more settlers advanced on the Indian nations, the vibration of their coming could only have created a psychic chill, like persistent footfalls on a future grave.

At first, the Native American tribes retreated in front of the European advance, but, as it became clear that the white men would never be satisfied with the land they had already taken—and would never stop coming—many of the native peoples stood and fought. Under the leadership of Geronimo and Cochise, the Chiricahua Apache waged a protracted guerrilla war in Arizona and New Mexico, while further north, an alliance of the Lakota, Northern Cheyenne and Arapaho, led by Thatháŋka Íyotake—commonly known as Sitting Bull—defeated George Armstrong Custer and his murderous 7th Cavalry at the Little Big Horn (or, as the Lakota called it, the Battle of Greasy Grass Creek). Sadly this victory was only a short and temporary postponement of the inevitable. The Europeans were just too numerous and well armed. Outnumbered and outgunned, and unable to prevail in a culture clash in which victory was dictated by machinery and gunpowder, Native Americans retreated into mysticism and began to dance.

Wikipedia's entry on the Ghost Dance begins:

"The Ghost Dance was a religious movement incorporated into numerous Native American belief systems. The traditional ritual in the Ghost Dance, the circle dance, has been used

by many Native Americans since prehistoric times but was first performed 1889. The practice swept throughout much of the American West, quickly reaching areas of California and Oklahoma. As the Ghost Dance spread from its original source, Native American tribes synthesized selective aspects of the ritual with their own beliefs, often creating change in both the society that integrated it and the ritual itself. Perhaps the best-known facet of the Ghost Dance movement is the role it reportedly played in instigating the Wounded Knee massacre in 1890, which resulted in the deaths of at least 153 Lakota Sioux."

I was born fifty-three years after the massacre at Wounded Knee, and just twenty-two months before the Trinity nuclear test. For most of my childhood and all of my adult life, I lived with knowledge that, at any given moment, a great white light might burst from over the horizon, telling me, as my retina burned, that this was the absolute end of everything. Or, at least, the absolute end of civilization as we knew it, as they used to say in those 1950s, science fiction monster movies. This knowledge was probably what prompted me to wonder, more than once, if some special human instinct kicks in when everything we know and love is threatened with extinction. Do we all, down in some Jungian, universal mind, sense the possibility of annihilation and react accordingly?

I wish I had learned about Ghost Dancers in childhood, and that the story was taught in school of how a panic on the part of the notoriously corrupt Bureau of Indian Affairs started a chain of events that led to a confrontation between BIA reservation police and a crowd of angry Ghost Dancers, the murder of Sitting Bull, and finally the massacre at Wounded Knee Creek of 153 Lakota—mainly women and children—by that same 7th Cavalry by then armed with rapid-fire Hotchkiss guns. It wasn't, of course. Like any English schoolboy who liked to play cowboys and Indians, I was addicted to all the Western movies and TV shows in which Indians were guttural, backward savages with bows and arrows, and were slaughtered on a weekly basis by Errol Flynn, John Wayne, Richard Widmark, James Stewart, Kirk Douglas, and Randolph Scott down at the local cinema. I was a rebellious teenager long before I was able to cut loose from all the MGM and RKO folklore, and grasp that the celluloid, six-shooter, screen heroes in the big hats were, in a more accurate reality, little more than ethnic-cleansing death-squads, and that many had already been driven kill-crazy by the fire-power horrors of the Civil War.

I'm not exactly sure when I made the connection between the Ghost Dancers and my generation of rock'n'roll kids who wondered if they could change the world. Was it overweening vanity to compare the Native American Ghost Dances of the late nineteenth century with the social, political, and metaphysical movements in the second half of the twentieth? The parallel wholly depends on acceptance of the premise that both were generated by a sense of impending annihilation. Native Americans sensed the clear and present danger of their entire way of life being erased by a brutally alien culture. Twentieth century youth faced—and still face—the equally plain possibility of absolutely everything being fried to a crisp in a nuclear holocaust.

If anyone here in the twenty-first century doubts how much the threat of thermonuclear warfare infiltrated the awareness of those born during, or in the aftermath of World War II, I can only say you should have been there. In the decade or so after Hiroshima the pop images of nuclear destruction wholly permeated popular culture. In B-movies nuclear tests were responsible for giant insects and shrinking humans, not to mention the sixty-year career of Godzilla. Post-apocalyptic visions became a subgenre of science fiction. Hobbesian nightmares set vicious dog-eat-dog survivors in violent competition for the last remaining relics of the former civilization, and simple necessities like food, water, gasoline, or sexual partners were rare and desperately sought-after prizes. The nuclear spectre even wove its way into the Westerns. The fast-draw, gunfighter showdown on the main street at high noon was easily recognized as a full-blown analog for nuclear superpower confrontation and the doctrine of Mutually Assured Destruction (MAD).

In what was laughingly called the real world, American school children were drilled by a cartoon turtle named Bert in what to do if the bombs ever started falling. Bert the Turtle made it clear a nuclear attack could come at any time, and without warning. If the atom-flash came, the kids should instantly stop whatever they were doing, duck under a table, or crouch next to a wall and assume a fetal position while covering their heads with their hands. This was—according to both the turtle and the government of the United States—how one survived an atomic war.

Mercifully, other voices were being heard to counter the atomic disinformation of Bert the Turtle. They were those of Elvis Presley and Little Richard, and young people started dancing. The mode of the music had changed and the walls of the city seemed about to shake. Our dance began as nothing more than a feeling, the whisper of a promise that, on a deep unconscious level, change could be accomplished. The drums were beating and rock'n'roll was at the very heart of this new mood. It swelled with a massive potential power. In stoned moments we fancied it a fulcrum to move the world. Statements like these can now be ridiculed as clichés, but—back in the day—no-one questioned them. Rock music could light its own firestorm.

We knew that there had been other viral dance crazes, but rock'n'roll was different. It wasn't the Charleston or the jitterbug. It was much, much more. Bastard child of the blues, it could channel an undertow of anger along with a good time, and hinted at the same unfocused rebellion that smouldered from the films of Marlon Brando and James Dean. In *The Wild One*, when asked what he's rebelling against, Brando's Johnny Strabler had the succinct answer. "What have you got?" It was far snappier than explaining how the real target was the regimented, post-World War II consumer society, where everyone was expected to think and act alike, and totally distrust crazies on Harleys in black leather jackets.

In what liked to call itself the "free world," the brave new scenario for the second half of the twentieth century, was a glossy uniformity. More pleasant than Orwell but almost as totalitarian, it was the dream of corporate capitalism in the process of expanding from national to global. The drugs of choice would be nicotine and alcohol. Sexual repression and tightly managed media would be the tools of control. Populations would be racked and stacked, either in high rise housing projects, or endless, sprawling, car-culture suburbs. They would wear the same clothes, read the same magazines, go to the same movies, and watch the same inane television. The energy use would be catastrophic, but since those chickens wouldn't come home to roost for another fifty years, who gave a damn?

Meanwhile the MAD balancing acts between two superpowers hung poised—a frozen war—just to make sure no one grew too comfortable. First-time home-owners of the postwar American affluence dug holes in their back yards and installed steel and concrete fallout shelters. They stocked them with canned good, bottled water, and small arms, fully prepared to fight their neighbors with shot-guns over what was left. And they learned it all from the Hollywood post-nuke fantasies at the drive-in. Amid such repressed madness, Elvis Presley, his gold suit and slap-back echo, made total sense.

The early rock'n'roll that started a generation wondering about possible alternatives to what Henry Miller called the "air-conditioned nightmare" was, in terms of content, close to mindless. Gene Vincent's 'Be-Bop-A-Lula' was no revolutionary manifesto, and yet it contained such intense and malcontent echoes even the squares felt threatened. Like the BIA agents confronted by Ghost Dancers, those in charge of the twentieth century knew something was happening even if they didn't know what it was. The BBC banned the single, and restricted all rock'n'roll radio to a maximum of four or five hours a week—until forced to do otherwise by offshore pirate radio ships. If the first rock generation needed confirmation that the spirit of their new music went much deeper than its vinyl surface, they only needed to observe how quickly authorities decided rock was somehow subversive.

Rock'n'roll came under pressure. US Congressional hearings on payola in the record industry directly targeted it, and DJ Alan Freed was broken by Federal prosecutors. Rumors also circulated of secret deals cut between the government and Colonel Tom Parker so Elvis—tamed and emasculated—could be drafted into the Army without delay or bad publicity as an example to the nation's youth.

Elvis was drafted, Chuck Berry was jailed, and Little Richard went crazy and searched out Jesus, but rock continued to roll like the rising tide. Bob Dylan came out of the Woody Guthrie Midwest bringing a sense of literacy that was first political and later surreal and allegorical. He opened the doors for the music to become dangerously articulate. Nothing we could say could not be sung. Lennon/McCartney, Jagger/Richards, Pete Townshend, Neil Young—an army of singers and songwriters was suddenly on the march. A guitar army—a phrase coined by Jimi Hendrix and popularized and politicized by White Panther founder John Sinclair—was advancing on the entrenchments of power.

From *Mad* magazine to the Beat Generation, from New Wave cinema to *Dr. Strange*, from sexual freedom and the contraceptive pill, to the Free Speech Movement and Lenny Bruce, revolution appeared ready to roll on multiple fronts. The emperor's nakedness was going to be exposed. It was here we found the connection to the Ghost Dancers. Both the Ghost Dancers and the post-nuke generation looked for alternative solutions. After the destruction of their tribal economies, the Indians were supposed to turn into subservient replicas of the white man. They didn't. They danced into the spirit world and had to be stopped with Hotchkiss guns. In the aftermath of World War II and the dawn of the Atomic Age, the plans those in power had for us were more complicated but equally demeaning.

The more we explored alternatives—via psychedelic

drugs, constant marijuana, exercises of the mind, and strange encounters of the body, the better we knew it. We were dancing to the music and might also need to be stopped by Hotchkiss guns. In the underground press we were developing our own media. Some thought we followed blindly, like the children in Arthur C. Clarke's novel *Childhood's End* who do not speak and follow the alien spaceships. But we were not blind, and were also very noisy. We had our instructions and our communications. When Jim Morrison used the imperative "speak in secret alphabets" we knew exactly what he meant. In around 1968, some pundit claimed that rock'n'roll music was the primary source of information for a generation. I forget who made the claim but I wouldn't argue with it.

Popular culture was being reshaped from its youth up, subversively, organically, and wholly out of control, and, for a while, it seemed to be on a global level. Young people speaking their minds, but also out of those minds, and all too often revealing fatal weaknesses. Parts of the counterculture were corrupted by drug prohibition into a criminal drug-culture. Heroin became all too readily available in inner cities that were both volatile and vulnerable. Gentrified, Gordon Gekko squares took up cocaine, and the world became far too familiar with Colombian cartels and automatic weapons. On a different level—but with similar intent—the corporate music industry attempted to repackage rock'n'roll, harmlessly divorced from its original revolutionary posture. Fortunately the next generation down the timeline would retaliate by rekindling the rage with punk, and our new version of the Ghost Dance would continue to the sound of the Ramones, the Clash, and Patti Smith.

At around the same time, the original form of the underground press fell victim not only to harassment and lawsuits, but also the generally increasing diversity of media. Topics once covered in the underground mags and tabloids had publications of their own. Gay and women's issues were a perfect example. It started to seem as though the underground readership had been whittled down to bikers, stoners, and fans of the *Fabulous Furry Freak Brothers*. Corporate print was also borrowing the tricks of the underground on a wholesale scale, and even hiring previously underground writers. We writers allowed ourselves to be hired, but not without shame, angst, and alcohol. We could console ourselves that, by appearing in large circulation magazines, we could spread the good word far wider. Certainly the rebels who had been recruited as hired guns in the commercial music press were able to do a lot to promote punk to a much larger audience, but the sense of having sold out never quite went away, although our landlords and bartenders were happy that we were now receiving paychecks.

And so our Ghost Dance flowed, in and out like the tide, a cycle of cultural upheaval that would, in turn, be debased, defused, and distracted, clear to the end of the twentieth century and beyond. The Reagan/Thatcher era was a peak in greed and imperial certainty. Blair/Clinton produced at least the illusion of improvement, but then the Blair/Bush alliance took the world to new peaks in vicious absurdity. In the worst of these times, booze, opiates, or even a combination of the two, could look damned attractive. I freely admit, along with many of my peers, I sought whiskey-insulation when the good fight turned out to be no quick victory but a lifelong process. At times the Ghost Dance became little more than a drunken stumble. Some might say it stumbled and fell, but I prefer to think that we just shape-shifted and mutated to function in a world that was changing so fast that not even those in power could keep pace.

No one expected Soviet communism to lose its footing so fast, and collapse under the cost of the nuclear arms race. In the 1960s, while hippies danced in the West, the Red Guard marched in China, proving Chairman Mao was the only world leader who could recognize the global youth revolt and manipulate it to be a part of his own Cultural Revolution. But then, after Mao died in 1976, China moved towards a strange and barely understood hybrid of communism and capitalism that made it the world powerhouse of consumer manufacturing. These drastic changes in China also added to the frightening toll on the environment. The bill for the world's industrialization in the nineteenth and twentieth centuries was becoming due, and a new ideological gulf appeared between those who saw a planet headed for climate change and rapid ruin, and those who used their corporate profits to continue a polluting, depleting, business as usual. Rain forests burned and polar bears stood on melting iceflows, while oil companies mounted massive PR campaigns to convince us that nothing was wrong. The Ghost Dance became visible again as the Greens joined in.

Nothing, however, could match the changes in technology. One lesson the counterculture learned very quickly was that technology is ideologically neutral, and belongs to whoever uses it. The multinational corporations might have had financial and legal control over new and expanding media, but as choice increased, they were moved away from the narrow and easily managed uniformity that had been their original goal. Cable TV and the VCR freed viewers from the dictates of prime time and corporate schedules. We still watched the same shows, but we watched them when we damned well liked. By the mid to late 1980s, the personal computer became a crucial feature in an increasing number of homes, and then, just a few years later, the Internet blew into town, based—with extreme irony—on a military communications system for use after a nuclear war. Al Gore's information superhighway rolled up to the door bringing more traffic than was imagined a decade earlier. From fraud to voyeurism, from stockmarket analysis to conspiracy theory, from mail-order to metaphysics, from banking to *shibari* bondage, the web opened the gates of Eden on gardens of virtual delights, and global pop culture would never be the same again.

The humble telephone even horned in on the act, growing in power and sophistication until small handheld devices—smaller than the communicators on *Star Trek*—could access the Internet and much more besides. Mobile phones now come equipped with many multiples of the computer memory available to the entire Apollo moon project. Web pages mutated into blogsites. Social interaction sites like Facebook and MySpace became lasting fads, while Twitter reduced everything to 140 characters and put the collective attention span in clear and present jeopardy. But, at the same time, as global communication conglomerates did their worst, anyone with the price of their wares—both hard and soft—could play. A mind-bending mosaic could accommodate every shade of belief, illusion, or obsession. In one sector the net hosted the mathematics of string theory and the membranes of multiple realities, while in another bible-belt fundamentalists claimed that the universe was created 6,000 years ago and would end with the Rapture. All can join in, although all may not be either sane or honest.

The near-infinite digital dreamscape of the Internet made so much possible that it seemed like the perfect medium for the Ghost Dancer. Philosophical insurgents could appear out of nowhere, make their point and then vanish again without trace. This view may have been an overly romantic one. Many feared that the net, with its porn and its potential for piracy, would simply be yet another means of corporate manipulation of an already close to mindless popular culture. As early as 1999, Zack de la Rocha complained of "a monstrous pop culture that has a tendency to commodify and pacify everything." He failed to realize, however, that his own band, Rage Against The Machine, functioned and even succeeded at still plying the old rock'n'roll rebel trade within the monster, and that, via the net, pop culture could simultaneously encompass everything from the IWW to the CIA. A decade later Barack Obama's presidential campaign proved that not only was the Internet a forum for ideas, but could also maintain highly effective political pressure groups and fund raisers like *moveon.org*.

The freedom of expression afforded by the net isn't without a price. From Nigerian scam artists to identity theft, crime is rampant, but the path of freedom has always been down mean and shadowy streets, with a fair share of footpads and cut-purses. And even more complex dangers lurk in the electronics of the twenty-first century. Computers never forget and all too easily give up their data to total strangers. Data mining is both a major commercial industry, and a preoccupation of too many government agencies in too many countries, maybe only a shot away from the thought police. While rock stars who are brought down when their credit card numbers are found on the hard drives of kiddie porn operations deserve all they get, the rest of us, with no dark secrets to conceal—except maybe our opposition to the way our so-called leaders run things—have little to fear. There's simple safety in numbers; they can't round up all of us.

The Internet has brought us—we the people—unprecedented access to media of our own. It enables us to publish what we like, when we like, and how we like. Subversion is possible for anyone with a computer, and the blogosphere is now a serious challenge to the mainstream media. The oldtime underground print could never, even in its wildest dreams, imagine how bloggers can shoot holes in the official versions of events. Propaganda expects to be believed, but when it's examined and challenged from a million different points of view, its power and plausibility is diminished or removed.

The consternation of China's current rulers at the prospect of free speech on the Internet confirms the degree of threat it poses to any regime seeking to control the ideas and communications of its people. Despite the deals the Chinese government has cut to restrict services, Internet guerrillas, from sex bloggers to political dissidents, just keep on coming. The incalculable amounts of saved data and the quantum volume of communications make monitoring the Web wholly impossible. Ultimately the only solution would be to actually dismantle the technology, and that simply isn't going to happen unless it's replaced by a better mousetrap. Internet services are, of course, owned and operated by capitalist corporations, and although they may attempt to curtail content, other providers will happily step in with less limitations. The comment of V.I. Lenin still applies. "The Capitalists will sell us the rope with which we will hang them."

And let's not forget the computers themselves. As they grow more powerful and highly developed they may well have a say in the fate of humanity. Futurist Ray Kurzweil predicts that "machine intelligence will surpass that of humans around 2045." We can only hope that they won't emulate the fictional HAL 9000 and decide that humans are detrimental to the mission and eliminate us.

Yes, my friends, the Ghost Dance continues and will go on as long as the dancers know the end may be looming. Not only must the proliferation of nuclear weapons be halted and reversed, but global corporations—and whatever China has become—urgently need to wean themselves off policies of damage and destruction in the name of profits while we still have a habitable planet. Until that golden day dawns, we can only keep on dancing.

This book of memories is dedicated to all the guitar players and all the girls and the memory of all of those who have gone before and are not forgotten, and also all the cats who have been such vital companions.

16

Part One

A Rock'n'Roll Insurrection

althouth the media dubbed the warm months of 1967 the Summer of Love, it was—for me, at least—also a time of crystallizing anger. The spring of that epic year was when the rebel found his cause. The sense that all was very far from right with the world ceased to be idealistic and turned personal. I had worn a half-formed snarl of teenage resentment like a philosophic motorcycle jacket since I'd been old enough to buy my own cigarettes, but suddenly I began to feel threatened.

In the first months of 1967, authority in the United Kingdom decided to crack down what would later be defined as the rock'n'roll counterculture. Harold Wilson's labour government may have swept away the old conservative, blue-blood corruption after a prostitution scandal, and England had won the World Cup, but that didn't stop those in power coming to the conclusion that all of the sex, drugs and boogie that was being so readily embraced by the youth of the world was detrimental to the national well-being, and something drastically needed to be done about it.

On a celebrity level, drastic meant an attempt to jail the Rolling Stones and John Lennon. On the street, it meant police officers assuming the power to stop and search anyone whose looks they didn't like, or to break into homes on much the same pretext and ransack the contents. Rock shows and nightclubs were raided. Prominent counterculture figures like John (Hoppy) Hopkins, who had founded the underground newspaper *International Times* (*IT*) and UFO, London's first psychedelic club, were targeted for arrest and imprisonment. Previously the confrontation between the emerging drug-culture underground had, in most of our minds, been a naively abstract affair. We were dumb-as-a-post revolutionaries who made a nuisance of ourselves, hoping to goad those in authority to reevaluate their attitudes, but didn't for a moment expect them to retaliate by taking us down.

When I wasn't trying to pilot my band, the Deviants, into the air, I was hanging around at *IT* trying to make myself useful. The raids and busts—and also our own stupidity—however, were making me extremely angry, and everyone around me knew it. It was suggested that I write something, and, ever-game, I did exactly that. The result was a piece headlined "Pop In A Police State." It was gauche, clumsy, but definitely heartfelt. I had made a start and had this massive suspicion that maybe, with a lot of practice, I could actually do it. By this time the police raided the *IT* offices with the intent of closing the paper down, my anger had grown even more intense. But I had seen myself in print and there was no stopping after that.

POP IN A POLICE STATE

THERE WAS A TIME, LONG AGO, WHEN POP STARS WERE nice, albeit thick young men, who were safely kept in check by their managers. The worst things they were ever accused of were a certain preoccupation with death/sex/movements of their hips and possible homosexual relations with the aforesaid managers. But then there followed the less acceptable brigade; the long-haired ones, the ex-art students, the university drop-outs, the beatniks trying to make it rich. This lot knew a few things. They hadn't come straight from the building site or secondary modern, and they produced what was probably the most honest music since the start of the rock'n'roll era. They stomped all over the nice tidy flower bed where sex is spelt l-o-v-e when you do it, and in-ter-course when anybody else does.

Pete Townshend smashed 200 quid guitars almost nightly. Mick Jagger's body spelt "Fuck you if you don't know!" in semaphore. The Beatles refused to remain lovable mop-tops, and Bob Dylan wrote songs of violent anarchy. The kids of course loved this. If Townshend, Jagger etc., could get away with this stuff, then just maybe the revolution that began with James Dean and Elvis Presley was getting somewhere. The straight people muttered "tut tut" and masturbated secretly over pop star's Sunday paper "sexual exploits" and got their second hand kicks.

Then the *News of the World* decided to give the straight people a real orgy for a couple of weeks and so they ran a series called "Pop Stars and Drugs." Now, sex is okay, the straight people like to read about sex, but drugs—drugs are scary, they turn a man into an animal, they are bad for business—why, if the younger generation turned on they would be unmanageable.

On the day after the concluding piece in the *News of the World* series, Keith Richards' country house was raided and Richards, Mick Jagger and Robert Fraser were later charged under various drug laws. The same day specially trained narcotics squads (with specially trained dogs) were introduced into police forces in all parts of the country. The following week parties, clubs, cafés, and private homes were raided by the thousands, and dozens were charged with possessing drugs. Two weeks later *International Times* and Indica bookshop were also raided. Eight days after the *IT* raid, teenagers in the Harold Dog coffee bar were segregated, stripped naked, held in the dance hall, and subjected, one at a time, to the closest possible searches.

This became a pattern of action which was used at clubs all round the country. It suddenly became a crime to go dancing to pop groups, the penalty being to be searched in this obscene manner. The drug raids on private homes continued, and almost every pop group that went through London airport was subjected to a complete search. The Rolling Stones were searched yet again by French customs. Dave, Dee, etc., were frisked by Australian customs men, along with Eric Burdon, who was accused of corrupting the minds of Australia youth. Group vans all over England were pulled off the road and searched. Many groups were subjected to raids simply because they were a group, they were vulnerable, and they made good publicity for the police. Steve Marriot of the Small Faces was pulled in together with his girlfriend Chrissie Shrimpton.

The final move was made on the day Jagger, Richards and Fraser appeared in magistrates' court. Another Rolling Stone, Brian Jones was arrested and charged with possessing cannabis.

So where do you go from here? There are two alternatives. You can either be direct or you can be sneaky. Or you can do both, which is often the best alternative. Pop groups, of course, could turn themselves in en masse as users of narcotics. The country would become very dull, however. It is not nice in prison and not everyone fancies the Pete Seeger let's go-to-jail-for freedom bit. The real answer is to do the opposite. When they think you're hiding come into the open. When they want you in the open, hide.

It's a matter of bug the cops but don't get busted. Turn on before you go. You can't get busted in a club if you are not holding—only don't get too stoned to notice a plant. Make smoke-ins work. The cops are unable to bust 2,000 people; make sure, however, that the joints are not at the extreme edge of the crowd. Hide your address book as well as you stash. Be creative in concealing narcotics, only don't get too proud of your ingenuity and tell everyone. Spray aniseed on police dogs. Get high by other means. And best of all—if a cop touches you, instantly remove all your clothes to facilitate the search.

Let's make no mistake, we are living in something of a police state. The police are playing a game, the government is playing a game. There is no "Bring people into line Act," so the drugs and obscenity laws are being used as a stock prod. The leaders of the herd are being busted—Jagger, Jim Dine, Brian Jones, Donovan, the newspaper that you're right now reading, with the hope that if the flock are harassed a bit, the sheep will fall into panic and confusion, and eventually return to the straight and narrow. If this action doesn't succeed—and it doesn't seem to except in so far as it makes life uncomfortable—then the police state has two alternatives. It can either give up and withdraw or else really force the pressure, put curfews on under-twenty-fives, draft the non-straight into a labor corps. If this happens the only answer is street fighting. Maybe as Dick Gregory says: "It's gonna be a hard summer."

International Times, June 1967

ROCK: ENERGY FOR REVOLUTION

❑ Oh yes, those first writings were gauche, for sure, but as **IT** survived the attentions of the cops, and the newspaper continued to publish,

WHEN I FIRST BROUGHT HOME ELVIS PRESLEY AND Chuck Berry albums my parents didn't much like it. They made the mistake of thinking rock was a passing craze, like the hula-hoop, and not paying it too much attention.

Today rock is so powerful a force that it will draw a

MICK FARREN

quarter of a million people to sleep in the open for days on end. It can spread tolerance or invoke violence. It cannot be ignored. Rock brought a generation closer together, but in many ways it· alienated us from the previous one. Our parents have never really understood rock'n'roll. They never understood it because rock is not something you understand, it is something that you feel with your body, and you know.

Eldridge Cleaver of the Black Panthers called it "a generation of whites getting back into their bodies." Some of our parents could never feel what rock was about, but the energy made them uneasy. The unease that showed in the fifties when priests condemned Elvis Presley, and TV cut Billy Fury off from the waist down, and in the sixties with the BBC giving you Malcolm Roberts when you wanted Jefferson Airplane, and with the Rolling Stones being arrested, and in the seventies it shows as attempts to ban pop festivals.

In the last five years a large slice of the young generation has openly rejected the current values of society as morally indefensible. Many of the original hippies' Utopian dreams were destroyed as all manner of organizations and individuals found ways of profiting from the kids and their new lifestyle. A lot of people were eager to profit from peddling a product that was "underground," "psychedelic," or otherwise "groovy" although all but a few—a very few—were far from eager to use those profits in any way that benefitted the underground community. A commercial image of phony love began to replace any real ideology, while on the street the genuine love generation began to face the reality that, for the long-haired kids, there were few jobs and very few decent homes, that they were easy targets for violence and abuse, and that arrest and imprisonment were an ever present threat.

The use of amphetamines and barbiturates undermined the spirit of the community even more and the hard fact of real poverty became familiar as the hippie areas of large cities took on an increasing resemblance to long haired ghettos. Frank Zappa's vision of "the tide of

I stayed around for a while, and briefly acted as de facto editor. Did I know what I was doing? Not a clue, but it hung together. Somehow. Time passed and **Melody Maker**, then the leading weekly tabloid music paper, seemed to think I was something and offered me a double page spread to indulge in a rant. To be absolutely honest the **Melody Maker** piece was nothing more than standard rabble rousing of a kind that, by 1970, I was really all too adept. My excuse was that the editors of the music paper had commissioned it, and, since this wasn't the underground, I was being given a chance to rouse a whole new rabble. It came with a nice picture of me and I was inordinately pleased with myself.

hungry freaks" began to become a cold truth. The freaks began to realize that if no one else cared about them it was down to them to start the struggle for themselves. The black community had already got themselves together to demand some of that good living and it was with all this in mind that John Sinclair founded the White Panther Party in Detroit in 1968.

The problems of our society in Britain are different to those in the US. In many respects they are less extreme. Different methods are needed to solve them, and it will be pointless to attempt to carbon-copy the attitudes of American militants. Despite differences in British and American societies, both are based on the same principles and the same sickness is present in both. In the two cultures there is a definite need for a real alternative to the life-long, mind-twisting routine of office or factory. In both cultures a large minority does not get enough to eat, and have inadequate homes. Both cultures increasingly curtail personal freedom, both are overcrowded and in the process of poisoning the air, the water and the soil. Our parents are making only meager attempts to cure the sickness in their society and so, by default, the responsibility shifts to this generation.

One of the unique products of this generation is rock'n'roll. Our music is already a source of energy and a means of generating solidarity. The crowd at Woodstock had to treat "the next man as their brother" in order to survive the weekend. They had no choice. It could be that we won't either. In addition to energy, rock is also a major industry which earns millions every year. This money can either increase corporate dividends and artists' and promoters' personal fortunes, or it can be put to use so our generation can be put to use and can begin to try to solve the problems that are closing in on us. It is too late for any of us to cop out. There is now a choice none of us can ignore. If we carry on as we are now we are a frightened overcrowded species on a dying planet. If we work on the principle (and this is really the only revolutionary principle) that the man next to you really is your brother, and that you need each other in order to survive, then maybe, even at this late stage, we may still have a chance to become a free and dignified people.

Melody Maker, October 1970

FRAGMENTS OF JIM

I ONLY SAW JIM MORRISON PERFORM TWICE. EACH TIME, even off stage, he gave the appearance of a man who was acting in his own private movie. Maybe in some secluded place he was able to drop the self-inflicted role; or maybe the Morrison movie occupied all his waking hours. Certainly all the evidence shows that while there was even one person around to watch, Morrison performed.

The first time I saw him was at the Roundhouse. It was a Middle Earth all-night spectacular that starred the Doors and the Jefferson Airplane—the most ambitious project yet tackled by the flower punks and psychedelic wheeler-dealers who rode herd on what was laughingly called London's underground rock business. Invested with all the phony urgency of an event that aspired to be The Year's Biggest Bash, being there was mandatory. The love punks, the radical chic, the freak elite and the dealers jockeyed for position. Everyone wanted a space to see and be seen. And it was imperative that this space should be suited to, if not slightly above, each individual's station in the tribal pecking order.

It was clear right from the first that there was no love lost between the Doors and the Airplane. In the first wave of backstage gossip came the news that a high-level tactical battle had been raging all afternoon over who should go on first. The Doors had won—by a strategic use of stage setting. Their roadies had arranged the Doors' thirty-odd Acoustic speakers, meticulously matched black, Rexene-covered monoliths crowned by a baby-blue high frequency horn, like the pillars at a Nuremberg rally. The Airplane had little choice, with their somewhat ragbag assortment of hip-

Jim Morrison boasted that his preoccupations were "chaos and disorder," he seemed to be bent on making himself the incarnation of the rising angry rock'n'roll revolt. Many saw this endeavor as, at the very least, a mixed blessing. The question is still asked. Was Morrison a clown or a shaman, a cultural revolutionary, or just another entertainer with rebellion as his shtick? For many years after his death, his grave in Père Lachaise Cemetery in Paris—close to the magnificent edifice erected over the mortal remains of Oscar Wilde—had no permanent marker, but was littered with mawkish garbage strewn by the morbid, the second-hand sensation seekers and the hippie tourists. It seemed that was how rock treated one of its martyrs. Or maybe just Jim.

pie-built cabinets, to work around the Doors' fait accompli.

Both bands had obviously approached the London concert determined to emerge as The Stars. Both were already hippie legends and both were anxious to consolidate their reputations. The Airplane had brought the entire Joshua lightshow from the Fillmore West. The Doors simply had Jim.

In another time and another place, Jim Morrison might have been content to be Frank Sinatra or Elvis Presley. He had a pleasant, resonant voice, he was pretty and went down well with the girls. It was, however, 1967 and California. Dylan, the Beatles and the Rolling Stones had driven rock'n'roll a long way from innocent entertainment. The wide-eyed optimism of the flower power acid freaks was giving way to the confusion of abortive youth revolution. A year earlier, the fires in Watts had been clearly visible in the Hollywood hills. Young men were being dragged off to Vietnam to die in a scarcely understood war. Detroit had exploded. Paris would all but fall to an unhappy alliance of Stalinist unions and Maoist students, and in Chicago the police would prove the accuracy of the title "pig" by attacking unarmed yippies. Unrest was spreading across the Western world, and Morrison, if not offering himself, was ready made to be a symbol of the upheaval. If he didn't go out and seek the role, he certainly didn't resist. The Doors declared themselves "sexual politicians," and expressed an interest in "all that was anarchic, chaotic and against authority."

The Lizard King became totally identified with the romantic ideal of revolution and, in so doing, just about summed up the built-in contradictions that dogged the sixties.

Morrison's revolution was straight from the Hollywood mold. Hollywood is very fond of revolutionaries provided they don't disturb the status quo. In Hollywood, the rebel is not the individual who changes society. He is the one who gloriously destroys himself in the attempt. He is the noblest suicide of them all.

These were the postures that Morrison adopted. His revolution was acid, sex and death, a terminal revolt that ignored Lenin, Bukharin, or Chairman Mao. The highest act was dying rather than living for the new society. Of course Morrison wasn't taken seriously, in a political sense, on anything but the most comic book level. Few actually believed he would personally lead them into the Promised Land. What he did do was to present a rhetoric and mime that exactly typified the thoughtless, emotive confusion of the sixties youth revolt. Unlike Dylan, he didn't question. He saw no other point of view than that of the Lizard King's narrow perspective. On record, Morrison moved from the sinister Oedipal rage of 'The End' to the preposterous demands of 'When The Music's Over' and on to the premature victory shout in 'Five to One': "We're gonna win, we're taking over."

On stage, for the few moments Morrison had total control, objectivity was suspended. His histrionics, the prowling, the long insolent stares, the lunges at the mike, and the spasmodic twitching leaps, ceased to be absurd. He took the audience to a high place and showed them the countries of the earth laid out before them. On that level even authority took him semi-seriously, and joined in the act. He was arrested at LA airport after a disturbance on a plane. He was arrested at the Troubadour after forcing himself on stage and indulging in a drunken political harangue. In New Haven, Connecticut, he came closest to real confrontation (apart from the Miami incident). It was December. He came on stage in a brooding rage and told the audience how he had been maced, along with a girl in a backstage dressing room. "We started talking and we wanted some privacy and so we went into this little show room. We weren't doing anything. You know, just standing there talking, and then this little man in a little blue suit and a little blue cap came in there. He said 'Whatcha doin' there?' 'Nothin'. But he didn't go away, he stood there and then he reached round behind him and brought out this little black can of something. It looked like shaving cream. And then he sprayed it in my eyes. I was blinded for about thirty minutes."

As Morrison finished, three policemen walked onstage.

He held out the mike. One of them took it. The other two grabbed Morrison. Bill Siddons tried to separate them. As the police tried to drag him away, Morrison's sense of theatre didn't desert him. He fell into a crucifixion pose. Photographers in the pit were quick to respond. The photo became an icon of the rock revolution. Morrison was charged with causing a breach of the peace, giving an indecent and immoral exhibition and resisting arrest. Fights started to break out between audience and cops.

Of course, when you got down to it, it was just another mutual fantasy.

At best, Morrison's revolution was just a bunch of crazy kids being urged on by a drunken clown in a leather suit.

Sections of a longer, two-part story that appeared
in *New Musical Express*, September 1975

CHE IS DEAD

❑ The short note I wrote marking the death of Che Guevara in October of 1967 was never published. Within days it would be clear that the man and the image would instantly become a global rock icon, just like Jim Morrison, but also totally unlike Jim Morrison.

CHE GUEVARA WAS MURDERED IN A SCHOOLHOUSE IN the tiny Bolivian hamlet of La Higuera. His killer was Mario Teran, a Sergeant in the Bolivian Rangers Special Forces, who had drawn a short straw after, according to legend, his superiors—including Felix Rodriguez, the CIA agent who had coordinated Che's capture—proved too chickenshit to do the deed themselves. On the first attempt, it's alleged that Teran so botched the job that the badly wounded Guevara screamed "Shoot, coward, you are only going to kill a man." After the killing, Rodriguez the spook stole Che's Rolex watch, his only possession of any value, as a souvenir. Then his body was lashed to the landing skids of a helicopter and flown to neighboring Vallegrande where it was laid out in the local hospital and displayed to the press like a trophy in a big game hunt.

Not previously published

MICK FARREN

GARBAGE

We got garbage
We got garbage
Why don't you try some?
Try some garbage?
Garbage can make you feel so good
Make you feel like you think you should
Garbage can make you feel so large
Put two cars in your garage
(Can't you feel it?)
Why don't you pick it up?
(Can't you feel it?)
Why don't you hold it in your hand?
(Can't you feel it?)
Why don't you fondle it?
(Can't you feel it?)

❑ The reality couldn't be avoided that, in my own revolution, in those early days, I remained an absolute beginner. I wasn't Che and I wasn't W. H. Auden; but I also wasn't Joseph Goebbels and I wasn't J. Walter Thompson. But maybe—both in print and rock'n'roll—I was learning to be a propagandist.

Written for the Deviants' album *PTOOFF!*, 1968

BACKLASH

IF THEY HAD BEEN PREACHING BLOODY REVOLT THE HIP-pies could not have received a more hostile response from the rest of society. As the hippies grew their hair and worked out their own styles of dress, the man in the street began to react to their presence with every kind of abuse he could think of. They were filthy, they stank, they were perverts, cowards, the men were queer, the women were whores. Long haired kids were fired from their jobs (to many this was no great loss), denied social security, refused service in bars and restaurants. The attempt at a totally peaceful way of life made the hippie fair game for every Saturday night drunk with an itch to beat someone up.

The redneck was not alone in his hostility to the drop-out. Media and business adopted the familiar dual role of on one hand attempting to sell the hippies as much gar-bage as they could handle, while on the other using them,

❑ Unfortunately the opposition was also learning…

like blacks or Jews, as a bogeyman to keep the rest of society in line. At the same time as love beads, peace badges, hippie bells, rock records, kaftans and psychedelic posters flooded the stores, sections of media and marketing made many a fast buck by running "Beautify America—get a haircut" campaigns and publishing anti-hippie books and magazines with sentiments like—"The public parks must be cleared of this filth. Hippies must be made to clean up their garbage and then thrown in jail."

From the book *Watch Out Kids*, 1972

YOU'VE GOT TO HOLD ON

❏ The conflict swayed back and forth. I was also learning that rock'n'roll was a highly effective outlet for my rage against the repressive machine, and it turned out to be a lesson that would hold me in good stance not only at the chaotic end of the turbulent 1960s, but also a decade later, when the same rock'n'roll anger became even more steel-edged, jailhouse-tattooed, and naked.

The night burned with terror in my eyes
My foes leap at my throat in their surprise
The words rang at the start of dawn's decay
The truth sang its song at the break of day

It's a long time coming but you gotta hold on
It's a long time coming but the past is gone

Head reeled at screaming waves of doubt
As the worms turned to make as though to shut me out
But the white light of the world was at my side
And they fell back driven by the surging tide

Chains broke as the words of youth we sang
And the day broke as into the street we ran
The lords saw their need had gone for good
As we saw things the way the poet said we would

It's a long time coming but you gotta hold on
It's a long time coming but the past is gone

Written and recorded for the Deviants'
album *Disposable*, 1969

MICK FARREN

WHY CAN'T YOU BE TRUE?

CHUCK (CRAZY LEGS) BERRY, TOP TEN CONTENDER FOR the title "King of Rock'n'roll," has been referred to as the greatest black folk poet of the twentieth century. The first shock when you meet him is that he sure doesn't act that way. Folk maybe, but poet? Hardly. In fact, there's an old fashioned cockney word for the general attitude that ol' Chuck seems to take in the face of the press. The word is leery.

For those who aren't familiar with it, it usually indicates one who employs a mixture of evasion and cunning that appears to afford him a great deal of smug amusement and self-gratification. This may be being a little hard on Chuck, but in terms of talking directly to the media he is by no means Mr. Communication. Admittedly the corner of the fairly crowded bar of a large international hotel is not the best place to get an interview subject to relax, get loose and open up. You do get the impression, however, that Chuck Berry wouldn't open up to an interviewer if you were both drinking 100-year-old brandy in a private room in the most expensive whorehouse in town, and *NME* was picking up the tab.

Even across a crowded bar, you can't miss Chuck Berry. There's no mistaking the moustache, the haircut and the sideburns. Even if he wasn't wearing a blue striped denim Levi's suit among all the lightweight worsteds and double knits. There's no one else with the same flat-footed, slightly stooped walk that, on stage, evolves easily into the legendary duck walk. After sitting down and shaking hands Chuck came out with his very first ploy. He tapped the tape recorder with an exceedingly long forefinger, grinned impishly and shook his head.

"Uh-uh. Use the pencil and paper."

"You don't like tape recorders?"

Again Chuck shook his head. It was not an auspicious start to any baring of the Berry soul. Hardly even to Chuck's advantage, unless, of course, he's paranoid about people bootlegging the sound of his voice. I couldn't think

❑ I once met Jim Morrison in a London pub on Kings Road called the Chelsea Potter in the company of a mutual friend. Jim was drunk, and pretty much everything I expected. Chuck Berry was quite the opposite. The given intelligence is that it's usually a mistake to meet your idols because the odds are that you're going to be disappointed. In the case of Chuck Berry it was all true and then some. I was sitting across a table from the man who had done more than most to make me and Keith Richards—and hundreds upon hundreds of others—what we were that day, and—even cutting Chuck a break for having led a hard life—I wished I was someplace else.

of any other reason for the game. "You realise that you're more likely to get misquoted this way?"

Chuck didn't appear to care. It looked like it wasn't going to be an over-cordial session. The only way out seemed to be to come straight to the point. "There's been a lot of criticism lately, in Britain, that you don't ever bring your American band on tour over here."

Berry tilts his head to one side. It's that familiar gesture he uses on stage, coupled with putting his hand to his ear to listen to the audience singing along. On stage it's cute, if overused. Across a space of maybe eighteen inches, it's grotesque. I phrase the question more directly. "How come you don't bring your American band to England?"

"I did last time over."

This takes me back a piece. I can't, for the life of me, recall a tour when Chuck Berry played with anything but an under-rehearsed English pick-up band. I knew I hadn't missed a Chuck Berry tour in at least four years.

"Some of the British bands you've used have come in for a good deal of criticism."

"How? What criticism?"

"That basically they were either under-rehearsed, or simply not up to backing you." Chuck went into a long and somewhat rambling response. It boiled down to the idea that if the band wasn't any good, all he could do was to refuse to go on with them. If he refused to go on, then that let down his fans.

"I don't even know if the ones who'd bought tickets would get their money back."

Fair enough, except for a couple of points. The first being that Chuck Berry must be one of the very few potentially top-line performers who are content to play with the nearest pick-up band. The second is that, from all reports, he declines to rehearse with his backing musicians even if it means putting together a show that's only minimally polished. At this said point in time, Chuck doesn't know whom he's going to be playing with. He says he has to look at his date sheet.

"Don't you ever feel that you'd like to get up with a really good band and just cook?"

This is, after all, the man whose playing has influenced more people than probably any other musician in the latter half of the twentieth century, excluding maybe Charlie Parker and Jimi Hendrix.

"Feel what?"

I repeated the question.

"It's up to the promoter who I play with." Just like that. I have to confess I'm off-balance. It's like meeting Van Gogh and he claims he did it all with Paint-By-Numbers.

"You don't have any control over whom you play with when you come to Europe?"

"No."

We seem to have run headfirst into a blind alley. I start again from another direction. "There hasn't really been any new material from you for a long time."

"Material?"

"New songs."

I pointed out that as far as I could remember there hadn't been a significant new Chuck Berry since the *I'm a Rocker* album. Had Chuck been writing anything of late?

"I've been writing, but there's been problems."

"Problems?"

"The publishing company. Things have been transferred."

Chuck has vagueness down to a fine art. He gives out the minimum information, in its most oblique form. He also volunteers nothing, and all the time he's looking straight at you and smiling his foxy smile. Has he written or recorded anything new in the last couple of years?

"I've been writing and recording."

"Will any of it see the light of day?"

"I don't have control over that. It's all with the publishing company."

"So you've no idea when we'll be likely to hear it?"

"It'll come out some day."

"How much material is there?"

"I got two albums on the shelf."

"What kind of music is it?"

"Chuck Berry music."

"It's what we've all grown used to?"

"It's new songs."

"They're like your other songs?"

"You mean rock'n'roll?"

"Yeah, rock'n'roll."

We seem to be waltzing round and round and getting nowhere. Every approach to any part of the inner Berry is blocked. The pointlessness of it is plain frustrating. Chuck treats the interview situation as though he was on the witness stand. He doesn't even want to talk about his music. His voice becomes almost sing-song. "It's rock'n'roll, and some isn't rock'n'roll."

"What's the stuff that isn't rock'n'roll?"

There's a long pause while Chuck just smiles. Finally...

"It's all kind of things."

"Like what?"

Another pause, again the slight sing-song. "There's romantic music, there's jazz, there's Western music, there's swing music."

It's another dead-end and Chuck knows it. He sits and smiles. The blocking, the circling around and the fooling around might be amusing. Okay, so maybe uppity white boy writers need to be taken down, but, hell, this is Chuck Berry. The man doesn't seem to be aware of his own legend and his own power. He may be having fun, but he doesn't seem to realise that there are people here willing to hang on reverently to every word, if he was to start talking. Surely he doesn't think that his ideas, opinions and memories are evidence to use against him? I try another shot. What about his other business interests? Would he wax lyrical about his amusement park?

"How much of your time do you devote to music these days?"

"I spend about forty percent of my time on music."

"And the rest?"

"I have some other businesses back home."

He actually looks a little more animated. Maybe these are his real pride and joy. "What are they?"

"Video."

"Video?"

"That's right."

He seems almost proud. Could Chuck be heavily involved with TV software? "What kind of things are you doing with video?"

"You know what video is?"

"Yes, I know what video is, I was wondering how you were involved in it."

"Surveillance."

"Surveillance?"

"Surveillance and some commercials."

Another bizarre image, Chuck Berry spending the majority of his time running a company that installs anti-shoplifting devices in liquor stores and supermarkets.

My mind flashes back to one drunken night in Dingwalls. I was talking to Lee Brilleaux of Dr. Feelgood. Eventually we got round to the subject of Chuck Berry. We unashamedly waxed so eloquent that to listen to us you would have thought that he was a cross between God and Milton. Now this superman was sitting beside me telling me proudly about his surveillance business. I wonder if flattery might get him to open up.

"Chuck, there are people in this country who look at you as one of the greatest influences on rock'n'roll." Chuck doesn't look particularly interested. "I wouldn't know about that, I just do what I do. Writing, doing my thing."

"What about the Beatles or the Stones? They both did your songs and talk about you as a major influence on their early work."

"They didn't only play my songs. They played Little Richard's songs, all kind of people's songs. I didn't influence anyone."

Just like that, Chuck Berry seems to dismiss his contribution to rock'n'roll—"*I didn't influence anyone.*" I make one last try.

"When you hear people playing your songs, say Jimi Hendrix playing 'Johnny B. Goode,' doesn't it have some kind of effect on you?"

"Affect me? How should it affect me?"

"Well… for instance, does it give you ideas for what you're writing?"

"You mean like I should write 'Henry B. Goode'?"

It seems impossible.

"No, no, nothing like that, I just wondered how you felt."

"I don't feel nothing."

It's becoming clear that, in terms of communication talking to Chuck Berry is a waste of time. It seems that his paranoia is so firmly entrenched that he won't talk about anything. I ought to give up, but I guess I'm just dumb. I make one more effort. "You've been playing rock'n'roll for over twenty years now. How much has it changed over that time?"

"Not a lot."

Again the foxy smile came back. "I used to travel by car, now I travel by plane."

It's time to stop. I try a final shot. "You did some time in jail?"

Chuck goes stone-faced.

"No."

"No?"

"No."

This is actually a lie. Documented history records that, somewhere towards the end of 1959, Chuck brought an Indian girl from Texas to work the Chuck Berry Bandstand Club, the joint he ran in St. Louis. As she was only fourteen-years-old, this contravened the Mann Act, which related to the transportation of minors over the state line for immoral purposes. Apparently Chuck sacked her after a short while and she immediately told the police, who suspected her of being a prostitute, the whole story. A court case followed and there are supposed to be records which show that Berry eventually went to jail in February 1962 and stayed there for two years. Chuck has always denied this and often tells people that he was acquitted. His defence was that he thought the girl was over twenty-one.

It is certain, however, that he did wind up in a striped suit. Producer Ralph Bass, in a *Melody Maker* interview, said: "Berry spent some time in the can, while in a recent

TV documentary Chuck himself claimed that he had spent a long time inside and he had taken the chance to study various subjects."

It would probably be safe to say that a good deal of Chuck's devious attitude stems from these prison experiences. In his songs and in his life in general he has always promoted the American ethic of work hard, make a buck and be a good citizen. Just when he was on the very brink of achieving this goal he found himself savagely shattered by the American Way of Life in the form of Federal authority. Chuck Berry is never going to stick his neck out again. After that there seemed little else to do except wind up the interview. So long Chuck, thanks for talking, good luck with the tour, blah, blah.

I went away sad and depressed. I had just been face to face with one of the early giants of rock'n'roll and the situation, from the start, had been like a cop interviewing a petty criminal.

New Musical Express, May 1976

ENTER THE LEATHER

MY FIRST ENCOUNTER WITH THE POWER OF THE BLACK leather jacket came when I was maybe fourteen or fifteen, I can still clearly remember the first time I bought one. I'd seen the older guys in school and on the street who wore them; they were the ones who looked cool and, overtaken by adolescent hero worship, I wanted to be just like them. But part of the attraction was also that the leather jacket was frowned upon, proscribed and legislated against. I'd also seen stills of Marlon Brando in *The Wild One* and from the perspective of the time, he was as far as it went. (Marlon was also legislated against. *The Wild One* remained banned in the UK until 1967, presumably to deter young boys like me from emulating the Brando character. It didn't work; it only made me all the more eager.) It was a time when I was seriously fighting the dress code on

❏ Heroes can help set a young lad on the path to insurrection, but sometimes rebellion can be nurtured by a inanimate object if the symbolism is strong enough, and the role of the rebel, with or without a cause—at least in the youthful imagination—could be a matter of just striking poses in front of a mirror and wishing for adventure.

two fronts. Both my teachers and my folks seemed bent on turning me into a junior gentleman—a potential bank manager or advertising executive if ever you saw one. For my part, I was equally determined to become a greaser hoodlum. It was a time when everything hip and teenage was against the rules, a time of sneaking out of the house with a pair of skintight black jeans hidden under baggy gray flannel pants.

I bought the jacket in a small, backstreet men's clothing store, hard up against a railway bridge in a medium sized seaside town in Southern England. It was hardly the concrete jungle but it passed at the time. The store specialized in tacky, juvenile delinquent fashions—polka-dot shirts, stardust peggies, dayglo socks and lurid suits that usually fell apart after a couple of weeks. I paid for it out of my own money, cash that I'd squirrelled away from what I was paid for crawling out of bed and delivering newspapers at some ungodly hour in the morning. In the prevailing situation, there was no way that my folks were going to spring for a motorcycle jacket and, indeed, there would even be repercussions when I got it home. It was all too obvious that it was my provisional membership card to the Bad Boys, an introduction to the kids they didn't want me hanging out with. I'm sure my normally level-headed mother saw it as the rash step onto the slippery slope that led all the way down to drugs, degradation and cheap women. So, for that matter, did I. That why I was so all-fired keen.

It was something of a ceremony. I stood in front of the store's full-length mirror and slipped off whatever jacket I was wearing. (It isn't part of the memory. It was probably some tweed sportcoat of which my mother totally approved.) I struggled into what was going to be my first cool garment. The leather creaked with newness and smelled like the interior of a factory-fresh car but there was more than adequate compensation. It had a red silk lining, just like Dracula's cape. I think I remember making that connection at the time. I also remember the label. The jacket came from D. Lewis Ltd. of Great Portland Street, London. It was the Bronx model. As I stared into the mirror, I couldn't believe myself. Admittedly the mirror was tilted up to produce the flattering effect, but I looked great. My legs seemed longer, my shoulders seemed broader. I flipped the collar up, I looked so damned cool. Mother of God, I was a cross between Elvis and Lord Byron. The old guy who was taking care of me asked me how I felt. I lit a cigarette. I'd been smoking for a year or so, but this was the first time I'd ever lit one while I had an adult's total attention. Jekyll was already becoming Hyde. I told him grandly that it was okay. He really had only the most minimal role in my fantasy.

Of course, to the casual observer, this little scene would have appeared a trifle ridiculous, an awkward kid preening in front of a mirror in a new leather jacket. (And there's nothing so unfortunate as a brand new leather jacket.) When I got it back to the neighborhood there were those who told me to rub it with a brick. (This, incidentally, is nonsense. Only time will age a leather jacket.) Much of this leather jacket mystique is a very subjective business. You may be walking around looking like a jerk, but inside you feel like Billy the Kid's bad brother. Even the worst of fools, devoid of all determination and style, can put on the most badly cut, evilly tailored, imitation bike jacket, and feel himself capable of taking on the world. It's only when this capability is put to the test that the trouble starts. All too often the world doesn't treat the fool with the seriousness that he believes he deserves, and this is where the seeds of disaster are sown, where the violent, ugly, antisocial punk is created.

I wasn't, however, thinking about any of this. For me, it was an occasion. I was like the young squire in the days of chivalry, receiving his first suit of armor. The cold mornings of my paper round were, I guess, my equivalent of the traditional knight errant wearing out his knees all night in a freezing chapel keeping vigil over his armor and weapons before going out and breaking heads. The feeling went with me out onto the street. I'd had the straight sportcoat or whatever wrapped, and I was wearing the leather jacket. I immediately felt different. The reflection that glanced back at me from the shop windows and the occasional mirror showed a whole new body shape. Boy, at least in his own imagination, had been turned into Man. The whole top half of my body was heavier and more capable while my legs were free, in their tight jeans, to play any games that they could think up. I swaggered, I scowled. The jacket molded to my moves. The highlights in its finish seemed to accentuate those moves and I fondly believed that I was bad, maybe even menacing. I flattered myself that people were stepping out of my way. Nobody was going to mess with me. Inside my private fantasy, I had moved on from the make-believe world of cowboys and Indians and into the quasi-real world of teen gangs and switchblade justice.

But do remember, I was extremely young at the time, and I'd just discovered narcissism.

An excerpt from the book *The Black Leather Jacket*, 1985

THE SUBVERSIVE APPLICATION OF JETEX FUSE

❑ Not all of my insurrections took place in the 1960s and 1970s. Some came much earlier. Maybe it was a product of living in a world that could vanish in one huge pyrotechnic flash, but, before puberty, before my first rock'n'roll record— not to put too fine a point on it—I liked to blow things up. Before the great explosion of rock'n'roll, I occupied myself with other explosions.

Jetex was crucial in the development of my pre-teen personality, and thus, when I discovered an actual print ad for the Jetex motor on my favorite website I was both surprised and uplifted. The Jetex motor was a cheap, solid-fuel burning, rocket-propulsion unit for toy planes, cars, and boats.

My first encounter was with a Jetex powered car that was supposed to run on a line—at quite alarming speed— in circles around a central tether. Although it was my car, my stepfather insisted on setting the thing up and lighting the Jetex fuse. And, needless to say, he fucked up. The car was being run on a very uneven patio. It hit a bump, went straight up in the air for some distance and then came back down again, scared the dog, and pretty much wrecked itself, although the Jetex motor was still intact.

My second Jetex experience was with something called the Dan Dare Jetex Space Rocket that was launched from

MICK FARREN

a spring-loaded ramp, supposedly released a parachute after it had achieved what Werner von Braun called brenschluss, and floated gently to earth. It came in kit form. My grandfather and I took almost a full month of one summer to complete the asbestos-lined, balsa wood construction. But we mistimed the first launch, and the rocket fell off the ramp before the motor ignited, and then it lay on its side, burning grass and spewing smoke until the fuel ran out.

The second launch of the Dan Dare Jetex Space Rocket was much more successful. The rocket went up a hundred feet or more before the fuel was spent. Unfortunately the chute didn't deploy until far too late in the fall to stop it ploughing into the ground. After it was glued back together, the Dan Dare Jetex Space Rocket made one last flight, with an incendiary device aboard to blow it up in midair. Which gets me to my real romance with Jetex. Or, to be more precise, Jetex fuse.

At age eleven, I was a mad bomber. Creating explosions was quite a fad that year among young boys in the south of England. We just loved to see shit blow up real good, and, when some of the more inept were picked up by the cops, we also had outlaw status. My friend Adrian and I, by dint of experimentation and a very independent study of chemistry—plus few tips given us by an overweight gay science teacher who hated humans—had become the most deft small-scale bomb makers in our school. Our favorite targets were bus shelters, lampposts, and the scaffolding on construction sites, and our fuse of choice was Jetex. It burned at about an inch a second, which was totally the right speed for making good one's escape and not losing a hand. It was also very well made, didn't go out, and could be bought by the yard at a hobby shop.

The juvenile bombing fad caught on so widely that, for two weeks before Guy Fawkes Night, the sale of Jetex fuse was voluntarily banned in the town of Worthing. Cops visited the school and issued dire warnings. Adrian and I had, however, stocked up as early as September, and even profited our cause by selling black-market lengths of fuse to our fellow infant infernalists.

At puberty, I largely gave up explosives in favor of girls and rock'n'roll. Probably just as well. Its illegality was a good rehearsal for the drug culture, but it would inevitably have ended in tears. A few times in later life I had encounters with Jetex fuse, but those are other stories.

Doc40, 2009

WHAT ARE YOU REBELLING AGAINST, JOHNNY?

❑ Just as the roots of youthful frustration extend beyond rock'n'roll, they also embraced individuals who didn't actually tote electric guitars or moon-howled into live microphones, but, all the same, supported the same ethos.

MARLON, MARILYN, ELVIS, AND JAMES DEAN WERE THE towering quartet of pop turmoil's pantheon; the primary icons of the post-atomic, post-World War II conflict between suburban subdivisions of conformity, and the madness of Mutually Assured Destruction. All four are now dead and gone. Dean was a fast and beautiful corpse who never aged nor did any wrong. Marilyn lasted longer, but took the desperate pill exit as she imagined her superpowers waning, while Elvis left the building by a similar side door, but in far worse condition. Only Marlon survived to see overripe old age, and depart the coil aged all of eighty, having played not only the leather jacketed Johnny Strabler, and the guilty and inarticulate Terry Molloy, but also Don Vito Corleone, Colonel Walter Kurtz, Mark Anthony, and Superman's father. At the same time, though, in his private life, he seemed incapable of coping with an extended and dysfunctional family that degenerated to murder and suicide.

Marlon Brando was simultaneously blessed and cursed, and, maybe worst of all, he was also possessed of a perversity that caused him to curse his blessings and embrace his curse. Certainly that's one underlying thesis in the three-hour documentary *Brando*. Marlon Brando had the good fortune to be born one of the most handsome individuals on the planet. If the film clips, newsreels, TV interviews, and home movies of the young Marlon hadn't made this abundantly clear, it's confirmed by Angie Dickinson, one of the dozens of famous, but also highly perceptive, interviewees who provide the narrative thread for more footage of Marlon Brando than has ever before been assembled in any one show. The first time Dickinson encountered Brando, she vividly remembers he was one of the most physically beautiful humans beings she had ever seen, and admits she would have fucked him on the spot if she hadn't been married at the time.

Brando was not only beautiful, however, he was also blessed with a dangerous brain, and, for those who subscribe to the idea that creativity stems from childhood deprivation, he had an alcoholic mother and a son-of-a-bitch father who deemed him uncontrollable and shipped him off to a military academy where, with an early teenage perversity, he fell into acting. Heading for New York, he took the usual young actor's trail of poverty, slept with a staggering number of women, and studied, first at the Actor's Studio, and then at the New School's Dramatic Workshop, where he became the star pupil of the legendary Stella Adler.

James Lipton and the ceaseless *Inside The Actors Studio* has taught some of us more than we need to know about the process of acting, especially the Stanislavski method of using personal memory to replicate emotion. We learn more of the same in *Brando*, but here we actually see the clip in question and then luminaries like Robert Duvall, Dennis Hopper, Martin Scorsese, Johnny Depp, Jane Fonda, Edward Norton, and an articulate if awed and reverential Al Pacino describe how, in his early days, Brando gave the impression of painfully ripping the metaphysical essentials of each performance from someplace deep inside himself. Even Sir John Gielgud, in an ancient clip, waxes lyrical about Brando's performance in *Julius Caesar*, while Quincy Jones likens him to Miles Davis, in that both these giants had no patience with rules and simply reinvented them. The consensus of opinion was that Marlon Brando was the greatest actor of the twentieth century—when he wanted to be.

When his power was flowing, Marlon was mesmerizing—and *Brando* provides enough archive material, some previously unseen, clearly to demonstrate that power. We see rare clips of him attracting initial attention in the play *Truckline Café*, and then taking Broadway by storm in *A Streetcar Named Desire*—with more unearthed clips of Marlon and a youthful Jessica Tandy as Blanche. We also are made aware that another of Brando's gifts was an historic timing. A revolution was taking place in the theatre, if not the entire culture. Tennessee Williams was writing the plays and Marlon Brando was there to act in them. Martin Landau, who palled around and drank with Brando while he was doing *Streetcar*, described how the excitement was palpable, but, having riveted audiences, and proved himself the consummate stage actor, Brando went off to do the movie of *Streetcar* and never came back to the theatre again.

For a while, Brando ruled Hollywood, and *The Wild One*, *On The Waterfront*, *Viva Zapata*, *Julius Caesar*, and *The Fugitive Kind*, established him not only as a new mode of movie star—a young and insolent alternative to established box office kings like Kirk Douglas, Burt Lancaster, and Rock Hudson—but also a significant—maybe magnificent—cultural symbol for the generation that would, within the course of the 1950s, embrace everything from beat poetry to rock'n'roll to turn the world on its ear. Martin Scorsese treats Brando as nothing less than a benchmark. "He is the marker. There's 'before Brando' and 'after Brando.'" From the Hollywood front-office point of view, though, Marlon Brando was far from being a benchmark. He was a royal pain in the ass, and he, in turn, did nothing to disguise his ingrained contempt for the entire studio process of creating and marketing motion pictures. Brando was the perpetual and relentless rebel in search of bigger and more worthwhile causes.

The rift between Brando and Hollywood widened after he had independently produced and directed the flawed but powerful *One Eyed Jacks*, and, as the world moved into the tumult of the 1960s, his political radicalism made him an even more suspect outsider. In *Brando*, no less than Bobby Seale tells how Marlon, not content with being on the front lines of the civil rights movement went all the way and embraced the Black Panther Party. Russell Means also recalls how, while members of the American Indian Movement were under armed siege by the FBI at Wounded Knee, Brando showed up to boost morale. Hollywood, on the other hand, now firmly believed the man who would be hailed as the greatest actor of the twentieth century was unemployable box office poison.

We have all heard the legend how Francis Ford Coppola was forced to put Brando through an impromptu screen test to secure him the role of Vito Corleone, and then, after Marlon had won an Academy Award for the part, he sent Sacheen Littlefeather to reject his Oscar because of Hollywood's years of demeaning Native Americans. The delight of *Brando* is to hear *The Godfather* stories, the *Last Tango In Paris* stories, and the *Apocalypse Now* stories retold by those who were actually there. Producer Leslie Grief and writer Mimi Freedman have pieced together a unique portrait of a man who could be both a comedian and a cut-up, but was frequently at war with everyone around him, and even with himself. Marlon Brando frequently expressed serious doubts as to whether acting was a legitimate occupation for a grown man, and yet, could emotionally turn himself inside out when fully engaged in a worthwhile part. As, later in life, Brando ballooned up to more than 300 pounds, many suspected that he was even rebelling against—and maybe deliberately destroying—the good looks that had brought him so many advantages in his youth.

The entertainment industry is never happy with idiosyncratic or wayward artists, and Marlon Brando was one of the most idiosyncratic and wayward in movie history. The suits loathed him, but every actor interviewed for *Brando*, from Johnny Depp, to James Caan, to Harry Dean Stanton agreed that he was the one that blazed the trail for the rest of them to follow, and *Brando* shows more than enough of Marlon the actor, to fully prove their point.

LA CityBeat, April 2007

A ROCK'N'ROLL INSURRECTION

WE WON'T GET FOOLED AGAIN

❏ I sometimes encounter a modern misconception espoused by pop historians and the like that we radical, 1960s, counterculture hippies (damn but I hate that word) all marched into a Maxfield Parrish sunset in total accord and agreement. In fact, nothing could have been further from the truth. We didn't fight among ourselves as much as the radical left, who seemed unable to order a round of drinks without breaking into ideological schisms, but we had our fallings out. This confrontation with Pete Townshend over the song 'Won't Get Fooled Again' started at a party at Keith Moon's futuristic suburban fun palace. I'm not sure whether the party was to celebrate the record's release or what. The epic of drunken and explosive surrealism certainly wasn't like any other record release party I could recall. In the middle of it, three of the **IT** inner circle—Chris Rowley, Ed Barker and myself—had engaged Townshend over the song's implied theme that revolution would inevi-

Dear Pete,

After rapping on you so heavily at Moon's party on Wednesday we felt that we would write to you as promised and lay out the reasoning behind the feelings of puzzlement and worry that we feel when playing the new single. Whereas the music is still strong kicking out aggressive music, the lyric is seemingly defensive and negative, even potentially damaging to the consciousness of kids who still strongly identify with the Who as an extension of their lifestyles. In fact it's calculated to bring down anybody seeking radical change in what we know you agree is a depressingly corrupt society. So why?

The problem of "Leadership" is discussed at length in most radical group circles, like for instance the Newton/Cleaver mess or the personality cultism around Hoffman and Rubin. These make a solid case for the old Dylan axiom, "Don't follow leaders and watch the parking meters," the problem is however that as you probably know yourself the accomplishment of most operations usually requires some dumb bastard to coordinate and get things done, whether it's billsticking, raising crops or newspapers or playing rock music at the right place and time and well. However, if the individual whose initiative produces results feels he has a right to special treatment and personal adulation from his fellow workers then some of "here comes the new boss same as the old boss" is perfectly valid.

So the first question is do you make this distinction? There are obvious leadership situations which have developed into a very bogus elitism, this is most prevalent amongst leading figures who have used the rock'n'roll business to communicate their ideas. In a lot of cases where a leader figure has attempted to impose a morally objectionable ethic on his audience and supposed "followers" the idea of "we're not gonna take it" comes strongly into play and it would seem that when such an individual loses touch and ceases to be a reflection of the gestalt of the street he is rejected—often very sadly. Either in outright fashion as with the MC5 or reluctantly as with Bob Dylan. There are however people who have come to prominence thru' their energies and abilities—Sinclair, George Jackson, Garcia even, who despite amazing suffering and harassment still are prepared to make themselves a vehicle to channelling ideas without extracting any heavy personal toll on the way.

Specifically the danger in the new single seems to be that it fails to differentiate between the megalomaniac and the courageous individual who is prepared to stand up and voice the sentiment "fuck you" to authority. The fact that the techniques of straight media make it impossible for anyone to voice a common philosophy without being elevated to an elitist position is unfortunate and something that may change as more and more kids get pissed off with the phoniness of news, TV, rich honky pop stars, etc.

Since the days of the High Numbers you have progressively become more famous, successful and wealthy by playing fine and mighty mean rock music and by reflecting the power that this generation has discovered within itself. The Who have become a brand name for change and perhaps even a symbol with which kids who are fucked over in the streets can identify with.

Obviously the artist has a right to his own particular opinions and ideas and to the expression of them but at the same time it seems reasonable to expect as a return from the artist a positive attitude to the problems he comments on. The artist is cushioned against the trips on the street and the problems of the people who attend his shows, in return he must strive to maintain the mental contact which keeps his art alive and kicking and directly meaningful to the audience. Are you expressing a desire to escape the pressures of your situation, to say in effect "all right I'm a Rock Star and nothing else and I can't help you"—because this is essentially a negative approach to things. No one really expects to see you opening a "problems of youth guidance service" but at the same time we'd be interested to know what use a self-realized man is going be to the community and the world in general.

Yours, Chris Rowley, Mick Farren, J. Edward Barker

tably lead to some stripe of brutal dictatorship. Alcohol and other stimulants precluded the conversation being resolved on the night, and letters were exchanged.

Dear Chris, Mick & Ed,

Just got back from the States with damaged hands and the anticipation of having to answer a huge pile of mail. I'm answering this first. I was amused and invigorated by our rap at Keith's. It's always funny to me to get into any heavy raps like that in the midst of such indulgent fantasia insanity. The invigoration, and I know you're going to go through the roof, is because you proved to me that everyone in the Grove is not dying of their own cloudy idealism.

I suppose if I wasn't cunt enough to be a Rock Star I would be round there with you. A lot of my people are. The fact is, and it's not really surprising, I'm not with you. Neither in your neighborhood nor frame of mind. It's weird how the extremes of Rock existence drag you through twenty years of life in a week. Joplin and Hendrix died of old age quite probably. The reason we, the Who, escape death is simple. We are English. We go to the States, we look, perform and then get back to the relative peace of green pastures. It gives us time and space to observe and reflect more accurately the changing balance of power.

You remain frustrated, we reflect that frustration. You get pissed at people dying in campus warfare just like mum and dad used to die in France and Germany so we reflect that feeling of being pissed off. It's hard I know to be essentially nonviolent and yet still feel very strongly that our strength, wherever it lies in us (the kids) has to be demonstrated. We have to be respected, feared and listened to.

The Who don't "return" a positive attitude to youth because it is expected of them or because they get rich from their music. They REFLECT the negative attitude which a lot of kids are taking to the fight for power which is being waged in their name, but not on their terms, not using their ethics. 'Won't Get Fooled' is partly a personal song but mainly a song which screams defiance at those who feel that any cause is better than no cause, that death in a sick society is better than putting up with it, or resigning themselves to wait for change. It mainly screams defiance at those who try to tell Us (the Who) what we have to do with money that isn't ours, power that belongs not to us but our audiences and lives that long ago were handed to the Rock world on platters. We fight to remain. Merely remain. We are human and feel the instinct of self survival. Not supremacy over existing leaders, the right to live a DIFFERENT life than they. Freedom and self realization are words I use a lot in my songs, you use them a lot in life too I'm sure, but what do they mean? The revolution in the Latin American countries was waged on Fidel principles for seven years before new leaders informed the revolutionaries that Fidel TOO had failed until he tailored his fight to the specific set of circumstances that existed in Cuba and not merely to emulate the Marxist catalog.

Today freedom and realization are surely words that apply to the inside of man, to man's ability to be aware that he IS free. I get a good buzz when you bring me to my senses, I know the song is negative, I've written quite a few before, but suggesting that there might be a possibility that the Who are trying to escape the pressures of our situation— that's libelous. We're the only fucking Rock band apart from the Grateful Dead that knows what is happening in the audience at a gig. We play hard, often, long. We think, we work, we worry, we give money away, we reinvest money in our music, in the road circus, we write, we record, we might even get a little negative at times, but we ain't fucking well trying to escape from nowhere. There is no escape from our own karma, we know what we have to do. We also know how the ground has to be laid in order for us to do this. Listen to our next single. It was recorded at the same session as 'Fooled' and is a planned predetermined follow-up. Read our frustration at not being able to truly push Rock through as the alternative society it deserves to be. Listen to the band play as the shotguns sing. You have no need to fret, you're not losing a rock band, you're not gaining new leaders, and you're keeping the Who. After digging your letter I understand, too, that we're keeping you, and that's good. Some time will pass before Christmas.

Love, Pete.

International Times, September 1971

BILLY THE MONSTER

In the autumn of 1967, **IT** and I temporarily parted company, and I took off with the Deviants. By a process that was hardly orthodox, even for the times, I was able to spend much of the next two years making records and playing live with the band. Although I still contributed rants and squibs to the paper, most of my writing was devoted to song lyrics.

Billy the monster
Billy the monster
Watch out Billy as you walk around.
There are ugly people living underground.
They'll defile your body and your brain,
And you will never be the same again
Billy the monster
Billy the monster
Billy didn't take our good advice
He went too far, it wasn't very nice.
Billy who was once like me or you,
He has now become a monster too.
Billy the monster
Billy the monster

Written and recorded for the album *Deviants 3*, 1969

IF THE COFFIN'S ROCKIN'

Times moved on and times changed. Far too many of the high hopes of the late 1960s turned into the high desperation of the early 1970s. These were not good times. Even death-rock attempted to make something of a comeback.

THE EXPLOITATION SIDE OF THE ROCK INDUSTRY, THE guys who like to preprogram teen crazes rather than have them happen spontaneously, are packaging up death for us again, and pushing it out on the media merry-go-round. Ever since James Dean rocketed to teen immortality after his death in an auto wreck in 1955, any rock impresario who was hard up for an idea would give the death trip a whirl. Not that the idea of a popular medium developing a preoccupation with death is all that unusual. If a poll was taken of what individual subjects attract the greatest consistent interest, you would almost certainly find sex number one with death a close second. It has boosted the careers of such diverse artists as Shakespeare and Sam Peckinpah. The surprising thing about this latest morbid flirtation is that it comes so quickly after Bowie and Cooper working out their terminal fantasies.

The current cycle of Coffin Rock seems particularly

MICK FARREN

tacky and lacking in taste. Needless to say it has originated in the United States. One of the more bizarre examples is a sixteen-year-old kid who seems to have studied every riff on *Electric Ladyland* until he is note perfect, and is now being promoted as being possessed by the spirit of Jimi Hendrix.

Another individual called The Phantom does a passable imitation of Jim Morrison, has made two singles containing all these baroque lizardskin clichés, and is the subject of rumors, dutifully spread by a crazed promo-man, that he is in fact the real Morrison, recorded from insane, or hideously disfigured, seclusion.

Mind you, death as a form of perverse entertainment is not really new. In the eighteenth century, a public hanging had the same pulling power, in proportion to the population, as Emerson Lake and Palmer. On a more mundane level, grand opera, possibly with an eye on the box office, made sure it was replete with murder and mayhem. As far as rock'n'roll is concerned, the golden age of the coffin song was the late fifties and early sixties. Who could ever forget those star-crossed teenage lovers, Tommy and Laura, Betty and Jimmy, Mark Denning and his Teen Angel—all transcending the problems of acne, and being too young to go steady, in glorious, Wagnerian auto wrecks?

There are all kinds of possible social and philosophical reasons why the late fifties should have produced such a crop of death songs. You could blame everything on a spectrum of causes from the nuclear Cold War to the change in social and family structures. There's probably a book there for some hip sociologist. The one thing that's clear is that all these songs viewed death as a means of escape or protest. In the Ray Peterson song, 'Give Us Your Blessing,' Jimmy's and Mary's bodies are found in the ditch, mutely reproaching their parents who forbade them to get married.

There was a strong element of "we'll show them" in most of these teenage wastings. Jimmy totals himself and his bike to show Betty's parents they can't mess with the leader of the pack.

The coffin song had heavy roots in the country tradition of hangings, shooting, and he-had-to-die-'cos-he-messed-with-my-woman. The first definable teen death song, 'Endless Sleep,' was a pure tear-jerk country ballad with a rock guitar laid on top of it. Thomas Wayne followed the same Nashville funeral route with 'Tragedy,' as did the Everly Brothers on 'Ebony Eyes,' right down to the spoken middle: "Will anyone having relatives on flight 1203 report to the chapel across the street." As the coffin songs moved more heavily into the lush grazing land of Clearasil and daddy's car, they began to develop a style of their own. 'Tell Laura I Love Her,' which established Ray Peterson as a one-hit wonder, got morbidly bouncy, while 'Last Kiss' by J. Frank Wilson, and 'Teen Angel,' both moved into a kind of mournful pre-Spector doo-wop.

Denning and Wilson may have had stabs at teen melodrama but it took the Shangri-Las and the legendary Shadow Morton to perfect the full pop art, soap opera magnificence of 'Leader Of The Pack.' Even 'Walking In The Sand,' where nothing is explicitly stated in the lyrics, still leaves you feeling as though something terrible is about to happen. It was as if the Shangri-Las brought the coffin song full cycle.

The strident chorus of "Gone" at the end of 'Leader Of The Pack' has a fatalism about it, a kind of resignation that almost implies that, so Jimmy totalled himself, so what? The scream of his tires was preserved in an electronic time-warp, like a fly in amber, and rock was able to move out into the healthy, virile sunshine of the early Beatles and Stones.

Any examination of coffin songs couldn't be complete with a mention of 'Three Stars' by Ruby Wright. When Buddy Holly, Big Bopper, and Ritchie Valens died in a plane wreck on February 3, 1959, the exploitation machine went into action bigtime.

The sickly religious 'Three Stars,' with its saccharine gospel chorus and drawn-out recitation—"On the right stands Buddy Holly with a shy grin on his face... Gee, we're gonna miss you, everybody sends their love"—must have been one of rock's worst three and a half minutes. Irony was piled on top of the tack when the late Eddie Cochran felt constrained to produce a demo of the same song a few months before his own death.

After the Shangri-Las the death cycle seemed to wither away. The new wave of hard rock spearheaded by the British bands swept aside the morbid fantasies. The only death preoccupations that remained were the dire warnings of global annihilation from Barry McGuire, P.F. Sloan and the more hysterical end of the protest movements.

The mid-sixties were comparatively free of doom epics. It was as though the high-powered creativity that flowered in London, New York, and Los Angeles negated the need of any new revival of the coffin cult.

It wasn't until the drug culture moved from self-awareness to self-destruction that rock once again hit the graveyard trail. The drug-connected deaths of Brian Jones, Hendrix, Janis Joplin and Jim Morrison, in a short space of time, threw the rock media into a frenzy of self-flagellation. What happened, where did it all go wrong? The reassessment of the subculture's attitudes came thick and fast. The violence at Altamont and the odd musician's flirtation with the violent end of the New Left brought the whole thing to boiling point. At the very end of the sixties, it became almost impossible to pick up a rock paper without finding some piece of necro breast beating. The hippies could recite the names of their OD'd heroes as though it was a litany. Some became even more direct. Tarot-telling hippie chicks were visited by Brian, Jim or Jimi in their bedsits. Way over in the outer limits, Charlie Manson and his secret legion heard snuff instructions where none existed.

A similar atmosphere began to permeate the music. The post-satanic Rolling Stones were among the first to warn that rape and murder were just a shot away.

Although always outrageous, the late sixties saw the Stones taking up their now familiar pose, halfway between Edgar Allan Poe and Chelsea Girls. As they spiralled further into twilight excess they seemed to kick off another cycle. The Ziggy Stardust epic, and the space age Grand Guignol of Alice Cooper are such recent history that they need no comment. There is no doubt that there was a certain rapport between the performer and audience.

Although Cooper would be the first to admit that part of the motivation for his macabre spectacles was getting the bucks, it would seem that both he and Bowie have more in common with Lenny Bruce and Fellini than with 'Tell Laura I Love Her.'

Death, it seems, is once again being paraded as a sales pitch. It's a tired gimmick, particularly when it could so easily be taken seriously. An examination of humanity's death fears has produced some music of dynamic worth. It has also produced the worst soap opera sobbings.

New Musical Express, June 1974

THE KIDS ARE NOT NECESSARILY ALRIGHT

❑ Among the living, corporate interests figured out how to wrest back the control that a few artists had very briefly enjoyed. Rock seemed in danger of ceasing to be any kind of "force for revolution," and was being transformed into nothing more than one more variety of consumer entertainment. The word "product" had replaced the word "music."

WHEN YOU SPEND A GREAT DEAL OF YOUR WAKING TIME hard up against the outpourings of the rock'n'roll industry, it gets difficult to believe that the music we've all grown up with is actually drifting away from the mainstream of everyday life. Unfortunately, if you do step far enough back to get modern rock trends into perspective with the general movements in society at large, the suggestion that contemporary boogie is fast becoming somewhat irrelevant cannot be ignored. Admittedly there's plenty of music about. There's more rock'n'roll coming out of radio than at any time since the golden age of the pirate stations. There are certainly more live bands on the road than ever before, and although there is a temporary slump in record sales, this in no way indicates that the actual playing of records has at all diminished.

It's not that, as Don McLean used to whine at us, the music's died. There is little danger of rock'n'roll imminently shuffling off this mortal coil. The real problem that could maybe do with a morsel of examination is the way in which rock has, over the last couple of years, come in off the street and cocooned itself in a cozy escapist world all of its own. It has always been possible to trace the history

MICK FARREN

of just about any period by listening to its music. The last great era of economic insecurity, the thirties, were documented at almost every level. Woody Guthrie left behind a vast and detailed panorama of the American working-class during the depression, Cole Porter produced a series of brittle insights into the urbanites' fear and cynicism, while in Europe, Brecht and Weill mapped the entire spectrum of class conflict.

The World War II period was a marked exception. As with most other media, popular music was forced into a soft propaganda role and reduced to the level of tinsel and sentimentalism. The music of the postwar period, however, immediately settled down to mirror the conflicts that were being bred in the crushing paternalism of the Eisenhwer/McCarthy/Churchill/Eden era.

In many respects the musical underground, which spanned such diverse artists as Charlie Parker, Hank Ballard and even Hank Williams, paralleled the moves that were being made by Kerouac and Mailer in the same way that Steinbeck and Fitzgerald paralleled Guthrie and Porter. This divergence in different sections of society eventually exploded into rock'n'roll, and music became a symbolic spearhead in the generation conflict that surfaced with the primal rockers. Chuck Berry, Cochran, Buddy Holly and writing teams like Jerry Leiber and Mike Stoller placed the emerging music firmly on the street and created songs that were a complete statement of the day-to-day highs and frustrations of that generation. Despite the machinations of hustlers like Dick Clark or Tom Parker, who tried to smooth it with a harmless, apple pie, candy coating, the energetic, gut level thread of rock'n'roll gathered momentum as it shifted into the sixties.

The Beatles, the Rolling Stones and Dylan all cataloged, and at times even predicted the behavior changes in a restless and often renegade core of the kids of the sixties. All of them came to success straight from the street and brought street language, street mannerisms and raw energy with them and injected it straight and undiluted into their music.

For a period of seven or eight years all these artists were able to write very directly as part of their generation. They were leaders, but it took no conscious effort. They were a part of what was going on and it seemed as if there was no way that they could do anything but become spokesmen for their peers. In the same way, the Who and the Small Faces totally summed up the amphetamine aggression of the mods. The Animals were an extension of the rough, tough, rather purist attitude of the northern industrial punks, and the Beach Boys built a whole musical style around the cultism that was the first stirring of California craziness.

When drugs and global upheaval hit in the middle of the decade, rock'n'roll was there with artists who represented just above every shade of opinion for that confused time. The Grateful Dead offered good time, falling-down-stoned, funky hippyism; Jim Morrison came through with sexual gothic; Jefferson Airplane cornered the market with fuzzy psychedelic romanticism; MC5 embodied the street corner, speed freak rebel, and the Stooges made a killing in delinquent vandalism. Rock was, for a time, the sole language of white youth revolt, and more than any other art form, it recorded the successes and failures of that particularly convoluted piece of rebellion. It was a time when even soul music broke out of its purely sexual terms of reference to begin to state the pride and anger that was dominating urban black consciousness.

Then the sixties slid into the seventies, and things began to change. Where rock stars would once chatter about drugs or Vietnam or Chairman Mao or the imminent downfall of capitalism, the outside world suddenly became just altogether too unfashionable.

The revolution ground to a halt, a few incautious militants went to the slammers, and not much more than a year after the Kent State killings, decadence was the new thing, or so they told us. That was the major change. Instead of the rock star reflecting what was going down on the street, he began to attempt to dictate it in advance.

The mods had wrestled fashion out of the clutches

of the haute couture houses and set it down among high energy grass roots. At the start of the seventies, a spurious rock'n'roll high society was trying to put it back into Blake's Hotel and the International Hyatt House. We were witnessing a limp-wristed sell-out. For a while the surreal, spangled Alice Cooper spectacle had its attraction, but it quickly became revealed that the Cooper ethic had much more to do with dollars than with Dada. Next came Bowie and the rest of the glitter crew. The commentators started to talk about how the new generation was experimenting with its innate bisexuality.

But was it?

Were there as many kids getting into ambidextrous sex as there were dropping psychedelics in '67? On analysis it would seem not. Max Factor didn't bring out a single brand of male eyeshadow. Was this really a great leap forward for liberation from the genital role, or was it just a bunch of creatively bankrupt rockers falling back on an elaborate drag routine to cover up that they didn't actually know what was happening?

Of course, just because the world passes an arbitrary ten year mark, and we start writing a seven after the nine on our cheques instead of six, it doesn't follow that all the idols of the previous decade turned back into pumpkins. Most are still around in force. A few died, and a few more ran scared to God, Krishna, Vishnu, L. Ron Hubbard or fat Maharajji. Some went crazy. The majority simply matured to the point where they realized they were no longer delinquent rockers, but grown up superstars. They started to write about where they were living.

Dylan recounted his confused attempts to raise kids and have a wife, Lennon ranted about simplistic politics, primal scream therapy and breaking up being hard to do, while Lou Reed kept us up to date with the saga of where the junkies go in the wintertime. Some of this may have been fine stuff. It is good to know what's going on in that rarefied world, but it didn't have much to do with everyday life.

Even when a punk fantasy was served up neatly packaged by, say, the Stones or Faces, it still had the air of vision carefully observed while peeking from the window of a penthouse suite.

So what of the new crop of punks? There really don't seem to be too many. Is it possible to look to Showaddywaddy, Mud or the Rubettes for a picture of the new generation? There seems to be little going on there except a revamping of stylistic quirks of the fifties, which, if these peoples' press releases are to be believed, most of them are too young to remember first hand. The alternative to the *Top Of The Pops* regulars seems to be either Ferry or maybe Feelgood, but once again we have to face the fact that both of them are primarily engaged in recherché stylistic jokes. Given a choice between Ferry and the more talented Brian Eno, it would appear that Eno is maybe closer to his tiny minority of ambiguous crazies than Ferry is to his new improved lost generation.

Even when the recording scene drifts into a sterile phase, you can usually hope to spot some measure of salvation in the bands working live. At present that seems to be denied us. From ELP to Hawkwind the prime function of most big touring draws seems to be to produce exactly the right noise for a particular section of public taste to bathe in when they're wasted. It's a laudable endeavor, but hardly communication on anything but the most simplistic level. So what does that leave us? A choice of Hello or Bruce Springsteen? It is an unpleasant fact that if Hello and their like are representative of the seventies youth culture, then God have mercy on our souls. Sure, they're young, they're very pretty, but as far as one can see, they're a manipulated product who know their place and don't talk back. With all respect, they do come on with all the flair and dash of Julie Andrews and give the impression that the seventies have produced a generation of teenage Uncle Toms.

Bruce Springsteen, on first examination, is a much more plausible candidate for new wave punkhood. What makes him a little suspect is the way his imagery is an amalgam of previous archetypes drawn from a range of classics that encompasses Herbert Selby, Bill Burroughs,

James Dean and, of course, Dylan. It could be that the only drawback with Springsteen is that he is laboring under too much pressure, exerted either by himself or by the commercial interests around him, to confirm to his "new Dylan" role. In fact his Fourth Street revisited pose is no more spurious than the young Dylan playing at Woody Guthrie. The real proof of whether Springsteen can cut it or not is in the response of the younger kids. If they wrap their little legs around his New Jersey engine in sensational ecstasy, the way our lot did with Dylan, then all is well. If not, then he will be relegated to just another nostalgic put-on for the Blonde On Blonde Memorial Society.

The very last ray of hope in this whole depressing examination is that maybe there is an MC5 of 1976 working out in a church hall somewhere. A cursory look round only revealed that nobody's working out anything anywhere. The youth of the nation just doesn't seem to be starting up bands with the alacrity and blind determination that they had a few years ago. There could be a mass of reasons for this. One is economic. Whereas once it was possible to equip a modest band with one fast hire purchase shuffle, a glance round the guitar stores makes it look as though you now need the solid backing of a well founded merchant bank to put a band on the road. Another answer might be the progressive relaxation in the sexual climate. A lot of established rock stars have cited some kind of sexual inadequacy as the reason they originally took up playing. Pete Townshend is a prime example. He has always admitted that he found his nose so brutally unattractive that he felt the need to seek safety behind a guitar.

It could be that in these liberal times the kids no longer have that kind of traumatic motivation.

Another, much more serious reason for the lack of new talent could be the current structure of the music industry. There are times when it really appears that over the last ten years we have produced a new strain of executive fat cat who is just as conservative as the old Tin Pan Alley breed who did their best to stop the flood of creativity during the early sixties. What once were maverick outfits have turned into big money operations with the big money reluctance to trust their technology and finance to a bunch of raw, ignorant punks from out of nowhere.

Of course, this is all speculation.

Before you pick up your pen to complain, gentle reader, look back over the first half of the seventies and see if you can define a solid, on-going thread in rock'n'roll that somehow syncs in with the broad stream of social attitudes. See one? No, me neither.

Neither, for that matter, did the scarf-toting kids I talked to outside QPR's ground at Loftus Road—football, after all, being the real crowd puller. They were fifteen and fourteen respectively. Two ten-years-on mutations of what mods once were. Fast talking and sharp, they made it perfectly clear that music was no great force in their lives. Their prime motivation was football. Sure they consumed music. They bought records, and owned something to play them on, but music was purely incidental. They followed no trends, could listen to the Tymes or Gary Glitter with equal enthusiasm.

Their idea of a good album was a K-Tel hits collection because you got a lot of good stuff for your money. They obtained most of their information from *Top Of The Pops* and the radio. They liked to have music around, but it was less important than Bruce Lee or birds. Is this the younger generation? It was certainly two of them. It is hard to say whether they were typical. The thing to remember, neighbors, is that *we* are hardly typical. We go to the trouble of reading a music paper. That shows a devotion over and above the call of duty. Most record buyers don't. It could be that rock'n'roll is sliding out of the preeminent position it has enjoyed for so long. It could be that the world is simply waiting for something new to appear, born from the waves like Aphrodite. If the latter's the case it is one hell of a long time coming.

New Musical Express, March 1, 1975

MICK FARREN

LET'S LOOT THE SUPERMARKET (LIKE WE DID LAST SUMMER)

Come on everybody, come gather round friends,
This is the way civilization ends.
Let's get together and do Death's dance,
And go loot the supermarket
While
We got the chance.

Times don't change but the haircuts do.
Same old bullshit for me and you.
Romp and stomp and hope to flash,
Hardtime summer when the sevens clash.

Bad old days come round again,
Half a minute and half a brain.
Too many old friends never came through.
Time we had the fun we're due.

Push and shove and stand in line.
Times get hard it's a spot of crime.
Scrabble, babble, buy a round,
Feels like you're surfing on solid ground.

Come on everybody, come gather round friends,
This is the way civilization ends.
Let's get together and do Death's dance,
And go loot the supermarket
While
We got the chance.

Written and recorded for the Deviants EP, *Screwed Up*, 1977

❑ Times did occur when a song—if maybe only in retrospect—could be a more accurate summation than any rock mag diatribe.

THE TITANIC SAILS AT DAWN

AS YOU CAN ALL QUITE WELL IMAGINE, THE READERS' letters that get themselves printed are only the tip of an

❑ The story, essay, call it what you will, that I wrote

A ROCK'N'ROLL INSURRECTION

for the **NME** in mid 1977, has been cited in a number of rock'n'roll histories as an active factor in the launching of punk. I disagree. By June of that year, the major punk bands, the Sex Pistols, the Clash, the Damned, and many more were together and playing shows. To tell the truth, I was being a little disingenuous in calling for something that was already happening. All I can say in my own defense is that my intention had been to spread the contagion of rabid, teeth grinding, electric-razor, punk guitar bands as far and as wide as possible. So there was a little sleight of pen involved. I just wanted it all to happen in a wider arena.

iceberg. The iceberg in this case seems to be one of a particularly threatening nature. In fact it is an iceberg that is drifting uncomfortably close to the dazzlingly lit, wonderfully appointed *Titanic* that is big-time, rock-pop, tax exile, jet-set showbusiness.

Unless someone aboard is prepared to leave the party and go up on the bridge and do something about, at least, a slight change of course, the whole chromium, metalflake Leviathan could go down with all hands. Currently about the only individual who seems to have the least interest in the social progress of rock'n'roll is the skinny, crypto Übermensch figure of David Bowie. Everyone else is waltzing around the grand ballroom, or playing musical chairs at the captain's table.

(WHAT IS HE TALKING ABOUT?)

I guess it's the absorption of rock'n'roll into the turgid masterstream of traditional establishment showbiz. For Zsa Zsa Gabor read Mick Jagger, for Lew Grade read Harvey Goldsmith. Only the names have been changed, blah, blah.

If that's the way of the world then keep your head down, make like William Hickey and drink yourself to death.

(OH GOD, DIDN'T HE GO THROUGH ALL THIS BACK IN JANUARY?)

That's right, he did. And short of picking up some change by doing it all over again and hoping no one will notice, it would be something of a redundant exercise.

Except that something seems to be happening that wasn't happening back in January. The aforementioned iceberg cometh. And that iceberg, dear reader is you.

Dig? I'm talkin' 'bout you.

Where once the letters that were dumped in the tray marked *Gasbag* contained smart-ass one liners, demands for album tokens, obscene ideas for the uses of Max Bell, or diatribes against Smith, Springsteen or Salewicz, now the tone has changed.

Stewart Tray of Manchester wouldn't go down and see the Stones if he was pulled there by Keith Richards. Mart of Oldham doesn't want to see five middle aged millionaires poncing around to pseudo soul funk/rock. Letter after letter repeats the same thing. You all seem to have had it with the Who, and Liz Taylor, Rod and the Queen, Jagger and Princess Margaret, paying three quid to be bent, mutilated, crushed or seated behind a pillar or a PA stack, all in the name of modern seventies-style super rock. The roar from the stage of, "I shout, I scream, I kill the king, I rail at all his servants" has been muted, mutated and diluted: "I smile, I fawn, I kiss ass and get my photo took." It was all too easy to accept that change, until you out there pulled the whole thing up short.

"We're not going to take it" wasn't coming from the stage with any conviction. Instead it was coming from the audience. Could it be that once more there's music in the cafés at night and revolution in the air?

It's hard to tell. Like it or not, *NME* is a part of the rock industry and, to an extent, suffers from the same isolation that is endemic to the whole business.

Certainly the massive rock gala of the last month has produced some kind of backlash. People have become tired of the godawful conditions at places like the recent concert by the Who at Charlton football ground. They're sick of having their booze confiscated and being ordered to stop dancing. Maybe they're also sick of seeing the vibrant, iconoclastic music whose changes did, at least, shake the walls of the city a little, being turned round, sold out, castrated and co-opted. Did we ever expect to see the Rolling Stones on *News at Ten* just like they were at the Badminton Horse Trials or the Chelsea Flower Show? It's not clear just how deep this resistance goes. There's no way of knowing whether the mail we've getting is simply another version of "Dear Esther Rantzen, I just found a sewer rat in my Diet Pepsi."

The only thing I know for sure is the effect the whole thing had on me. I woke up guilty and angry. Has rock'n'roll become another mindless consumer product that plays footsie with jet set and royalty while the kids who make up its roots and energy queue up in the rain to watch it from 200 yards away? The Who, the Stones,

Bowie, are, after all, my own generation. We all grew up together. I saw them in small sweaty clubs, cinemas and finally giant rock festivals. At the same time as everyone else they embraced politics, mysticism, and acid. Together we ran through the trends, fads, psychoses and few precious moments of clear honesty that made up the tangle of the sixties.

(ISN'T THIS GETTING A LITTLE... UH... SUBJECTIVE? IT'S ONLY ROCK'N'ROLL, AFTER ALL?)

Yeah, maybe so. There does, however, come a point when a cynical sold-out front has to drop for long enough to shout "Hold it!" Did we really come through the fantasy, fear and psychic mess of the last decade to make rock'n'roll safe for the Queen, Princess Margaret or Liz Taylor? Was the bold rhetoric and even the deaths and imprisonments simply to enable the heroes and idols of the period to retreat into a gaudy, vulgar jet set that differs from the Taylor/Burton menace or the Sinatra rat pack only in small variations of style. It's not so much the lifestyle of stars that is important. They can guzzle champagne till it runs from their ears, and become facile to the point of dumbness. They will only undermine their own credibility. The real danger lies in what seems sometimes to be a determined effort on the part of some artists, promoters and sections of the media to turn rock into a safe, establishment form of entertainment. It's okay if some stars want to make the switch from punk to Liberace so long as they don't take rock'n'roll with them.

If rock becomes safe, it's all over. It's a vibrant, vital music that from its very roots has always been a burst of color and excitement against a background of dullness, hardship or frustration. From the blues onwards, the essential core of the music has been the rough side of humanity. It's a core of rebellion, sexuality, assertion and even violence. All the things that have always been unacceptable to a ruling establishment.

Once that vigorous, horny-handed core is extracted from rock'n'roll, you're left with little more than muzak. No matter how tastefully played or artfully constructed, if the soul's gone then it still, in the end, comes down to muzak.

(OKAY, OKAY, WE'VE HEARD THE "MUSIC IS THE LIFE FORCE" MESSAGE PLENTY OF TIMES BEFORE. WHAT ABOUT A FEW SOLUTIONS FOR A CHANGE?)

"Well," he said, avoiding everyone's eyes, "solutions aren't quite so easy."

The one thing that isn't a solution is to look back at the sixties and reproduce something from the past. This is, in fact, one of the problems we're suffering from today. The methods of presenting the biggest of today's superstars were conceived in the sixties when the crowds were smaller and logistics a whole lot easier. When the Stones play at Earl's Court, or Bowie at Wembley Pool, we're seeing the old Bill Graham Fillmore. The difference is that the crowd is five or ten times the size and the problems of controlling it are multiplied by the same extent. The promoter's solution is to remove the dancing, freaking about, and general looseness of the old Fillmore days. Instead the audience is expected to sit still in their numbered, regimented seats, under the watchful ear of the security muscle.

The same situation exists when the Who play at Charlton or any other football ground. The stadium rock show is basically the open air festival penned up inside the walls of a sports arena. Again, from the promoter's point of view, it makes everything very much easier. There's no more trouble with ticket-taking or the collection of money. Security is simplified, and all the problems of overnight camping are avoided. Unfortunately it's the audience that now takes all the chances. They're the ones who take the risk of being crushed, cramped, bottled, soaked, stuck behind a pillar or a PA stack, manhandled by security, ripped off by hotdog men or generally dumped on. It's got to the point where the only celebration at today's superstar concert is taking place on stage. The only role for the audience is that of uncomfortable observers. There are more ways of taking the soul out of rock'n'roll than just changing the music. We're six years into the 1970s, and already the sixties are beginning to sound like some golden age.

A ROCK'N'ROLL INSURRECTION

(OH NO, NOT THAT AGAIN.)

Of course they weren't. If we could be miraculously transported back there, we'd probably be appalled at some of the dumbness and naïveté that went down. There were wrong moves, screw-ups, disasters and even straightforward robberies. The two things that did exist that don't seem to be prominent today were, first, a phenomenal burst of creativity that wasn't merely confined to the stage but extended into the presentation, the audience and even right through to the press and poster art.

The second thing was that from musicians to managers to promoters to audience, the whole rock scene was in the hands of one generation. It was by no means perfect, but at least the energy levels were higher, and the gap between star and fan wasn't the yawning chasm that it has become today.

From sweaty, shoestring cellar clubs through the multimedia extravaganzas like the Avalon in San Francisco, the Grande Ballroom in Detroit or the Technicolour Dream and UFO in London, clear through Glastonbury Fayre and even Woodstock, it was one generation taking care of its own music. The scene was sufficiently solid to ease out the old farts from the fifties who thought promoting rock was a matter of giving the "kids" the kind of safe product, the kind of thing that was good for them.

(AH-HA! NOW WE GET DOWN TO IT. FARREN'S TRYING TO TURN THE CLOCK BACK TO THE SIXTIES UNDERGROUND SCENE.)

No such thing. Even if I wanted to, that simply wouldn't be possible. The whole of the sixties underground, the free concerts and festivals, *Oz*, *IT*, the crazed fringe bands, and street theater would be largely impossible today. They survived financially in a tiny margin of a still affluent society that doesn't exist today. The seventies are without doubt an era of compromise. Even to get this piece into print it is necessary to use the resources of a giant corporation, and adapt one's approach accordingly. The real question of this decade is not whether to compromise or not, but how much and in what way.

One major lesson can be learned from the sixties, however, and that is that the best, most healthy kind of rock'n'roll is produced by and for the same generation.

There can be no question that a lot of today's rock is isolated from the broad mass of its audience. From the superstars with champagne and coke parties all the way down to your humble servant spending more time with his friends, his writing and his cat than he does cruising the street, all are cut off. If rock is not being currently presented in an acceptable manner, and from the letters we've been getting at *NME*, this would seem to be the case, it is time for the seventies generation to start producing their own ideas, and ease out the old farts who are still pushing tired ideas left over from the sixties.

The time seems to be right for original thinking and new inventive concepts, not only in the music but in the way that it is staged and promoted. It may be difficult in the current economic climate, and it may be a question of taking rock back to street level and starting all over again. This is the only way out, if we are not going to look forward to an endless series of Charlton and Earl's Court style gigs, and constant reruns of things from the past, be they Glenn Miller revivals or Bowie's stabs at neo-fascism. Putting the Beatles back together isn't going to be the salvation of rock'n'roll. Four kids playing to their contemporaries in a dirty cellar club might.

And that, gentle reader, is where you come in.

New Musical Express, June 1977

THE ALL-NIGHT GIRLS ARE BACK ON THE TRAIN

THE MUTANTS, THE DWARFS, AND THE ALL NIGHT GIRLS (that's right, the ones who still brag about escapades out on the D train, despite the fact that the amphetamines have turned their teeth brown and they've taken so many downers that orgasms are no longer possible) have always ❑ And when that something happened, it happened fast. By October of the same year, punk was in full flourish. The nasty rama-lama was back with cuts and bruises, bad breath, torn stockings, smeared lipstick, a dirty mouth, and a really bad attitude.

been with us. They probably always will be. If you wanted to stretch a point (the rubber, the rubber), you could say that the sleazoid motherlode was one of the most enduring themes in rock'n'roll, beyond, that is, love (l-u-v), drugs (spelled p-a-r-a-n-o-i-a) and paranoia (usually spelled d-r-u-g-s).

(Have you noticed the number of brackets in this first paragraph?)

You might think that it was the 1966 Bob Dylan who first mined the back alley vampire vein. On one level, you'd probably be right. Dylan was lucky, I guess. He came at a time when rock and the street were both starting to grow up. The boy from New York City, who looked so cute in his mohair suit, had lost the ability to keep his pockets full of spending loot. He'd degenerated to just another angel-head seeking an angry fix in the hungry etc. The teen hoods and motorcycle rowdies of legend were being forcibly turned into the gas station attendants, the overdose statistics, and brave boys in Vietnam.

But those are the sixties, and we've heard all about them, haven't we? We're supposed to be looking at the seventies, right? Okay, let's look at them.

The problem is that time doesn't readily allow itself to be sliced up into tidy ten-year segments. Nineteen hundred and seventy wasn't the opening of a clean new chapter, whatever anyone might tell you. There was still too much unfinished business from the chapter before. I mean, it took right through to 1971 for the hippies to wise up that they'd lost the revolution. Sleaze, however, is fairly easy to chop into segments. It is, after all, a fairly constant phenomenon. About all that happens to sleaze is that it gets progressively worse. At least, that's one of the main threads of the 1970s.

I guess a lot of people assumed, or maybe just hoped, that the geeks and ghouls and angry ratted-over poets would drift away after Dylan had taken himself off to Nashville to sing with Johnny Cash. There are certain people who always hope they'll go away. It's the same kind of people who got so awfully, awfully shocked at the antics of Rotten and the rest just a while ago. They're the people who refuse to believe that we're not all part of the G-Plan. So there we were, at the start of the seventies. The Stones, shell-shocked from Altamont, had holed up in room 1009, where they complained that they just couldn't get high. Elvis had decked himself in black leather to try and prove for the very last time that he was a human being and, as I already said, Dylan was doing his damnedest to become the very first all-Jewish country cousin.

For some people, those easy options just weren't open. In New York, Lou Reed was making his way from Severin the masochist (whip kissing on bended knee) to all the freaks who came from out on the island, shaving their legs, giving head and trying to be James Dean for a day. In Detroit, MC5 were fighting the law and the law was winning. Same time, same place, Iggy Pop (the Stooge, sometime Osterberg) was fighting himself and no one was winning. In LA, Frank Zappa worked on his groupies-as-the-path-to world-domination master plan, and in Paris? Jim Morrison was finally succeeding in drinking himself to death so the whole bloody trip in the blue bus could be marked paid and filed under H.

The stage was set, the credits rolled. Yes, my dears, 1970 was all ready to do its worst. I suppose if you were to search out the ground zero of rock sleaze, back in those early days of this wonderful decade, the place to look was the back room of Max's Kansas City. In those days, it was simply a drinking joint for the parasites who buzzed, for all the world like flies round a dead dog, in the general vicinity of the old Warhol factory, across the other side of Union Square.

At various points during Max's heyday, before it became an obsolete landmark for out-of-town teen tourists and first-time-in-New York British low rollers hoping to score with the broads, the Flamin' Groovies came out of Oakland and conspired to be bad. Sylvain, Thunders, Johansen and all (Dolls to you) conspired to be worse. Warhol looked on, and maybe brought Truman Capote slumming. Debbie Harry waited table. Patti Smith waited for a part in an art movie.

The denizens of Max's didn't have to look too far for inspiration. Just across the avenue, in the middle of the square, was enough lowlife to satisfy anyone who wasn't courting a genuine, dead on arrival, rock'n'roll suicide. Around the statue (General Grant? I've never bothered to look) and in and out of the gray bushes, the kids burned the winos and the junkies robbed the kids. Smack and sexual ambiguity constantly battled for the heavyweight theme crown of the horrorshow hot hundred. (In fact there weren't enough to make up a hundred, but what the hell?) White punks on dope or wearing your sister's dress? The choices were hard for concerned young adults in the third, fourth and fifth years of the Nixon era.

New York City didn't, however, have it all its own way. There were things going on elsewhere that were less than savory in the eyes of middle earth (the global silent majority, not Planet Hobbit, although, maybe, in the end, they ain't so far apart, dig?). In London, David Bowie preached sexual confusion. Alice Cooper stalked the Canadian border, leaving legends of chicken geek fun and pleasing the bikers.

Alas, paths, even in the twilight zone, have a habit of straying. The road from chicken molesting to golf with Groucho proved alarmingly short, as did the trail from Martian self-destruction to one man Herrenvolk. Some did attempt to keep the faith if faith is a word you can use in this context. The Dolls tried and failed and tried again. Brian Eno skipped in with warm jets and burning babies but had too fleet and complex a mind to become a permanent fixture in the night gallery. Even the Pink Fairies tried to make their mark, but all too often the mark was Russell Hunter's blood on the hotel room ceiling. Lemmy abided, as did a million nameless others. A band that went by the name of Third World War even preached the philosophy of machine guns in Knightsbridge a good four years before it was at all cool.

All this shuck and jive was the extent. By 1974, sleaze was far from acceptable. Why? you ask. Was it because the world had so righted itself that the fags, hags, halt and lame had been transformed in the light of clear new morning? Yeah, pigs fly. All that had happened was that the corporations had moved in. Global Leisure had decreed that the world had had enough of all this junkie street shtick. Crosby, Stills, Emerson, Lake and the Eagles were the sounds suitable for a balanced society.

Of course, this wasn't the way things went. Down in the King's Road and at Bleecker and Bowery stuff once again stirred. Patti Smith's chance had come, and Rotten had his chance to kick ass. The dam burst, the Ramones sped out with their own brand of just-add-water minimalism by numbers, Verlaine and Hell fought in the captain's tower. Blondie mourned the passing of bouffants and stiletto heels, Willy de Ville made like James Brown from space, Talking Heads moved in icy mystery, while ex-Doll Thunders used the UK as a springboard for a second coming.

It seemed fitting that the year that gave us Son of Sam also revealed that Global Leisure Inc. did not dictate the entire fate of modern music as we know it. Once again, the creeps were back. Sleaze went on. And where did it all get us? Well, I'm writing this in a DC 10 about eight miles above and a little to the south of the North Pole. (This might account for the story being more fanciful than factual.) Right at the same moment a gay bank robber is sitting in the airport in Atlanta, Georgia, threatening to kill eighty-seven people unless they let his boyfriend out of jail. He monopolized airtime all across the USA. It's only rock'n'roll, but it's drastic.

Need I say more? Have a nice day.

New Musical Express, October 1977

DON'T

☞ Don't trust anyone who is always on TV.
☞ Don't trust anyone who always has their picture in the newspapers.

And as we moved uneasily into the 1980s, I even compiled a modest list of things that one really shouldn't do.

☞ Don't trust anyone from New Jersey who wears a Van Halen T-shirt.

☞ Don't trust anyone who sings along with Neil Diamond.

☞ Don't trust anyone who sings along with Billy Joel.

☞ Don't trust anyone who wants you to do something unpleasant and tells you it's good for you.

☞ Don't trust anyone who claims to be in touch with God.

☞ Don't trust anyone who thinks Ronald Reagan is going to save us all.

☞ Don't trust anyone who thinks Paul McCartney is art.

☞ Don't trust anyone who thinks *The Horror of Party Beach* isn't.

☞ Don't trust anyone with a cowboy hat, a beard and beergut (particularly when they're bigger than you).

☞ Don't trust anyone who imitates dead rock stars.

☞ Don't trust people who know for a fact that a particular dead rock star is still alive.

☞ Don't trust dead rock stars.

☞ Don't trust any band that talks about its wonderful relationship with its label.

☞ Don't trust any record label that wants to seal the deal with a handshake.

☞ Don't trust anyone in white winklepickers.

☞ Don't pick a fight with a Willie Nelson fan in Austin, Texas.

☞ Don't trust anyone who thinks Elvis Presley is irrelevant.

☞ Don't trust anyone who thinks 'In The Ghetto' is significant.

☞ Don't trust people who like to be mistaken for Elvis Costello.

☞ Don't trust anyone who claims to have appeared on *Let's Make a Deal*.

☞ Don't trust anyone who thinks Sandy Shaw is important in the scheme of things.

☞ Don't trust anyone who tells you *Eraserhead* is their favorite movie.

☞ Don't trust anyone who listens to nothing but obscure English new wave bands.

- ☞ Don't trust anyone who listens to nothing but obscure California punk bands.
- ☞ Don't trust anyone who listens to nothing but Top 40.
- ☞ Don't trust anyone for whom the Black Sabbath/Blue Öyster Cult tour was the high point of 1980.
- ☞ Don't trust anyone who goes around armed.
- ☞ Don't trust anyone constantly seeking publicity for themselves.
- ☞ Don't trust anyone constantly seeking publicity for other people.
- ☞ Don't trust anyone who is considerably richer than you. Wonder, instead, how they got that way.
- ☞ Don't trust anyone considerably poorer than you. They are probably defective.
- ☞ Don't trust anyone who sleeps with a Kermit the Frog doll on their pillow.
- ☞ Don't trust anyone who has seen the movie *Alien* more than twice.
- ☞ Don't trust anyone whose car has black windows.
- ☞ Don't trust anyone who says "product" when they mean music.
- ☞ Don't trust anyone who admits to having owned a pet rock.
- ☞ Don't trust people who make lists.
- ☞ Don't trust anyone who kept a scrapbook on the Manson Family.
- ☞ Don't trust anyone drinking white port and swallowing reds.
- ☞ Don't trust anyone who raises reptiles.
- ☞ Don't trust anyone who likes having their picture taken with gangsters—or rock stars.
- ☞ Don't trust anyone who brings a Polaroid One Step on the first date.
- ☞ Don't trust anyone who you've never seen standing up.
- ☞ Don't trust anyone who arrives with their lawyer.
- ☞ Don't trust anyone who arrives with their mother.
- ☞ Don't trust anyone who still has a yellow ribbon tied to their property.
- ☞ Don't trust anyone who worries about static cling.

☞ Don't trust anyone who goes out of their way to badmouth the Clash.

☞ Don't trust anyone who steals jokes from Woody Allen.

☞ Don't trust anyone who cries through re-runs of *The Mary Tyler Moore Show.*

☞ Never lend money to musicians.

☞ Don't trust anyone who's never heard of Arthur Lee.

☞ Don't trust anyone who claims to be cloned.

☞ Don't trust anyone who keeps a Doberman Pinscher in a small studio apartment.

☞ Don't trust anyone who tells you bestiality is the now thing.

☞ Don't trust anyone who thinks John Belushi wrote 'Hold On, I'm Coming.'

☞ Don't trust anyone with L-O-V-E and H-A-T-E tattooed on their knuckles.

☞ Don't trust anyone who gets all their information from the *National Enquirer.*

☞ Don't trust people who claim to be able to get you backstage.

☞ Don't trust people who claim to be re-staging Woodstock.

☞ Don't go down in the basement!

☞ Don't trust late night talk-show hosts.

☞ On no account trust the born again. One birth in a lifetime is quite enough for anyone.

☞ Don't trust people whose pants don't reach their shoes.

☞ Don't trust people who claim Public Image Ltd. is the future of rock.

☞ Don't trust people who tell you rock is dead.

☞ Don't trust anyone who tells you he was Elvis Presley's doctor.

☞ Don't trust any song that rhymes "brain" with "pain."

☞ Don't trust anyone who tells you to "have a nice day."

☞ Don't trust any self-declared poets who front rock bands.

☞ Don't believe anything you read or almost anything on network news.

☞ Never eat at a place called Mom's.

MICK FARREN

☞ Never play cards with a man called Doc.
☞ Don't think twice—it's alright.

Trouser Press, 1982

ONE MORE TEENAGE WASTELAND

ONE OF THE PROBLEMS WITH THE WHO IS THAT they're just so damned lovable. In London, they're looked on with the kind of cockney fondness that's normally reserved for soccer stars, big-time criminals, and Michael Caine. The legend about how one of the town's most successful rock impresarios started on the road to riches by selling speed to the kids who came to see the band way back when at the Marquee Club is still repeated with relish. The Who are so lovable that they beat the late seventies generation gap. Even the Sex Pistols had to forgive their Uncle Pete Townshend.

The unfortunate part is that people who love the Who best of all are the most lumpen of American youth, the kind who thronged the IRT going out to Shea Stadium, the ones with the hair and the souvenir T-shirts worn like campaign ribbons, the ones who pour beer down themselves with the pre-hysteric determination of someone whose best idea is to end the night unconscious or in jail. It's an important event. It's been publicized, at least, as the last time they'll ever see the Who. Their idols are retiring. These guys (and they're a predominantly young male phenomenon) want nothing so much as to bay out loud when Townshend windmills his arm in his guitar god signature and bellow along that "it's only teenage wasteland."

There's nothing basically wrong with these kids except that they've perfected the knack of using beer and rock'n'roll as a means of making themselves totally nuts. Minds disengage, they go for the stage by any means possible, and the blind pushing and stomping starts. Even though the headline writers at the *New York Post* became more hysterical than any fan when they wrote about a

☐ Despite corporate attempts to sideline it as "New Wave," and the highly publicized implosion of the Sex Pistols, punk carved a major niché for itself in rock'n'roll to the point that, as the 1970s moved into the 1980s, the bands that had survived—notably the Ramones and the Clash—were very close to being part of the mainstream. In October of 1982, the Clash opened for the Who at New York's Shea Stadium where the Beatles had played their very last East Coast live concert on their final tour. The Who had intimated that this would also be the end for them. They were retiring, hanging up their guns, and stepping aside to let the Clash take over. The idea seemed too good to be true, and, of course, as history would prove, it was.

so-called "riot," and whoever was ultimately responsible for putting the Who on what looked like a four-foot high stage in front of a standing crowd of many thousands should perhaps be relieved of his or her job.

The artists who go this stadium route tend, whether they know it or not, to become captives of these mindless assemblies. Their live work is only heard in the open air or in the dubious acoustics of very big buildings, and though the crowds provide bursts of extreme adulation and fixes of intense energy, they are also possessed of a massive inertia that drags, stretches, and slows the music. The mindless like it ponderous. They like songs that start, with only a delicate guitar figure and some sobbing, histrionic singing, and, nine minutes later, have slowly built to the aural equivalent of the bombing of Dresden. No matter how they may holler for rock'n'roll, the mindless mass are suckers for this Godzilla dynamic. They love an anthem. It's a particular heavy metal lurch toward high art that has as much to do with Tchaikovsky's cannons as it does with Little Richard and is best presented with spectacular visual effects. In 'Behind Blue Eyes,' the Who have a perfect example which they are not ashamed to milk for every shuddering moment. They know they're playing to the same people who keep 'Stairway to Heaven' the most played song on US radio.

The way that the span of some eighteen years has slowed and weighted the Who is particularly noticeable when they bounce onto the stage to open with 'Substitute' rapidly followed by 'I Can't Explain.' These early hit singles are a forcible reminder of how they started and of how Pete Townshend was once a master of the sharp, stripped-down pop tune. In their club days, the Who were badder than any bad-ass teen band I ever witnessed. They were unique in that they arrived at a certain moment in both rock technology and the drug culture armed with Pete Townshend's instinctive grasp of what levels of aggression that moment might yield. There was a shimmer of juvenile angst and methamphetamine on the band, particularly on Townshend and Keith Moon, back in those days when guitars and equipment were sacrificed to their reading of Hubert Sumlin's six note guitar figure for 'Smokestack Lightnin''. They were a part of the dark, angry, sometimes psychotic side of swinging London that the tourist brochures always neglected to mention.

Both the strength and the curse of the Who is that they were too complex to remain just a bad-ass teen band with a neat line in volume and violence. They embraced every new influence as it came. For an instant they were psychedelic, and then they drifted into what was mainly Townshend's inflated idea of big art. From *Tommy* they went to Woodstock and on to the ballparks and stadia of the American heartland. As far as I'm concerned, it was in this teenage wasteland that the rot set in.

Just how far the rot actually went can be easily gauged by the new album, *It's Hard*. It's aptly titled. The Who have become complicated and labored. Townshend's alternating need to know (remember 'The Seeker'?) and need to confess, Entwistle's seeming distaste for all the trappings of stardom, and the general erosion of age seems to have produced a standardized late-model Who song that's long, wordy, medium-paced, based on an over-extended guitar or synthesizer figure, and lacking in both hooks and genuine power.

Although I haven't been particularly crazy about the Who's recent work (okay, 'Don't Let Go of the Gold'), what really surprised me about *It's Hard* was that although there are a couple of pretty items (notably the single and title track) there's nothing approaching a rabble rousing pop song, a robust rocker, or even a new anthem for the teenage wasteland. I fear that *It's Hard*—and it's a terrible thing to find yourself saying about the Who—sounds like an album that was made because it had to be, with little to offer bar sluggish, warmed-over riffs and midlife angst.

On stage, the Who are much more at their ease. They are able to parade their entire catalog of successes. The years have made them consummate performers, even though there are moments of confusion and even irony. What, for instance, is an aging, very wealthy Londoner doing out there singing 'My Generation'? (What, for that matter, though, is an equally aging though much less wealthy Londoner doing sitting here writing about it?) They've become a fairly incongruous bunch of rock stars. Townshend in his leather jacket and fifties haircut half fits the part, despite baggy pants and an expression of exhaustion. Kenny Jones is superb and workmanlike behind the drums, but he's a new boy and missed the years of dangerous excesses. John Entwistle looks more like a successful movie producer than one of the world's most celebrated bass players while Roger Daltrey, resplendent in a silver mohair James Brown suit, never stops jumping, bouncing, and running on the spot. He's like an overtrained bantamweight who's worked so much harder because he knows he's got a limited number of fights left in his career.

Mass adulation has endowed the Who with a number of bad habits. They extend when they ought to be snapping it together. Solos go on far too long and I see no reason why Daltrey should indulge in two major bouts of harmonica blowing. Even when things flag, though, the Who have it covered. The searchlights blaze out, the truly awesome effects come into play, and those sections of the crowd that may have been drifting toward boredom are whipped back up.

Stadium playing is an acquired art that not only requires expertise and experience but also the deployment of massive amounts of money. This was something that the Clash, opening the show, learned to their total cost. In the pre-event publicity it was pitched as some kind of dynastic event. The Who would abdicate in favor of the younger musicians, handing their pinball crowns to the Clash. On the night, the Clash received the same shaft as any other warm-up band that hasn't learned the tricks. Allowed minimal use of the lighting facilities, they all but vanished. Only Mick Jones, who by either luck or judgment had worn a red jumpsuit, could be seen clearly. Strummer and Simonon, in guerrilla drab, were invisible to all but the front rows. Racketing around Shea Stadium, their already dodgy vocals became painfully disorganized. By the end of

'Substitute' the heirs apparent were all but forgotten.

Two hours or more later, I'd about had enough of the Who. I'd been too long in this damp, uncomfortable environment with a lot of cops and kids and without so much as a beer. I started to wonder if I should miss the end of the protracted encore ritual and beat the rush to the subway. Then I was zapped. After a Townshend chord collection they burst into 'Twist and Shout,' a magnificent Beatles-style 'Twist and Shout' right at Shea Stadium. Not only was it a killer version, but it was presented with such a guileless, grinning sense of history that I started to believe, for the first time, that maybe history was being made. For as long as the tune took, I was prepared to forgive the Who all the sins that are listed above, and bid them a fond farewell. As I said at the start, the Who are just so damned lovable. There's one thing, though—if they pull a comeback in a couple of years' time I shall be extremely upset.

Village Voice, October 1982

THE SNUFF OF DREAMS

IT'S EASY IN MORE NORMAL TIMES TO TALK ABOUT THE price of fame. By very definition, the artist, the rock'n'roll star, is up for grabs. We carry a piece of him or her in our soul and in our memory. In the case of the Beatles, damn near all of us were faces in one of the crowds. The hysterical teenager at Shea Stadium may now be a thirty-year-old executive, but she still walks with the legacy. For millions of us, the most significant events of our lives frequently took place to a soundtrack of 'She Loves You,' 'Paperback Writer' or 'All You Need Is Love' coming from a background radio. John Lennon figures in all of our histories; we have all taken a piece of him for our own. Unfortunately, one particular maniac felt that he had the right to collect much more than his fair share.

There was a certain twisted logic about Elvis Presley dying on his bathroom floor with a stomach full of

❑ The shock that followed the TV newsflash still defies description. The idea that John Lennon could be shot dead on a New York sidewalk as he was going into his apartment in the Dakota building on Central Park West defied all belief. I was living in New York at the time, and my friends Boss Goodman and Larry Wallis were paying a pre-Christmas visit. Still hardly able to grasp the reality of what had happened, the three of us headed out into a Manhattan night that was a scene of chaotic grief. People wept openly in Greenwich Village bars. When they heard our English accents, bartenders wouldn't take our money, and other customers tried to explain that New York and America weren't really places of homicide and insanity. The next day, and very hungover, I received a call from my editor at the **SoHo Weekly News**. He wanted eight hundred words on Lennon's death and he needed it in the next two hours. Bleary and aching—still not quite believing—I acquired coffee and went to work.

Quaaludes. At least he was a victim of his own spiritual bankruptcy. There is no logic whatsoever in John Lennon being gunned down outside the Dakota. The spiritual bankruptcy in this case is that of a vampiric fan whose dreams became so warped that the only catharsis was to slay the man who made the music.

It had to be John Lennon, didn't it? John the cynic, John the lout, John the iconoclast. John the genius, John the working class hero. John Lennon who gave us 'I Feel Fine,' 'Good Dog Nigel,' 'Cold Turkey.' Nobody would ever go looking for Paul McCartney with a gun. John Lennon became part of our dreams because he couldn't resist publicly displaying his own wounds. We were all there when Lennon drove himself to the edge—we were allowed to feel his elation and his moments of despair. All over the world, there are people who have found their own problems easier to deal with because Lennon had been there first, and had written a song about it.

One of the problems that Lennon constantly experienced was that he couldn't separate his emotional life from his work. No artist can. Right now I'm experiencing the same dilemma. I want someone to blame, someone to hold responsible—someone more than "a local screwball." I can't quite believe that a human being as worthwhile as John Lennon was blown away by a smirking, barren, totally valueless lunatic who could find no other way to carve himself a place in history.

I suppose it might be possible to blame society for the death of its poets and heroes. We've all been sold fame so hard that there's some of the warp in all of us. The media constantly pump the message that the rich and the famous and the powerful are the ones deserving of adoration; that mass adulation is a substitute for individual love.

The major irony is that among all the so-called superstars of rock'n'roll, Lennon was the one who seemed to have managed to overcome the pressures, the strain and the terrors that might have sent him down the same route as Hendrix, Morrison, Joplin, and Presley. He seemed to be able to fight back the demons and come to terms with

MICK FARREN

the reality of being a normal, fallible and often terrified mortal, whose talent elevated him to a near-godlike status without anything but a mortal's emotional armor to protect him. Lennon appeared to have reached that position of peace that is only available to a man who has truly come to terms with himself. It's a monstrous thing that this peace can be so easily shattered by a single criminal act.

A certain level of commonsense says that the murder of John Lennon is nothing more and nothing less than the hundreds of other pointless, brutal and anonymous killings that happen every week every year. Of course, it never works that way. John Lennon has been blown away by a lunatic and that's something you can't just write off with sociology.

The anger has yet to subside. Right now I'm too numb to properly grieve. I'm more angry that a man who gave me so much pleasure, who totally offered himself to the world, should have his life ended from behind.

It's too early to really come to grips with what has happened. And it's hardly possible to give an assessment of John Lennon. Christ, I loved the man, and I only met him once. Maybe, though, an assessment isn't really necessary. In the final analysis, the measure of John Lennon can be clearly judged by the number of people who are grieving. The evil that killed Lennon has killed part of all our memories and all our fantasies. That self-serving little son-of-a-bitch has killed a part of all of us.

SoHo Weekly News, December 1980

Part Two

From The Barricades To The Bar

1n all the gin joints in all the world, the ones most amenable to bending oneself completely out of shape had to be in New York City. I've spent time in London, Los Angeles, New York, and Tokyo, and visited dozens of other towns and cities across the world, and I never found anywhere better suited to toxic self-destruction than the lower end of the island of Manhattan in the 1980s.

Of course, I had a lot of help. The Reagan era was in full swing, and a confederacy of fools and criminals had deemed that greed was (for want of a better word) good, and were willing to risk anything from global climate breakdown to World War III if it raised the Dow, and was good for the military industrial complex. They even re-classified ketchup as a vegetable in school meal nutrition guidelines. The ugliness that would grow into the political right of the twenty-first century was being nurtured and trained, while paper billions were being made down on freshly deregulated Wall Street by cocaine fueled young men who owned Ferraris, but had no furniture in their condos.

On the other side of the coin, the punk revolution was falling back in confusion, ducking the alpha-jerk, if not actually living on Chinese rocks. Patti Smith was still having her photo taken with Bob Dylan and William Burroughs, but Jim Carroll was making a name for himself by showing his track marks, and Johnny Thunders was fighting with Dee Dee Ramone over who ruled the Lost Highway, while Keith Richards drove past in his limo, and Lester Bangs grew more morose. Madonna had been loosed on the culture and it was hardly a happy environment for the artist.

My basic reaction was to retreat to my fortress of solitude and write, but that didn't mean that I wholly shut myself way. The energy of New York was far too intense to be a complete recluse, plus I had tradition on my side. Ask Samuel Taylor Coleridge, Dylan Thomas, Charles Bukowski, or Dr. Hunter Thompson. Literature has a long history of scribes who cannot help but head for the whiskey or worse when the pressure of the deadline bearing down on their imagination becomes intolerable, and, never one to argue with a sensible tradition of the trade, many a midnight, and even a necessarily idle afternoon, would find me in the Lion's Head, Dan Lynch's, the Bells of Hell, the Park Inn Tavern, Paul's Lounge, the Grass Roots, or the St. Mark's Bar & Grill. After the 4am last call, I might repair to an after-hours joint like Sophie's or Save The Robots, or places with no name where one could drink until well into the morning.

My liver may not have been overjoyed but, in all other ways, this proved to be a very productive alternation between isolation and a barstool. I am in no position to judge if what I created was literature, but I produced a half dozen science fiction novels, a couple of non-fiction books, a slew of magazine stories for publications as diverse as *Rolling Stone*, the *Village Voice*, *Twilight Zone*, *SoHo Weekly News*, *Trouser Press*, and the *East Village Eye*, and even a handful of episodes of a TV cartoon show called *The Galaxy Rangers*. Maybe vignettes from all the saloons and shebeens I treated as second homes spilled over into my prose and poetry, but how could it be otherwise if I was to be true to my craft.

AFTER MIDNIGHT WHEN THE BOYS AND GIRLS TALK ABOUT DEATH

"Anyway, there's this crazy guy who jumped the lights in a bright red Firebird. It's somewhere around 19th Street and Park Avenue South, just a bit north of Max's, and he just misses greasing this guy who's crossing the street by the width of a whisper."

Dolores was already drunk by the time the rest of us got there. She was relating the story to the bartender and two wandering bucket salesmen from the great American Heartland, but, then again, it was that time of night. Dolores' only competition was a rummy at the other end of the bar who looked like Charlie Mingus in a pork pie hat; he was trying to tell nobody in particular about how he once impregnated a polar bear, but he was having trouble making the words form. When you got down to it, Dolores had the room.

"So anyway, needless to say, the guy who's trying to cross the street starts yelling bloody Ratso Rizzo murder after the Firebird. I mean, who wouldn't if you've just been almost run over. The crazy driver must have heard him because he stamps on his brakes and starts to back up. Now, if it had been me, I would have taken off running. In a situation like that you know that this guy isn't backing up his car to hand you any prize for civic pride. The guy who was nearly run over, though, I got to tell you, he ain't me. He thinks he's got balls or something. He stands his ground, hollering and cursing. The Firebird gets right up by him, but he doesn't quit. Then suddenly, BLAM! BLAM! The crazy in the Firebird has pulled out a gun and pumped two bullets into him. Just like that."

Dolores silently shook her head as though astonished at the depravity of which mankind is capable. The rummy in the pork pie hat had one last shot at the polar bear fantasy and then he gave up. Dolores shook her head a second time. "I mean, can you believe it? There's people who have sunk so low that they'll actually kill someone just on account of they don't like the way that they drive."

"Some people are kind of touchy about their driving."

"He was probably one of the Me Generation. They take themselves very seriously."

"John Wesley Harding once shot a man dead because he didn't like the way he snored."

"They use that in some Time-Life book commercial. *Great Psychos of The Old West*. I guess they think it's a major selling point."

"It was different back then."

"Men were men."

"And women looked for solace."

"Everyone was less sane and armed to the teeth."

"So what changed?"

"Last week, over on the east side, some kid stabbed a guy to death because he didn't like his face. He was mugging him at the time."

"It's like child abuse."

"I abuse children every chance I get. Trouble is they abuse you back. Maybe shoot you too. Even the kids are packing pieces these days. The cops raided this high school in Staten Island and hauled away over 200 handguns."

"Love is never having to use wire hangers."

"Why are you all talking this shit?"

Vinnie took out his gum and parked it on the underside of the bar, leaving it for someone else's fingers to encounter. Vinnie had moved up close to Dolores and was trying to look down the front of her low-cut, ultra-tight, bright red, Whore-In-A-Babylon dress. Lately, Dolores had been affecting a somewhat overripe look that tended to attract single-minded individuals like Vinnie. The dress was set off by matching red, spike heel shoes and no stockings. She had exceedingly white legs. It was as though Dolores rarely saw the sun which, in fact, was the case. Like most of those present, Dolores pretty much kept vampire hours.

Something about the conversation seemed to have upset Vinnie. He was nervously fingering the gold religious medal that hung around his neck. "What you all want to keep on talking about death for?"

Vinnie looked nervous. Most of us tried to avoid getting Vinnie nervous. When Vinnie became nervous he also tended to become unpredictable. Nobody wanted to be in the same room as Vinnie when he got unpredictable. All except Lennie that is, who, after spending all day in the Baby Doll Lounge soaking up Miller Lite and straight tequila, was drunk and reckless. "Maybe death is all that we got in common—death and not being able to stay sober."

Vinnie scowled at Lennie and stuck out his jaw. "You saying I'm drunk? I ain't drunk, just drinking."

"That's your loss."

Dolores—having enough on the ball to realize unless she did something to deflect Vinnie, he was going to start machoing it out with Lennie and anyone else who didn't share his somewhat primitive world view—slid off her barstool and sashayed over to the jukebox. She fed money into the gaudy BAL-AMi, and, after a few seconds of electronic pause, it started in with 'I Know What Boys Like' by the Waitresses. The record was about Vinnie's measure. A small round guy in wire glasses and a duck billed baseball cap, who'd been sitting by himself reading *Soldier of Fortune* magazine, suddenly looked up.

"They were all on morphine."

"Who was on morphine?"

Nobody was quite sure what the small round guy was talking about, but the mention of morphine attracted their

MICK FARREN

attention.

"Those old gunfighters, the psychos of the old West."

Lennie sneered. "This sounds dangerously like the theory that everyone's a junkie."

"It's a Burroughs theory, actually. William S. Burroughs, that is."

"Nobody thought it was a theory of Edgar Rice Burroughs."

"Were they related?"

"Who the fuck cares."

"As a matter of fact, no."

"Burroughs figures that, what with gunshot wounds, syphilis and the general stress of life, most of the old time Western legends were doing morphine."

"Morphine?"

"Laudanum, tincture of opium, opium. It all comes to the same thing in the end. It probably accounts for why someone like John Wesley Harding could get so bad tempered that he shot a guy for snoring. He was probably coming down."

The jukebox was now playing 'Fascist Groove Thang.'

"So Doc Holiday wasn't called Doc for nothing?"

"He had the works. He gave them sweet taste."

"Burroughs has been threatening to write his magnum Western for ten years now, but he doesn't seem to be able to get past this thing about the young boys being hung."

Vinnie slammed his fist down on the bar. "Goddamn it! You're all talking about death again. What's the matter with you all? It's Saturday night. I don't want to hear about all this crap."

Lennie was as unconcerned as ever. "To be precise, we were talking about William Burroughs, the writer."

Vinnie grunted. "It's all the same thing. It's all the same stuff that I don't like. It's all the same stuff that makes me crazy."

It looked as though, this time, not even Dolores could distract him. Not that she was trying too hard. She didn't particularly like Vinnie and rather resented that, as a result of the one charitable gesture of deflecting Vinnie from fighting with Lennie, the whole bar had decided to appoint her as Vinnie's keeper. Just to prove that he had no sense of tact, taste or timing, Vinnie chose that moment to make a lunge for her. Dolores quit as Vinnie's keeper and slapped him away.

"Get the fuck off me, you oaf."

Vinnie appealed to the rest of the bar. "She won't kiss me."

"What the hell do you expect?"

"What about Yoko Ono?"

"She wouldn't kiss Vinnie either."

But the small round guy had found himself another topic. Everyone looked at him in surprise. It seemed that *Soldier of Fortune* magazine just couldn't hold his attention any longer. "So what about Yoko Ono?"

"I don't like the way she's doing things."

Old Sam looked at him sideways. "So what's it to you?"

The rest of the bar joined in. "Yeah, what's it to you?"

"Yeah, she had her old man gunned down right in front of her, what's she supposed to do?"

The bar, from being maudlin drunk was rapidly turning defensive and hostile. Most of the hostility was gathering around the small, round guy. About the only person who wasn't staring distrustfully at him was Vinnie. All Vinnie's meanness was taken up with Lennie who seemed to want to pick a fight and Dolores who had rejected him. The small round guy went on regardless. "I don't like the way she seems to be promoting herself as Lennon's widow. I mean, first of all, there was that album cover with the glass of water and the bloodstained eyeglasses, then there seems to be some kind of fuck-up with the Lennon memorial garden in Central Park and finally we get her film of Lennon on *Saturday Night Live*. It all seems too tacky."

"You've got a hell of a nerve." The whole bar, with the exception of Vinnie, was looking at him as though he'd just defiled the Virgin Mary. Only Lennie took a reasonable attitude. "You can't blame her. She's a natural promoter. What else can a conceptual artist be? She's doing a lot less to Lennon than they did to Elvis Presley or Jim Morrison.

What about that creep Danny Sugarman who seems to think he owns the rights on Morrison's memory?"

Vinnie stabbed an accusing finger at Lennie. "You're talking about death again."

"It's probably all we have in common."

"I swear to God, I'll kill you."

Like I think I said earlier, it was that time of the night.

East Village Eye, 1982

HALF PRICE DRINKS

Half price drinks and the early evening crowd comes
    walking through
Half price drinks and there's always one that makes a
    grab for you
Half price drinks and the band ain't drunk enough to
    sound like it was worth a damn
And me?
I just sit here in the corner wondering who I am

Half price drinks and some just use the place to come in
    out of the rain
Cheat on the wife and get back home on the midnight
    train
And the secretary trails back to flat and cat and midnight
    fear
And me?
I just sit here in the corner wondering why I'm here.

Did some fool call this the happy hour?
They never saw the drunks who couldn't make the
    journey home
Did some fool call this the happy hour?
They never saw the working stiff, early shift and so alone.

Half price drinks and the jukebox does big business on
    suburban pain

❏ And sometimes a simple song could say it all…

Half price drinks and the sleazy fumblings that ain't
worth the strain
Half price drinks? Did anybody promise you it'd end up
right?
And me?
I just sit here in the corner wondering how to make it
through the night.

Written and recorded for the album
Vampires Stole My Lunch Money, 1977

COCKTAILS FOR TWO

❏ In other circumstances, after a bath and shave, and with the benefit of clean shirt, a drunk can easily pass as an urbane and authoritative connoisseur.

A DATE FOR COCKTAILS, AT LEAST IN THEORY, CONTAINS all the ingredients for romance. It's right up there in the all-time big league, along with cigarettes bearing lipstick traces, brief encounters on night flights from the coast, and phone numbers hastily scrawled on napkins from nightclubs or matchbooks from five star hotels. The accoutrements are all in place, soft pink lights, deco decor, a discreetly attentive waitress, and a piano noodling in the manner of George Shearing—at a minimum, the jukebox turned down low and probably playing Bryan Ferry. Side by side on chrome and leather bar-stools or face to face across the table of a secluded booth, with blue drinks in chic little glasses, you let the seductive haze imperceptibly gather. The inhibitions start their slide and the wit begins to flow with a casual ease. You're bright, you're amusing, you're relaxed, you're even sophisticated. Getting to know you, getting to know all about you. The trouble is that you're also on the way to being drunk as a skunk.

Like so much that seems to be the height of sophistication at the time, the cocktail tryst is largely a matter of illusion, an illusion that has been primarily fostered by bar owners, the advertising agencies of corporate distillers, and Noel Coward. The ugly truth is that the cocktail is simply a deceitful method of gift wrapping serious booze. At the cocktail tête-à-tête, it's all too possible to pack it away with the determination of a would-be Jerry Lee Lewis on a shot an' a beer bender. It's only the veneer of civilization and the fact that your date is getting as brain-fried as you are that stops you looking equally loathsome. To the impartial, un-hazed observer you're not that bright and not that amusing. The wit could stand a good deal of editing and the waitress is hoping you're the kind of insecure lush who tries to impress by leaving a damn great tip. This is the real reason that men traditionally press drinks on women. They subconsciously realize what a ludicrous figure they must present, after a fistful of B&Bs, to one who only sips Perrier.

THE MARTINI
1/8 vermouth
7/8 (although there are those who believe that, actually, you need only show the vermouth to the gin)

When I was young and impressionable, I used to believe that the martini was the ultimately superior cocktail. Chill in its puritan beauty, the martini was the Grace Kelly of alcohol. The way it lay in its conical long-stemmed glass, clear and still with the faintest of opal blooms was close to Zen perfection. Then I started drinking them and discovered what a disaster they could be. Early in the movie *The Thin Man*, William Powell as Nick Charles announces that he already has five martinis under his belt. Myrna Loy as Nora, who is only on her first, smiles sweetly at the waiter.

"Alright, bring me five more martinis, Leo, and line them right up here."

Nora, at least had the good grace to collapse while Nick carried on regardless.

Collapse would appear to follow martini abuse as surely as Letterman follows Carson. I once played host, bartender, and token male to a martini party for a group of tailored, cultured women, none of whom was the kind to swill straight gin in public. The idea was to bring a little old-fashioned grace to our otherwise drab lives. The actuality was that, after three each, in one case four, all slid elegantly to the floor. Far from being sophisticated, the martini is essentially lethal.

THE MARGARITA
3/5 tequila
1/5 fresh lime juice
1/5 triple sec

Through the months of high summer, it's seemed impossible to walk more than three blocks in the city without passing a Mexican restaurant with sidewalk tables filled to capacity by bright young people facing mass quantities of franchised, frozen margaritas that have the consistency of a Slurpee and are consumed with much the same abandon. In the days when it was hip to drink tequila, biker-style, with a lick of salt and a suck on a lime, it was widely recognized that the stuff tended to turn life into a Sam Peckinpah movie, with all the attendant, slow-motion violence. The bright young people, whether they know it or not, are doing the self-same thing except the liquor now comes in the guise of a supermarket soft drink. (Downtown at El Internacional they make them blue with Curacao, which lends a certain *Star Trek* ambience.)

THE STRAWBERRY DAIQUIRI
1 handful of fresh strawberries
2 oz. sour mix
2 oz. white or dark rum

When fruit comes into the picture, the retrogression to infantilism runs faster and faster. Now we are dressed in Hawaiian shirts and getting drunk on what amount to milkshakes. The distance from fractious children at a nightmare, now-we-are-six birthday party is hardly great, right down to the fact that one of us may actually throw up. Much the same principles apply to pina coladas, mai-tais, and practically anything that comes with a slice of pineapple, a banana, or a small paper umbrella rising from, or floating on its surface. It most particularly applies to the Brandy Alexander, the chocolate shake of the cocktail lounge. Let's not forget that it was a nightlong diet of

Brandy Alexanders that moved the late John Lennon to storm into the Troubador in Los Angeles with a Kotex tied to his head. That night, little was left to imagine.

LONG ISLAND ICED TEA
1 splash vodka
1 splash gin
1 splash white rum
1 splash tequila
1 splash triple sec
1 splash sour mix
1 splash cola

If any date orders one of these things, the best policy is to immediately get up and leave, unless you were told in front that he or she worked as a road manager for a heavy metal band. Don't even make your excuses. All through history there have been variations on this kind of instrument of speedy destruction—the kamikaze, the menace, the jive bomber, all were the aesthetic equivalent of asking the bartender to give you a random mix of the first four bottles from the right on the middle shelf behind the bar—and they have no place in romance. In fact they are the stuff of conventions, suicide pacts, and waking in the morning with an extremely obscene tattoo on the inside of your left thigh and having no recollection of how it came to be there.

IN PARTING, I MUST MAKE IT CLEAR THAT THIS IS NO prohibitionist diatribe against the demon rum. Alcohol is, after all, heavily promoted as one of our few legal buffers against the swings and roundabouts of outrageous fortune. To drink or not to drink has to be a matter of individual decision. What does worry me a little is that the current cocktail vogue, with the exception of the martini—and the martini is not particularly part of that vogue—contains a certain level of hypocrisy. Hey, look at us, we're not really wrecking our livers, we're just having fun. Me? I drink straight Irish whiskey, become drunk, and bore my friends with both the regularity and rapidity of the practice. My only consolation is a certain glum honesty, that you might call truth in alcoholism. When that truth can no longer be faced there's little point in adding grenadine: AA is that-away.

Village Voice, September 1988

POOL TABLE VIGNETTE

❏ The value of intoxication for the writer is that what normally might be a momentary and hardly noticed tableau can expand into a faux significant vision that can be nursed and shakily preserved, and then lovingly recreated with any degree of embroidery when back at the keyboard.

SHE WAS A BRIGHT BLAZE OF IRRADIATED GOLD IN A Rembrandt whiskey haze of soft-focus amber, a fluid symmetry of impossible desire between the electric blue halo above the pool table and verdant green of its surface. The California blonde, practiced and willowy, leaned over the pool table to make her shot. The solid colors of the balls clicked at the command of her stick. She tossed her mane at each fresh position, short shorts, long legs, and when she turned to dust her hands with talc and then chalked her cue before dispatching the frame, the phallic implication was wholly overt. The bartender had either followed the direction of my gaze, or read whatever remained of my mind, because he winked as he poured me another shot of Jack Daniels and placed a bottle of Bud beside it, indicating that it was on the house.

"Catching the show?"

"Uh-huh."

"Ain't she a promise on stiletto heels?"

"A definite promise."

"She's a stripper from the Paradise. Calls herself Indira Candy. Does a whole mess of speed and then drinks to come down. She don't exist for herself unless someone's watching."

As she watched her next opponent in line rack 'em, she made a slight disdainful acknowledgment of her audience, the silently staring reptilian drunks, then she pouted, leaned forward, broke with a crash, and straightened in coolly understated triumph. I could only shake my head in open admiration. "And the love child of Fast Eddie Felson."

"Speed can give you a real focus behind a pool cue."

"Tell me she isn't as hot up close."

The bartender refused with a bartender's grin. "I ain't going to spoil your illusion."

A fragment from a never published novel

SEX & DRUGS & ROCK'N'ROLL

IAN DURY'S INSTANT CLASSIC REALLY CAME AS SOME-thing of a surprise. The surprise wasn't that he did it, but that nobody had thought of doing it before.

Since the beginning sex and drugs have been inextricably bound up with rock'n'roll music. In fact, those eminent psychiatrists, frenzied Bible Belters, and rabid conservative moralists who prophesied in print and pulpit that rock'n'roll was a "communicable disease," that it led to drug addiction, promiscuity, juvenile delinquency and the probable downfall of Christian values and civilization as they knew it were absolutely right. They may have got the reasons pretty ass backwards, but in substance they were right. Wasn't that, after all, why we liked the music?

Rock'n'roll—beyond any doubt—has always needed high octane fuel. Anybody who tells you different is a damn liar, and about as trustworthy as that godforsaken individual who passes up a joint or a mirror or whatever with a superior smile and the statement, "I don't use the stuff, I'm naturally high."

If you don't believe that rock'n'roll ran, right from the start, on one kind of scheduled drug or another, go ask Screaming Jay Hawkins, or Little Richard, or Johnny Cash or even Elvis (although that would admittedly prove difficult without the services of a high priced medium). Best of all, ask Jerry Lee Lewis.

Jerry Lee Lewis has to be the archetype and the ultimate survivor of that time when rock'n'roll was getting born in the back of a station wagon on some backroad of the South, en route to a one night stand in a high school gym or Legion hall. At the start of the sixties Lewis and his band, the Memphis Beats, were busted at a motel in Grand Prairie,

In the world at large, intoxication, taken to its most ultimate and exceptional levels, had, by the early 1970s at the very latest, become totally synonymous with rock'n'roll. Years later, in the TV comedy **Absolutely Fabulous**, the unreconstructed, alcoholic, chain-smoking, drug-abusing, fictional former party and Bond girl Patsy Stone would wax nostalgic about how "nobody drowns in their own vomit any more."

Texas, and charged with possession of 700 amphetamine capsules. This was in the days when being busted for speed meant a traffic offence, not a narcotics beef.

Before it had even begun, rock'n'roll was in the grip of its very first amphetamine cycle. It never had a chance to do anything but run the distance. The pattern was, after all, set up in front. At the start of the fifties, Hank Williams had dropped dead in the back of his limousine from too much speed. It was the drug of Dixie, the trucker's friend, the LA turnround in all shapes and colors. Too many good old boys had come back from World War II with a taste for the big bags of Benzedrine that the US Army and Air Force were prone to hand out to combat troops.

Alan Freed may have tried to shuck the world into believing that rock'n'roll was good, clean, youthful high spirits. The truth was Jerry Lee playing with a machine gun in his hotel, Gene Vincent and the Blue Caps crazy and crawling in some redneck town they couldn't even remember the name of, washing down pills with Wild Turkey or Rebel Yell Confederate bourbon and trying to persuade a waitress or high school cheerleader to come back to the motel and see if the South could rise again. Then having to split town early in the morning before daddy/husband/brother/boyfriend came after them with a pump shotgun or length of primary chain off a Harley Davidson because Peggy Sue was back home sobbing she'd been raped, after she'd been caught dishevelled and sneaking in through her bedroom window.

Of course, that speed cycle, like all other speed cycles, had to end, if for no other reason than to let another one start up again after a few months of lying low.

In London art schools and the coffeehouses of New York and San Francisco something new was going on. Smoke from a hand-rolled kept under the hand, made from the contents of a foil package bought with the thrill of fear from a romantic street dealer, was filling the air. A new generation of white kids had discovered dope, and was working its way through passages of their minds that mom, dad and teacher hadn't let on existed, if, in fact, they'd even known about them in the first place. Like all new generations of white kids who discover dope, they got to thinking. One of the first realizations was that Cliff and the Shadows or Bobby Vee were simply not easy on the ear. You just couldn't loll back and listen to a Dansette portable scratching on about some damn rubber ball going bouncey-bouncey, bouncey-bouncey. It could rot your brain and make you physically ill. It's easy enough to get sick and ill without having music that does it to you pouring out of the radio or the TV. You couldn't find it in the High Street Record Rendezvous. It had to be sought after in back alley specialist shops and word of mouth contact. Finding Chess R&B, Prestige jazz, Jimmy Smith, Chuck Berry, Howlin' Wolf or Charlie Mingus could be as much trouble and as much adventure as actually copping the reefer.

With a wind of change blowing through the Dansette's seven-inch speaker, the decks were cleared for action. The new generation of white kids who'd discovered dope said to themselves, "Why can't we play music like Jimmy Smith, Chuck Berry et al?" Of course they couldn't, but they could play something. Change was in the air. It was a new frontier, the white heat of technology; the planet was attempting to drag itself kicking and screaming into the second half of the twentieth century and cheap, red, electric guitars were in the window of the local record store. It was time to move and get down with the change.

Then JFK was iced on Dealey Plaza, and, as the joint went round a lot of people in a lot of basements realized that the faceless men who really run things weren't messing around. With an attitude of stoned, aggressive, paranoid optimism, a thousand Brian Joneses picked up their Futurama guitars and a thousand Johnnies started mixing up the medicine. Once again, rock'n'roll had to move back onto high octane fuel. Yes, you guessed it. A new speed cycle had started up.

Mod: a new five-ply mohair suit and purple hearts at a tanner, Georgie Fame and the Blue Flames and going to a go-go. You were part of the now. Know what I mean, John?

How many rock'n'roll empires were founded on flogging pills to the kids queuing up outside the Marquee to see the Who on a Tuesday night (maximum R&B)? Blocked was the expression of the time. Stumbling, glazed, stammering, incoherent and young, all style and aggression, but no brains. Go straight for it. The freak shall inherit the earth. Mods and rockers made the headlines in their actions of evolution, Cro-Magnon v. Neanderthal. Blue nylon against black leather. That was something that the tabloids could quite easily grasp. What the media missed was the movement that was formlessly growing in basements and attics all over the Western world.

Even before the hippies hit the streets, rock'n'roll was pushing at its outer limits, both in terms of lyric and musical structure. It wouldn't be any exaggeration to say that psychotropics had a major hand in the perception that brought about all this new ground breaking. Speed may have been the fuel for the live show, but marijuana was the great aid to the recording studio. A heightened perception coupled with a rapidly expanding technology and increasingly sophisticated recording techniques enabled rock'n'roll to go in every direction but down. The Beatles and Rolling Stones took the simple R&B structures that were the foundation of rock'n'roll and moulded them in elaborate and increasingly baroque directions. Dylan was writing lyrics that would have been scarcely believable to anyone in the fifties. Brian Wilson layered harmony upon harmony, bringing an unprecedented lushness to a simple vocal workout, while Jeff Beck, Eric Clapton and, a little later, Jimi Hendrix produced sounds from the electric guitar that were undreamed of by Duane Eddy or Hank B. Marvin.

All this experimentation alone would have constituted both a major achievement and a giant stride in the development of rock'n'roll. There was something about the sixties, however, that just wouldn't allow things to stand still. Only a couple of short years after the rock generation had first grappled with the new visions and perspectives revealed by marijuana, LSD-25 hit the street market and quickly grabbed half the youth of the West by the synapses. The effect of acid on rock'n'roll was immeasurable. The idea of actually translating the mind wrenching revelations of the new wonder drugs was an elusive prize. Numerous rock'n'roll bands grasped out but only a very few managed to come close to reproducing even a single facet of the psychedelic experience.

Jim Morrison of the Doors freely admitted that he "gobbled down acid like candy" during his days as a Venice, California, beach bum, when he conceived and wrote the major percentage of his songs. Morrison delved deep into the subconscious and used the images and fears that he found there to create a nightmarish, sinisterly erotic fantasy world where mystic killers roamed dreamlike highways, virginal princesses sacrificed themselves to black leather monsters, cities burned, violence was always lurking just below the surface and reptiles abounded. Morrison presided over his strange creation in the role of his lizard king character.

Pink Floyd took an almost diametrically opposed position. Half hidden by the first lightshows, and motivated by the brilliant but far-from-stable Syd Barrett, they produced a cold, aloof music that evoked images of both the glittering icy void of deep space and the chill isolated corners of the paranoid mind.

On a gut level, Jimi Hendrix, another self avowed psychedelic stunt pilot, came close to the jangle, the loop and the curve experienced by the acid saturated brain. Hendrix, more than all the other guitar gods of the late sixties, had such a physical rapport with his instrument and equipment that he seemed almost capable of weaving dreams out of the magnetic fields of his banks of Marshall amps and communicating them directly to the audience. This, coupled with Hendrix's overt sexuality, made him able to strike all manner of responses from his listeners.

Acid, however, like marijuana, wasn't the ideal drug for a coherent live show. Maybe the Grateful Dead could tank up on psychedelics and play a five or six hour show of erratic brilliance, but they were definitely the exception. More often than not, a bunch of acid before a show could lead to scattered impromptu outbursts of the kind that Jim Morrison was famous for, or else total confusion and breakdown of even the slimmest musical continuity. A typical case was Eric Burdon who, at a legendary San Francisco concert, spent more than an hour on stage, unable to do anything but wander, awestruck, around the stage gazing at the lightshow and murmuring "Gosh, wow" periodically into the microphone.

Again, amphetamines became the favored fuel for the live show. The useful familiar pills did their rounds, but in addition to the well known Dexedrine, spansules, Drinamyl and the rest, a new super-upper appeared on the streets. Methedrine quickly proved to be the big brother of all the other forms of speed. Either in clinical ampoules, bootleg pills, capsules or powder, it was more powerful than anything that had previously gone the illicit distribution route.

The major medical use for Methedrine was only emergency injection to revive victims from a state of technical death due to heart stoppage. In other words, it was for waking up corpses. The speedfreaks didn't see it that way. If taken in sufficient quantity, methedrine could produce a manic, hallucinatory state that might be a whole lot of fun at the time, but could be so physically and mentally depleting that the various hippie ghettos of the Western world suddenly needed to get used to an entirely new breed of damage cases.

At its most terminal, Methedrine could produce extreme and often violent paranoia and hallucinations as scary as alcoholic DTs. From a juddering, stammering mess the wacko speedfreak now had the potential to turn himself into a full blown, wild eyed psychotic. Surprisingly, Methedrine claimed only a limited number of rock'n'roll victims. Most of them came from the lower echelons of touring bands. Even before meth mania had reached its peak, the big stars had moved on to the smoother, less instantly damaging and infinitely more expensive joys of cocaine.

The meth ethos did however, produce a wave of suitably demented music. Favorites among the San Francisco speedfreaks were an outfit called the Blue Cheer. A prototype of today's heavy metal bands, the Blue Cheer relied on sheer volume to punch across their point, boasting anything up to 2,000 watts of guitar amplification. Legend has it that at one concert a dog who happened to walk on the stage dropped dead of a brain haemorrhage. Their music scarcely translated onto record, and even the semi-hit 'Summertime Blues' lacked the awesome weight of Blue Cheer's live sound.

Worldwide, the speedfreaks' favorite recording had to be the Velvet Underground's notorious cut 'Sister Ray.' Nobody could deny that it fitted the mood exactly. In its twenty-minute duration the song screeched its way through a high velocity ribbon of the most disquieting jangle the world had ever heard. All across the planet, in grungy basements, with four amps of meth, and an auto-changer set to repeat, 'Sister Ray' played over and over again. Of course, nobody listened to the music too much, not even the almost inaudible, but oft repeated, lyric line "I'm searching for my mainline." The freaks were too busy babbling into space. The record wasn't there for aural gratification, more to heighten the illusion of jagged, high-power madness.

By very definition, the meth craze had to wear itself out in short order. The rock'n'roll narcotic top ten ground round until it was pointing in the diametrically opposite direction. Heroin became the number one fashion turn on.

The downer temptation has always been strong in rock'n'roll. In a world that is always overcrowded with people jostling in search of the magic point that is exactly where it's at, liable to go crazy without warning and attempting to run twenty-four hours a day, sleep, and a certain measure of psychological space, become premium needs. In the days of Marilyn Monroe, Seconal provided the answer to those needs, but, in the late sixties, the more sensual down of Mandrax or Quaaludes replaced the cruder barbiturates. A handful of downers after the show made the hotel room party easier to handle and the few hours sleep before the car, truck or plane a lot less elusive.

Unfortunately, downers have two major drawbacks. The first is that they just won't allow themselves to be confined to one portion of the user's life. They have this tendency to spread out and take over. The second is that downers come closely followed by tolerance. The combination of the two cause too many fine musicians to turn themselves into stumbling, vomiting avocados. Some managed to ease themselves out of this less than attractive mess. Others, like Paul Kossoff, didn't.

There was another alternative when the daily pill intake got too intense. Heroin was simpler, easier, more to the point and, in the long run, much more deadly. Certainly smack does hold the pressures at bay and gives the user not only mental space but cocoons him in a psychological capsule that pain is unable to enter as long as he keeps taking the medicine.

The one thing that heroin doesn't protect against is death. The long roll call of dead rock stars can only attest to the vulnerability of the junkie, whatever his or her income or status.

Possibly one of the main problems of the seventies was that no new drug appeared on the streets to jerk the consciousness of rock. For over half the decade, both music and drug consumption seemed to stabilize and turn in on itself.

Experimentation was constricted to flirtations with glittering homosexuality, right-wing politics, and other drugs like animal tranquillizer or angel dust. For the most part the successful consumed cocaine, the unhappy used heroin, the struggling took speed and downers and just about everyone used as much booze and marijuana as they could lay their hands on.

Just as it began to look as if the seventies weren't going to produce anything of value, the new wave broke. A new generation of feisty young kids marched into the picture with new ideas, new fashions and more raw energy than had been seen since the mid sixties. The music, which had previously been moving through an unadventurous and inward looking phase, became stripped down, energetic and quite prepared to kick out at old or redundant ideas. Once again rock'n'roll seemed ready to face the strain.

The new wave also brought back the need for fuel. Failing to find any exciting chemical innovations, the punks, just like their spiritual fathers before them, turned back to the tried and trusted standby. A new amphetamine cycle started, proving that the direction of rock'n'roll is probably more circular than linear.

"Wait a minute," you say, "didn't the title of this piece say something about sex?" True, it did, but this is, after all, a family magazine.

Home Grown, 1979

LOST JOHNNY

You only get a single chance
The rules are very plain,
The truth is well concealed inside
The details of the game,
You can hear it coming,
You can see it from afar,
It's pale and it glimmers
Like a faded movie star
And up there in the castle,
They're trying to make her scream,
By sticking thumb tacks in her flesh
And cancelling the dream,
Can you find the Valium?
For chrissakes bring 'em soon,
Lost Johnny's out there,
Baying at the moon

The time has come for you to choose,
You'd better get it right,
Berlin girls with sharp white teeth
Are waiting in the night,
But keep your weapons handy
It surely can't be hard,
There's always trouble lurking
When you leave your own backyard
Underneath the city,

❑ The theme of wretched excess was also the order of the day when Lemmy and I sat down to write this song—me the words, he the music—because he was short of an original track for what would be his last album with Hawkwind.

The alligators sing,
Of how the tarnished crowns remain,
On skulls of ancient kings
Can you find the morphine,
And make it goddamned brief,
Lost Johnny's out there,
Looking for relief

That Larry looks so evil,
And you know he really tries,
But every time he makes a play,
That vital number compromise,
And Lucretia buys her underwear,
From a store where no-one goes,
She makes it big in photographs,
On the strength of what she shows,
And here inside the waiting room,
The radio still screams,
And we're all gobbling Nembutal,
To modify our dreams
Can you find your credit card,
For god's sake make it quick,
Lost Johnny's out there,
Trying to turn a trick

Recorded by Hawkwind, 1974, and later
by Motörhead, myself and others

THE CONTENTS OF ELVIS' STOMACH

❏ Much of the romance goes out of the extreme when the extreme becomes part of an autopsy. Elvis Presley is the subject of much more detailed examination in other parts of this book. In this short inclusion

Codeine—at a concentration ten times higher than the toxic level
Morphine—possible metabolite of codeine
Methaqualone—Quaalude, above toxic level
Diazepam—Valium
Diazepam metabolite
Ethinamate—Valmid
Ethchlorvynol—Placidyl

MICK FARREN

Amobarbital—Amytal
Pentobarbital—Nembutal
Pentobarbital—Carbrital
Meperidine—Demerol
Phenyltoloxamine—Sinutab (a decongestant)

the contents of his stomach
after his death are treated
as a piece of found poetry.

Published 1990 as a guerrilla flyer in New York

LENNIE AT THE TOPLESS BAR

LENNIE IS ONE OF THOSE HALF EATEN, DISCARDED CIGA-
rette pack kind of people who you figure probably ran out
of ambition round about the age of nine. I heard that he
had a wife once, but that she gave up on him within weeks
of the wedding. Most days, of late, you can find him, afternoons, drinking in a dump of a topless joint called the
Baby Doll Lounge (not the Baby Doll Lounge on West
Broadway, the other one). He'll sit in that place half the
day, paying double price for his booze just because he'd
rather look at the waitresses' sagging titties than go to a
regular joint and listen to the bartender talking about how
the world has got itself screwed. Over the years, Lennie
must have pissed away a small fortune on sweaty and less
than perfect mammaries, which is kind of surprising since
Lennie knows an incredible amount about how the world
has got itself screwed and could talk to even the most terminally opinionated bartender for hours if he so chose.

As you can probably imagine, Lennie doesn't look like
much. For as long as I can remember, he's worn this black,
two-piece, thrift shop suit that not even Elvis Costello
would want to get into. I suppose Lennie couldn't really
afford to be a dandy if he drops all his money sitting round
in topless bars. The pants on the suit are a lot too short. In
the summer he exposes an expanse of not-too-clean dayglo sock. In the winter he stuffs the pants into a pair of
heavy duty engineer boots. It's not only Lennie's clothes
that mark him as some kind of jumped-the-rails lowlife,
he also has the exceptional repellant expression into which

❑ Meanwhile, back in New
York in the 1980s, and this
time at a topless joint…

his face tends to fold. There's a nasty vacancy about it that gives anyone sitting opposite him the impression that he's about to drool out of the corner of his mouth. I could never quite figure out how the topless waitresses tolerated him.

Both Lennie's clothes and his vacant expression are, in truth, something of a bluff. Although he prefers everyone to think so, there's nothing vacant about Lennie. Quite the reverse, he has this straight-edge, razor-sharp, rat-trap mind, and alarmingly accurate sources of information that he steadfastly refuses to reveal. Witness about six days ago, Lennie drags his attention away from *Lash Magazine* through which he'd been thumbing for a good half hour and blinks pale, watery, Gollum eyes. "You all realize that the suckhead Christians are turning into a full-scale fucking plague. They aren't fucking around, Jack. They're out to fuck us, make no mistake about that."

With that he lapses into a temporary silence. This is one of Lennie's ploys for attention. Everyone around the table nods with drunken encouragement. It's not often the Lennie launches into a tirade, but, when he does, it's usually worth keeping your mouth shut for the duration.

"You hear about Bob Dylan, huh? I mean, Bob Dylan, think about it. He's forty this year and he's so fucking hallelujahed-out it passeth all understanding. I heard it from this engineer who worked with Dylan in LA."

This in itself is something of a mystery. Lennie hasn't been near LA in living memory. "If the engineer wanted to bring beer into the studio he had to keep it in a different refrigerator to old Bob's Perrier, and if he wanted to actually drink the stuff then he had to do it when Bobby wasn't around because it seems like the middle-aged born again can't take even the chance of getting alcohol contamination even by remote. You gotta serve somebody? Shit! And, while we're on the subject of Christian suckheads, how many of you have caught the act of James Watt, Reagan's Secretary of the Interior, he's going to let strip mining rip along with wilderness raping, and all manner of wild environmental unpleasantness because he's so far gone in Jesus' Sunbeams that he don't believe the planet's worth bother-

ing about. We don't have to worry about future generations because the Second Coming, Armageddon, Night of
the Living Dead, the Day of Judgment, all that Rapture
and Book of Revelations shit is only a matter of years away.
Check Jerry Falwell and the rest. They've got the End of
the World down on a timetable. Nuclear war, the whole
bit. And then there's another of Reagan's boys called Jer-
emiah Denton who wants to turn family planning clinics
into chastity centers where kids get help to keep their vir-
ginity."

Lennie pauses for breath and to flag down a passing
beer. "Of course, that says it all. Sex has always been a
problem with Christians. Ever since they massacred the
agnostics. They've always tried to prohibit fucking and
drive everyone crazy. They're suckheads and today the
suckheads are back with a vengeance. Trouble is, everyone
else has got their head so far up their ass that they should
worry about the ring around the collar. Sex is the crux of
what the Christians are at…"

"We thought you didn't have anything to do with sex,
Lennie."

Lennie scowled. "I don't, but that might just be because I
ain't run into Brooke Shields in a garter belt and high heels."

It wasn't a pleasant picture.

"Goddamn Christians even got the TV networks on
the run. They said the word boycott and the networks are
running like sheep. They can pull stuff like boycotts, too.
They're the first of their kind getting it down on computer.
Bigotry goes cybernetic."

Did I remember to tell you that when Lennie ain't sitting around in the Baby Doll Lounge paying double price
for his beer, he's lying in bed watching TV?

"ABC has already announced that they've canned all the
jiggle shows for the next season. Do you realize what this
means? There'll be nothing on TV next season that can't
get past the Christians, nothing but wholesome, family entertainment."

Lennie's face is a combination of horror and disgust.
His voice is starting to rise in both pitch and volume. "You

know what that means? *No tits on TV!* That's what it means, and I'm telling you right now, I'm mad as hell and I ain't gonna take it."

He waves his fist at the suckhead Christian wolf packs. "On *titties* I take my *stand.*"

East Village Eye, 1981

LIES, DAMNED LIES, AND MARIJUANA

All this concentration on New York City and its 4am closing time should not be allowed to obscure the fact that recreational intoxication has a history that goes back to prehistory and beyond, and—according to Dr. Ronald Siegal of UCLA—even extends into the animal kingdom. (How else did my cat Finn discover that Japanese catnip is highly superior to American catnip?) I figure just about every possible word has been said about marijuana, and what follows is, I guess, about the shortest herb summation I ever consigned to a keyboard. The tide of possible legalization ebbs and flows. In the UK, dope is reclassified as a dangerous drug. Los Angeles on the other hand has 187 pot shops dispensing "medici-

Since March of 2003 we have been listening to George W. Bush and his surrogates offer the American People a progression of reasons for invading the sovereign nation of Iraq, and the resulting bloody mayhem. The rationales, the excuses, and the all too obvious lies have progressively eroded support for the war, until, as we move into the fifth year of the conflict, considerably less than a third of the country believes what comes out of the White House. As wretchedly disastrous as the falsehoods about Iraq have proved to be—from WMD to spreading the gospel of democracy—they can only pale in comparison to the lies that have been told about marijuana, if only by the duration of the deceit.

Pity the generations of potheads, who—for a full three quarters of a century—have been derided, damned, demonised, incarcerated, and even killed over a harmless herb, for a sequence of changing reasons, many of which are even less plausible than the ones our current president uses to justify having combat troops in Iraq.

And while Bush had his entire crew, plus the whole PNAC neocon manifesto, to create his lies about Iraq, the decades of disinformation about pot can be traced back to a single individual. When, in 1930, a former railroad investigator, Harry J. Anslinger, was—via family connections—named director of a new division in the Treasury Department, known as the Federal Bureau of Narcotics, its function supposedly to regulate the supply and taxation of cocaine and opiates. Anslinger, however, seemingly a full blown megalomaniac, dreamed of a vast and all-powerful agency with police powers to rival J. Edgar Hoover's FBI, and set about to creating exactly that.

His strategy was simple but effective. He would instigate a public panic in which the innocuous drug marijuana would be mythologized as the root of all evil, and its eradication would become a matter of national security. Thus began one of the longest running exercises in state-sponsored mendacity in US history. The demonizing of marijuana even had a practical side. Prior to heading the Federal Bureau of Narcotics, Anslinger had been a prohibition agent. Alcohol prohibition was clearly going to be repealed in the next three years, and many of his former colleagues would need jobs.

Anslinger's propaganda campaign was not subtle, but he had enlisted the sensationalist aid of the Hearst newspaper chain, and was also firmly backed by the pharmaceutical corporations. One of his more lurid harangues told how *"a gang of boys tear the clothes from two school girls and rape the screaming girls. A sixteen-year-old kills his entire family of five in Florida. In Colorado a husband tries to shoot his wife, kills her grandmother instead, and then kills himself. Every one of these crimes had been proceeded [sic] by the smoking of one or more marijuana 'reefers.' Marijuana is an addictive drug which produces in its users insanity, criminality, and death."* His mythic doctrine was encapsulated in the 1936 kitsch movie classic *Tell Your Children*—later renamed *Reefer Madness*—in which dope leads to sexual frenzy, dementia, and finally homicide. Today we laugh, and turn it into a musical. Under Anslinger it was a tool in the establishment of the intoxicant police state that still flourishes.

Anslinger was also extremely happy to play the most evil of race cards. *"There are 100,000 total marijuana smokers in the US, and most are Negroes, Hispanics, Filipinos, and entertainers. Their Satanic music, jazz, and swing, result from marijuana use. This marijuana causes white women to seek sexual relations with Negroes, entertainers, and any others. Reefer makes darkies think they're as good as white men."* He even emphasized political horrors as *"marihuana leads to nal marijuana,"* but also a coterie on the City Council militating to shut them down. But I guess when the stoned are involved nothing is ever easy.

pacifism and communist brainwashing."

Anslinger ran the Federal Bureau of Narcotics from 1930 to 1962—"drug czar" in everything but name for an unprecedented thirty-two years, during which his almost theological doctrine of marijuana being "evil" shaped all official attitudes. It was only after his retirement, and the massive embrace of pot by the young of the 1960s—both as a recreational high and an anti-authoritarian symbol—that it became obvious Anslinger's crudity needed modification.

Hundreds of thousands of kids were smoking dope, and the country had not been plunged into an orgy of rape and slaughter, but now demands that pot should be legalized were met with the new argument that this was impossible because it was a "gateway drug." Dubious government sponsored studies had observed a majority of sampled junkies smoked dope before becoming addicted to heroin, and thus concluded that, while marijuana might cause minimal harm, it was dangerous because it led to the use of harder drugs. What these studies ignored was that most marijuana smokers never used another illegal drug, and also, applying the government's own methodology to a wider range of intoxicants, the real gateway drugs used by most junkies prior to their addiction were beer and cigarettes.

For a couple of minutes during the Carter administration, the chance of some nationwide decriminalization appeared distantly possible, but then the Iran hostage crisis ushered in the Reagan era with Nancy Reagan's "just say no" campaign, and a total return to the Anslinger doctrine of the "evil weed." The Federal Drug Administration issued a flat edict that "marijuana was of no medical benefit," and maintained that position despite overwhelming evidence to the contrary. Bush the Elder did everything he could to prove himself the valiant drug warrior, including invading Panama in what became known as the "biggest drug bust in history."

Even Bill (I didn't inhale) Clinton did nothing to stop the Drug Enforcement Agency making bizarre claims that marijuana potency had increased ten-, twenty- or thirty-fold since the 1970s and was therefore a much more dangerous drug that must remain illegal. He also did nothing when, as individual states declared medical marijuana legal, the DEA stormed in, arresting cancer patients, growers, distributors, and closing legal cannabis clubs.

Any mention of the Netherlands as a model for an alternative pot policy elicited knee-jerk fury from both Republicans and Democrats, who would bluster that the Dutch experience had been a complete disaster and Amsterdam was a hell of an addiction. They seemed blind to the reality that the Dutch had achieved a healthy tolerance toward alternative lifestyles, were able to protect marijuana users from the marginalization that accompanies arrest and prosecution, and had created a separation between the retail markets for "soft" and "hard" drugs.

Even when UCLA pulmonologist and marijuana expert Donald Tashkin, after conducting the largest study of its kind, unexpectedly concluded in 2006 that smoking marijuana, even regularly and heavily, did not lead to lung cancer, and that the chemical THC might kill aging cells and keep them from becoming cancerous, Federal health and drug enforcement officials still used Tashkin's earlier work on marijuana—that he had now refuted—to make the case that the drug is dangerously carcinogenic and should remain illegal.

After a lifetime spent with the illegal weed and the lies and deceptions keeping it so, little hope can be extended for any sudden about-turn to sanity. Which is a pity, because the government's lying stupidity over marijuana has alienated a whole stratum of citizens. And that's the truth.

LA CityBeat, 2007

LES FLEURS DE MAL

IT'S BEEN MY FAIRLY WELL INFORMED OBSERVATION that opium—for all practical consumer purposes—is almost unknown in the USA, except for a few unconventional and very relaxed botanists who grow dark eyed pop-

❏ The following piece was an early note for an erudite essay on historical drug use that was never written

because the magazine for which it was destined went out of business.

pies, and lacerate and milk the *fleur de mal* for their own consumption. In the haste and disorder of the New World, those with a taste for opiates opted for the hunched, criminal, and always messy life of the needle and the spoon. They cooked their dope and shot, sending the rush from vein to heart, and thence to the receptors in the head. In Europe, on the other hand, opium is a gourmet rarity that showed up every now and again, usually as an unexpected bonus with the hashish supply. Paris seemed fairly well assured of its quota. The city of Communards, Jacobins, the *Belle Epoch*, Hunchbacks of Notre Dame, and Jean Genet had its special subterranean places.

And opium, unlike all of its trashy, rock-and-powder chemical cousins, whose cheap habits spread from tenements and trailer parks to the palatial homes of rock stars, was too scarce and exceptional to present the problem of a jones. You had it and then it was gone, and there wouldn't be any more for months, if not years, so get over it. Goodbye Ruby Tuesday and the Lord Buddha bless you. I have always envied those habitués of yore; Coleridge and De Quincey, Doc Holliday playing Fan Tan, and Lord Alfred Douglas chasing the dragon in the dens of Limehouse. A twentieth century boy could grow imaginatively wistful for the eighteenth and nineteenth centuries, when a poet could walk the earth with a flask of laudanum in the pocket of his frock coat and a twelve-inch pipe in his knapsack, and it was nobody's business but his own.

Not previously published

CARVED GODS AND DRAGONS

❑ And opium, of course, can be the stuff of highly deviant dreams.

"I'VE TRIED TO ESCAPE FROM THIS PLANET ON A NUMBER of occasions."

"No shit."

"Each time the aliens caught me and brought me back."

As the woman talked, apparently without end or continuity, Max drew dreamily on the long ornate ivory and hardwood opium pipe, with its carved gods and dragons, and brass mouthpiece. "Motherfuckers those aliens. I hope you avoided the anal probe."

She didn't appear to hear him. On the other hand, Max may not have actually spoken, only fantasized that he did. She frowned. "I also escaped from the nuns. A number of times. But they always caught me too."

Max shook his head as if to clear it. He had totally lost the thread. "Nuns?"

"I was raised by nuns in a Catholic orphanage of great barbarism. The benefits were few and the penalties severe. They administered enemas for our health and cruelly whipped us for the most minor infraction. I'm not sure which was worse, the nozzle or the cane."

Max didn't feel he was obliged to say anything. He merely contemplated the images the woman was creating, and

"Those nuns…" She shook her head in search of a word strong enough to express her contempt. Her English was poor and her vocabulary small. "… those *bitches* in black and white were *enjoying* themselves. I used to wonder what they did when we couldn't see them."

"Something to wonder about."

"They had this trick…"

"Trick?"

"If two girls were caught doing… well, you know… what young girls do in a gender segregated school."

"I can hazard a guess."

"The unhappy pair would be bent over opposite ends of a table to receive their punishment, arms outstretched, and gripping each other's wrists. Can you imagine that?"

Max nodded simultaneously drawing on the pipe. Stoned as he was, he could easily and vividly imagine it.

"They would thrash one while the other watched, while the other one could actually feel her reaction, and then…"

"The positions would be reversed?"

"Exactly."

"Perverse."

Fragment of an unpublished novel

THE PICTURE ON THE MOTEL WALL

❑ I have never found it that hard to craft fiction from scenes in a contemporary bar or pub. All you need is a half decent recall and a talent for embroidery of dialogue. To enter the mind of the chemically deranged is a much more interesting challenge. Joe Gibson was the hero of my 1999 novel **Necrom**, in which he was buffeted through the branes of alternate dimensions by all manner of hallucinatory and paranormal entities. In **Necrom**, the reader was free to decide whether Joe's adventures were a narrative of the fantastic or just the delusions of advanced psychosis. Revisiting him in this short story, the same decisions have to be made. Is the story really happening, with Joe inhabiting a functioning science fiction world, but seeing it through the eyes of someone who has spent "three days on a strict regimen of trailer-park amphetamine and Wild Turkey"? Or is he imaging what's happening to him as a side-effect of amphetamine and Wild Turkey. Then there's the third alternative

JOE GIBSON CLOSED THE DOOR BEHIND HIM, AND SAGGED back against it with a sigh. At least he was in out of the night. The room he had rented was in the back of the highway motel, and that gave him a small measure of temporary concealment, although, since he'd discovered that his name and description had been given to Donnie and the Wipeout Gang, no hidden place any longer existed in all of the real world—or even those that were less real—where he could truly feel secure. Apparently the Skull & Bones wanted him so badly that they'd hired the ultimate best to get him. In the long run, no one had ever eluded Donnie and the Wipeout Gang. Joe Gibson didn't believe that he was going to be the first to beat them, but he could try. He really had no other option. His only consolation was that he was finally out of the state-run mental facility. He had been nothing more than a sitting duck in those neon-bright, rat-maze, disinfectant corridors, where, if he had attempted to explain about the danger that was undoubtedly coming at him, the staff would have instantly had him gurney-strapped, restrained, and under full lockdown.

If he had told any of the thug orderlies or unblinking psychiatrists about the Wipeouts they would have immediately red-flagged him as having succumbed to a bad case of dementia in addition to all the other psychoses for which they already had him diagnosed. The great irony was that dementia was actually one of the Wipeouts' favorite weapons for softening-up and disorientating the target. They would talk to you from your TV or appear in surreal shimmering color on your own computer screen, or, infinitely worse, make sinister alterations to small and mundane, randomly selected, physical objects, just to let the victim know that they had him or her down-cold and defenseless.

After maybe a minute, Joe straightened up and stepped away from the door and into the room. Joe's jaw moved as though on nervous automatic, chewing on his most recent stick of gum as though his life depended on the motion,

MICK FARREN

and, in some respects, it did. After three days on a strict regimen of trailer-park amphetamine and Wild Turkey, he had a choice of either chewing gum or talking to himself, and if he talked to himself, the conversation would probably be more than he could handle. He didn't bother to slip on the chain lock. The thing was so flimsy that it would not hold back any determined assault by a brawny shoulder or determined boot for more than three and a half seconds at best.

Joe dropped the flight bag on the bed. It contained the few essentials he had purchased back along his route of flight, plus the notes, and computer disks he had on the Skull & Bones, all the documentation that had been stashed for so long in the left luggage locker. When he had made good his escape from the state facility, he had not been exactly able to bring much out with him, and if he had not managed to hold on to the late Moriarty's Visa card, either the Wipeouts or the regular cops would have had him days ago. In addition to being on the lam from the Wipeout Gang, Joe Gibson was also listed as a fugitive mental patient.

Concealing the card through his incarceration had not been easy, and he could never have pulled it off had he not been as wise as he was in the ways of institutions and asylums. It was a mercy in that it meant he had a limited sum of running money, and that the purchases and ATM withdrawals he made along the way were only creating the transaction trail of a dead man. He took off his new sunglasses and the black cowboy hat he had bought—the combination he had been using to hide his face from casual scrutiny. He tossed the sunglasses on the bed beside the bag, but he placed the hat more carefully on the side table so it covered the old fashioned General Electric motel phone. He didn't need any hats-on-the-bed when so much else was already against him. Finally Joe looked around the room, and nodded sagely. "Bates Motel, Mk III. Definitely Mk III."

He had been in a great many cheesy motel rooms in his time, and this one was exactly what he expected; dirty paint, a queen-size bed, an old RCA TV probably suffer-

that he is just plain psychotic in a nightmare of his own devising.

ing from color distortion, a bedside table, a small built-in closet, a rudimentary dressing table, one of those frame things on which you could place an open suitcase, and an interior door that opened on a minuscule bathroom. To Joe's mind, every one of these back-road cabin flops was a Bates Motel, but each came with subtle variations, and, long ago, he had started to grade them—Bates Motel Mk I, Mk II, Mk III, etc. Since the Original Occurrence, he had spent almost all his time in either Bates Motels or institutions. The grading system was one of the tricks he used to keep sane in the face of the unacceptably unnatural.

"Or is this maybe a Mk IV?"

One item, a picture on the wall above the head of the bed, defied the normal Gibson categorization. The framed painting was supported by dirty string hung over a bent and rusted nail that had caused a crack in the plaster, and he had never seen anything quite like it in any motel room before. That a painting hung over the bed was not unusual in itself. In fact, it was fairly standard. Usually they were the mass produced horses in the surf, tropical sunsets, disquieting clowns, or nicotine stained abstracts, castoffs from the next level of lodging houses like Holiday or Ramada Inns. Also they were normally bolted to the wall as he had discovered on the odd drunken occasion that he had attempted to steal one. On rare occasions, he would encounter a more idiosyncratic piece of art, a portrait of Elvis Presley or John Wayne on black velvet, or some daub by a friend or relative of the proprietor. Once, in Detroit, his normally hot-sheet room had been decorated by a nude, honey colored lady sporting an enormous puffball Afro. Gibson had even stayed in a motel near Rachel, Nevada with a portrait of a gray alien on the wall, but that had been locally predictable in a place where the majority of guests were UFO conspiracy tourists headed for the perimeter of Area 51.

This current picture, however, was quite different to all of the above, and Joe found it distinctly disturbing. Indeed, it was disturbing enough for him to turn on the bedside light for a closer inspection. A small child waited at the right of the composition, an unhappy, Cinderella-like, Edwardian waif, in buttoned blouse, tattered skirt and sash, hands clasped behind her back as though miserably anticipating the arrival of some cruel step-parent. To the left of the picture, a bucket and mop stood in a spillage of slopped water. Either the little girl had just finished mopping, or was expecting instructions to commence the hated chore. The wall behind both bucket and waif showed cracks of age and neglect, with plaster fallen away above the line of the baseboard revealing the underlying laths.

Joe's first reaction was that the picture was a psych-out set-up by the Wipeout Gang, an implanted, shock'n'awe device to cultivate the terror paralysis with the knowledge that they were already one step ahead of him, but then he surprised himself by holding back, with an unexpected reserve of strength, from immediately leaping into the abyss of paranoia. The picture was weird, but by no means weird enough to be Wipeout work.

"Yeah, brother man, you're being paranoid." Paranoia was understandable after all that he'd been through in the years since the Original Occurrence, but he figured the picture needed one more element to make it anything more than an odd, but perfectly innocuous painting. He was about to turn away. He needed the refuge of mindless TV, and a hot shower. He needed to go into his flight bag for the still half-full bottle of Wild Turkey, to pick up the phone and see if it was possible to order a pizza, and maybe cop some more speed, because the one thing he didn't need was the risk of sleep, and the chance of dreams.

Then the first bead of gelatinous green liquid—like the thick and sluggish blood of a reptile nightmare—appeared from under the right hand corner of the picture's frame. It was followed by a second and a third. A fourth disgusting glob emerged as the first began to viscously run down the wall. As the others followed the call of gravity, each tracking its slime trail, Joe knew that this was the added element he would have expected from the Wipeouts. This was the message that he had dreaded for so long. They had him. Finally he was acquired. They'd locked on. The actual capture—and the unthinkable that would follow—was now preordained and only a matter of time. Joe's courage tried to rise to meet the inevitable, but it could not hold against the fright-tide of pure panic. For Joe, though, with all of his history, panic did not come in any orthodox form. He didn't gasp, reel or run. Instead, he carefully pushed his hair out of his eyes, and removed his gum. Then he sank slowly to his knees, and, only when he was settled in that pose of submission, Joe Gibson started to scream with the fullest force of his horrified lungs.

Written for an anthology, *Framed*, 2003

EXCERPTS OF AFTERLIFE

❏ I attempted a similar tactic of entering the mind of the chemically deranged in my 1999 novel **Jim Morrison's Adventures In The Afterlife**, but this was a little more complex than the horrors of the unfortunate Joe Gibson since the two central characters—Jim Morrison and Aimee Semple McPherson—were both dead and occupying multiple afterlives. This is a brief excerpt.

IF JIM HAD INDEED ACHIEVED HIS XANADU, IT WOULD have to be a stately pleasure dome of night and mysterious mist, as far, far down in Coleridge's caverns measureless to man as it was possible to go. It would hug the crags and surf and romantic chasms of ice and fire, where Alph the sacred river seethed at the apex of its ceaseless turmoil and crashed into the kraken depths of the great and sunless inward sea.

His Xanadu was a savage place and holy, both brutal and enchanted. A beast within a city, rampaging at its heart. Above the ring of Fenders and dulcimers, Bechtstein grand music loud and long, and the crash of dancing timpani and rocks, the voices of women soared as they wailed for their doomed and demon lovers amid a perfect chaos and a tranquillity of disorder chat even Jim himself had never been quite able to visualize. The stillness of his dope-fiend vision was the peace in the ultimate eye of the hurricane. Why had he never thought of that before, made it his objective! The magic of the pipe had brought it all into such clear focus and sharp perspective. Previously he had only closed his eyes in holy dread and ridden upon the storm with his cold silver-ringed fingers locked into the mane of the nightmare. Around him, all was a spiral of magnificent fury. Fountains gushed scarlet flame and

MICK FARREN

reptiles slithered about their business of corruption and seduction, but at the center of it all, he had finally found the strength and stability of the truly and fantastically free, free to waste an infinity of time if he so desired. Free to regard his right foot for a millennium if he so desired. To reinforce this bold discovery, his own face came toward him, with a woman, *the* woman, dark curls and pale, ready to reveal, repeating that it was true, it was all true, voice muffled but becoming clear, through the mirage of the ion-charged mist of Avalon and no one cried, "Beware! Beware!" at his flashing eyes and floating hair or wove a circle around him thrice because he on honeydew had fed and drunk the milk of paradise

"Okay. Enough, *mon ami*. You're slipping into borrowed poetry. Time to wake and move."

And Xanadu was gone and Jim was out of the dream and into a place of ice and freezing cold. "Fuck you, Hypo-dermic! I was just starting to enjoy myself."

From the novel *Jim Morrison's Adventures In The Afterlife*, 1999

THAT BAAAD COCAINE

AS I WRITE THIS, THE TABLOIDS TELL ME WE'RE HAVING a cocaine war in New York City. Not that there's anything novel about a cocaine war—any commodity that is highly illegal and of such market value that $50,000 worth can be stashed in the lining of a satin tour jacket is bound to cause a few fatalities now and then, but an unfortunate juxtaposition started me thinking. On Saturday night, for my sins, I was watching TV—the first show in the *Billy Crystal Comedy Hour* series. When Crystal (whose main claim to fame is having played the gay character Jody in *Soap*) got together with guest star Robin (Mork) Williams, every second gag was about coke—jive-ass stuff about Hollywood homeowners snorting their driveways clear after a freak blizzard—the kind of thing that passes for

❑ "Standing on State Street, looking down Maine, looking for the woman with that baaad cocaine..."

risqué on prime time.

Two days later I picked up the *New York Daily News*. The front page screamed a story about how a Colombian, his wife and their two infant children were shot dead in an execution-style hit when their Mercedes was pulled over on Grand Central Parkway. Investigating police searched the couple's Queens apartment and found 140 lbs of cocaine, a million dollars in loose cash and a small arsenal of automatic weapons. At least two other related murders followed, and the media speculated that the drug warfare common to Miami's demimonde had come north to the Big Apple.

Bit of a dichotomy, what? Within forty-eight hours we have Mork and Crystal (and, at other times: Johnny Carson, *Fridays, SCTV, Saturday Night Live et al.*) being daring with snort sniggers while whole families are blown away with a cool million stashed in the wardrobe. Something would appear to be a little skewed.

If you're wondering what this has to do with rock'n'roll, you must have been living in Tibet the last dozen years. Cocaine has been a rock'n'roll staple since before there was rock'n'roll. It was a favorite among thirties swing band members and forties bopsters. It replaced acid as the vogue drug when psychedelic quests into the unknown ceased to be fashionable. (Remember 'Casey Jones,' the Grateful Dead's tuneful *mea culpa?*) Through the rock star excess of the seventies the twin symbols of "making it" were unlimited coke and oral sex from top fashion models. Even puritanical punks took to coke like ducks to water (did someone say like pigs to shit?) as soon as their incomes were sufficiently substantial.

And musicians weren't the only ones who wanted to teach the world to sing. The powder permeated the whole business. Executives and flunkies, managers and booking agents all seemed unable to start a conversation without the ritual request, "Y'got any blow?" (Check the traffic to the toilet at any rock joints that specialize in showcase nights for business and media.) Cocaine even reached the typing pool, where secretaries tooted it off makeup mirrors.

Cocaine's appeal is that it is the ultimate product for

consumer capitalism. It produces a state of noisy euphoria that can turn rapidly to megalomania. It's so damned expensive that it provides a natural status high. Despite its illegality, part of the fun seems to be letting everyone know you're doing it. The rolled $100 bills, the elitist rituals, all contribute to the slightly scary concept that the cokehead (particularly the corporate cokehead who is all too common in most branches of the entertainment industry) is not getting stoned but consuming money in its most refined form.

Cocaine has never attracted law reformers the way marijuana has. The substance has always been bracketed with heroin—probably because both are white powders—and only defended publicly by social extremists. I've never understood why past governments were so down on the drug. Rather than turn users antisocial, cocaine makes them more aggressive wage slaves. The only reason this drug commands $100 or more a gram is because wealthy people want it and it is illegal. Cocaine costs pennies to manufacture— and pennies are all that the South American peasants who produce it receive. The big money is made in coke's transportation and sale. The rationale for such huge profits is that those who make them risk massive prison sentences.

At the moment, coke profits support organized crime and near-fascist Latin American governments. If the cocaine business were run as a legitimate corporation, it's been estimated it would make number five in the Fortune 500. Indeed, Colombia's drug-based "black market" economy is now larger than its legitimate coffee-based trade. Without the huge input of drug money, the country would be on the verge of fiscal collapse; the situation has become so blatant that it no longer seems to embarrass the country's rulers.

The only reason this state of affairs can exist—the only reason a coke dealer can have a million bucks stashed away in his flat like chump change, and the only reason ruthless individuals will stage private wars over these profits—is that the drug is illegal. If cocaine weren't illegal it would simply be a relatively inexpensive stimulant. No murders, no million-dollar profits, no sensational headlines and no chemical chic.

The logical answer would be to legalize the stuff and regulate its sale the same way liquor sales are regulated. Unfortunately, in the current climate and with the current administration there is little point in talking about logic. Equally unfortunately, until somebody does talk logic, both the killings and risqué jokes will go on.

Trouser Press, May 1982

SOUTH OF THE BORDER

DRYDEN

❑ But the problem with cokeheads is that they tend to go to extremes—extreme extremes. Remember the bumper sticker? "My other car is up my nose."

I once knew this heroin dealer in Istanbul. He kept three king cobras in a glass tank like an aquarium. Big mean poisonous motherfuckers that'd kill you as soon as look at you. Always hissing and spreading their hoods.

(DRYDEN gestures like a cobra spreading its hood.) Son of a bitch used to hide all his dope and his money under the gravel in the bottom of the tank. Figured that anyone trying to rip him off would never have the balls to stick their hand in the cobra tank.

MILNE
When the fuck were you in Istanbul?

(DRYDEN doesn't look at Milne.)

MILNE
(grins knowingly)
You were never in fucking Istanbul.

DRYDEN
(shrugs)
Actually it was Trenton, New Jersey. The guy was some old time hippie asshole with a big beard, looked like Jerry Garcia with bulimia. I only said Istanbul to improve on the story. Shit always sounds better if you set it somewhere exotic, you know what I mean?

MICK FARREN

CHA-CHA
What you mean is that you're a fucking liar.

DRYDEN
I'm a weaver of lurid tales, kid.

(The phone rings, a European-style double ring.)

From the play *South Of The Border*, 1993

THE CYCLE OF SEDUCTION

WITH HEROIN, THERE'S SOME KIND OF TEN TO TWELVE year cycle. Things go along pretty much as before and then suddenly—pow! There's a whole new generation of dope fiends out there, fucking up and overdosing and everything else that goes with the junkie territory. The media gets hysterical for fifteen minutes. Senators and congressmen start screaming for more jail time or the death penalty; you get a brief upsurge of police activity, and then it all goes back to business as usual. This is not to say that both heroin and addicts aren't always with us. Of course, they are. It's just that each time a new generation discovers the drug, it produces a fresh blip on the radar, and that's when the trouble starts up all over again.

The romantic image of opiates was in place long before there was Keith Richards or Johnny Thunders, or even Charlie Parker, William Burroughs, Lenny Bruce or *The Man With The Golden Arm*. From the very moment that opiates first arrived in Western Europe and the United States, regular or recreational users were invested with a certain dark and dangerous romance—Byron, Keats and Shelley, William Wordsworth, Samuel Taylor Coleridge, Thomas De Quincey, Dante Gabriel Rossetti, the beautiful and damned Lizzie Siddal, and the rest of the opium consuming Romantics and Pre-Raphaelites. Even the gunfighter Doc Holliday was set apart from the rest by his flask of laudanum. Oscar Wilde's fictional Dorian Gray

❏ Moving from the folklore of one white powder to another—Bolivian flake to Chinese rocks—I thought I perceived a rotating romance.

not only had a portrait in the attic, but also hung around the opium dens of Limehouse, Victorian London's Chinatown, to confirm his transcendental decadence.

In the sixties, when the hippies, at least initially, condemned heroin as a drug without the slightest redeeming social or artistic merit, the romance still lingered. Lou Reed may have scandalized the flower children with the song 'Heroin' on the Velvet Underground's first album ("I'm going to try for the kingdom if I can / Because it makes me feel like I'm a man") but, in a matter of months, large numbers of them would be trying for the selfsame kingdom.

Even on the other side of the coin, among the prohibitionists, the lawmakers, and the enforcers, the myth and romance prevail. Far from taking the approach that the problem, whether medical, social, or criminal, is that of a simple if addictive chemical, all too often heroin is portrayed as something almost supernatural, evil distilled to molecular form, the black prince of narcotics. The language used is frequently more biblical or grandly military than medical or legal. The talk is "horror," "evil," the word "narcoterrorism" is coined. The constantly repeated phrase "war on drugs" was turned from metaphor to alarming reality when George Bush, determined to arrest an alleged drug trafficker who also happened to be the president of a sovereign country, ordered 24,000 US troops into Panama, and expended the lives of 202 civilians and 337 soldiers (314 Panamanian and 23 American), to get his man. As Tom Wicker observed in a scathing argument in the *New York Times*: "539 people lost their lives as the primary cost of putting handcuffs on one thug,"

Ed Leuw, the eminent drug policy researcher for the Dutch government, attempted to explain actions like Panama in the book *Drug Prohibition and the Conscience of Nations*. "The drug war can only be understood as a holy war—and the important thing about a holy war is to fight it, not to win it." In this context, we begin to see not a law enforcement effort to prevent citizens from socially or medically harming themselves or others by unacceptable methods of intoxication, but millions of citizens being classified as heretics by virtue of their choice of ingestible chemicals. "The level of barbarism has not yet been as widespread as in other holy wars, barbarism is growing."

From a cover story in the *LA Reader*, 1994

JUNKIE ROMANCE

So you want to act like Johnny
So you want to act like Keith
So you crave some soft cocoon, boy
For your Charlie Parker grief
And you court the adoration
Of the ones with no esteem
In a hollow point delivery
Dope fiend self-inflicted dream

It's a junkie romance, kid
Alive on Avenue D
It's a junkie romance, Kid
Nothing ever comes for free

She shoots up through her stocking
See her thighs as pale as death
And you can't feel her breathing
But there's frost upon her breath
There's an old time Rx croaker
The doctor? Yes he's in
A drugstore substitution
For the thing the priests call sin

It's a junkie romance, kid
Alive on Avenue D
It's a junkie romance, Kid
Stone dead on MTV

❏ The intention of this song was to expose the spuriousness of the down at heel, Sid & Nancy, heroine romance of doomed junkie lovers. Sometimes, especially when I've seen the response from the audience when Wayne has played it live, I wonder if it actually had quite the reverse effect.

Written for Wayne Kramer's album *The Hard Stuff*, 1995

TO DRINK AND DRIVE IN LA

But back in the routine groove of alcohol the habitual barfly can talk forever about the commonality of the bars in New York, the cafés of Paris or the pubs of London, but in LA we run into a problem. A bar in LA is very much like a bar in New York or London, except for the blinding sunlight that tends to stream in each time the door is opened. It's getting there and getting back that's the problem, and, since a car is required, that will bring you into immediate conflict with the LAPD, the CHP and the LA County Sheriffs. The City of Angels very adequately proves that booze and car culture simply don't mix.

THE GIRLS GIGGLE, THE APPLE MARTINIS ARE SHAKEN, celebrities revolve in and out of rehab, and some do token time in the county lock-up. But even in the heat of summer, the bars are crowded with a hard drinking, big spending clientele, and the booze flows like there's no tomorrow. (Does the booze know something we don't?) And yet, Los Angeles has a highly ambivalent attitude to alcohol.

On the one hand, this town has a well-promoted pride in its pantheon of drunkards. Any roster of lauded inebriates will include luminaries like Errol Flynn and Charlie Bukowski, Tallulah Bankhead and Jim Morrison, Bette Davis and W. C. Fields, Spencer Tracy, most of the Barrymore family, Lee Marvin, and Sam Peckinpah—not to mention visiting lushes like Tennessee Williams, F. Scott Fitzgerald, and all those famous and legless rock stars at what used to be called the Continental Hyatt House.

On the other hand, LA does not make life at all easy for the intoxicated. For a city this size, it does not have bars in abundance, unlike London, Paris, or New York where, in some neighborhoods, you can render yourself royally hammered on the same street without consuming more than a single gin in the same joint. The real problem, like so many others the LA Basin is heir to is, of course, the great-but-failed, car-culture experiment of the twentieth century. When Ford and General Motors descended on SoCal in the wake of World War II, ripped out the Red Cars and built the freeways, no planner considered the problem of how, when the automobile reigned supreme, one was supposed to get home from the bar after four shots of Wild Turkey and attendant beers without risking arrest for DUI, and a whole mess of jurisprudence chewing on your ass.

The answer, in any civilized city, is, of course, a taxi. In Amsterdam or Tokyo, one hardly has to gesture before a cab is at the curb. In LA the wait can potentially be until hell freezes over. Not only are the cab companies a post-Soviet law unto themselves, but are also governed by ar-

MICK FARREN

cane and unfathomable regulations about where each cab line can and cannot pick up passengers. Even a call from the bar doesn't totally guarantee a ride. Evil Barbie dolls and their boyfriends, who just happened to be standing at the curb, have stolen pre-ordered taxis out from under me.

The sheer geographic size of LA also exacerbates the problem. If the hotspot *de jour* is in Silver Lake and you're in West Hollywood, making the scene constitutes an excursion, even an expedition. The official answer is the designated driver, but, in reality—in any quartet of liquor-loving degenerates—no one wants to be nursing a god-damned club soda all night, and that rare being, a genuine non-drinker who doesn't mind spending a long evening with a bunch of drunks is a pearl without price.

The outlaw answer is to play the criminal odds, but, with too many black & whites ominously hiding in side streets near popular watering holes just before 2am closing time, the odds are against the DUI in the making, and, of course, drunk driving is hardly ethical.

One reasonably inexpensive system of moving to saloon to saloon is cab sharing. Solo bar hopping by taxi can become prohibitively expensive, but split three or four ways, it starts to become fiscally more feasible. This may actually be the long term answer to wrecking one's liver in LA and not going to jail for one's trouble. A super improved cab service catering to the nightlife might be the salvation of all of us who drink, but live below the limo level. Already City Cab are running late night TV commercials stressing they will chauffeur the intoxicated.

LA CityBeat, September 2007

BUSTED

IN THE INSTANT THAT HE SAW THE CRUISER, SAM KNEW that he was not going to melt into the night behind this one. Even a block away the police car spelled trouble; all capitals. The old bull alpha was up and in control and he

❑ And, in LA, even being drunk and on foot can be a legal matter, baby.

was determined to accept no shit from any uniform, no matter what the ultimate cost. The rest of Sam's personality was in no condition to argue. Even without the old bull's china-shop belligerence, grief was the near-certain outcome of the encounter. Sam was on foot, in the night, lost, and hardly had an excuse with which to bless himself. He was drunk, he'd just fled an after-hours joint where he'd incited a brawl. What more did they need to roll him to jail? That's why they used to call them rollers. The very state of being without a car was an arrestable offense on a bad night in LA County, and who would call this night particularly good? The black and white slowed to walking pace while still twenty or thirty yards from him, and Sam reflected how the police cars in Los Angeles, with all their lights and exterior gadgets always had an air of an over-accessorized Terminator-mobile. They were designed to intimidate and Sam admitted that, in his own petty-Bolshevik way, he was intimidated. Couldn't they cut a deal on the intimidation? No chance. He even stopped walking, seeing no point in maintaining the pretence that he was a law-abiding evening stroller, even though, in his own way, he was. Or was he? Did he still have the speed? Or any other drugs. He believed everything had been consumed. Recall was less than perfect, but he didn't imagine the three barracuda strippers would have left him anything. Otherwise why would they have tossed him out of their car? Whatever the way of it, the moment to be checking through his pockets and throwing out the incriminating was long gone. The cruiser stopped and the high beams and military spot cut in making Sam feel like a cross between a prison break and Judy Garland in concert. He put up a hand to shade his deer-in-the-headlamps eyes, but this must have been incorrect and suspect behavior because the car's built-in bullhorn boomed.

"STAND EXACTLY WHERE YOU ARE AND KEEP YOUR HANDS IN SIGHT AT ALL TIMES."

All Sam could think of was Paul Newman in *Cool Hand Luke* and mutter to himself: "Yes sir, boss. Freezing it up here, boss. Hands in sight, boss."

The driver's door opened and then the passenger door five seconds later. A silhouette slowly advanced into the light, hand right over the high holstered Glock that was the prevailing epitome of cop cool, while his partner remained a dark shape back at the car. As far as Sam could see, one was tall, blond and Aryan with a Tab Hunter-style crew cut of a kind that was only worn in the twenty-first century by LA cops and a certain speciality of gay hustler/porn model. The other was a short, handsome Latino with a pencil moustache and weird eyes. Sam wondered which one would prove to be the out-of-his-tree sociopath-with-a-badge. His money was on the Latino, and he was marginally glad it was the Aryan approaching him. The two cops just radiated paranoia, disguised as methodical care. Okay so armed psychos were all over the place, but how much were they figments of the cops' own vanity? Or perhaps life was imitating art imitating life imitating art, over and over world without end until everyone needed an AK47. Sam knew his life was probably in danger, but the old bull was belligerent.

"Please step over to the car." The blond cop gestured to the patrol car with its blazing lights as though Sam might not have noticed it before. Sam gave a slight shrug and did as instructed.

"Please place your hands on the car."

At least he hadn't been told to assume the position. Sam had always found it too arrogant an assumption that one knew what the position was. Surely one was an amateur until proved professional? Sam placed his hands on the hood of the car. So far the old bull alpha had played the game and the rest of Sam was grateful. The Latino with the moustache expertly patted him down then stepped back and indicated to his partner that Sam was unarmed.

"Turn out your pockets."

At this the old bull baulked. Sam kept his hands on the hood, but turned his head to look at the Aryan. The rest of Sam listened aghast as the old bull alpha finally and apocalyptically broke his silence. "Listen. Why don't you just fuck off and just leave me alone? I'm a harmless drunk with a bad case of culture shock trying to find his way home. I know I should be playing the game but, in all reality, isn't this a total waste of our collective time, comrades?" At least, that was what he had intended to say. Sometime in the middle of the phrase "just leave me alone," his head was slammed hard into the hood of the car, and the rest came out as part thought and part muffled mumble. Sam had to concede one thing to the old bull. He went right on trying to talk, even when Sam was seeing stars, although Sam couldn't be sure if the real object of the exercise was preservation of pride or attempted suicide by cop.

From an unpublished short story

CELEB-HAB

□ Or they could toss your sorry ass in rehab…

THE STORY GOES THAT SOMETIME IN THE 1980S, ROCKER Jerry Lee Lewis checked into the Betty Ford Clinic to dry out from booze. Early in his stay he was presented with a mop and bucket and informed he'd be swabbing hallways. The Killer immediately walked out and never looked back. Two decades later, VH1 presents us with a very different picture on the reality show *Celebrity Rehab With Dr. Drew*. In an idyllic setting, showbiz shrink Drew Pinsky—a suave, better educated, and less aggressive version of Dr. Phil—conducts endless soft-centered group sessions with the quasi-famous—including actor Daniel Baldwin, porn star Mary Cary, and Jeff Conaway, late of *Taxi*, who seems to sign up for any celeb problem show—and the narcissism of the patients is only rivalled by the prurience of we-who-watch. Between these sessions with Pinsky, the participants lounge by the pool endlessly discussing their rotten relationships, or text each other from their rooms. But the reality of this reality series seems wide open to question. I have visited friends in rehab, and the ambience resembled a Ukrainian minimum security prison, not the flower decked luxury spa where *Celebrity Rehab With Dr. Drew* takes place. Maybe it's different for

MICK FARREN

the semi-famous, but, although the participants bemoan their bouts with substance abuse, their primary addiction appears to be an unconquerable need to be on TV at any cost to their dignity or plausibility.

LA CityBeat, 2007

STANDING BY AMY

I HAVE BEEN WORKING ON MY NEW BOOK (ON THE SUB-ject of drugs as it happens) all the livelong damned day, so I don't have to much to say except, even loathing award shows as I do, I was delighted that Amy Winehouse picked up five Grammy awards, providing proof that, counter to all the fashionable hypocrisy and propaganda, one can still actually be psychotic, stoned, drunk, self de-structive, and an all round mess (plus being ratted out by a tabloid newspaper and tossed into dubious rehab) and still produce, if not great art, at least some of the best music around. Needless to say, the sobriety gestapo, led in this instance by the miserable Natalie Cole, is moaning that an alleged and incarcerated drug addict should not be so honored. Nice one, Natalie, let's lower the poor girl's self-esteem a bunch more notches when she's trying to save her own life. Ah, fuck 'em. I've had more than enough of the self-righteous dictating what is acceptable behavior for the artist and what's not, and degrading and diminishing all who disagree. (But get well Amy, we need you.)

❏ Or you could be Amy Winehouse…

Doc40, September 2008

DRUNK IN THE MORNING

Feels like there's sand under my eyelids
Feels like I've spent my life on my knees
Feels like I should be getting a pension
Feels like I ate some old brass keys

❏ Certainly this song could not have been written about Los Angeles.

Think I'll walk off drunk in the morning
Do all the things I ain't done yet
Singing some song by some old French singer
Singing some song about no regrets

Think I'll go see crazy Billy
Think I'll ride the cross-town bus
Maybe I'll just stay here in the barroom
Run out of money and cause a fuss

Maybe I'll hide
Maybe I'll run
Maybe I'll stagger
In the light of the sun
Maybe I'll stumble
Maybe wander
Maybe I'll be back
When the day is down

Maybe I'll visit dumb sweet Linda
Maybe she'll just take me in
Mumbling delight in her deep dark cellar
Losing yourself can't be no sin

Think I'll walk off drunk in the morning
Do all the things I ain't done yet
Singing some song by some old French singer
Singing some song about no regrets

Written and recorded for the album
Vampires Stole My Lunch Money, 1977

AGAIN THE LAST PLANE OUT

❏ Back in the late 1980s, at the end of the Reagan era, I wrote some scripts for a kids' TV cartoon show

EVEN THOUGH GASOLINE NOW COST MORE THAN GIN, an olive drab GM truck, belching smoke and spattered with mud the color of dried blood, pulled up in the main square, outside the bar, and government soldiers in World

MICK FARREN

War II vintage helmets, and ragged, sweat-stained fatigues, with the striped shoulder flashes of the Simba Division, began unloading a few thousand red, green, and yellow loyalist flags. The flags were small; just paper triangles on little sticks, the kind handed out to crowds at political rallies. They were left in an untidy heap of open disorganized boxes, stacked against the plinth of the repeatedly torn-down and then replaced statue of the city's supposed founder. As the truck pulled away to the grinding of a dying gearbox, a twitchy teenager with an MI6 was left behind to guard the boxes of flags. For some reason, the occurrence outraged Lenny the Addict. "Now what dumb shit is this? Who the fuck needs flags? Jesus fucking Christ, half these fuckers don't have food or paper to wipe their asses on. Flags?"

Although the question wasn't actually rhetorical, Lenny the Addict didn't require an answer from anyone in particular, just a general rustle of agreement. While heat vied with humidity as the primary cause of discomfort, he could hardly expect any more animated response from the patrons of the bar at the Hotel Europa. It was hot and the civil war dragged on. Lenny the Addict was drinking the local squeezings, probably the cheapest high in the hemisphere, husbanding his hard currency against the remote possibility that a connection yet to be named might sell him some morphine syrettes. And when Lenny the Addict was drunk—as opposed to stoned—he talked. Yancey Slide, who was drinking maybe the only good scotch in the city, slowly turned his head, looked at the flags, but declined to speak, making instead a sound somewhere between a sigh and a snarl. Yancey Slide was nearing his threshold of intolerance for Lenny the Addict. Okay, so at least one token junkie was needed at the downfall of any city, but Slide couldn't understand why Lenny the Addict needed to keep him company. It wasn't as though Slide could be of any use to the skinny degenerate.

Dolores Haze was a different matter. Slide could always tolerate her company. In fact he would privately admit to an indolent and largely theoretical attraction to the wom-

called **The Galaxy Rangers** on my very first 64k computer. It wasn't the most scintillating work I've ever done, but it proved enough of a challenge to be interesting, and, it was very well paid if you worked fast, and, hey, now I had a computer. The only problems were created by the fact that a portion of the show's funding came from a company in Texas run by uncompromising Christian fundamentalists, who felt a constant need to issue memos that adjusted the show's moral navigation as they saw it. These edicts from the money men were mostly treated by the writers as irksome wastes of time, but easily bypassed because the fundamentalists were also fundamentally stupid. A near-mutiny broke out, however, when the Texans attempted to ban bars and saloons from a show that was essentially a western-in-space. "Where," we demanded, "are our characters supposed to interact if they don't have saloons? Sitting in the bloody street on their ridiculous robot horses?" (Yes, neighbors, the show featured its heroes and villains riding around on robot horses.) Ultimately a compromise was reached. We could have our saloons, but no on screen drinking and no saloon girls. The conflict, however, did reinforce just how crucial the inn, bar, or pub is to so many works of fiction where random strangers need to meet and engage. The circumstances are what make the difference. The atmosphere in a thinly disguised Hollywood shot and beer joint is going to be very different to a hotel bar in an African nation—not a million miles from the Congo—at the very bad end of a prolonged revolution.

an with the complex and highly unconventional history. She looked over the top of her heart-shaped sunglasses at the arrival of the flags, and then shook her hair loose, creating a sudden waft of unexpected perfume. This week her hair was the most plausible ash-blonde that could be created with the limited resources still available in the capital. Her lipgloss and nail polish were a dark magenta. Slide respected Dolores Haze for two things. She was always able to discover cosmetics no matter how dangerously unstable the political situation, and she was always plugged in close to the heart of the prevailing rumor mill. "The latest is that the Simbas flip-flopped and now the functional majority of the army is supporting Zidika, whatever that might mean. I guess our new president is planning a rally for the CNN cameras."

Jorges, the one-eyed bartender who looked a lot like a heavyweight, eye-patched version of the Artist Formerly Known as Prince, maintained his own totalitarian regime in the bar at the Hotel Europa, deciding absolutely how many drinks a customer could expect in return for a Rolex or a DVD player. He kept the TV above the bar tuned to CNN. Right now, a report on the situation in the capital was being aired. A tall, attractive, and, above all, dry reporter stood in front of the burned-out Opera House. The setting was familiar, but the story the woman with the hair-job and the radio mike was telling to the world bore no resemblance to the situation as observed from what was left of the bar at the Hotel Europa.

Dolores Haze pinned the credibility problem in an instant. "That CNN bitch isn't sweating. Three minutes of exposure to any reality in this place, and you're sweating like James Brown. I'll bet good money she hasn't ventured out of The Internationale since she got here."

Dolores Haze was absolutely right. Only The International—or, as it was more usually called, the Time Warner embassy—had air-conditioning. Everyone else in the capital was sweating. The Hotel Europa's AC had been dead for almost a month. It had gone when the building had been hit at ground level by a stray anti-tank rocket during the street fighting when Tetsu's people had pulled back to the North Side. The air had gone, as had an entire plate glass wall. That they had intermittent electricity to run the TV and watch the disinformation hit the airwaves amounted to a blessed mercy, "I mean, shit, if you aren't in the relevant temperature, how the fuck are you going to understand anything?"

As Dolores Haze castigated the TV a bead of sweat ran down the inside of her right breast. Slide was drunk enough to happily watch the beads of sweat run down the insides of Dolores' breasts for hours. Her white cotton dress was damp and all but transparent. Slide didn't know what to call the garment. He wasn't hip to couture. To him it looked retro-fifties, like the one Marilyn Monroe wore in *The Seven Year Itch*. That movie had been set in a New York City heat wave. Marilyn kept her panties in the icebox. High-August New York heat waves were bad, but nothing compared to the capital in a change of regime. Slide allowed himself a short whiskey fantasy. He and Haze were making slick night-heat liquid love on the creaking bed in his room in the middle of an air raid. Desperation and damp sheets sheltered them as explosions blossomed, sirens howled, searchlights probed, and a blast three blocks away blew the windows in, covering the two of them with diamonds of broken glass. It was unlikely to become reality, however. Not that Haze wouldn't be willing, but air raids appeared to be a thing of the past. All factions in the civil war had run out of even antique warplanes, and the Hueys-for-hire had mostly headed back to the coast, knowing they were unlikely to be paid.

Lenny the Addict interrupted Slide's voyeur daydream by deciding Dolores' information was a personal affront. "So the Army's backing Zidika? So what? What the fuck does the Army mean anymore? Like, where's that junkie Major who was selling me my fucking morphine now that I need him? Most of the bastards who haven't deserted are in business on their own account, and some, as I'm learning to my cost, can't even take care of business. All that signifies now is the AK Youth."

In this Lenny the Addict was absolutely right. Everyone knew all real power lay with the kids, the AK Youth, as they'd come to be called. The fifteen-, fourteen-, twelve-, and eleven-year-olds; the killer children with the Dracula eyes, and time-release caps of a complicated descendant of Ritalin actually sown into the flesh of their arms. These were the children who detonated Semtex like it was firecrackers at Chinese New Year, and took pride in hacking off the right arms of surrendering prisoners with machetes and pangas.

Here in the capital the very stars in their courses were directed by whether the baby machine gunners had been smoking heroin, or crack, geezing meth, or drinking needle beer, and the rattle of their AK47s was so unpredictably random, Slide figured it gave both unpredictable and random a bad name. Their reasons for slaughter exceeded all in the murky and unfathomable night, and when they drummed and chanted, rhyming in contemporary dementia, they raised dark and ancient gods to sanctify and offer sacrifice. They even seemed to speak their own unique language, as though traditional tongues were too slow and too linear for their wired and tweaking speech centers. All childhood had been lost in the ebb and flow of apparently perpetual warfare. Some of the mercs claimed that on an especially holy day, the AK machine gun kids would eat their own wounded.

"And anyway, who the fuck is going to show up for a rally to honor Zidika, for chrissakes? Who'd dare?"

Yancey Slide didn't move. He didn't want to move. He'd been at the bar so long, he had his hunch curled to perfection; elbows precisely rooted, and boot heels hooked into the crosspieces of the barstool just so. He preyed over his Johnny Black on the rocks like a ravaged vulture guarding his own. He had two more bottles stashed in an arrangement with Jorges. That was Yancey Slide for you. Where everyone else was drinking Tikky, or squeezings, or some leftover abomination from the dusty bottom of the bar like bubblegum schnapps, Slide had Johnny Black. Some claimed he wasn't human except in the most superficial sense, and if it was said to his face, he never argued.

"They'll Shanghai a bunch of kids from out of the bush. Hand them the fucking flags, and tell them if they cheer loud enough, and wave the flags hard enough, they'll feed them, and, if they don't, they'll kill them."

"And then?"

"What then? For those kids there is no then. The concept of now is pretty fucking precarious. They'll turn them loose in the city with the rest of the scavengers, or they'll draft them, or they kill them anyway."

"All for a thirty-second image on CNN?"

"The one thing there's plenty of is people. You could say the bottom's dropped clean out of the people market."

Dolores Haze made the flat and obvious statement. "It's time we took the hint and got out of here."

Lenny the Addict nodded. "We gotta get out of here."

Although Lenny declaring he had to get out of there sounded straightforward enough, it was more complex than many might imagine. Lenny the Addict not only had to get out, but he had to choose a destination with some care. If he wound up in some Hottentot burg where he couldn't cop opiates within the first few hours of leaving the airport, he would find himself sick, shaking and royally fucked. Slide knew this had to be one of the primary churning conundrums in Lenny's loop-the-loop, squirrel cage brain. Not that Slide could spare much sympathy for Lenny the Addict. Now that even the Russians were narco-players, dope was pretty much every place that could boast an airport capable of bringing in a 747, and the life of the globe-trotting dope fiend was a hell of a lot easier than it had been a few years earlier.

Lenny turned to face Slide directly. "How long do you think planes will still be coming in and out?"

Yancey Slide shrugged. What the fuck did he know? "Three, four days, maybe a week."

Dolores Haze had been fucking the door gunner of a freelance Huey crew who'd been looking for a doomed romance before pulling out. He'd given her the inside scoop on the state of Patrice Lumumba Memorial Airport. "The e-vac vultures are lining up on the taxiway. Everything from antique DC3s to piece-of-shit Gulfstreams creaking from hundreds of over-the-limit air miles. They've moved everything from cocaine and rock bands to Chinese software pirates. Right now, they'll take anyone at a price. The real trick is getting out there. There's checkpoints and roadblocks all the way, HIV-positive regular army looking for a shakedown, technicals who finally ran out of gas, AK kids using passing cars for target practice, or laying mines just to see shit blow up. The highway to the airport is decidedly hairy any way you look at it."

Slide gestured to Jorges to pour him another Scotch. All the gin joints in all the third world seemed to be haunted by the same ghosts when the veneer of civilization really began to peel. The white mercs had staked out their turf in the far back of the bar, where a boom box was playing death metal. The mercs were mainly Eastern European; Ukrainians and Serbian Chetniks, plus some Libyan-trained Irishmen. The thrill seekers and psycho killers with their Street Sweepers, matched Suomis, and CZ 25s had long been shredded to history. The Soldier of Fortune amateurs with the Death or Glory tattoos never had what it took. They held on to grenades too long, stepped on landmines, were speared by bamboo pongee sticks, painted themselves into impossible tactical corners, or, in some of the more extreme cases, were fragged from this mortal coil by their own comrades.

Slide was surprised Hertz the German had survived so long, and was still one among the slumped figures in camouflage fatigues, scuffed jump boots propped up on tables, trying to drink away the thousand-yard stare. With the mutant Doberman that was always at his side, he was an extremely unpleasant showboat even by Yancey Slide's expansively lax standards. Slide found conversation with the German close to impossible. He had a habit of sexually juvenile non sequiturs. Out of the blue he'd make remarks like, "The sound of the cane on taut rubber is singularly distinctive, *nicht wahr?*" According to fairly reliable rumor, Hertz had this game he played with his women of simulated necrophilia. First inducing insulin coma and then, as he put it in his thick stormtrooper accent, "bringing the bitch back with a sucrose shot."

Right at this moment Hertz was turning his blond-beast, Nazi charm on the stranded script girl from the French documentary film crew who had arrived in the capital a week earlier. As parlor ex-Marxists they thought they could shoot footage of the AK Youth, but had been quickly set straight and, luckily for them, without too much loss of life. While they were packing to go, the script girl had engaged in a screaming Gallic fight with the director, and a prolonged pouting sulk had resulted in her losing her ride out, and now she was thrown to the wolves of her own resources and survival skills. From where Slide sat, she didn't seem to have many of either, except for a passing resemblance to a dark-haired version of the young Brigitte Bardot. Would she get the insulin treatment from the German? Would that be her supposed ticket to comparative safety? Slide wondered if a single cc of the drug remained in all of the city, unless, of course the German carried his own stash. Slide didn't doubt, even without the drug, Hertz had plenty more unnatural tricks up his abominable khaki sleeve.

The dark-haired Bardot, as she laughed with the German, head to head, lips close to lips, had no clue what she was really getting into, but in this she was not so unique. What the fuck did any of those assembled imagine they were doing there or really getting into? Some had the excuse they were only doing their job, plying their trade, or following their avowed calling. The mercs would maintain the atrocities just went with the job description. The journalists would likewise deny all accusations of advanced auto-wreck voyeurism, and claim they were simply relaying the story to a concerned world, or recording all for posterity. Lenny the Addict would blame his presence there on some disastrous counter-synchronicity of wrong turns and missed connections because Lenny, a perpetual victim of fate, was never responsible for his actions, and his being in the capital was at least a huge and hideous misunderstanding, if not an actual conspiracy.

In the area of conspiracy, James Jesus Valentine, the Europa's CIA spook-in-residence, had more than once copped the tired plea that he was only in the capital obeying orders, protecting the vital interests of the United States. Slide was at something of a loss to figure how exactly the vitals of the US were being protected by Valentine's current and lopsided conversation with Misty Mona, a bizarre, popeyed, drag-queen homage to the post-Supremes Diana Ross. He couldn't see what concern there might be at Langley, the State Department or the White House with Mona's whacked-out-on-Tikky-and-Benzedrine reflections on the cosmetic advantage of using Lee Press-On Nails on her toes when wearing open-toed sandals. Valentine was, however, famous throughout the capital as a master of plausible deniability, and for having an answer for everything. If challenged he would coolly respond that he was preparing a report on how the rules of entropy dictated no city could fall without a quorum of drag-queen adventurers in attendance.

Slide had Jorges pour him another shot from his private stash. He hoped the booze would take him past the stage of seeking explanations for what, in truth, completely defied explanation. Back in the seventies, legend told how a couple of New York cops had found a dead gorilla in the South Bronx. They hadn't even tried to offer reasons or theories, and Slide knew that was ultimately the best way. If he searched for reasons for too long, he would eventually wind up asking himself why he was there in the capital, and that was a question he knew he shouldn't even consider from a distance, let alone approach.

In general terms, Slide figured the material paradoxes were a part of the attraction. All in the Europa Bar were, to one degree or another, vultures picking over the carcass of an imploded nation-state. A Harry Lime romance of uncut diamonds and tainted penicillin. Just before everything ran out, crude economic law dictated a sudden rush of exotic consumer variables would hit the darkest strata of the black market. An abrupt plethora would occur: Cuban cigars; Beluga caviar; A-list celebrity porn; Durban Poison; Napo-

138

MICK FARREN

leon Brandy; primo flake; cut price gold and gems; and lately, in the modern world, deep-frozen body parts, as the elite of the *ancien regime* freed up their terminally hoarded goodies to pay the freight up the political gravity well. In the capital this was happening with a vengeance. Word was Zidika himself had personally purchased—from a strange individual who dealt in such things—a pair of genuine French government colonial-issue guillotines, cherry-perfect down to the tall polished oak-beam frame, the steel blade, and the rubbed brass hardware. Formal public executions, with full and bloody pomp and circumstance, could start anytime, and anyone even tenuously connected with Tetsu and the PRP had an unseen, unwritten, but wholly tangible death warrant hung round their necks and they just hadda, hadda, hadda get away.

Flesh would also need to be factored into the equation. A byproduct of any local apocalypse was always a hot and cold human buffet fit for the imagination of the Marquis de Sade. In the ad hoc culture of collapse, where torture and murder were merely items in the tool kit of maintaining power, the strangest of the passionately strange were able to indulge whims previously unimagined. Just two nights earlier a human being had run through the square and past the bar, blazing like a gasoline torch, and everyone had assumed it was the work of the lone and secretive Iraqi, late of the Republican Guard, who liked setting fire to women and teenage boys, supposedly fire-cleansing them for Allah or Zoroaster. Slide's best theory, though, was that it really had very little to do with either sex or plunder. When order and structure collapsed, a form of energy was released, and this was really what drew them, and on what they all fed.

On television the sweatless and sanitary CNN reporter was explaining how troops loyal to President Zidika were rapidly restoring order in the major cities. This prompted a former SAS man to mutter "Bollocks" in a thick Scottish accent, but then even he fell silent as all eyes turned away from the TV to the missing window and the square beyond. Slide groaned inwardly, and swallowed his shot of scotch, as five ominous figures followed their shadows across the threshold and into the bar. Lenny the Addict let out a short fearful breath.

"Oh shit."

One of the new arrivals was a regular army captain in a reasonably clean and complete uniform. Simba division again. He led a handcuffed and badly beaten prisoner by a short length of rope tied around his neck. The prisoner's head was covered with a flour sack. Two eyeholes had been cut for the unfortunate to see out; the traditional and accepted mask of the informer. Clearly the hooded one's life was being spared for at least as long as he could be led round the bars and cafés to identify his former colleagues and comrades. The captain and his prisoner, however, were not the primary reason the interior of the Europa had lapsed into such deathly silence, and Jorges had even used his remote stealthily to turn down CNN's audio. The captain and his prisoner had an escort of three young AK kids, the eldest of whom couldn't have been more than twelve. The tallest and most senior, despite the heat, wore a black PI trenchcoat over VC shorts, and a Marilyn Manson T-shirt. His Air Jordans looked practically new, as did the Mac 11 held down by his side. The gun seemed to have only recently come out of its Cosmolene. Some motherfucker was shipping in new materiel despite the embargo. His two companions were less sharp in T-shirts and ultra-baggy fatigue pants. One had jump boots and the other was barefoot, although the barefoot one did sport an old A3 flying jacket, and a red bandanna wrapped around his head. Both were armed with battle-scarred but totally serviceable Kalashnikovs.

Taking advantage of the distraction and human silence, a jade-green lizard made its way down the crumbling plaster of the wall behind the bar. As the informer studied the assembled faces, seeking candidates for Zidika's new guillotines, Slide couldn't help but make a move of minor defiance. He took one of Dolores' cigarettes, and lit it with his Zippo, the one with the Jack Daniels logo that had traveled with him over more than half the planet. Doombeam eyes from the black trenchcoat swivelled and focused, but Slide was not about to be stared down by any twelve-year-old, no matter how homicidal. He met them squarely. The youngest began to raise his AK, but the trenchcoated leader made a cool-it gesture, and psycho-speared deep into Slide's eyes, letting the beam carry its message. This was no child. The kid in the black trenchcoat was as old as Attila the Hun. In his world survival itself was a near-insupportable luxury, and all that remained was feral calculation and random death. Look at me, old-timer, then marvel and fear. You are history, and I am the face of the new millennium. I am primal, but you scream. We are here now, in this sorry city, but how long do you think it will be before you see these eyes in Paris, London, or Patterson, New Jersey?

The hooded informer broke the spell by pointing to a frightened individual with pomaded hair and a Little Richard moustache sitting two stools down from Lenny the Addict. He had once been number three in the hierarchy of Tetsu's Office of Public Order, but now he was just a fragment of the past, fit only for speedy disposal. The man froze as he was identified. A fly landed on his left hand, but he didn't appear to notice. As the captain beckoned him to his feet, his bladder gave way, staining the leg of his linen suit, and leaving a moisture trail on the barroom floor as he was led away. Slide let cigarette smoke drift from his nostrils as everyone in the Europa uniformly exhaled. Even the mercs in their paramilitary bravado knew they only lived because the three kids hadn't been in a mood for massacre.

Dolores Haze turned to Slide. "I think it's high time we braved the road to the airport."

"Again the last plane out?"

"You want to stay and see what happens next?"

"It had occurred to me."

"Are you even human, Slide?"

"Are any of us human, my dear Dolores? Aren't we just a pack old twentieth century ghosts gazing aghast at the inevitable future."

Published in the anthology *Carved In Rock*, 2003

THE LITERATE HANGOVER

☐ At times I have seriously considered the possibility that Christianity is really only an analog of alcohol or maybe vice versa. Easy pleasure is followed by the pain of retribution, sure as night follows day, or that old Hank Williams concept of honky-tonking on a Saturday night followed by church on Sunday, although I don't think Hank made it to too many churches. Whether this is correct or merely the product of atheist prejudice, a terrible price does have to be paid. The more wretched the excess of the night before, the more hideous the suffering that comes with the morning light. The only consolation in all this—aside from codeine and Valium—is the clear evidence that the hangover has produced some fine writing. But isn't that the way of it with pain? Ask Iris Murdoch or the Marquis de Sade.

"There is only one cure for a hangover, and that is to drink a bottle of very, very dry champagne the next morning."
—Dean Martin

"THE PLOP-PLOP WAS PAINFULLY DEAFENING, AND THE subsequent fizz approached my pain threshold. The morning was one in which even Alka Seltzer was an ordeal."

Writing about the hangover is amazingly easy. Far easier, in fact, than writing about the drunk that preceded it. The hangover is present, lucid and indelible. With the hangover comes a terrible Edvard Munch clarity. The clarity is what makes the pain so awesome, and the guilt-wracked fog of obscured memory so dark and threatening. The idea that alcohol is nothing more than a chemical analog of Christianity (or vice versa) becomes totally plausible. A peak of euphoria is followed by a deep vale of tears, retribution, lamentation, and the agony of the damned.

Attempting to accurately portray intoxication from the intoxicated's point of view is hard, since drunks rarely maintain the same point of view from one moment to the next. He or she is adrift on a sea of swaying incoherence, nearly impossible to reproduce except in broken English, or small subjective vignettes of how gravity warps out of whack. The only true grandmaster of literary inebriation was, of course, the late Dr. Hunter S. Thompson, who could reproduce the high drunkard's logic as well as the hallucinating hungover horrors, but, Hunter was Hunter and we will not see his like again in our short lifetimes.

The hangover may actually be so easy to write that it represents something of a health hazard to the jobbing scribe. Back in the days when I labored in the salt mines of rock journalism, I and a couple of other scribblers developed a critical technique by which we went to a show, partook of the optimum ambiance, and then rated the performance by the intensity of the next day's suffering. Maybe imprecise, but the readers understood, because these were the halcyon days when music was still meas-

MICK FARREN

ured by its excesses. Keith Moon drank cognac for breakfast, Keith Richards was still the Witch King of Angmar, and 'Sister Morphine' was a communiqué from the front. Later, when too many peers became so grimly clean and twelve-step sober, and health was equated with virtue, the hangover ceased to be anything to boast about. No more the next-day Jack Daniels hero. One risked being talked about as having "a problem," and suffered in diplomatic silence. Which is never easy, particularly as so many aspects of the modern world are best regarded with the jaundiced eye and toxic glaze of malevolent morning, especially when looking west to Washington.

Best ever hangovers in literature? The alcoholic journalist Peter Fallow in Tom Wolfe's *The Bonfire of The Vanities* comes close to the fictional crest, as does the musician Larry Underwood in Stephen King's *The Stand*, but my personal, and admittedly highly subjective prize has to go to the monumentally hard-boiled headache with which Mike Hammer awakes at the start of Mickey Spillane's *The Girl Hunters*, when Hammer has been a down-and-out rummy for seven years, but must sober up and go rescue Velma from the Commies in the Kremlin. The choice in movies is packed with even more contenders. Obvious nominations have to go to Jack Nicholson in *Easy Rider*, Dean Martin in *Rio Bravo*, Lee Marvin in *Cat Ballou*, Paul Newman in *Harper*, and Nick Nolte in *North Dallas Forty*. (Although Nolte is actually suffering the effects of not only booze, but also Percodan, steroids, and playing wide receiver in an NFL game.) The top honor, though, has to go to Jane Fonda as the washed-up actress, Alex Sternbergen, in Sydney Lumet's *The Morning After*, when she confronts every drunk's worst nightmare—that somewhere in the density of the blackout, she has committed an unremembered murder.

Best hangover in song? Simple. Has to be Johnny Cash's 'Lonesome To The Bone'...

The sun is roughly risin'
On the roofs of Stagger town
The time for sweatin' poison out

Is just now comin' round

The mention of sweating poison reminds me that no discussion of the hangover is complete without touching on possible cures. Some swear by black coffee, Valium, or hot showers. John Belushi thought a Turkish bath was the perfect balm, but look what happened to him. I favor a large'n'greasy diner breakfast, Coca Cola, and codeine if I can get them, but the unfortunate truth is that only two things cure a hangover. One is time, and the other—be it the very, very cold dry champagne cited by Dean Martin at the head of this piece, a cold beer, a Bloody Mary, a Greyhound, a Margarita, or a suicidal Sam Peckinpah shot of straight tequila—is simply to go out—call it hobby, habit, or hair-of-the-dog—and have another drink.

LA CityBeat, 2008

Part Three

The Corridors Of Power

I have neither trusted nor desired power. At its most honest, it seemed to require oversized Greek pillars and a hollow marble echo to sustain itself, and, when it was less than honest, it was capable of just about any atrocity. Routinely capable—which made it all the worse. I was never particularly attracted to the concept of power. Being expected to tell others what to do and order them around on a whim or a theory held no appeal. Quite the reverse. I have no desire to issue orders and even less to receive them. To separate the two would be hypocrisy. Fame I might cop to. I wouldn't have minded being famous, especially when I was young and had lungs, but the idea of wielding power was a complete anathema.

I would never argue with the oft-repeated remark by Niccolo Machiavelli that "it is better to be feared than loved, if you cannot be both." I have even less trouble with the even more frequently quoted remark by Lord Acton, "Power tends to corrupt, but absolute power corrupts absolutely." My position is that the desire to rule over others is rarely prompted by altruistic motives so the potential for corruption is present from the get-go. I have also noticed too many of the worst sons-of-bitches who come to power take Machiavelli's advice and employ the fear option early and often. I suspect this is maybe because the majority of power-seekers are most motivated by their own deep-seated fears. Which prompts me to suspect we live in an era of chickenhawks, of men and women of bellicose rhetoric, but who are terrified of all and any threat to their personal safety.

I'm well aware that the armed guards and Secret Service spooks with their Uzis and earpieces are now such a part of the territory that even corporate chieftains and rap stars have them, but I cannot shake the feeling that the powerful are, at the same time, also the fearful. In the wake of the September 11, 2001, attacks on the World Trade Center and the Pentagon we heard all the rumors about US Vice President Dick Cheney and his multiple bunkers, with their state of the art high-tech and maybe even high occult protection. Something in the nature of leaders and power had plainly changed over the two dozen centuries between Dick Cheney and Alexander the Great, who led his Macedonian forces into battle riding at the head of his cavalry.

And since we've already raised the spectre of Dick Cheney, let's continue with a reaction to his handiwork.

NOW AIN'T THE TIME FOR YOUR TEARS

THE TIGRIS AND EUPHRATES BURN IN MY LIVING ROOM. There are killing fields by the rivers of Babylon, there's war in the Garden of Eden. The history book cycles of death prove stubborn and eternal, and this is the third war in my life to which I feel at least a witness.

Born at the end of World War II, I lost my father to that one, and then I did my stoned and level best in the mass movement to halt the insanity in Vietnam, but now the tanks are rolling and the bombs falling all over again. Right now, I can think of no rock'n'roll tune, no CD or battered 45, that can reflect the combination of fear and fury that dogs my mind like the hellhound of a Robert Johnson nightmare, and the sure knowledge that this spurious conflict was never about democracy in Iraq—that it was merely a petrodollar payday, and a military industrial burn-off. The real battle for democracy—or the lack of it—will be fought back in the US. As the bombs grow smarter, and leaders more arrogantly stupid, I truly fear these sons-of-bitches actually do want to conquer the world.

On TV channels of managed news, finessed by the next Dr. Goebbels, I watch ruthless hollow-men playing crude, corrupt midwives to a New World Order, but I have yet to imagine a suitable musical score for the unfolding horror. Not Richard Strauss bombast, not 'Guns of Brixton,' NWA nor Public Enemy, not even the youthful, ear-bleeding wrath of Pete Townshend, the spite of Lou Reed, the rolling thunder of the Stones in their prime; who among them is adequate to the task? Maybe Jimi, but Jimi is long gone and was ultimately a peaceful soul.

Long ago, I saw Bob Dylan perform 'Masters of War.' Ol' Bob was in a nasty mood that night, and had the band tuned to a wrathful howl. *"And I'll stand over your grave 'til I'm sure that you're dead."* That was closer to the noise in my head, because, as of now, I am nobody's pacifist. A repressive horror bears down. The stench of the new McCarthyism streams from Fox and CNN at short attention-span speed, and accompanied by the theme from

Gladiator. And damn me if all the night-vision pride and blitzkrieg glory isn't punctuated by an older Bob, in new mode, singing how he's sick of love in a Victoria's Secret commercial.

Better look to the less compromised Hunter S. Thompson to confirm my fears. "This country has been having a nationwide nervous breakdown since 9/11. A nation of people suddenly broke, the market economy goes to shit, and they're threatened on every side by an unknown, sinister enemy. These are not philosopher-kings we're talking about. These are politicians." The politicians of the fixed election—of power at any price—pose like the righteous of God, but I can only see an opportunist gang of greed-is-good, corporate crusaders, following the ancient and bloody eastward trail of Alexander the Great on their computer maps; Bush, Cheney, Rumsfeld, Ashcroft, and the dark eminences Perle and Wolfowitz (who must have watched *Rollerball* far too many times when they were kids), plus, to my eternal shame, the dancing attendance of the leader of the British Labour Party.

These men are not only waging their war, but are conjuring an ugliness among the people, and opening the floodgates to a new brutality in which those timeworn other weapons of mass destruction; racism, misogyny, bigot-religion, homophobia, and the threat of poverty, are dragged out to divide and confuse, while the Bill of Rights is shredded, and neighbor is encouraged to rat out neighbor.

Yes, I would happily stand over their graves until I'm sure they are dead, and dance if I want to, because these men have yet again turned freedom into nothing left to lose. I would like to take comfort in Gandhi: "There have always been tyrants and murderers, and for a time they seem invincible, but in the end they always fall." But I don't have the patience of the Mahatma. The time is for some fighting talk of our own.

And where is the fighting talk of rock'n'roll in this terrible twenty-first century? Well muffled, brothers and sisters, coming as it does by courtesy of the mighty Clear Channel and the like, who have seemingly warned the too-malleable tour talent about how they'll pull the plugs on any antiwar talk.

Hell, I've had the plugs pulled on me more times than I can remember. The drummer refuses to stop and a riot starts. Did poor Jim Morrison die in vain? So far it has been the movie stars manning barricades; Martin Sheen, Susan Sarandon, Sean Penn, and Janine Garafolo have been putting their futures on the line, being told by TV pundits to shut their ignorant mouths, as though an actor is not entitled to an opinion, and everyone has forgotten the resumé of that old right wing cowboy Ronald Reagan.

It takes Michael Moore to "disgrace" the Oscars while Bono stands mute. Elvis Costello (God bless him) snarls his way through 'Peace, Love, And Understanding' while guest-hosting the Letterman show. A Dixie Chick blurts her Texas shame for having Bush as a homeboy, but is then forced to recant like some twelfth century nun faced with the instruments and the fire. I hear Eddie Vedder has been sticking it to Bush on Pearl Jam's Bush League tour, and this has resulted in everything from rousing cheers to mass walkouts depending on which managed news channel you're watching, or what web page you're reading. Thurston Moore has his website, and Steve Earle stands tall, but why is Bruce so damned quiet when the shot-and-beer boys from New Jersey, in the Motörhead T-shirts, are baying for the blood of towel-heads and peace-fags—"America, love it or leave it, motherfucker!"—and gung-ho for a crack at Syria or Iran.

But watch out, it moves too fast, the aftermath will be on us before we know it. JFK understood, and so did Khrushchev, but the Crusaders of this New Order are too aggressively dumb to comprehend that the Beast of War takes on a life of its own, shrugs off all control, and the only power that remains in their hands—if they're lucky—is the choice of striking or not striking the match in the room full of gasoline.

I feel like a fool, regurgitating the clichés of my youth, to actually ask if rock'n'roll is going to be part of the problem or part of the solution, but much more is at stake here than me appearing foolish, or risking any cultivated cynicism. One of the few perks of not dying before you grow old is that you don't have to fear being mocked as a fool. I no longer give a damn. I know the music I love is at its very pinnacle when it's played with a no-prisoners passion, and bellows the battle cry of freedom directly into the mouth of Hell. That is a law immutable.

So c'mon, everybody. You've taken the drugs, and you've taken the cures, you've fucked and forgotten the names of the lovers, and you've all made far too much money. Like it or not, the time to hesitate is once more through. There's even a rumor that Bush is back on the bottle. Gotta save the bloody world again.

Rock's Backpages, April 2003

LUNATICS WITH NOTHING TO LOSE

The Director of the Agency faces the Committee
Gentlemen, we have a problem
That we can no longer ignore
We have attempted to
Psycho civilize the lower bell curve
Of the indigenous population
But we have to face the unfortunate side effect
That even with the introduction of Mortal Kombat
And fifth generation anti-depressants
Plus the chemical additives in the water supply
And the TV subliminals
Instead of a docile subspecies
We seem to have created a line
Of lunatics with nothing to lose

The Director of the Agency paces the marble floor
Of the conference room of the committee
I cannot emphasize the point too strongly
We have done everything within
Our capability to reduce the attention span

❑ I have often suspected that the real motivation of those who seek power is a fear of how the world is full of other people, a fear so chronically intense that they come to believe a sense of safety is only possible if they control absolutely everything absolutely.

And induce greed as the sole motivating factor
To create hostile divisions
Of race, gender, belief, and preference
To burn out empathy, and desensitize them
To the concept of mortality
Hopelessly confuse violence and sexuality
And negatively sanction wilful individuality
By the use of quasi-legal narcotics
And the threat of a lethal and lingering retro-virus
According to our projections
We should have reached the point
Where they would allow themselves
To be driven like sheep
Yet our studies reveal increasing numbers
Of what can only be classified
As lunatics with nothing to lose
The Director of the Agency regards the committee
Over the cold frames of his designer glasses

The blame for this aberration
Can be apportioned later
Our most pressing need now
Is to order an increased presence
Of control forces in the major centers of population
Prior to the transition
To a more restrictive and prejudicial
Structure of government
The camps must be activated
And the Nightwatch put on full alert
The time for Malathion—gentlemen—is past
The helicopters must commence to do their worst
I am aware this involves design jumping
And forward shifting the timetable of our masters
But, for our own protection
We can only treat this deviation
With absolute seriousness

For if we don't, make no mistake
We ourselves could become victims

MICK FARREN

We ourselves could be
Dragged out—gentlemen—and hung by our feet
From municipal street illumination units
By mobs of lunatics with nothing left to lose

Not previously published

WHISKEY DRUNK IDIOTS

I'VE ALWAYS HAD THE UNEASY FEELING THAT, WHEN IT came to the unthinkable, ultimate showdown, nuclear powers might just behave as badly as drunks in a bar carrying guns. When one whiskey-drunk idiot pulls his gun and starts shooting, the others just can't stop themselves doing the same. Okay so Kennedy and Khrushchev skated by in the Cuban Missile crisis, but that was just two of them. These days, the barroom is a lot more crowded.

A fragment

❑ A moment comes in most people's childhood—we hope in infancy—when they wise-up to the fact that their parents are not all powerful, all seeing superbeings, and are, in fact, decidedly fallible. For some reason, all too many of us never experience the similar revelation that many of our leaders are pretty bloody stupid.

ETHICS OF BARBARISM

THE END OF 2002 AND THE COMMENCEMENT OF 2003 have hardly been kind to the rock'n'roll generation. John Entwistle provided the first shock. At the start of the Who's 2002 tour, the band's seemingly indestructible bass player, who once rejoiced in the nickname "the Ox," did up a line of coke in his Las Vegas hotel room and dropped dead. Then, at Christmas, Joe Strummer of the Clash not only keeled over from a fatal heart attack, but was forced to endure the postmortem mortification of having an uninvited Courtney Love make a total spectacle of herself before his family and friends. A matter of days after Strummer's demise, a second bombshell came from the Who. Guitarist and composer Pete Townshend's name and credit card number surfaced in the dragnet of the FBI's Operation Avalanche child pornography sting. Pete

❑ In the year 2001, instead of following the monolith to Jupiter, America detached from reality and attempted to take the rest of the world with it. Those of us who remained awake stared in disbelief at how the new century was shaping up. Except "up" didn't have much to do with it.

claimed that he was only doing research for a book, but the incident created strange resonations for all of us who ever owned a copy of *Tommy* or *Who's Next*.

The news that Phil Spector had been arrested for murder was received with far less humor, and set those of us who could still remember to wondering how the mastermind behind 'He's A Rebel,' 'River Deep Mountain High' and 'He Hit Me (And It felt Like A Kiss)' came to gun down poor Lana Clarkson, who's main claim to prior fame was the lead in the movie *Barbarian Princess*. He shot me and it felt like a kiss? What the hell had the man behind the Wall of Sound been into in his suburban Castle Dracula in Alhambra, California, with its Transylvanian turrets and high, maximum-security walls, that had led him allegedly to firing the fatal shot? Markie Ramone attempted to explain on CNN how Phillip had indeed once pulled a piece on the Ramones, but that had only been drunken R&R fun. Back in the late sixties, just a few months before the Stones played Altamont Speedway, Spector had been one of the celebrities on the Manson Family's supposed hit list. Now he was on the other end of a homicide investigation.

In just a couple of weeks, we saw press photos and TV newscasts of two major rock icons looking old and pathetic in the back of police cars. These visions were more than enough to spawn a feeling that a form of madness was loose, or to trigger a bout of where-did-we-all-go-wrong introspection, and bring on those nagging doubts that maybe the so-called conservatives were right, and all the blows that had been struck in our youth for supposed liberation had been empty or in vain.

Fortunately we only have to look hard to the right, to the other side of the ideological fence, to where our Republican contemporaries are now running the country, for confirmation that the outbreaks of craziness, incarceration, and death among my rock'n'roll peers are nowhere close, either in incidence or intensity, to the epidemic of post-yuppie psychosis that rages in the corridors of state, where the maintenance of power would appear to be harnessed to a snarling coalition of TV-fascist totalitarians, short attention-span pragmatists, and fraudulent corporate bagmen. Brett Easton Ellis' *American Psycho* and his attendant demons-from-the-id still have the same homicidal intent and expensive haircuts, but are now cloaked in a superior middle-aged certainty, and, in private, a smug and smiling amorality. I recognize them from way back. They are the same college boys who kept Ayn Rand and Machiavelli on the coffee table, but probably never read either, quoted Sun Tzu without understanding a word, and dismissed Henry Kissinger as a closet liberal.

Then they graduated to invade Wall Street like Armani Huns in the roaring eighties, when greed, for want of a better word, was good. They drank Chablis and single malt, snorted coke, but passed on the introspection of marijuana, or the cosmic self-criticism of acid, and, as I suspected at the time, would resort to date rape with little provocation. Twenty years on, they are cleaner, more sober and even meaner. Greed is no longer merely good, it has become imperial. To them, all things appear possible, whether you're pissing away fortunes in Washington or at AOL Time Warner, when confronted with a population they see as terminally dumbed down to mindless preoccupation with *American Idol,* and the denouement of *Joe Millionaire,* when not lurching to victim mass hysteria in the face of a first real taste of domestic terrorism, or maudlin mourning the symbolic loss of a crashed spaceship.

In an editorial that circulated by email at the end of January, the venerable Kurt Vonnegut shared a similar view of the current power structure, but, as a breed, they seemed to take him more by surprise. "*Our country might as well have been invaded by Martians and body snatchers. Sometimes I wish it had been. What has happened, though, is that it has been taken over by means of the sleaziest, low-comedy, Keystone Cops-style coup d'etat imaginable. And those now in charge of the federal government are upper-crust C-students who know no history or geography, plus not-so-closeted white supremacists, aka 'Christians,' and plus, most frighteningly, psychopathic personalities. Unlike normal peo-*

ple, they are never filled with doubts, for the simple reason that they cannot care what happens next. Simply can't. Do this! Do that! Mobilize the reserves! Privatize the public schools! Attack Iraq! Cut health care! Tap everybody's telephone! Cut taxes on the rich! Build a trillion-dollar missile shield! Fuck habeas corpus and the Sierra Club, and kiss my ass!"

Anyone who, in addition to the invention of Ice-nine, has the World War II Dresden firestorm on his resumé, and survived the most devastating air raid in human history prior to Hiroshima, while simultaneously a prisoner of the Nazis, must be taken a little bit seriously. John le Carre, the master of the espionage novel is also hard to dismiss as a bleeding heart liberal, but, writing in the London *Times*, his thoughts are almost identical to Vonnegut's. "*America has entered one of its periods of historical madness, but this is the worst I can remember: worse than McCarthyism, worse than the Bay of Pigs and in the long term potentially more disastrous than the Vietnam War. The reaction to 9/11 is beyond anything Osama bin Laden could have hoped for in his nastiest dreams. As in McCarthy times, the freedoms that have made America the envy of the world are being systematically eroded.*"

That Kurt Vonnegut, and John le Carre should pause from whatever they do all day to warn of what's being put over on us in the name of Homeland Security and Traditional Values can only be encouraging. Since September 2001, over on our left side of the barbed wire, we have been afraid of debate. Apologetic Susan Sarandon voices of reason have been raised only to be screamed down by Ann Coulter, and the other shrieking harpies of the right, who howl "treason" when what they really mean is "loyal opposition," and would convene a lynch mob if one expressed what's truly in one's heart—that the only traditional values the Bush junta embrace are those of a gang of drunken Chetniks on a looting rampage. One only has to watch *Crossfire*, to see that even the value of debate itself has become highly questionable. The ground shifts and the arguments do indeed have the irrational mutability of madness or a nervous breakdown.

All eyes are on the polls and the approval points, and any story will do in a pinch. As the defence budget continues to rise from its already staggering $364.6 billion, the Religious Right might well promote the assault on Baghdad as a biblical Fall of Babylon, and the Crusade of Millennium, but then, far from putting any distance between themselves and their *700 Club* allies, the True Believers of Gekko will just wink and smile, and happily invoke God as they move in like Tony Soprano, making sure that their transcendently rapacious military industrial skim is being skimmed to the max. The real difference is that Tony, with his distorted mob morality of obedience and *omerta*, will admit, if only to his psychiatrist, "I'm a fat crook from New Jersey." The Bush gang consistently cloak themselves, shameless and uncaring, in a nebulously belligerent, red, white, and blue. It is on this lack of caring or shame that Vonnegut primarily focuses in his editorial. "They cannot care because they are nuts. They have a screw loose! And what syndrome better (than psychopathic personalities) describes so many executives at Enron and WorldCom and on and on, who have enriched themselves while ruining their employees and investors and country, and who still feel as pure as the driven snow, no matter what anybody may say to or about them?"

An understandable core of feeling could be present among those of us out in left-field that maybe we ourselves might be partially to blame for allowing these psychopaths anywhere near the reins of government. Our generation has had its rock'n'roll president, who, in hindsight, presided over a period of comparative peace and prosperity only to have it all brought to naught in the obliging but too-talkative mouth of Monica Lewinski, and Bill's opening for the Stones at a benefit in LA. The guilt that we may have blown our chance, so to speak, might be one of the reasons, that, while we have finally started to protest Bush's War, we are still not prepared to think the unthinkable; the unspeakable fear that, having fixed the last election, the implacable triumvirate of Cheney, Ashcroft, and Rumsfeld might be fully capable of cancelling the next one. If GWB's handlers seriously thought their dyslexic boy was in danger of losing the next election, maybe, in pure panic and dread, to First Lady Clinton, how long would they hesitate before whipping up a state of emergency in which the constitution itself was suspended? It's only the classic course of dictatorship, and *habeas corpus* is selectively suspended already under the terms of the Patriot Act.

I have never before written a piece in which I have actually quoted Julius Caesar, but I am as worried as Vonnegut and le Carre, and Caesar's comments are too apt to go unmentioned, so treat this as something of a first in a new magazine. Julius Caesar was, after all, the noblest Roman of them all who brought about that crucial and perhaps fatal change from the rule of the Senate to the rule of the Emperor—before a conspiracy of Senators stabbed him to death in a last ditch attempt to preserve pre-Christian democracy. *"Beware the leader who bangs the drums of war in order to whip the citizenry into a patriotic fervor, for patriotism is indeed a double-edged sword. It both emboldens the blood, just as it narrows the mind. And when the drums of war have reached a fever pitch and the blood boils with hate and the mind has closed, the leader will have no need in seizing the rights of the citizenry. Rather, the citizenry, infused with fear and blinded by patriotism, will offer up all of their rights unto the leader and gladly so. How do I know? For this is what I have done. And I am Caesar."*

Metro, 2003

CONSERVATIVE DREAMIN'

☐ In 2001, a PhD called Kelly Bulkeley conducted a study on the dream lives of opposing political groups and found that Republicans reported three times as many nightmares as Demo-

I'VE BEEN ENTERTAINING THE IDEA THAT I'M DEALING with an Elmer Gantry, a cynical and successful media opportunist making her way through the book and TV circus, and doing very well by going to extremes. But, at one point, she becomes very animated, as if she really believes *she* is the victim, threatened by a ruthless liberal elite.

"My enemies are accusing me of saying dissent is trea-

MICK FARREN

son," she bristles. "Of course I'm not saying that, but in point of fact, you know, there were massive antiwar protests, across the country. The only dissent that anyone is trying to squelch here is my dissent from the proposition that liberals love their country. You can't say that. How dare you? Everyone is trying to intimidate me, and they've used the myth of McCarthyism, McCarthyism! McCarthyism... to prevent anyone from asking this question. Do liberals love their country? That's off-limits. That's the one thing you can't ask.

"I'm the one people are trying to silence," she goes on. "Not the antiwar protesters. People burning the American flag, denouncing our war aims. Flying to Baghdad. They're invited on Fox News, even they see O'Reilly, Hannity, and they're all saying, you have a First Amendment right to dissent. Well, so does David Duke. We don't slap him on the back. I want to start arguing about this again. They need a little tough love right now. I'm the one people are trying to silence, not antiwar protesters. It's a taboo to question them. They're like children who need discipline. So, I'm applying the tough love."

I can only blink through a silence of my own. Ann Coulter is white, wealthy, and successful. She has her health, and she dines with people who at least advise those who rule the world. She has personally assisted in an attempt to bring down a president. If any woman is part of the elite, she is. And yet, when the hyperbole approaches outburst, I am almost convinced she truly thinks she's victimized.

And she has come to this victim conclusion while George W. Bush, to whom she demonstrates unwavering loyalty and who she places beyond criticism, has been riding high. As the guerrilla war drags on in Iraq, the deficits become unmanageable, and Bush may face being forced to ignominiously pull out or hand over control to the U.N., I don't like to speculate how Coulter and her kind will react. Fear tends to beget hate, and, at least for the moment, she has enough media access to communicate this hate to a public that is pretty damned confused already.

For conservatives, these have been the good times. If

crats. "The dreams of the people on the political right reveal them to be insecure, anxious, conflict-ridden, and emotionally repressed. When they are not terrified of imaginary threats they cling to the comforts of the status quo. They seek a kind of power through their political views that they lack within their deeper selves." Two years later, I interviewed Ann Coulter the strident ultra-right pundit who I believe I once called a "shrieking harpy." In the middle of a confrontational but totally civilized conversation, and quite without warning, she confirmed the Bulkeley research when she melted into a near-fugue claiming she was the victim.

we traitors have our way, it will all be downhill from here, and I'll guarantee that the likes of Ann Coulter will descend with neither grace nor equanimity.

A segment from *LA CityBeat*, September 2003

THE BLACK ARTS OF ELECTION

□ Down the years, while staring at the History Channel, I have idly, but quite fruitlessly, wondered what went on in the mind of (say) Adolf Hitler, or Mao Zedong, or Margaret Thatcher—or Gandhi and FDR, for that matter. How many nightmares did they have? These inner processes are, of course, totally unknowable and probably wholly alien. We can only judge our leaders by their actions. It can only be a game of proof and puddings. Here in the democracies we are wise to note the lengths to which our elected leaders will go to subvert the democratic process.

THE PHONE RINGS IN LOWER MIDDLE-CLASS WEST VIRginia during a commercial break in prime time TV. "*You may be concerned to know that, if elected president, John Kerry will ban the Holy Bible in America.*" Welcome to the spook show. The political process enters a realm in which rational thought is overtaken by impressions, and subconscious suggestion has its way with fear and cultural superstition. John Kerry orders a Philly cheese steak with Swiss, no onions, and his manhood is impugned. Real men go for Cheez Whiz and onions. It's a small thing, but part of a larger on-going operation that has including Carl Cameron's fabricated Fox News story about Kerry's "French manicure" after the first TV debate. Every effort has been made to brand Kerry the Vietnam vet as somehow effeminate, and play to a deep and ugly homophobia.

We'll never know if the phone banks motivating the Bible Belt with biblical crank yanking were authorized by Karl Rove's central command in the Bush campaign, or just local improvisation doing what was known back in Nixon's Watergate heyday as "rat-fucking." The Cheez Whiz story, and other attempts to feminize the challenger, could only have emanated from Rove's office, because the president himself confirmed his potency in a good-old-boy, Philly vernacular soundbite. Bush takes his cheese steaks "Whiz and with."

These are the stories that feed directly into the left's anxiety-attack vision of Karl Rove as the near-invincible Prince of GOP Darkness, directing the apocalypse from atop his Dark Tower, like Sauron the Manipulator. The strategic mastermind behind the battle to reelect George

W. Bush is credited with a control so complete that even language is bent to his will, as dictated to a wormtongued news media. Karl Rove, at twenty-one, dropped out of college and into politics, and became an early protégé of convicted Watergate player Don Segretti—the man who invented the term "rat fucking" in the first place. Rove has been linked to The Swift Boat Veterans for Truth, attacks on John McCain's mental health, and back in the Texas day, the whispering that Democratic Governor Ann Richards was a lesbian. Rove remains, for many, a prime suspect in the outing of CIA agent Valerie Plame, and even Republicans tend to reinforce his image as Bush's Dark Lord. "He dominates a campaign," fellow Republican strategist David Weeks told the *Washington Post*. "Nothing ever happens that he's not aware of."

"The Republicans have the best propaganda out there since Lenin, and they just make stuff up and they keep repeating it, and hope people are going to believe it."
—Howard Dean to Associated Press, September 11, 2004

Of course, manipulation of the dark side is nothing new in US politics. Lyndon Johnson's campaigning is the stuff of Texas legend. In 1948, Johnson ran for the Senate against fellow Democrat Coke Stevenson, and the story goes that Johnson told an aide, "Go out there and tell 'em Coke was caught having sex with a farm animal."

The aide seemingly protested. "But you know that's not true!"

"Of course it's not true!" snapped LBJ. "That's not the point. Tell it anyway, and make him deny it."

The tale may be one of little more than the shit-kicking nastiness of old style stump-ranting, but Johnson also approved the famous 1964 TV commercial in which the little girl picked flowers while the spectre of nuclear annihilation loomed. The impression was clear although not literally stated. GOP candidate Barry Goldwater, a hardliner of the Old Right, was too crazy to be in charge of the nation's arsenal of nuclear weapons. Goldwater lost to Johnson, and politics reached a new benchmark in its relationship with television. The seeds were sown for one of Karl Rove's prime directives. *"Remember that emotion is a window into the soul."* Where previous political advertising had simply sold the candidate, it now moved to the Madison Avenue state of the art, cultural connection or emotional response made the pitch. Politics was another product in the marketplace like breakfast cereal, automobiles, beer, and steak knives, and, after the technique had worked so well for Johnson, there could be no turning back. Political campaigns even had the advantage of the First Amendment. Commercial claims for their "product" were not subject to FCC truth-in-advertising regulations.

"You may recall the 2000 election brouhaha when an attack ad by the Republicans flashed the word RAT over the visage of Al Gore. It was so fast you had to slow the tape to see it, rousing accusations of subliminal advertising by Democrats (Bush was unfazed, saying his campaign was not using 'subliminable' advertising.)"—Keith Olbermann, MSNBC

Richard Nixon, running for four more years in the chaos of the Vietnam War, looked to black-bag operations and the intelligence community. Wire tap, burglary, forgery, character assassination, and even IRS audit were tricks of CREEP's electoral trade, but would eventually be Nixon's downfall, if only by the intervention of karma and the *Washington Post.* The overt racism of the 1988 Bush-Quayle, "Willie Horton" commercial played to straight racism. Ronald Reagan used his Hollywood skills to sell platitudes. Bill Clinton campaigned on MTV and aspired to a rock star charisma, but was tarnished by a rock star attitude to casual blow-jobs. All helped design the landscape of the modern election. No campaign strategist would ever openly admit having studied the real dark side of the political force, but a nodding acquaintance with classic George Orwell, Joseph Goebbels, or Stalin is evident in the brute psychology that is being applied to what can only be defined as the lizard brain of the electorate.

The lizard brain is what takes over when the rest of the mind is inundated, tired or distracted. It senses threat on sub-verbal levels and becomes poised for fight and flight.

As James Moore, the coauthor of the book and current TV documentary *Bush's Brain* puts it, "Rove knows that we are all too busy worrying about our jobs and retirement and health care or paying for our children's college education that we don't have time to pay attention to the details of issues. Few of us read the 3,000 word stories in the newspaper. We read the headlines. We watch the news with the sound turned down. We're too busy." Over the years, we have taught our upper brains to tune out much of the electronic babble—especially TV commercials—and too many of our opinions are formed by the sub-verbal, half-seen impressions that are replayed day after day, and repeated ad nauseam. In California we have had it comparatively easy, but, in Ohio, between March and late September 14, 273 political ads were aired on Toledo's four leading TV stations. How anyone in a swing state can still form a coherent opinion under such a weight of bombardment has to be open to question.

"*War plays to some fundamental urges. Lurking beneath the surface of every society, including ours, is the passionate yearning for a nationalist cause that exalts us, the kind that war alone is able to deliver. When war psychology takes hold, the public believes, temporarily, in a mythic reality in which our nation is purely good, our enemies are purely evil, and anyone who isn't our ally is our enemy. This state of mind works greatly to the benefit of those in power.*"—"War Is a Force That Gives Us Meaning," from an essay on the psychology of war by Chris Hedges, veteran war correspondent.

In a nation at war, all deals are off, and the potential for emotional manipulation goes into overdrive. John Kerry reports for duty at the Democratic National Convention, and rocker John Fogerty plays his Credence classic 'Fortunate Son' on the Vote For Change Concert Tour sending resonances through everyone old enough to remember. The Sinclair Broadcast Group follows up on the Swiftboat assault on Kerry's service record, ordering its stations to preempt regular programming to air the documentary *Stolen Honor: Wounds That Never Heal*, that chronicles Kerry's 1971 testimony before Congress and links him to a freshly re-demonized Jane Fonda. In the gray areas of implication and illusion, the 2004 presidential race has been fighting two wars at the same time. One in the bloody present and another in Vietnam, thirty-five years ago. And yet it is not a Vietnam War I recognize. Even movie-memories of *Apocalypse Now* and *Platoon* are erased, along with the recanting of Robert McNamara, as talking haircuts on my TV characterize the debacle as an heroic stand against the Red Menace, and not a disastrous intervention into a distant and misunderstood civil war.

Bush stayed home, but Kerry, who volunteered for combat, is labeled a traitor. The LBJ strategy of "let him deny it" has advanced to Orwellian "doublethink"—the totalitarian art by which two seemingly contradictory statements could support a conclusion, if only by shameless repetition. In recent weeks, George Bush has taken a shine to the phrase "he can run but he can't hide," and repeats it with relish. At first, it referred to Osama bin Laden, but when Osama became an un-apprehended embarrassment, it was applied to terrorists in general. Then, during Debate III, John Kerry was suddenly the fugitive. "He can run but he can't hide" became the favorite sound bite, and the carefully vetted crowds at the Bush rallies went wild. The thread defies all rationality, but, in the TV-zombie flicker, it subconsciously links John Kerry to bin Laden.

"The truth is useless. You have to understand this right now. You can't deposit the truth in a bank. You can't buy groceries with the truth. You can't pay rent with the truth. The truth is a useless commodity that will hang around your neck like an albatross."—Jeb Bush quoted on Buzzflash.com

Part of an *LA CityBeat* story, 2004

HELL MOVED CLOSER, AND EVERYTHING TURNED UGLY

THE BUSH MACHINE STANDS IN MENACING RESERVE like the fiscal equivalent of an SS Panzer division, with the capacity, I understand, to spend a million bucks a day on the SOB's reelection all the way clear to November. Shee-it, I know with that kind of money, I could probably fix anything. I even wonder about today's rumor that the real reason Dick Cheney is running all over the planet trying to convince the world that he has no plans to conquer it is only to thwart a palace coupe, that in which Bush would dump Cheney in favor of Rudy Giuliani as VP. It could so easily have been concocted in some evil White House sub-basement, and tossed like a bone of false hope to the opposition. Kinda like the python giving the mouse a fleeting but erroneous idea that it might not be swallowed and digested after all.

One of my problems, of course, is that Democrat primaries always take me back to 1968, when the Dems milled about like chickens in the rain, as cities burned and the SE Asia war raged, and Hubert Humphrey presented himself as the natural successor to LBJ, while all the time the dark prospect of Richard Nixon bore down on us. But, wondrous day, a white knight in the shining form of Bobby Kennedy suddenly made it seem as though democracy might actually work one more time. Then finally the shock, horror and a scream of "No! Not again!" as, in the moment of winning California, he was gunned down in the kitchen of the Ambassador Hotel by yet another implausible lone gunman (with a cleanup by the LAPD and a young-but-rising Daryl Gates) and the sun went out, Hell moved closer, and everything turned ugly.

Fragment from *Doc40*, 2004

❏ Or looking for the same thing from a different angle and with a more emotional attitude…

MEDIA CAN WORK FOR ANYONE

❏ Back in 1972, when no one in my neck of the ideological woods would so much as consider moderation, I had my first book published. **Watch Out Kids** gave me a chance to offer a summation of all the thoughts and ideas that I'd be generating and developing with my work at **IT** and being on the road with the Deviants. Even after a decidedly intense exposure to the realities of the world and the way it worked, some of that naïveté still remained. If only we could explain it with sufficient clarity, the squares would see the error of their ways. We could quite believe that those in power would propagate poison simply because it fitted their unimaginable agendas.

It is the system that forges a relationship between otherwise unrelated individuals. Media, however, are subject to a great amount of spatial distortion. Take the example of the Vietcong who is shot in the head regularly by a South Vietnamese colonel in TV documentary shows. He is a TV personality, an international symbol, millions of individuals are intimately familiar with the instant of his death. They know nothing else about him, no other information, no background. His death has been translated into a cipher. His death and Jayne Mansfield's tits both provide raw material for whoever creates for media.

The property of media to freeze the individual in an instant situation and then to relay this situation repeatedly is what modern propaganda is about. The essential situation may be fact. The inference placed on the situation by juxtaposition is quite possibly spurious. Example: John is black. John is a rapist. Blacks are rapists.

The artist is subject to this freezing situation every time he commits himself to creation. Every action is only the one between the action before and the action after. Transferring it to media is apt to give a single action overemphasis.

Make way for the essential paradox.

For the first time in human history the nature of social organization has been questioned in its very essence rather than in its structure. This is revolution in terms of basic principles rather than methods.

This is total revolution.

Man, as a work unit, has always been viewed as the principal factor in the production of his own needs. Thus all previous social change has been concerned with the distribution of material possessions (either equitable or otherwise).

Up the workers!

It is a technical fact that man need no longer be concerned to such an extent (that is, to the extent of eight hours a day plus) with the production of his own life support.

The robots are coming—make way for the robots. The

MICK FARREN

only barrier to the elimination of the essentially degrading toil that for the last Christ-knows-how-many centuries has been the necessity for the majority of the human race to survive, is one of a purely social nature. The current rulers of twentieth century civilization seem incapable of working out the methods for the basic social reconstruction that is necessary for a leisure orientated civilization.

It's about time we had a new civilization. The human race is technically capable of supporting itself at a high standard of living. The major cause of famine is organized human greed. I often feel that in a historical context we are witnessing the decay of a great civilization. We are in the position of Rome in 400 AD. It could be that us hippies are the barbarians within the gates. This would indicate that it is down to us to acquire as much information as we can to equip ourselves to survive the coming dark ages with some degree of culture and comfort. The lemmings have a great and groovy method of population control. The trouble is that it's a bit hard on the individual lemming.

Later for jumping in the sea.

Leary points out that the rulers of this planet have a basic working principle that ecstasy is dangerous. The principle manifests itself in censorship, drug laws, sexual repression.

Why??

Our current rulers have an overriding prejudice against the needs of the individual taking any kind of precedence over the needs of the mass.

But why??

The mass—society, the state, the people—does not fundamentally exist. These words are collectively nouns which save time when dealing with a large number of individuals. Obviously individuals of the same species have, to a great extent, common or similar needs. Thus these needs can be catered for at a mass level. This is the function of civilization. What this current civilization has become criminally blind to is the fact that each and every individual has unique needs and desires that are entirely his own. These needs cannot be catered for at a mass level, they can only be worked out in terms of the individual himself.

We are all perverts—we are all afraid.

Our rulers and their attendant bureaucratic machine find these unique individual needs a time wasting and inconvenient factor in their manipulation of the mass. They, by the very nature of their trip, cannot conceive that these individual needs have to be considered. They find, moreover, that a population that is maintained at a high level of frustration is easily manipulated. Thus the idea behind the current government of humanity is to eradicate any original or unusual desires in individuals by labeling the individualist abnormal and causing him to suffer social or legal victimization. In addition to this, the attempt to repress common needs for sensual or spiritual release by denying the means of release and offering either titillation or a planned substitute. These methods create a malleable population.

He who don't get laid is a sucker for patriotism: proverb.

Our leaders have one flaw in their characters. Although their system of repression works extremely well, they seem prone to personal greed and dishonesty to themselves whereby if they can detect a short term material gain in a situation which is potentially dangerous to their system, they will allow the situation to continue or even develop.

There is always someone who will sell guns to the Indians.

The system, it cannot even be tied down to individuals, that rules our planet is corrupting and polluting the land, sea and air. Animal life is being destroyed. Humanity is being misused and distorted until it is almost impossible for it to live with anything but a pretence of dignity. In the West a generation is being turned into criminals, in Asia, Africa, and South America the same generation is having its land, its home, its standard of living, in some cases its very life, destroyed by the global chess game that is an apparently essential part of the system.

For the most part, those of us who are aware of this situation can only make a feeble attempt to bring down the system. We can only use what media are available to give vent to our impotent anger. The juxtaposition of our efforts in media are nonetheless still controlled by the ruling system, and by its control of that positioning it is more than able to contain our efforts.

In every medium, from machine guns to color TV, the system out-numbers and outmaneuvers us. Art has become a luxury, and the attainment of any degree of perfection in my craft as an artist is blocked by constant impotent fury at the system. The *New York Times* will inform us about pop music, books will rest on a lot of hip coffee tables, and the system will continue. We will all compromise in order to survive and the system will still continue.

The feeling of community that was about to emerge three years ago has scattered and split. If that singleness of purpose can be recaptured and developed it might enable us to survive and hold tiny pieces of territory in which we could live according to our own ideals, and by living in this way we may remind the population that an alternative to the system actually exists.

They will try to crush any part of the alternative society that they cannot buy.

Frank Zappa got written up in the *Sunday Times* while John Sinclair rotted in jail—last Tuesday they showed us Attica prison victims' blood on TV—the Sunday supplements carry Lenin's biography but no contraceptive advertising—you get your picture in the paper but don't have enough money to buy a copy—last summer the musical *Hair* was a focal point for hippie beggars. Media can work for anyone but they mainly work for the system.

Watch Out Kids, 1972

WE THE PEOPLE

It was the end of *Donahue*. It had been one of those discreetly prurient, sexual confessionals that are such a tidy combination of Phil's Catholic upbringing, liberal sensibility, and watch on the ratings. The subject had been the ménage-a-trois and, from the stage, the audi-

❏ A decade and a half later, the refusal to see error of any kind was so shamelessly manifest that we knew the fix was in and the manipulation—like a dayglo, MTV version of Orwell's Ministry of Truth—was big-time, and could only grow. And, maybe as a byproduct, reality TV was being spawned.

ence, and over the phone lines, all manner of individuals had recounted every imaginable variation on the romantic triplex—imaginable, that is, within the parameters set by Standards and Practices for afternoon viewing. The usual audience members stood up and said their predictable pieces into the proffered radio mike. The fundamentalist wanted to know where God stood in all this, and the concerned conservative demanded to know how they could raise their children in such an awful situation. All this was fairly routine. There's a *Donahue* show of this sort at least once a week. The only untoward moment came just before the closing credits. Phil looked into the camera with professional impishness and grinned, "You'd be surprised who's in the audience," intimating that, included in their number, were people with even stranger stories than they had heard already. The audience reacted as though they'd been goosed. They looked around. The creatures were in among them but they had no way of telling who was who. Were they dangerous, were they diseased? I have seen the deviants and they are us.

It was around that point that it occurred to me how these shows, *Donahue*, *Oprah*, *Geraldo*, not to mention the ravening and soon to be syndicated *Morton Downey Jr.*, could, taken as a whole, be giving us a very strange image of ourselves. These mutated talk-shows, along with, I guess, *The People's Court*, are the only TV shows that present us, the general public, in any context other than hysterically striving to win the Buick Regal; or as bemused bystanders at the scene of a news story. ("He was such a nice guy, I can't believe that he shot twenty-nine people, right here in the Fatburger.")

On *Donahue*, *Oprah*, *Geraldo*, and *Mort*, the general public—or at least a selected slice of the general public—is the motivating force of the show. This could be interpreted as an act of TV populism and, indeed, these shows are frequently sold to us as exactly that. The unfortunate part is that these shows, dependent on their need to titillate, present a section of the population that is, for one reason or another, flying in the face of the norm. They come to the screen only passing as plain folks. They may look like the Joneses but, very quickly, they reveal their fixations, their abnormalities, and their dirty little secrets. The cumulative effect of all this is to subliminally convince the protracted viewer that everyone out there is a little weird. An image starts to grow of the suburban avenue on which, behind closed doors, every third house is a bed of exotica. You can check them off. This one's the home of the channeler, next door are the S&M swingers, and down the street there's the Satanists' split level. (Perhaps it's no accident that Phil Donahue and Oprah Winfrey almost offer stranger-than-fiction reinforcement to the hothouse plotlines of the soaps that they follow in the time schedule.) Far from populist, on close examination, this all starts to reveal a potential for mutual distrust that is little short of frightening. Are neighbors and coworkers really what they seem, or will they turn up on *Oprah* next Tuesday advocating man/sheep love?

Village Voice, June 1988

A GENTLEMAN RADICAL

FOR A LONG TIME I HAD A PHOTO CLIPPED FROM A MAGazine pinned to a bulletin board. It was probably taken somewhere around 1960. Three men smiled for the camera. On the left was Tennessee Williams, on the right Gore Vidal, and in the center John Kennedy. At the time, Kennedy was either running for president or had just been elected. The grouping said much about twentieth century iconography. All three came from the World War II generation, the one now rapidly passing. Lately these parents and grandparents—the ones whose lives were disrupted by old-style dictatorship—have been celebrated and idealized, but, having been raised by that generation, my memories of it are not as fond. I recall small-minded conformists who became bent out of shape by everything from Little Richard to the length of my hair.

❏ We tend to depend on the media for our vision of the world. What other choice do we really have? We can't go to the war zone and see for ourselves, and, beyond that, all is merely rumor, propaganda, or hearsay. For an intelligent, measured, and also extremely witty analysis of how power is wielded in this world, I can recommend nothing better than an afternoon spent in the company of Gore Vidal.

THE CORRIDORS OF POWER

The men in the old photograph were, however, something else again, definitely deserving of idealization, and all products of what Gore Vidal—the lone survivor of the three—called a golden age. "1945 through 1950 was the only time we have not been at war in my lifetime. Five years. That's all we had. In '50, we got the Korean War. After that, nothing but war. Between '45 and '50, we were ahead in music with the whole world. We were ahead in poetry. We were ahead in the *ballet*, something we've never been noted for before; ahead in the theatre, with Tennessee and Arthur Miller. There was, in five years, this great burst of culture, because we had been repressed—first by the Depression for some twenty years, and then by World War II."

Of the trio in the picture—and this is not in any way to denigrate him—Vidal is hardest to define. Kennedy was the consummate politician and, later, the assassinated boy king. Williams is counted among the great playwrights of the English language. But what exactly is Gore Vidal? Excellent company, perhaps, but something of a cultural Jack-of-all-trades. Now approaching his eighty-first birthday, he has spent a long and infinitely productive life shuttling among a variety of roles. He has written twenty-five novels under his own name, five more under pseudonyms, plus a collection of short stories. He has had seven plays produced, crafted movie and television scripts—including having a subversive hand in the screenplay of *Ben-Hur*—and his essays, articles, monographs, memoirs, and other works of nonfiction and political commentary are too numerous to count. He has acted on the stage and in a number of movies, including *Bob Roberts*, *Gattaca*, *With Honors*, and Fellini's *Roma*, and he appeared in the film version of Williams' *Suddenly Last Summer*, in addition to adapting it for the screen.

Vidal was also an early TV personality, quick to recognize the power of television as a tool of self-promotion, and he became a regular on the early talk-show circuit, trading quips with the likes of Johnny Carson, Merv Griffin, Mike Douglas, and Dick Cavett. His love affair with the small screen extended as far as *What's My Line, Laugh-In,* and *Playboy After Dark,* and, even today, he continues to bring his august presence to *Real Time with Bill Maher* and *The Daily Show with John Stewart.* He has even sat still for Sacha Baron Cohen's wigger-moron shtick on *Da Ali G Show.*

Gore Vidal's heavyweight exposure to the mass TV audience came in 1968, when he and right-wing pundit William F. Buckley Jr. were hired by ABC News to provide point-counterpoint political commentary on the Republican and Democratic national conventions in that troubled year. As the Chicago police gassed and clubbed war protesters on the streets, Buckley and Vidal came close to blows in the studio, with Vidal calling Buckley a "crypto Nazi" and Buckley responding by calling Vidal a "queer" and threatening to "sock him in the goddamn face." In a subsequent essay, published in *Esquire* in August 1969, Buckley attacked Vidal as an "apologist for homosexuality" and trashed Vidal's novel *Myra Breckenridge* as "pornography." A month later, Vidal countered with an essay of his own, in which he denounced Buckley as "anti-black," "anti-Semitic," and a "warmonger." A lawsuit ensued, which would be settled to neither's satisfaction, and then, amazingly, the whole matter resurfaced just three years ago, in 2003, when *Esquire* published its *Big Book of Great Writing* that included Vidal's original essay. Buckley launched another libel suit, which the magazine settled for a total of $65,000.

This furor and TV feud at the violent end of the 1960s set Gore Vidal on the path to what he has become today—the gay, patrician, highly erudite preserver of all that is worthwhile in traditional American dissent. Although he would probably dislike the characterization, Gore Vidal is an American institution whose voice is still crucial in these grim and oppressive times.

My own first brush with Vidal came during my early teens. A sleazy store at the bad end of my English hometown specialized in books and magazines remaindered in bulk from the USA, and, if you looked hard enough among the pulp fiction, the go-go girlie mags, and the *Archie* comics, you might come up with a Beat Generation gem, like a Digit paperback of Burroughs' *Junkie*, or an Olympia Press edition of De Sade's *Justine*. I discovered Vidal's novel *The City and the Pillar* racked with a mess of print-porn paperbacks with titles like *Party Girl*, *Pagan Urge*, and *Caged Lust*. I had no idea, as I walked away from the store with a *Black Hawk* comic, *Famous Monsters of Filmland*, a copy of *Swank*, and *The City and the Pillar* in a plain brown bag, that this was a notorious gay novel. Indeed, I had no real idea there were such things as notorious gay novels—and no clue that the book's publication had cause such fury in American literary circles that the *New York Times* refused to review Vidal's next five novels. The book, however, did much to offset the institutionalized homophobia that was standard issue to the British schoolboy of the time. I also found myself totally convinced by what seemed to be Vidal's underlying theme—that one should not dwell upon the past, because the future was what counted.

From then on I consumed Vidal wherever I found him, from the inevitable *Myra Breckenridge* and the allegorical *Two Sisters*, through the heavyweight historical novels like *Burr* and *Lincoln*, to the satirical science fiction of *Duluth*, and, of course, the constant and invaluable political commentary. No part of this, though, has prepared me for the eventuality that I would find myself, in the summer heat of 2006, driving up to his house in the hills—his permanent home since he gave up his cliffside villa in Ravello, Italy—and ringing the doorbell of the Hollywood faux-Spanish house that might have been that of a well-heeled client in a Raymond Chandler novel. The English schoolboy is completing one unexpected circle.

This afternoon meeting with Gore Vidal is on the second or third day after the outbreak of hostilities between Israel and Hezbollah. The news has just broken that the US government is expecting its citizens to pay for their evacuation from Lebanon, and Vidal, despite seeming tired and frail, and also walking with difficulty—"I have a titanium hip"—is furious. He makes no attempt to contain his towering contempt for George W. Bush, his principles, and his henchmen.

"We need a real American president, not this bad joke," Vidal says. "I think he did himself in with the 25,000 Americans trying to get out of Lebanon. The Norwegians got their people out. The Swedes got their people. The French got them out. Everybody, every other nationality is out, with less logistical problems than ours, and it's Katrina number two. Not only does he pay no attention to anything; he doesn't give a damn. It is clear to me by his activities, first in the Katrina affair, and now in his total indifference to 25,000 Americans marooned in Lebanon, he does not like the American people—he really *dislikes* them. You can just see him when he gets out there. He is so uncomfortable. He will not go to a funeral of any of the soldiers that he's sent off to be killed. He has no response other than loathing. They're in his way. Things he wants to do, he can't do. Like cut brush, or whatever it is he does in that little place of his."

Regrettably, current events and anger at Bush overshadow our entire encounter. In theory, sitting with Gore Vidal should offer the possibility of a hundred stories and anecdotes of the famous and notorious with whom he's rubbed shoulders, but to depart from the crisis of world politics is wholly impossible. That's the way of things in this wretched summer.

"Little Bush says we are at war, but we are not at war, because, to be at war, Congress has to vote for it," he fumes. "He says we are at war on terror, but that is a metaphor, though I doubt if he knows what that means. It's like having a war on dandruff—it's endless and pointless."

Vidal pulls no punches. "We are in a dictatorship that has been totally militarized. Everyone is spied on by the government itself. All three arms of government are in the hands of this junta. Plus we have a media more vicious, stupid, and corrupt than at any previous time." He lapses into a parody of Bush's phony Texas drawl: "I'm a wartime president, wartime president, wartime president. Why doesn't somebody say, 'There is no war'?"

But, in fact, someone has just said there is no war—no less than Alberto Gonzales, Bush's own attorney general. While the media were focused on the explosions in Haifa and Beirut, Gonzales faced the Senate Judiciary Committee over the legality of the National Security Agency wiretaps, and, under pressure from California Senator Dianne Feinstein, haltingly admitted that the country was not, in legal terms, at war. Most of the world had not been watching, but Vidal had missed nothing.

"There's no war. Gonzales—who proved to be even dumber than one suspected—said that to Feinstein... did you see that? It was on C-SPAN," he says. "Gonzales was before the Judiciary Committee, and she said something about FISA [Foreign Intelligence Surveillance Act], that court which Bush refuses to use to get permission for warrants on everybody, and Gonzales really—usually he's very good at being slithery—put his foot right in his mouth when he said, 'Well, of course, that was designed for wartime, and this is not wartime.' No, there is no war. There are no wartime powers. Bush pretends that he has certain inherent powers as Commander in Chief which allow him to do anything he wants to do... torture, wiretap, imprison without trial."

Vidal becomes passionately emphatic. "There are no *inherent powers*. There are *enumerated* powers in the Constitution, and each one is *written out very clearly*. A child of five could explain to Bush about his enumerated powers. But I don't think they can find a child of five who wants to expose himself to the tedium of explaining the Constitution to the president."

The degree to which Vidal detests Bush might seem obsessive in someone less sophisticated, but he uses the weapons of wit, charm, and intelligence to remain and sound entirely rational. A part of his contempt may also be rooted in his own experience. He fought in a war, freezing in the Aleutians during World War II, and he has lost someone close to him in war. The dedication in *The City and the Pillar* is to "J.T."—Vidal has revealed that these are the initials of Jimmie Trimble, his lover at St. Albans prep school, who had died in the Battle of Iwo Jima in 1945. In his memoir *Palimpsest*, Vidal wrote of Trimble's death: "Forever after, I was to be the surviving half of what had once been a whole." He knows the truth about war, and has no tolerance for those who don't, yet are prepared use it as a tool of power.

"[Bush and his cronies] are all sissies. Remember that," he says. "These are people who've never been in an army. The men behind the war in Iraq are cowards who did not fight in Vietnam. They've run away like the president, who I refer to as the Yellow Rose of Texas. They're weak little people with an agenda—which is: 'We've gotta show our muscle around the world. Running out of oil? We'll take it. Show how tough we are. We're macho.' And we're also *dumbo*, and that is the problem."

The rarest pleasure of talking to Gore Vidal is to witness his acute sense of history. While most historians slice the past into bite-sized decades or easy political eras—the Clinton period, the Reagan era, the Nixon years—he sees the past as a continuous process that leads inexorably to the present, and on to the future. It is no surprise to him that American service people should be killing and dying for Big Oil in Iraq. It's merely one more inevitable incident in the long thread of US corporate imperialism.

"We behaved badly always—Central America in particular, but Latin America too," he says. "We'd taken them for granted. United Fruit was ripping them off, paying no tax, and they couldn't run their governments because Chase Manhattan was collecting all the money to service old debts. The great Smedley Butler, Commanding General of the Marine Corps in the early twentieth century, he always said, 'I was an enforcer. As head of the Marines, I was an enforcer for Chase Manhattan. I was an enforcer for Standard Oil.' He said, 'Al Capone had only five city districts in Chicago; I had five continents.'"

Vidal fluidly cites historical examples—from the Founding Fathers to the Civil War to the New Deal and FDR (a man he seems to simultaneously revere and dislike)—as they relate to the modern world. When I ruminate that Bush—or, more likely, Rumsfeld—might actually use a nuclear weapon just to prove that he could, Vidal has the historic reference at his fingertips. "Harry Truman did. Truman received a unanimous 'no' from all the commanding officers of World War II—from Eisenhower in Europe to Nimitz in the Pacific. Every one of them, including the mad Curtis Le May, said, 'Don't do it. Japan is already asking for a peace treaty. They surrender.' But Truman wanted to scare Stalin, so he dropped not one but two bombs. And really let the world in for hell. And we're objecting to Iran getting a little nuclear bomb? It would be nice if they didn't have it, yes. It would be nice if we didn't have it, too."

He makes it clear that his innate respect for history has been the driving force behind some of his best known fiction. "In fact, it is to correct bad history that I have spent thirty years writing *Burr* and *Lincoln*, *1876*, and all those books. You can be more truthful in fiction. Professional historians, by and large, have their prejudices, which condition everything they write because they must always be looking for tenure. Once they have tenure, they must maintain it. They must not rock the boat. They must not take political stands. That's why we have no intellectual class."

The common mistake is to assume that Gore Vidal is a true-blue Democrat. But, at best, his affiliations with the party are by default. He has run twice for office on a Democratic ticket. The first time was in 1960, when he ran for a congressional seat in upstate New York. The second was when he entered California's 1982 Democratic primary for the Senate, and finished second in a field of nine, polling a half-million votes but losing to former California Governor Jerry Brown. When I ask him why he never attempted such a thing again, Vidal wryly shakes his head. "The moment of truth for me came from Alan Cranston—quite a good senator. And he said, 'You realize what you're doing if you get elected? Let me tell you. If you get elected for a first term—six years—every week you have to raise $10,000 if you want to run again.' That's six years, every week—fifty-two weeks a year, six times fifty-two—you do the math. And this was in 1982. Ten thousand dollars a week for six years. I said, 'How do you get time to do anything?' Cranston replied, 'Oh, you don't. You call people for money.' This didn't sound healthy to me, so I never even thought about it again."

"There is only one party in the United States, the Property Party… and it has two right wings, Republican and Democrat," he says. "Republicans are a bit stupider, more rigid, more doctrinaire in their laissez-faire capitalism than the Democrats, who are cuter, prettier, a bit more corrupt—until recently—and more willing than the Republicans to make small adjustments when the poor, the black, the anti-imperialists got out of hand. But, essentially, there is no difference between the two parties."

Vidal sees Bush and his neocons only being halted in their tracks when the nation runs out of money. "We'll just default," he says. "There's really no way out. I think the financial collapse—which seems to me to be on its way—will at least stop the wars. We cannot go into the military adventures. Cost too much. We haven't got the men to fight the wars. Don't think we'll find them. I don't think we can hire that many Albanians, you know, to pretend they're American soldiers, but it will get to something like that."

As I review all that's been said, and all that I've read, I start to believe that maybe the only word to define Vidal is *radical*. With his charm, his elegance, his wit, and his art collection, he hardly conforms to the popular image of the radical. He's no wild-haired Abbie Hoffman or rumpled and academic Howard Zinn. Gore Vidal is something currently unique, a gentleman radical. As someone in Vidal's entry on *Wikipedia* puts it, he "is a radical reformer" with "a disdain for privilege and power" who wants to return to the "pure republicanism of early America"—a secular, egalitarian democracy with an elegant and comprehensively crafted Constitution, and leaders honestly elected by, for, and of the people. He is a radical striving for the revolutionary concept of a civilized America, and who, incidentally, once wrote "in a civilized society, law should not function at all in the area of sex, except to protect people from being interfered with against their will." And also once remarked in an online interview, "As you may by now suspect, I don't think we [the US] are civilized."

Vidal's new book, *Point to Point Navigation*, will be published in November. It is, essentially, a companion volume to his *Palimpsest*. When I carelessly refer to *Navigation* as an autobiography, Vidal sternly corrects me: "A *memoir*."

Gore Vidal is always precise. And—goddamn it—do we have serious need of his precision in this slovenly era of trash and duplicity.

LA CityBeat, August 2006

POWER AS ILLUSION

And duplicity in government is most often used to instill either fear or blind ignorance, and to disguise what those in power are really up to. And what they are all too often up to is interfering in the private business of their own citizens.

THE STORY MAY BE APOCRYPHAL, SINCE MOST HARD EVIdence was subsequently destroyed, but, if there's any truth in it all, the tale speaks volumes about the nature of large scale surveillance within a police state, and mass manipulation by the fear that one is being constantly watched by those in authority. During the violent chaos of 1989 that surrounded the fall of Communism in Romania, and culminated in the executions of dictator Nicolae Ceausescu and his wife Elena, a large crowd occupied the Communist Central Committee building in Bucharest. While the majority of the mob seized Ceausescu's writings, official portraits, and either burned them or hurled then out of windows, one group broke into an office supposedly used by the Securitate to tap private phones in the city.

The Securitate were one of the most feared secret police organizations of the Cold War era, considered quite as brutally efficient as the Soviet KGB, or the East German Stasi, and yet an engineer who supposedly looked over the equipment before it was ripped out and smashed, estimated that Securitate operators were unable to tap any more than two dozen phones at one time. For decades, all Romanians—or at least all Romanians who could afford phones—had assumed that, at any time, their lines would be tapped and acted accordingly. As it turned out, it was paranoia rather than realty that struck fear into the population and kept them on the Ceausescu straight and narrow.

POWER AS TECHNOLOGY

MENWITH HILL IS THE ECHELON NERVE CENTER where, as members of the public chat on the phone, surf the Internet, or engage in routine online transactions, they unknowingly leave behind trails of personal details that are automatically captured and retained in computer logs. Intelligence analysts at each of the respective "listening stations" keep separate keyword lists to help them analyze conversations or documents flagged by the system, which are then forwarded to the intelligence agency that requested the intercept. The interception and interpretation of signals by the Department of Justice, the FBI and the Drug Enforcement Administration intrudes into all forms of communication including broadband Internet access and Voice Over IP. Although the number of intercepts currently being made by Echelon is highly classified, some idea can be gleaned from the fact that as early as 1992, in the wake of the first Gulf War, the system was intercepting two million messages per hour, of which all but around 13,000 were discarded before being refined down to the 2,000 that satisfied forwarding of investigative criteria. These were whittled down further to a mere twenty messages that were read and examined by analysts. Fifteen years ago, Menwith Hill station was intercepting seventeen-and-a-half billion messages a year, and thus any projection today that takes into account the massive growth of all types of communication through the 1990s and up to today, makes the data flow through Menwith Hill close to unimaginable.

The astronomical volume of intercepts does, though, lay to rest any idea that shadowy NSA operatives are actually listening to the world's telephone calls and reading every piece of email. What Echelon primarily deals with is flow patterns and clusters of chatter. Pattern recognition software might, for instance, detect an unusual high volume of calls between (say) Cairo and Frankfurt, Germany, which might be flagged for further investigation, and sorted according to selected criteria in a radiation-hardened underground facility called Steeplebush 11. Word or phrase recognition software (the Echelon dictionary) would then come into play to decide if samples need actually be replayed in realtime by human operatives. This is not to say that specific individuals are not subject to Echelon scrutiny.

POWER, A HISTORY LESSON

IN REALITY THE CREATION OF SYSTEMS WHEREBY CITIzens were manipulated by those in power to spy and report on other citizens is as old as civilization itself. While the masses were illiterate and no methods of mass communications existed, this internecine surveillance was largely limited to those with power in the society—the aristocracy, the educated elite, plus, of course, their slaves, servants, and concubines, because only they had the ability to threaten the status quo. In Imperial Rome or feudal Japan, the mob might need to be placated with bread and circuses, or crushed by military force, but they hardly need to be constantly watched. This state of affairs really only began to change when societies became more mobile, and the first printing presses facilitated the rapid spread of ideas.

As with so much of our history, this change really began with the Crusades, and took hold during the Renaissance and the Reformation. The clash of cultures in the twelfth and thirteenth centuries, when Christianity first squared off against Islam, put a huge menu of new and radical ideas into motion. Europe was opened up to new directions in mathematics, astronomy, dress, architecture and cuisine. Even religion was openly questioned, and the inevitable schism between Catholics and Protestants would ultimately result in open warfare, as whole cities were put to the fire and their populations slaughtered in the name of the true faith. The famous order *"Neca eos omnes. Deus suos agnoset"*—that became loosely translated as "kill them all and let God sort it out"—was issued by Amalric Arnaud, the Abbot of Citeaux to Simon de Monfort while purging the town of Beziers in Southern France of heretics at the behest of Pope Innocent III. After some 20,000 townsfolk had been either burned or clubbed to death in order to eradicate an estimated 200 heretics, the Papacy was finally forced to recognize that there had to be a more subtle way of enforcing religious conformity. Out of this recognition was born what became known as the Inquisition, and in the religious sector, spies and informers found themselves working in a growth industry, the main product of which was mass fear. The Catholic Inquisition and its Protestant equivalents basically invented the concept of what, hundreds of years later, George Orwell would call "thought crime."

Three excerpts from the book *Who's Watching You?*, 2007

WHO'S WATCHING WHAT YOU'RE WATCHING?

PORNOGRAPHY HAS BEEN ATTACKED BY EVERYONE FROM feminists to fundamentalists to Al Qaeda, accused of debasing the moral standards of the culture, and giving free reign to man's most base and animal instincts. When the computer and the Internet came into the picture, the accusations grew in both number and volume. Far from being relieved that pornography was now being consumed behind closed doors in online transactions that involved no one except the vendor and subscriber, the furor only increased. With porn now online, the dubious old time sleaze-flick movie theaters, and hole-in-the-corner adult bookstores became out-of-date anachronisms, but that still didn't satisfy the moralists, evangelists, and decency crusaders.

❑ Mass surveillance is usually assumed to be the work of government or law enforcement acting on the government's behalf. Unfortunately it has started to emerge over the last decade that private enterprise has also moved in on the act. Some measure of the extent of commercial spying was revealed—somewhat surprisingly—by the porn industry.

A whole new wave of complaints was levelled at the adult online industry, some true, some possible, and some implausible nonsense. Unwanted and unexpected porn spam was being randomly sent to kids and little old ladies. Porn websites were committing all manner of credit card irregularities, and planting spyware, adware, and Trojan horse viruses in our PCs. Teenagers were being deliberately targeted so, by the time they were adults, they would be helpless smut addicts. About the only accusation not levelled against porn was that it was anything but either a solitary vice, or the mutual recreation of consenting couples. In theory, porn should be a private matter, but in a world where anything and everything we do on our computers can be logged and stored on some massive database, against which we have absolutely no recourse, privacy has become history. As we open the lid of the laptop, an inanimate presence watches and records.

And, for once, this ceaseless surveillance is neither the work of law enforcement nor some extra-legal government agency, but a vast and immensely profitable segment of the private sector, dealing in what has become politely known as data brokerage, but is really nothing more than cash-driven spying. Pop paranoia has always focused on the Federal Government as the keeper of unwarranted records on citizens who have committed no actual crimes. The FBI, the CIA, and, more recently, the NSA, have always been feared for their potential for becoming an "American Gestapo," turning the nation from a democracy to a totalitarian "Big Brother" state. Here in the twenty-first century, corporate entities—but motivated by income rather than power—are quietly fulfilling some of our most basic societal fears, and run virtually unregulated.

The largest and most perfect example of a data mining operation is the company known as ChoicePoint. Based in Georgia, ChoicePoint buys information from anyone willing to supply it, and then resells to anyone willing to pay. Its clients include insurance companies, government agencies, corporate marketing departments, advertising agencies, and even private investigators. The *Wall Street*

Journal recently reported that ChoicePoint provides personal information to thirty-five or more government agencies, and also has several multimillion dollar contracts to sell personal data to law enforcement groups.

In the last ten years, since 1997, ChoicePoint has steadily accumulated a huge share of commercial data brokerage by acquiring thirty-eight other businesses, and is now one of the biggest players in the game. These acquisitions include major data retention organizations such as Pinkertons Inc., National Data Retrieval Inc., CITI Network, Bode Technology, Accident Report Services and many more, and their takeover has given ChoicePoint a combined database so comprehensive and detailed that it may outstrip any information system amassed by a national government.

ChoicePoint and operations like it also conduct their business with the same obsessive secrecy as any part of the Federal intelligence community, but a small tip of this large and sinister iceberg was revealed early this year when AOL, the nation's largest Internet service provider, and a division of Time Warner, admitted they had given away private search engine data on some 658,000 "anonymised" users. Privacy defenders became apoplectic. One news report ran "AOL has released very private data about its users without their permission. While the AOL username has been changed to a random ID number, simple analysis can easily determine who the user is, and what they are up to." As anyone who maintains so much as a blog tracker is well aware, search engine requests can be self-revealing in the extreme, ranging from "Mexico City UFO sightings" to "teen girls in handcuffs."

The AOL revelations were rendered even more shocking, coming as they did on top of a less widely publicized admission by ChoicePoint that, in February 2005, the company had "accidentally" sold personal information on at least 145,000 Americans to a criminal ring engaged in identity theft. This was a little too much for even the shadow world of data brokers, and ChoicePoint was forced to issue a statement defending its business practices.

Unfortunately the company's press release proved to be a classic example of twenty-first century corporate double-speak. ChoicePoint *"reserved the right to sell sensitive information to support consumer-driven transactions where the data is needed to complete or maintain relationships... to provide authentication or fraud prevention tools to large, accredited corporate customers where consumers have existing relationships... and to assist Federal, state and local government and criminal justice agencies in their important missions."* But what exactly were *"consumer-driven transactions"* and when is data *"needed to complete or maintain relationships"?* Even *"relationships"* were not defined. To many reporters, the wording sounded close to the euphemisms of old school Cold War intelligence jargon in which "plausible deniability" and "extreme prejudice" were used as substitutes for the plain English of words like "deception" and "assassination."

When a business can issue statements that baffle the media, the general public has little chance of understanding what's being done to them. The great misconception is that computer surveillance is conducted in real time, or at least any action is studied and analyzed shortly after it's made. This is far from being the case. A consumer who logs on to the "wrong" porn site is not going to suddenly find an FBI morality squad at his door. Most of data stored on private individuals is never seen by a human being until requested by a customer, usually when one applies for a loan, opens a bank account, becomes involved in divorce proceedings, or some other lawsuit, or runs for public office. Only then does it become revealed (for instance) that a pillar of the community has a private taste for downloading girl-on-girl lesbo porn.

Reality, however, does not stop ChoicePoint from using fear in its advertising, and—as happens so frequently—citing child protection to defend their actions. The company claims, for instance, that it protects against predatory paedophiles, and that many missing children have been found through its database. But at a hearing before the California Senate Banking Committee, in March 2005, ChoicePoint was asked for the numbers of these lost children it had rescued, but no answer was forthcoming.

Worse still, it would appear that much of the data obtained by data mining is also far from accurate. According to a report by the watchdog group World Privacy Forum, ChoicePoint's reports have a "high error rate." In WPF's sample, ninety percent of the reports contained errors, many serious and others plain ridiculous, including one individual being assigned the wrong sex. Behind the high-minded smokescreen, ChoicePoint, LexisNexis, Acxiom, and those like them, gather all the information they can on all of us, good, bad, or ugly. They have little interest in its accuracy and sell it to anyone who will pay the price, like a cash-driven secret police force, currently unchecked by regulation or legislation.

Sadly computer surveillance doesn't end with huge, all devouring, corporations. To find true "Big Brother," real-time spying, one need look no further than the home and the workplace. Surveillance at work has become close to a way of life, with more and more employers checking that their workers are not sending private emails, instant messaging friends, downloading streaming hentai, or playing online blackjack on company time. Low cost monitoring technology and a recklessly amoral business climate encourages firms to watchdog their workers in the name of supposed "efficiency." Unfortunately, according to a Privacy Foundation study, the simplest way for an employer to watch the hired help is to watch all of them. Monitoring just those employees who exhibit suspicious behavior is expensive, so most employers opt for the cruder but more cost effective "continuous, systematic surveillance," and everyone receives the Big Brother treatment.

Computer-monitoring programs with impressive names like Shadow, SpyAgent, Web Sleuth, and Silent Watch—that vary in price from a few hundred to a few thousand dollars—form the base of an emerging multi-million dollar, "employee Internet management" industry. For two grand, the Spector company offers their 360 model that *"records websites visited, emails sent and received, chats and instant messages, keystrokes typed, files transferred, documents printed and applications run. In addition, through a first of its kind surveillance-like camera recording tool, Spector 360 shows you in exact visual detail what an employee does every step of the way."*

For the real police state in miniature, though, the home is the place, especially homes that have succumbed to the pitches for the domestic versions of Spector or Web Sleuth. Yet again children are the core of the sales pitch. What are little Johnny and Jane doing all alone in their rooms with their laptops and webcams? Are they being victimized by sexual predators, or planning to blow up their high school in some goth/guerrilla chat room? The first line of defense offered is the keylogger, simple software and a plug-in that monitors each keystroke made on a computer's keyboard. All typed text, URLs or commands are recorded, keystroke-by-keystroke, and saved in the logger's miniature hard drive. At some later time, the keylogger can be removed, and the parent can access every action that has been performed on the computer.

Or, at least, that's the theory, but when the *New York Times* reports teen and even preteen boys organizing their own webcam peepshow porn sites, and being paid via gift vouchers for Amazon.com, and other online shopping malls, one can only wonder just how much of a clue many Internet-age parents really have about what their children are up to.

The hugely popular MySpace has recently come under intense media scrutiny as a kind of cyber jungle, rife with sexual predators and unregulated weirdness. A website calling itself wiredsafety.com is replete with horror stories of the insidious spread of MySpace.

"Mom accidentally came upon her eighteen-year-old son's MySpace page. His 'Friends' section had girls pictures everywhere. They were provocative pictures, with provocative write-ups. Mom later found out that her son had introduced MySpace to his eleven-year-old sister. She had her own page and own friends. Although her page appeared hugely innocent in comparison to his, she would get daily messages that discussed penis sizes, breast augmentation, etc."

What we are really seeing is, of course, adults interfacing with children and teenagers online and being shocked at the degree of their kids' sophistication. Much sentimental rhetoric is spouted—usually by individuals and groups who want to ban, censor, or control something—about the innocence of children, but little is said about appalling and apathetic naïveté of parents. Owned by Rupert Murdoch's News Corp, MySpace describes itself as "*a social networking website, offering an interactive, user-submitted network of friends, personal profiles, blogs, groups, photos, music, and videos.*" What we're not told is that MySpace is causing more problems than just the unwelcome parental revelations. MySpace leaks data like a rusty bucket. Its web pages, containing multiple profiles, pictures and other intimate details, that can be effortlessly lifted for anything from nuisance pranks to identity theft. Employers have been using MySpace as a free background check, and young college graduates ruefully complain that they have been turned down for jobs because they had unthinkingly posted accounts of keg-parties, and sexual conquests. (Gee, we never thought anyone in the real world would actually see that stuff.)

The psychology of the way both adults and children feel the need to gather in online cyber communities to bare their souls (and also their bodies and innermost secrets) on sites like MySpace and Facebook is well beyond the scope of this story, but it has a spawned a growth industry in specific monitoring software. Families can happily spy on each other and create their very own Big Brother environment. Parents load software to spy on the kids, while the kids install counter programs. Electronic suspicion rules, and, of course, the same software is also being put to use by suspicious spouses and jealous lovers to spy on supposedly cheating husbands, wives, girlfriends and boyfriends, establishing a generally unhealthy atmosphere of unwarranted cyber snooping and domestic paranoia, and, in some anecdotal cases, nothing short of domestic violence, misery, and divorce.

So can anything be done to curb an area of computer

technology that makes the online porn business resemble a paragon of virtue? The answer is, regretfully, not much. A new regime in Washington after 2008 might do something to strengthen and enforce existing privacy laws, and even institute new ones, but there is so much money in snooping, spying, and data mining, that it will be hard. Also, legislation is wholly incapable of keeping up with technology. As always, I pin my hopes on human ingenuity and deviousness. We will learn to outfox the snoops and data pirates. They can ferret out what they think is essential while we cunningly figure ways to effectively conceal what we don't want them to know.

AVN Online, 2007

THE BEST POLICE FORCE THAT MONEY CAN BUY

❑ The human macro-system on this planet may be controlled by multinational corporations, national governments, and the military industrial complexes and intelligence communities who dance attendance on them, but down on the more mundane ground, on the streets where most of us live, it's the cops who wield the power—in some cities the power of life and death. (And if you don't believe that, explain the syndrome of "suicide by police officer.")

I DON'T KNOW ABOUT YOU, BUT I'M CLOSE TO BURNED out on the antics of the Los Angeles Police Department. As atrocities go, the mini-riot after the UCLA basketball team won the NCAA tournament a few weeks ago amounted to very little in the grand scheme of things. Nothing more, in fact, than just another dreary indication that the LAPD is apparently incapable of learning from its mistakes or in any way connecting with the fact that, although its members may be the principal guardians of law and order, they do not actually own the streets, and that we, as citizens, might have a few residual rights to go about our lawful business, or even our lawful fun, without being at risk from indiscriminate beatings or random arrest.

OK, so the kids in Westwood became a tad rowdy. Perhaps some store owners feared for their window glass, and a KIIS-FM van certainly did get trashed. On the other hand, similar scenes occur in most cities around the globe following a major victory by a local sports team. The police in Munich, Osaka, or Sydney don't immediately blitz the neighborhood with tear gas, rubber bullets, and a Kevlar-

MICK FARREN

clad riot squad. Even in Britain, where violent soccer hooliganism has been a clear and present problem since the late sixties, the police manage to handle victory celebrations with a great deal more tact and diplomacy.

As every Beatles fan knows, the city of Liverpool is anything but a sleepy backwater. Unemployment and public drunkenness are high, and the Liverpool constabulary extends no kid-glove treatment to any potential breakdown in public order. Liverpool does, however, have one of the greatest soccer teams in the world, and its coppers are highly experienced in sport-related crowd control. One has only to watch the TV news coverage when the Liverpool team brings home the Football Association Cup to realize that the key to the successful management of such a hard-drinking, spontaneous street event is that the police are seen to be participants in the celebration. Individual officers pose for photographs, smiling and allowing themselves to be hugged and kissed by intoxicated female fans. The message is clear: The Liverpool cop is also a citizen and is as proud as the next guy that his team is number one.

Beneath the public relations exercise, a watchful presence is maintained. Pairs of mounted officers play a major role, using their better visibility and the psychological effect of their horses to spot knots of potential troublemakers and cut them off from the crowd, quite literally like cowboys cutting steers from the herd. At no time do they resort to the kind of paramilitary, street-clearing skirmish line employed by the LAPD in Westwood.

Over the last few years, we have watched Los Angeles' finest violently brutalize striking janitors in Century City, fire tear gas and rubber bullets into the crowd at last year's downtown Cinco de Mayo celebrations, and then repeat the performance when the Mexican soccer team won its playoff in the 1994 World Cup. It's almost impossible to drive around the city for any length of time without seeing LAPD or sheriff's deputies holding our fellow citizens— usually male minority youths—spread-eagled against a wall or sitting humiliated in the gutter while the officers search their cars and persons for drugs, weapons, or whatever contraband might be the subject of current hysteria.

Over and above the smaller incidents is the Rodney King debacle, which started as a small group of officers indulging in some sadly familiar Nazi-boy fun, and ended with more than sixty people dead, a half-billion bucks in property damage, and a collective trauma from which the city has yet to fully recover.

The sum total of all this is that the citizenry of Los Angeles probably has the worst us-and-them perception of its police department of any city I've ever known. For many years, law enforcement theorists have identified this kind of "army of occupation syndrome" as one of the major ills that can infect a big-city police force. After the riots, when Daryl Gates was handed his hat and the suggestion that he retrain as a talk-show host, and Willie Williams was brought in from Philadelphia, a lot of lip service was paid to the concept of community policing. On the ground, however, little appears to have changed. In my community, the sheriffs continue to roust and harass the drag queens and rent boys on Santa Monica Boulevard, and, when the weather gets warmer, the helicopters will again clatter over Plummer Park in the dead of night, irritating the sleeping homeless, and interrupting my late-night TV viewing, making me feel as if I'm in Saigon waiting for a mission.

The unfortunate perception that Los Angeles police officers are a bunch of spit-shined, robotic town bullies—or, as my girlfriend's lawyer put it, with deadpan cynicism, "the best police force that money can buy"—can only counteract the basic maintenance of Los Angeles as a workable and inhabitable environment. Certainly the great majority of us seem to be willing to believe the worst. We are ready to buy Johnnie Cochran's conspiracy theories or that, at the O.J. Simpson celebrity crime-scene-of-the-decade, vital evidence was handled with all the finesse of Larry, Moe, and Curly. It becomes extremely easy to give credence to urban legends like the deputy sheriff who shot the blind wino's dog when it growled at him, or to accept the current media speculation that Chief Williams, far from being the brave new broom, is nothing more than a fat freeloader.

The bottom line is that a police force has to get down with the population it claims to protect and serve. It cannot function efficiently when a majority of its rank and file live in far-flung suburbs and look at the inner city with distance and contempt. The status quo has, so far, given us law enforcement that proved ineffectual during the riots, is tainted in the O.J. case, and appears to be viewed by a large section of the populace on a spectrum that starts at fear and ends at loathing. God save us from the kind of chaotic hell that might break out should anyone blow up our Federal Building.

LA Reader, April 1995

PILLAR OF FIRE

Shake's gotta case of Colt 45 an' I got an AK47
Shake's gotta VCR to go an' I got an AK47
Bud's gotta brand new pair of Reeboks
An' I got an AK47
Bud's gotta pipe an' Shake's gotta lighter
An' I got an AK47

The warning's plain for all to see
The writing crowds the wall
Now greed has spawned disaster
And pride precedes the fall
The rapid fire of destiny
Takes history by the hour
Now you and I have chained ourselves
To the pillar of fire

The deputy's got a shotgun
The Marines got CS gas
The cops have got a swagger
Says you can kiss my ass
Politician now ain't nothing

❏ The most recent Los Angeles riot, that broke out in the spring of 1992, after the Rodney King incident and the acquittal of the cops involved, was one of those extreme occurrences that bring out both the superlative and the very worst in people—proving, if nothing else, that Hobbes made his Leviathan just too simplistic. The cool detachment of the poet also came into play. Obsessively watching the local TV news to see which way the mob was headed and what neighborhood would burn next, I noticed how nighttime lens-distortion by the cameras on the TV news choppers gave each burning building a vertical halo reaching for the sky. It had a terrible beauty and became the motif for this song.

But another word for liar
The only truth is in the light
Of the pillar of fire

Rising from the jewelfield
Rising from the plain
Rising from the liquormart
Rising from the pain
Rising from consuming rage
Rising from the mire
Rising from Los Angeles
An awesome pillar of fire

The Huxtables can't save us
Willy Horton takes the point
St. Theresa of the Roses
Works a topless joint
Can't trust no ballgame hero
Until he's on the barricade
And Eddie Murphy's having lunch
With Himmler in the shade
And high above the carnage
Cold eyes lack all desire
While you and I in fascination
Approach the pillar of fire

Shake's gotta case of Colt 45 an' I got an AK47
Shake's gotta VCR to go an' I got an AK47
Bud's gotta brand new pair of Reeboks
An' I got an AK47
Bud's gotta pipe an' Shake's gotta lighter
An' I got an AK47

Written in 1992 in wake of the riots.
Recorded by Wayne Kramer in 1995.

MICK FARREN

666

THE BLONDE HAD AN UNCANNY ABILITY TO REMAIN AL-most totally motionless. She was already on stage, naked but for a purple drape, as the audience/congregation took their seats for the Fortieth Anniversary High Mass of the Church of Satan. She held a Vargas-style calendar pose, stretched out on her right side, head tilted, partially sup-porting herself on her arm, one leg extended, the other bent under her. She could almost have been a mannequin, except, now and again, the pendant pentacle that hung be-tween her breasts flashed slightly in the stage lights. In a perfect world she would have been a comely devotee, im-mobilized in an occult trance, but the truth was more pro-saic. She was a model, Leola Jossi, hired for the gig, and just extremely good at what she did. Which was to keep very, very still for approximately ninety minutes, and func-tion as human scenery for the Satanic ceremony.

In addition to Leola Jossi, the Church of Satan had also engaged a quartet of armed security guards, and the in-vitation-only arrivals were frisked for concealed weapons before being admitted. Were these rent-a-cops merely to heighten the drama? Maybe, but in a world where a pro-life, pro-gay Episcopalian Priest—a friend of a friend—has received so many death threats he wears a Kevlar vest under his surplice, who knows what homicidal zealots might do if they knew that Lucifer was being invoked in the heart of the city?

The invitations stipulated dress was formal, and pre-ceremony cocktails were served in the theater's foyer where muted conversation melded with discreet piped-in bebop. It could have been a high-end art opening except for all the pentagram pendants round the necks of the well dressed crowd. (I was also wearing a pentagram, except it was under my shirt on a leather thong, along with an Elvis talisman, a voodoo heart, and the key to the Tardis, but those were just my usual protective totems.) The only Sa-tanic pop-culture reference I could apply to this select and affluent gathering were the uptown friends of Minnie and

❏ Not all power stems from simple politics or direct reaction to oppressive authority. There are many who believe that power both extends to and emanates from the occult and the paranormal. Scientology has a huge influence on Hollywood. The Bush family males are all members of Skull & Bones, and then there are the rumors of se-cret rooms in Dick Cheney's bunker equipped for strange and arcane rites. On June 6, 2006, I attended a black mass in the Silver Lake neighborhood of Los Angeles.

Roman Castevet in *Rosemary's Baby*, but even that was something of a stretch and, anyway, where was Rosemary?

After the audience was seated, I could see nothing except the dimly lit figure of Leola Jossi, but with the darkness came a half-second frisson. I didn't really expect a daemonic emanation, or that I'd fall victim to a conjured succubus, but this was my first Satanic mass, and a boy can hope. Anticipation was heightened by the music of Lustmord, an electronic fusion resembling an early and particularly depressed Pink Floyd, and a humpbacked whale familiar with Bach fugues. Finally the church hierarchy, filed in from the rear of the theater. The hoods of their robes hid their faces and they carried candles, but a lifetime of watching Hammer horror diminished the drama. I had seen it all before, and with Christopher Lee in the starring role.

The audience was initially instructed by Magistra Peggy Nadramia on how to respond at various points in the service, and her warm-up—like telling the goys at the Seder what was expected of them—put us somewhat at ease. She even threw in a gratuitous Pee-wee Herman reference that evoked the only laugh of the evening. The mass was divided into three thematic parts—Compassion, Lust, and Destruction—and at the end of each, three supplicants were led to the stage to make their requests of Satan. A Hugh Grant-looking young Englishman wanted to be "the Casanova of my neighborhood," a corporate wannabe craved a highly paid job, a nervous young woman desired nothing more than to be happy. A guy who looked like an East European car dealer wanted major hurt put on some people who had fucked him in a deal. The only altruistic request was an inarticulate plea for the environment. Cynicism set in. The High Mass was turning depressingly middle-class, a self-realization seminar with occult trappings. I figured that approaching a Mafia Don on the day of his daughter's wedding might yield more practical results.

The only truly human moment came when a woman, clearly suffering an emotional crisis, prayed for her husband to love her. I later saw her being helped to her car in tears. Did she gain any comfort from the Satanic mass?

Maybe as much as from a therapist or a more conventional encounter group. She had come and she had asked for help, and sometimes that's really all solace requires. But solace and theater are not the same thing.

Gongs were struck, a bell rung to the four points of the compass, a sword flourished—although more a long dagger than Excalibur—but the performance was oddly static. Where was the soul energy of the Reverend Ike, or the Bible pounding stagecraft of Jimmy Swaggart? I've seen Episcopalians with more juice. But my primary problem is with the text. The High Mass is based on the rituals created by Anton LaVey who founded the Church of Satan in a flurry of notoriety in the mid 1960s. It's little more than inverted Catholic litany, with a pinch of H.P. Lovecraft, a recipe for pretentious and ponderous poetry.

The 1960s also saw the rabbinical Zen grandeur of Allan Ginsberg, and Jim Morrison, as the Dionysian delinquent, calling down concho belt chaos and mojo disorder with his *Celebration of the Lizard*, and this quasi-ecclesiastic mélange is minor league in comparison. LaVey was making his occult bones at the same time as Bob Dylan was completing *Blonde On Blonde*, Lenny Bruce was being hounded to death by the defenders of decency, the Warlocks had changed their name to the Grateful Dead, Ken Kesey and the Merry Pranksters were on the bus, and Owsley Stanley III was making the best acid on the planet. Anton Szandor LaVey and his Church of Satan—at its zenith—attracted celebrities like Jayne Mansfield and Sammy Davis Jr., while an ex-con called Charlie Manson cast covetous glances at LaVey's operation, and a hippie chick called Susan Atkins—later a knife-wielding Manson slaymate—posed nude at a LaVey ceremony. LaVey was part of this cultural explosion. The only real twenty-first century energy was finally generated at the end of the Destruction phase, conducted by Magister Rex Diabolos, who actually has horns permanently implanted in his forehead. On his command, the audience/congregation rose to its feet, right arms extended, fingers in horned salute.

"Hail Satan!"

"Hail Satan!"

I have some very serious reservations about straight arm salutes, especially en masse. Last time I found myself hemmed in by a pack of hail/heils I had foolishly infiltrated a neo-Nazi punk gig (Skrewdriver, if I recall) and barely escaped with life and limb. I'm not, in any way, equating the Church of Satan with Nazism old or new, but this mass gesture—the salute and the call and response—generates a weird energy that just plain makes me nervous. While the believers lined up to collect some kind if souvenir tokens, I headed for the bar.

The choice of various Satans is a wide one. In the biblical chronology, he's right there in Genesis, the serpent of Eden tempting Eve into a fig-leaf bikini, but also endowing humanity with self-awareness, not unlike Prometheus who, after bringing the gift of fire, suffered horribly at the hands of the gods. From then on, the Evil One has so many personae it's hard to keep up. Is he the horned demon of medieval folklore? The Beast of Revelations, or Lucifer Son of Morning, the fallen favorite from Milton's *Paradise Lost*? Or is he the diabolic maestro who, in the nineteenth century, made Niccolo Paganini the greatest violinist of all time in return for his immortal soul, and, 100 years later, the devil who met Robert Johnson at the crossroads, or scared the shit out of Jerry Lee Lewis when drunk out of his mind in Sun studios? Is he the motivating force behind Norwegian death metal, a bad-rap, third century rewriting of Mithras, or the gleefully urbane Al Pacino in *The Devil's Advocate*? Could he even be the secret consigliore of Dick Cheney?

And why celebrate 6/6/06? This Number of the Beast from Revelations is the product of one of the most savagely pernicious books of the Bible, an insanely vicious piece of ancient science fiction, written by the half-starved and possibly hallucinating John of Patmos, exiled in a Roman Gulag, and maybe eating the fungus on the wall of his cave. It is obsessed with mass destruction, retribution, sex, and death, and although it is currently the paranoia-inducing favorite of Rapture believers, and evangelists like

Pat Robertson who also like to play Armageddon politics, it was not always so. In the fourth century, bishops led by St. John Chrysostom wanted Revelations excluded from the New Testament because of its potential for abuse. No less than Martin Luther loathed Revelations, considered it "neither apostolic nor prophetic." Don't Satanists, by accepting the 666 mystique, also put themselves in an unbreakable symbiosis with Christianity?

Christians—especially fundamentalists—will tell you Lucifer is all of the above. Satan employs every seductive form to ensnare his victims, and this multitude of manifestations proves the fiendishness of his infernal plan. But Christians must come under suspicion of extreme bias— or worse—where Lucifer is concerned. For centuries, the devil has been the convenient excuse to brutally torture and horribly execute hundreds of thousands of inconvenient midwives, wisewomen, freethinkers, and rebels against theocratic orthodoxy? And these witch-hunts are far from being confined to history. The Reagan era saw the "Satanic Panic," during which born-again Christians scoured heavy metal albums for secret messages, and claimed (eagerly abetted by media shills like Geraldo Rivera) to have uncovered repressed memories that indicated a Satanic underground honeycombed the entire US, and thousands of unfortunate victims, many young children, were being slaughtered in Satanic rituals.

Estimates of the Satanic bodycount ran as high as 60,000 dead, until an FBI spokesman pointed out this was close to triple the national homicide rate, and the Bureau had yet to find a single plausible body. These claims may be laughable, but the moral panic that surrounded incidents like the 1983 McMartin Preschool case in Manhattan Beach, when children were manipulated supposedly to recall underground tunnels and Satanic private jets, or the West Memphis Three who, in 1993, were convicted of murder after prosecutors used Pink Floyd lyrics and Stephen King novels as evidence of Satanic conspiracy. As recently as 2004, Scott Peterson attempted but failed to convince a jury that Satanists were the "real killers" of his pregnant wife Laci. Satan also figured in the trench-coat folklore of the genuinely dangerous. Richard Ramirez, Charlie Manson, Klebold and Harris, these are poster boys for the counterculture's nihilist trailer park. The disturbed and inadequate, the self-serving energy leeches, the teenage cat mutilators, can use the same symbols and language as an excuse to indulge their deep seated viciousness. "Hail Satan" can cover a multitude of sins.

A section from *LA CityBeat*, June 2006

THE PEREZ GIRL

☐ Henry Kissinger, when asked how he always had good-looking women on his arm at public events, replied in that trademark accent that "power was the ultimate aphrodisiac." In this short excerpt from a novel that I never finished, the character is the leader of the secret police in a fictional country in Central America who is planning a coup that will make him its dictatorial head of state.

ESTERO GLANCED BACK THROUGH THE DOORWAY BE-hind him at the young girl who now lay curled among the disarray of black silk sheets in one half of the huge king-size bed. She was the personal, private side of his sense of well being and accomplishment. The girl's name was Isabella Perez, and she was the supposedly chaste and protected daughter of one of his staunchest and most conservative backers. At some point, Perez, the father, if he didn't know already, would probably hear some whisper of Estero's liaison with his daughter, but he would never have the courage to either confront Estero, or withdraw his political support. Such was the freedom that came with power based largely on fear. It was possible to take a man's most prized possession and that man would be too afraid to even react. In many respects, the Perez girl was a symbol of the city, the country, of all that was about to come to him, and, for that reason alone, Estero had taken a silent delight in way that she had given herself to him with such adoration and blind faith. He had also noted that, judging from her behavior, deep in the black bed, she was hardly as chaste as her father apparently believed, and her family's moral protection must have been greatly less than absolute. The eager and accomplished upward thrusts of her pelvis and the convulsive gripping of her vaginal muscles told of an experience and enthusiasm hugely at odds with the supposed convent innocence of such a daughter of a so-called "good family."

She had cried out in pain just once during their lovemaking. He had hurt her a little, quite deliberately, just enough to demonstrate that what they were doing was also about power, the power that he controlled and that she received as she lay spread beneath him, shuddering, abandoned and helpless. He knew it was his power that she'd craved, and that power was the reason that she had been so instantly willing to come with him to wherever he might decide to take her. If she'd wanted tenderness, if she'd desired affection, she would never have been drawn to a man like him. Her lust had been for his power, pure and simple. She wanted him to move her in the same way that he had moved the mindlessness of the mob.

From an unpublished novel

HOW VICKI MORGAN ALMOST BROUGHT DOWN RONALD REAGAN BUT WAS MURDERED INSTEAD

WHILE CIA DIRECTOR CASEY MIXED IT UP WITH TERrorists, and Oliver North went about his illegal international intrigues in the White House basement, a 1983 sex scandal cast yet another shadow of doubt on the Reagan-era. Model and party girl, Vicki Morgan had been the longtime mistress of Alfred Bloomingdale, the founder of the Diner's Club and heir to the Bloomingdale's department store fortune. Bloomingdale was also a close friend of Ronald Reagan, an unofficial advisor, a member of his personal "kitchen cabinet," and an appointee to the Foreign Intelligence Advisory Board. On July 7, 1983, Morgan was found beaten to death in her Hollywood apartment. Her roommate, Marvin Pancost, immediately confessed to the slaying. Initially, it seemed to be nothing more than another sordidly pointless Hollywood murder out on the fringes of showbusiness, but then some bizarre rumors began to circulate.

❑ Political power and sex scandal will go hand in hand as long as politicians sell a spurious moral rectitude to the electorate. Bill Clinton all but fell when the simple liaison with Monica Lewinski was revealed, but if Vicki Morgan's alleged bondage parties had become public it could have decimated American conservatism.

A year earlier, when Bloomingdale had been hospitalized for throat cancer, his wife Betsy had attempted to end his relationship with Morgan by cutting off the money Bloomingdale had been paying her. Vicki immediately retaliated by threatening to go public with the story of her relationship with Bloomingdale. Apparently it had been more than just a one-on-one romance. Vicki had acted as hostess at regular S&M, whip and bondage parties thrown by Bloomingdale for prominent figures in the Reagan administration, and she had videotapes to prove it. She went to the William Morris Agency with a tell-all book proposal, but this project was supposedly derailed by powerful Hollywood figures looking to protect Reagan's interests. Vicki then threatened to go directly to the media, but died before she could make a public statement. Five days after the murder, attorney Robert Steinberg claimed that he had the Bloomingdale orgy tapes, but was unable to produce them when ordered by a court. They had been mysteriously stolen from his briefcase.

Marvin Pancost was convicted of the murder on the strength of his confession and that should have been the end of the Vicki Morgan story, except that weird tidbits of information continued to surface. Pancost turned out to have a history of confessing to crimes that he never committed, all the way back to when he tried to take the blame for the Manson Family, Tate/LaBianca murders. The LAPD investigation of the Morgan murder was revealed to be a badly botched job. The crime scene had not been sealed for twenty-four hours, and was a gem of police negligence. These items were more than enough to start the conspiracy mill grinding and fingers were again pointed at the CIA. The most popular interpretation was that someone in the Reagan camp had used Bloomingdale's intelligence connections to enlist Agency help to silence Morgan, before copies of the sex party tapes could find their way to tabloid TV and maybe bring down the supposedly ultramoral Republican presidency.

From the book *The CIA Files*, 1999

MICK FARREN

COME WITH ME TO THE CASBAH

THE FOLLOWING SMALL WONDER CAME IN TODAY (AS A forwarded email) from Henry Cabot Beck. Spam that serves as the come-on, the hook for what has become known as the Nigerian Scam can often be highly implausible, but this illiterate wonder was a gem of the genre.

DEAR Citibank Members,

This E-mail was sent by the Citibank server to veerify your E MAIL addres. You musst clmoetpe this prsecos by clicking on the link below and enttering in the smal winddow your CITI-bank ATM Card number and Pin that you use in the local ATM Machine. This is done—for-your pcertotion G because some of our members no logner have accses to their email adrssedes and we must verify it.

Aside from qualifying as the most inept webscam of all time—or at least to date—this loony clip also started me thinking. I'm well aware that my imagination tends towards over-cook a lot of the time, but that's how I earn a living (distant laughter), and also how I keep myself sane (more distant laughter), but it serves as yet another reinforcement of my fantasy picture of the Internet. Al Gore dubbed it the Information Super Highway, conjuring, for me at least some rolling, big-deal perspective that had elements of Robert A. Heinlein's *The Roads Must Roll*, the world of the clone-makers in *Star Wars: Episode II*, the Venusian city of Mekonta, and Osaka International Airport, all clean and chrome, plexiglass, and airstream tubular, with order and efficiency, a precision of integrated and organized traffic. And maybe that's why Old Al found himself incapable of defeating chump-chimp George W. because at least Bush, probably courtesy of Dick Cheney, and with rich-boy contempt, could see a little, if iniquitous, vision of the true unkempt nature of reality.

For me, the Internet has always seemed far more like a Middle Eastern bazaar, a souk or casbah, part futur-

❏ The sense of isolation and powerlessness is the raw clay out of which despots mold societies. It may seem as though they have it all their way, but when that helpless feeling comes upon you remember once again the words of the Mahatma. Gandhi was always positive. "There have always been tyrants and murderers, and for a time, they can seem invincible, but in the end, they always fall." Governments become bloated and sluggish and if the people stay on their toes and are not paralyzed by intimidation, they can often take control of an innovation before the rulers have even figured out what it is.

ist, part medieval, a space-floating Interzone, unplanned, asymmetrical and labyrinthine, although easily negotiable by those who know, with narrow accessways between gimcrack structures, whose flaws are hidden by hypnoswirls of niteglo color, and all the whores, hustlers, cutpurses, deadrabbits, footpads, swackdogs and gutter jumpers at which an adventurer could ever hope to shake his swordstick.

Quack croakers with dirty instruments want to enlarge your penis, brothel-shills do it with domestic beasts, and that's only the promise of better things inside, swarthy bunco artists whisper of fortunes in Nigeria, and politicians with corrosive blood want your money even more than they want your vote. Sexualized cartoon hentai-children retail their tears in darker alleyways, dancing in come-to-me display for dangerously scarred and mind-numbed teenage gunpersons on R&R from the carnage of their Xboxes, while dealers in long coats of a million pockets whisper transactionally of every dubious pill known to man and crustacean, to calm your mind, roll up your eyes, or keep you fucking to Sunday. Pop-ups like dirty gray beggars need beating, while mules look for their forty acres, and the gambling games tell you there's ninety minutes in every hour and 100 seconds in a minute and the odds are in your favor. And you should believe that when pigs eat your brother.

And in the middle of it all, there's *Doc 40's Own Cozy, Leather-Jacket Gin-Joint, Twenty-four Hour Global House Party, and Medicine Show*, offering sharp conversation, bad ideas, honest politics, cheap stimulation, dirty concepts, and links to revolution, right out on the stairs. The girls are smart, the women wicked, the men at least reasonable, poets cut up, the aliens behave themselves, the cats help themselves, the fire escapes work, and there's never a cop around even if you need one. And that, my friends, is why I attempt to keep it all going. Even if it is only a bunch of freaks on a stream of electrons. Come on back now, y'hear.

Doc40, 2004

MICK FARREN

THE ALL-SEEING EYE

WHEN THE EXECUTION OF SADDAM HUSSEIN BECAME inevitable, I wondered how soon a video clip of the hanging would appear on YouTube. I was essentially joking, but, as reality played out, DVDs of the hanging were on sale on sidewalks of Sadr City within forty-eight hours of Saddam's death, and the Western cable news channels were showing every part of the now famous "unauthorized" camera-phone footage, except for the sprung trap and former Iraqi dictator's actual drop into the abyss. Plainly the CNN rule on prurient death was the same as for prurient sex—cut before the consummation. Far more important, however, was that a very crucial line had been crossed in news management in a world where truth is often an inconvenience and must be spun, sanitized, and as predigested as baby food before being served to the public.

Had the camera-phone never recorded the noose (another traditional use for hemp, by the way) being placed around Saddam's neck, the assumption would have been—first as news, then as history—that the execution was conducted with, at the very least, the death row decorum of *The Green Mile* or *Dead Man Walking*, with dress uniforms, a blindfold, a pre-set script, practiced choreography, and maybe a final cigarette. Only those involved would have known that it was, in fact, a homicidal cluster fuck with masked thugs screaming abuse, and only Saddam himself maintaining any vestige of dignity. Propaganda was betrayed by the ubiquitous and miniaturized recording device, something that will happen with increasing regularity from here on out, and may actually constitute a major and far-reaching revolution in what we know and when we know it, that radicalizes every level of communication, all the way from news to art.

(The purpose of this piece is not to discuss the death penalty, but—since it can't be ignored in the process—I feel obligated to make clear I am totally opposed to its use under any circumstances. It fails as a deterrent, it is administered with haphazard inequality, and, as judicial

❏ The stream of electrons can seemingly take us anywhere—whether we want to go there or not.

revenge, has no place in a civilized society, since it lowers the culture to the moral level of the criminal. If, however, we collectively insist on putting criminals to death, I do feel that sentences should be carried out live on television, so at least we all see what is being done in our name. And by the same token, anyone who enjoys a good steak should maybe visit a slaughterhouse.)

The camera in the hands of the amateur civilian—as opposed to the sanctioned media—can be a powerful, and even dangerous tool, and a potential challenge to the status quo. In 1963, when John Kennedy was murdered in Dallas, Abraham Zapruder was the lone cameraman. While others filmed earlier moments in the motorcade, Zapruder alone, with his 8mm Bell & Howell Zoomatic, recorded the fatal headshot that cast so much doubt on the Warren Commission's conclusion that Lee Oswald acted alone. Collusion between *Life* magazine and the federal government kept the film totally under wraps for a full six years, and then prevented it from being aired on national TV until as late 1975, a dozen years after the assassination.

In 1991, twenty-eight years after the JFK killing, the VHS camcorder had become so common that, when George Holliday saw a crew of LAPD officers abusing a motorist named Rodney King in the Lake View Terrace area, he was able to make a permanent record of the crime. At the subsequent first trial of the officers involved, defense lawyers were able to persuade a Simi Valley jury to disbelieve the evidence of their own eyes, and in so doing, sparked some of the worst rioting in this city's history.

If these incidents teach us anything, it has to be that those in authority view the motion picture or video camera in the hands of the public with suspicion and discomfort. From a Rolling Stones concert to a National Guard patrol in Baghdad, a camera phone can record and disseminate the event, and there's damned little that anyone can do about it. The Rolling Stones don't like it and the Pentagon likes it even less. Both organizations know they're losing control of the shape and flow of their own imagery, and, in a world where data is a cash commodity and perception is paramount, this is cause for serious concern. Mick Jagger is unable to collect royalties while the Pentagon loses it's capacity for propaganda spin.

Not that authority doesn't have cameras of its own. Anyone who has run a red light at Hollywood and La Brea, and then received a ticket in the mail along with an incriminating picture, is well aware that some electronic DMV version of Big Brother is watching and recording our traffic transgressions, and, as Winona Ryder learned to her cost and humiliation, most major stores and retail malls employ extensive surveillance systems. Maybe from a supposedly ingrained sense of privacy, the US has been relatively slow to move into the Big Brother business. The British currently lead the field with between two and three million cameras watching its citizens, and anyone going about their business in central London will be under virtually non-stop scrutiny by either private security or law enforcement. There's little consolation in our lagging, however. What happens in London today will be happening in Hollywood or Culver City tomorrow.

In all of this, the twenty-first century may well be showing us the shape of things to come. On one hand we have a booming industry in systemized surveillance, while, on the other, citizens brandishing camera phones potentially turn Big Brother on his head, making all things visible, and empowering average citizens to become news reporters, paparazzi, visual artists, or pornographers. The clips created by camera phones and similar technology is not even subject to the editing and censorship process of mainstream media. Back in the early 1990s, George Holliday's potentially explosive cassette of the Rodney King beating required a local TV channel, and ultimately a national network, to air the damning visual evidence. Today any video clip can be easily uploaded to YouTube, or a similar Wiki-style online site with only the most minimal censorship.

The cry is, of course, that this overabundance of random electronic recording is the death of individual privacy. This might indeed be true, except many of our concepts of privacy are largely illusions of fond hindsight. From Richard Nixon, to Joe McCarthy, to Cotton Mather, America has never shown too much respect for a citizen's privacy, and, in the small town so beloved by US folklore, everyone took—and still takes—a vicious interest in their neighbors' business. The trade-off for having cameras constantly pointed at us may well be a multilevel cultural revolution. The digital distortion of cell phone visuals and security cameras have already become part of the filmmaker's palette, and we can only guess at the post-punk, body modification subculture's ultimate response. Neo-pagans and techno-primitives could easily advance from piercings and tattoos to the cyberpunk predictions of implanted processors, body-wired hard drives, miniature video cameras, infrared vision, and a new breed of electronic street-art outlaw—truly masked and anonymous—thwarting the watchers by walking around in a haze of their own electronic distortion.

We all know the Chinese curse of living in interesting times. We can only wonder if an interesting future is equally ill-omened.

LA CityBeat, January 2007

ELECTRIC BAKUNIN

❑ Maybe all we need is the ability to walk blindly into the unknown and make use of anything we find there.

THE NEW ELECTRIC ANARCHY? ONE PERSON'S VIRUS IS another's empowerment. From Nero to Nixon, despots have feared the mob—could the videophone, YouTube, Blackberry Internet *et al* be the New Mob they must rightly fear? The voting machines may be fixed, but every politician will be open to scrutiny and ridicule twenty-four/seven. Perhaps ol' Mikhail Bakunin, the great anarcho-syndicalist, was just a century-and-a-half in front of himself when, in 1866, he called for "the absolute rejection of every authority which sacrifices freedom for the convenience of the state."

Doc40, 2007

MICK FARREN

HUMANITY V TECHNOLOGY
(WE MAY HAVE ALREADY SURRENDERED)

"Nothing can change the shape of things to come."
—Max Frost

"Belief can be manipulated, only knowledge is dangerous."
—Bene Geserit maxim

"It can only be attributable to human error."
—HAL 9000

ON THE EVE OF WATERLOO, WELLINGTON CAUTIONED his officers about "running around like wet hens." A cool simile, and still apt, after 190 years, when applied to our media, as we enter this brave new 2006. Tech is in such uproar that few can factor it into their thinking. 2005 saw unprecedented, multi-leveled upheavals in mass communications. At one end of the spectrum, the *Los Angeles Times* dropped in circulation, downsized its editorial staff, and gave up its online edition to free access/no subscription. At a far extreme, highly illegal, if enterprisingly twisted young boys sold webcam voyeur sex, quite without any recourse to adults except as customers and Internet providers. Change shakes windows and rattles doors. Something is happening here that is probably exponential, but does any one have clue as to what it is?

If current floundering augurs anything, the answer is "the hell we do." While Netflix eats the video store, Hollywood thrashes like a dying ape, creating movies that look like video games, and wondering why the XBox generation fails to show at theaters. In a world that dreams of liquid crystal home cinemas with cheap Chinese hardware, and where game CGI is better than the last Charlize Theron movie, movie houses full of popcorn reek and babies on cell phones lose their appeal. Print and The Electron go head to head with the end maybe sooner than many expected. Daily newspapers show battle fatigue, and make undignified advances on the youth market, trying to

❑ The majority of the power structures currently running this world have roots that stretch all the way back to the nineteenth century. Both Marxism and capitalism were products of Victorian smokestack industry, and early indications are that neither is making an exactly smooth transition to the high-speed, headlong, and unstoppable progress of twenty-first century techno-development. Newspapers flounder while what might have once been their readership reduces their attention span to the 140 characters of Twitter. The global economy teeters on the brink of the unthinkable as market traders treat money as an abstraction. And who the hell really knows what's happening in China?

prove they're not twentieth century relics. But everybody knows that The Electron will win, if only because The Electron says it will.

The Electron's Labyrinth, however, is not without conspiracy and conflict. Cable television/Internet providers slither fat in local monopoly, but phone companies are straining at the government leash to deliver programming to subscribers. Fundamentalists—via the FCC—have been led to believe they have oversight of everything, and now complicate every regulatory move with absurd stipulations of morality, and make the chances for even marginally intelligent solutions close to hopeless. The New American Century is hardly a golden age of clarity and vision. Communications are a massive sector of global *Rollerball* capitalism, and operate with the same tooth'n'claw audacity that allows a Bechtel monopoly to sell the Bolivians' their own rainwater by order of the World Bank.

A president of the United States, who is leery of science, uncomfortable around smart people, and distrusts the Internet, still dominates a congress so shamelessly corrupt it gives new meaning to Bob Dylan's old maxim "everything is legal as long as you don't get caught." And they all do business with the equally corrupt Comrades of Beijing, who believe they can control cyberspace, but are threatened by sex blogger Mu Zimei, and hackers like the Hongkong Blondes, and a Second Cultural Revolution might actually succeed, unless Google gets bigger and smarter, in which case we may well he headed to either Utopia or the Matrix. Or both.

In a recent letter, Felix Dennis, self-made print-billionaire, and publisher of *Maxim* expressed the belief that print, in many of its most familiar forms, will become obsolete in the foreseeable future, but that nothing radical would happen "in the next couple of years." He saw sufficient cushion for industries to adapt. The proprietors of daily and weekly newspapers might disagree, having, of late, sustained more bites to their flesh than a drunken teen in a shark movie. The single chomp of Craigslist may have hit vital organs, as a nation that once paid newspapers for its want ads—jobs, apartments, buy/sell, hookers, and personals—now increasingly logs on to Craigslist for free.

The Craigslist empire grew out of software designed by Craig Newmark in San Francisco that could automatically add email postings to an expanding website. Launched in 1995, with a mission to "restore the human voice to the Internet, in a humane, noncommercial environment," the system can now boast three billion page views per month in multiple cities. Classified advertising might seem minor to the outsider, but, within the newspaper industry, this loss of traditional hard-cash represents a body blow from which recovery may not be easy.

Newspapers, however, aren't the only area of print where previously undisputed turf is being conceded. The days of the reference book may already be numbered. Instead of reaching for *Leonard Maltin's Movie Guide* to check the dates, spellings, and casts of films, I now fast-click to the Internet Movie Database. It's a no brainer. The Electron wins because the electron offers speed. For more general information I have Wikipedia, "the Free Encyclopedia" on a hot button, and it's faster and more complete than any printed desk encyclopedia. Doubts may have been voiced as to how an encyclopedia can be accurate when it is created and updated for and by the people, but constant use tends to confirm Wikipedia's exactitude, and the entry on me (which makes me profoundly happy) is accurate, if short, and written with enough mild cynicism to keep me in my place.

The times that Wikipedia has been used for mischief—most famously the guerrilla rewrite of the entry for Donald Rumsfeld that bathroom-walled the Sec of Def as a child molester—were used as evidence that Wikipedia was just another treasonous liberal conspiracy. The problem, in reality, however, was trolls, the bottom feeding posters-of-mindless-messages who roam the entire net, defacing anything they can reach, like inner city taggers without the flair or color. Trolls were, in part, responsible for the collapse of Michael Kinsley's "Wikitorial" experiment at the

Los Angeles Times, they brought down the message boards on Howard Stern.com with their dumb-bastard overload, and currently keep webmasters and checkers at IMDb, Wikipedia and Craigslist on their toes. But trolls are one of the prices we pay for Internet freedom, and are generally viewed as infinitely preferable to any FCC-style oversight, if that was even possible.

With Wikipedia and Craigslist, so-called liberal web conspiracies have created functional resources, and without charging the consumer or hustling advertising. Donations need only cover tech and management. Nerds work on their obsessions, and don't require a salary. A post-capitalist business model? Hasn't *Star Trek* already been there? (Don't laugh yet.) Richard Mason says it all on Cal Tech's Robotics website. "Characters often describe the Federation as if it were a perfect socialist (or at any rate, post-capitalist) society, where there is no money and nobody wants for material things." In one TV episode, Captain Picard elaborated on a microwave oven-looking device into which you simply entered the code, and anything—a perfect martini or a perfect rose—materialized out of stray atoms. After such an invention, Picard indicated, money became pointless.

If not pointless, money certainly poses a problem on the contemporary Internet. Irrespective of content, some sites make truckloads of cash and others make none. The grim truth is that folks don't like to pay for anything online except porn, gambling, or shopping. All else—especially news items—is like paying for the peanuts in a bar. William Gibson's fictional cyberpunk imaginings may have been slightly off target, but a vision of endless cyberspace, populated by a million lightpoints of capricious blogs, and the slightly denser glow of more centralized information at the *Huffington Post*, *Drudge*, and *Wonkette*, still indicates that, if the mainstream media sail in like big-buck battlestars, they'll have problems with their navigation. The Internet has proved so skilled at circumventing attempts at control, it may actually be where freedom truly rings. On the other hand, many on the political right see this free choice as the tool of Satan, and, in this, they have some strange allies in modern late-model Chinese communists.

Beijing's new-look totalitarianism was recently rocked by a sex-blogger called Mu Zimei. Mu Zimei was originally Li Li who wrote a Sex Tips For Girls column for the Chinese fashion mag *City Pictorial*. Mu Zimei was the name Li Li used when, last spring, she started up a far more explicit blog of her hot-sheet adventures among China's rich and famous on the nation's top Internet site, Sina.com, and attracted ten million daily visitors to her tales of blowjobs and threesomes. While the government made no comment, Sina recognized a good thing and ran even more of Mu/Li Li. Official displeasure was finally expressed in oblique Chinese fashion, via an editorial on November 16, 2005, in the state-run *Beijing Evening News* that warned "the blind pursuit after this kind of phenomenon will mislead people into thinking that the authorities are turning a blind eye."

In her blog, Mu Zimei defended her right to sleep with whomever she fancied and to write about it. "I think my private life is very interesting. If a man does this it's no big deal. But as a woman doing so, I draw lots of criticism." Sina.com backed off, down-played its Mu promotion, but allowed her blog to continue. Not good enough apparently, because the government then moved to ban a print anthology of her work, despite a massive advance sale, and Sina was ordered into a period of old-fashioned Maoist self-criticism. To defuse more escalation, Mu voluntarily shut down her website, but she also told the foreign press that she had "other offers and hoped to continue writing, assuming the government did not ban her writing altogether."

For the moment, Mu Zimei lays low, but a market force has been revealed. China has sixty-eight million "netizens" on the Internet, with an annual growth rate approaching thirty percent, and they want what Mu offers. Dissident hackers with names like The Cult of the Dead Cow and The Hong Kong Blondes have meanwhile been infiltrating Chinese police and security networks just to prove they can. Link them with Mu—or the next rebel blogslut to challenge the status quo—and the creation of the unstoppable may be in motion. Unless, of course, Google decides to take a side in some virtual-future Tiananmen Square.

Folks who once loved Google are growing nervous. The revelation that the huge and near-indispensable search engine had rewritten some of its programs to accommodate political censorship by the Chinese government didn't sit well. Others simply saw its infinite capacity to store data as approaching the metaphysical. Already it's loading entire libraries into its vast new book-search, customizing our web ads, and Google Earth will take you to a simulated spy satellite picture of your very own building if directed. (Although not on my four-year-old laptop.) Google must already know more about any one of us than the FBI, and will ultimately know absolutely everything, which, to a few, will make it God. Even those who worry can't hide their respect. While debating the theoretical dangers of a challenge to Microsoft by a Google operating system, Thomas Y. Lee, professor of operations and information management at Wharton College is openly admiring. "Google has hired really, really smart people. When you put that many smart people in one place, neat things happen."

And one of the potentially neat things may well be this heavily rumored Google Operating System, duking it out with Microsoft for the favor of PC manufacturers. Balaji Padmanabhan, another Wharton professor, sees a Google system as part of "a move toward PCs that don't have a lot of software installed on them, where most applications can run off a network." How a systems war would impact the consumer remains to be seen, but, since the Google OS would have the user more plugged into Google than ever he or she was to Microsoft, concern is kindled that we may be putting too many of our most basic eggs in the Google basket. And the comfort and freedom of any Google basket is also questioned after Google's response to reports that—after acquiring an interest in Baidu.com, a Chinese search engine—they had intentionally excluded headlines of government-banned Chinese web sites from Google News. Their statement turned out to be a gem of corporate-global doublespeak. "*Google has decided that in order to create the best possible search experience for our mainland China users we will not include sites whose content is not accessible, as their inclusion does not provide a good experience for our News users who are looking for information.*"

A good experience, however, is often in the perception of the beholder. One person's heaven is another's purgatory. In the cyberspace vision, Google begins to look strangely maternal. A vast and synergetic mother system extends umbilicals of fun and data to the entire planetary population, feeding our human curiosity and need to delve—but maybe leading us in predetermined directions we know nothing about. The very name of this wholly faceless but intimate entity is babytalk. The word Google is comforting but meaningless, and, almost without knowing it, we are already modifying our behavior. Our love of stuff diminishes. Once we had CDs in jewel cases, and rolled joints on album sleeves. Now the music we own is an abstraction, a title on an iPod. The stuff we do acquire is frequently more electronic hardware to expand the modification of our minds. I've even observed—although the research is highly unscientific—that online readers are uncomfortable with long essays, and initially scan webtext with an am-I-interested speed-read. TV has already raised two generations with attention span disorders, so are we natural-born lazy slobs or merely adapting? Google knows more than we ever will, world without end, and may simply be preparing us for the day when it's smarter than we are. And—dare it be said—self aware? But that, of course, would be science fiction. Or the futurist predictions of Ray Kurzweil of the Singularity, coming in thirty years, when we humans will meld with our computers.

But you're okay. You're still reading a newspaper. Like, ink on paper, right?

Or are you?

LA CityBeat, 2006

216

Part Four

Elvis Died For Somebody's Sins But Not Mine

for a few months, while I was a resident of Manhattan, I attended a psychiatrist. It went with the territory. The relationship was not a happy one and it did not last. I knew it was going bad when she asked me a question that so totally missed the point I wondered if she had even bothered to aim. "You wanted to have sex with Elvis Presley?"

I do not recall if I made any attempt to keep the contempt out of voice, but I doubt it. "No. That's absurd. I wanted to be Elvis Presley."

The problem was that she was talking sex and I was talking fame. The psychiatrist, despite all her training, did seem to grasp the basic principle that, when fame is the desire and the spur, sex doesn't matter. Carnal lust becomes wholly irrelevant. Where fame goes, sex—plus a whole lot more—will automatically follow. I left the psychiatrist for a number of reasons, and one was certainly her total failure to grasp the nature of fame, and how the entire concept might well be bending twentieth century culture completely out of shape.

I'd started early. When I was about eight years old I wanted to be the first man on the moon. I like the idea of being a spaceman. (The word "astronaut" had yet to be invented.) But the real point was that, if I was the first man on the moon, I'd be remembered forever, like Christopher Columbus. It was a version of immortality, a hedge against death. Andy Warhol hadn't helped any by, a few years later, giving with one hand and taking away with the other. He had promised that, in the future, everyone was going to be famous, but it came with a kicker. Everyone was only going to be famous for fifteen lousy minutes. In a single sentence, he had anticipated both Paris Hilton and the diminishing attention span.

Andy had tied a Gordian knot of media-driven paradox. Immortality would be instant, but extremely finite. If you wanted to see the paradox in action you needed only to look south to Graceland.

At some point in the early 1970s, a research study on mass communications had discovered that the three most recognized images on the planet were the faces of Jesus Christ and Elvis, and then the Coca-Cola logo. Meanwhile Elvis himself, arguably the most famous living human in the world, appeared so fucked by fame that he was busily attempting slow suicide by overdosing on Percodan, animal fat, and sugar. By the time Elvis died in 1977— and with all that his death would reveal—the proposition had to be entertained that maybe fame was not a form of immortality. Indeed it might ultimately prove to be a stone killer.

ELVIS PRESLEY IS DEAD

IT WAS ONE OF THE WORST STORMS TO HIT LONDON since God knows when. The thunder rolled, lightning flashed and the rain hammered onto the roof. There's something about a storm that brings a sense of doom. It fitted so perfectly. When the ITV newsflash sign came on the TV screen everyone looked up. When the flash sign was immediately followed by a still of Elvis Presley, a quiet voice breathed,

"Oh, my God."

"Reports are coming in that Elvis Presley, the rock'n'roll singer, died this evening at his home in Memphis, Tennessee." We all looked at each other in disbelief.

"Elvis is dead!"

It didn't seem quite credible. And yet it wasn't the kind of shock that followed the news of JFK being cut down. There had been so much speculation about Presley's mental and physical health that his death was unpleasantly predictable. It was almost impossible to know what to think. My first impulse was to pick up the phone and call a couple of people. I tried two numbers, but they were both busy. Obviously other people had reacted the same way. It was the kind of news that demanded to be passed on. Elvis had always been there. For more than two decades he'd maintained a unique position in too many people's lives. Despite all the depressing rumors it scarcely seemed possible that he'd gone, that Elvis Presley was dead at forty-two.

I guess the only word I can use is numb. Numb, and just very slightly embarrassed at the way I was reacting. It wasn't the ordinary kind of grief that you feel for a personal friend. There was no voice telling me that I'd never see Elvis Presley again. Jesus Christ, I'd never seen him, ever. I didn't even regret that I'd never get the chance to see him. The Elvis Presley I'd have given my right arm to watch was the wild hoodlum in the gold jacket who vanished into the US Army and never returned. I'd mourned his passing many years ago.

I think, to be absolutely truthful, any grief for Elvis Presley has to be bound up with a grief for my own early youth. It's grief for that long vanished innocence, that virgin state in which it was possible to discover rock'n'roll for the very first time.

The moment when I first heard 'Heartbreak Hotel' coming out of the radio was an experience that's impossible to reproduce. It was a time when the radio didn't add up to much more than *The Archers, Journey into Space,* and *The Goon Show.* The readily available music was all 'Que Sera,' 'Love And Marriage,' and 'How Much Is That Doggie In The Window?'

After 'Heartbreak Hotel' all that changed. Music had the power. It may have taken another six or seven years for Bob Dylan to articulate it, but right from the start it was obvious that the times were changing. If it needed a confirmation, it was right there in the way Elvis was condemned out of hand by parents and pulpit. Elvis Presley was far more than just an entertainer. He was something different to Frank Sinatra or Bing Crosby. He'd picked up the teenage banner that had been dropped by James Dean. He not only picked it up, but he picked it up and ran with it. From the way he combed his hair to the sneer and the snapping knee, he was the beginning of the rebellion. You stopped thinking about being a chartered accountant and began to wonder if, just maybe, you could be Elvis.

Of course, the passing years brought disappointments. He came back from the army to make all those awful films and often equally awful records. The greatest white R&B singer the world had ever seen decayed before our eyes into a Hollywood clown who appeared to have no respect for his work, his audience or himself. If it had been anybody but Elvis Presley he probably would have been quietly forgotten, but he was just too big for that. If it was only in the middle of the night, when listening to the old records, the magnetism still came alive in those attempts to recapture the first careless rush. It was a haven of simplicity in a world of 'Visions Of Johanna' and 'Have You Seen Your Mother, Baby.'

Presley had racked up so much affection in the fifties that it was even hard to blame him for his dire output. More often than not the blame was laid at the door of Colonel Tom Parker. It may not have been logical, but even when he did his worst, it was hard to believe that it was Presley's fault.

Elvis worship lay dormant in a lot of us during the sixties. Just how many of us became noticeable when, at the end of the decade, our man seemed about to make a comeback with records like 'Promised Land,' 'Burning Love,' his TV special, and his return to the live stage at the Las Vegas Hilton. As it turned out, Presley didn't come back to us. His return was for the blue rinse and double knit set. He was fated never to return to rock'n'rollers and overgrown juvenile delinquents who had sweated out their adolescence with him.

Once again the decay started. His public behavior became erratic. It looked as though instead of coming back, Elvis Presley had dipped his toe into the real world, but had quickly withdrawn it again. The rumors flowed out from behind the high walls of his guarded mansions. They talked about his custom built blondes, his drugs, his neurotic eating and violent temper tantrums. His marriage came and went, and the figure who was once a hero turned, bit by bit, into a petulant, overweight pampered child. It was sad. It was like watching an old friend, whom you hadn't seen in a long time, slowly going to pieces. That may have been sad, but it was only a fraction as sad as the thought of Elvis Presley, maybe the biggest idol the world's seen yet, dying alone and disturbed in his luxury prison. There's just no way that you can help an idol. Maybe, in the final analysis, the world can't support an Elvis Presley all the way to a fulfilled and peaceful old age.

The clichés come thick and fast at a time like this. Some of them are even true. Without Elvis Presley history would certainly have been different. Jagger might have become an estate agent, Dylan a rabbi, Lennon a bricklayer or Johnny Rotten a judge. He probably was one of the tiny handful of artists who actually affected the course of human affairs. Maybe the load was too much for him to carry. I don't know. None of us can really imagine how it feels to walk around being Elvis Presley every day of your life.

All this isn't what's really important. All I know is that the death of Presley has produced a kind of dull hurt that's hard to pin down. I can't exactly define why or how it hurts. All I know is something that used to be important to me has gone.

I guess that's the measure of the man and what he meant. At least, what he meant to me.

New Musical Express, August 1977

BUT LOVE ME

I MUST HAVE BEEN ABOUT SIXTEEN YEARS OLD, GOING to one of my very first all-night parties. I was in my first fledgling garage rock'n'roll band by this point. The guitar player was a kid with glasses who went by the name of Chub. His folks were wealthy, they had a big house, and most importantly, they were going to be away for the weekend. It was like the Eddie Cochran hit. Come on everybody. We'd all told our parents different stories to account for our being out all night, and early on Saturday evening, we converged on the home of Chub's family for what we devoutly hoped would be a feast of drunkenness and debauchery.

The truth was that we were too young and too callow for anything approaching true debauchery. We didn't know that debauchery takes years of practice. All we managed was to get beer drunk and stupid and ineptly paw at any of the girls present who were willing to let us. Around two in the morning, a lull ensued. Some of the kids had passed out, some were immobilized, some necking and groping. For some time, nobody had enough together to even put on a fresh record. After maybe fifteen minutes of listening to our own collective snoring, breathing, whispering, giggling and grunting, someone finally managed to collect

❏ My first inkling of the impact of Elvis came when I was a dumb teenager and three-parts drunk. Even through that neophyte haze, I couldn't miss the unique power in his voice that would precipitate him to such unknowable—but oh so very seductive—levels of fame.

themselves sufficiently to put on Elvis—the second album. Whoever did it may have been thinking more clearly than I imagined. Instead of dropping the stylus on the first track on side one, 'Rip It Up,' the record started with the plaintive moan of 'Love Me.'

"Treat me like a fool, treat me mean and cruel, but… love me."

I swear to God, after that first line, a sound came from every young woman in that darkened room—from the floor and the depths of Chub's mother's couch, a swooning gasp, something between a sigh and a groan. It was as though they'd experienced a shock, somewhere out where pleasure meets the threshold of pain. At that moment, I realized beyond any shadow of a doubt that Elvis' voice did things to people.

From the book *The Hitchhiker's Guide To Elvis*, 1994

WELL BLESS MY SOUL, WHAT'S WRONG WITH ME?

❑ The death of Elvis Presley may have come as a shock, but it was hardly a surprise. More than a year before his death, I wrote a fairly lengthy essay attempting to define by what paranormal power Elvis was able to maintain his career when he did almost nothing of any creative worth. I was allowed to talk about isolation and mismanagement on the part of Colonel Tom Parker, but drugs were an area that was closed to speculation. The most

WHEN AN ARTIST HASN'T PRODUCED ANYTHING OF note for something like fourteen years, the world begins to judge him on just about anything but his talent. When no original work is forthcoming, a superstar tends to be evaluated by his fans, his tastes, his vices and his private life. This is exactly what happened to Elvis Presley. During the latter half of the 1950s he virtually turned popular music inside out. Then he was drafted into the US Army. When he returned to civilian life his career came to what almost amounted to a full stop. With a couple of notable exceptions, nothing he produced from 1962 onwards had any creative power whatsoever. His work turned into a constant rehash of a tried and trusted formula.

The gap between his work and the mainstream of rock widened to the point where Presley became a strange archaic figure, maybe fascinating as a peculiar phenomenon, but hardly valid as part of the on-going path of modern music. To put it bluntly, he became the last surviving dinosaur, whose rampages through the Las Vegas hotel lounges were entertaining spectacles, social curiosities, but hardly works of art.

A lesser individual would not have survived. He would have been quietly buried in the rock encyclopedias as another star who went nova and quickly burned out.

Probably the most amazing thing about the two-decade Elvis Presley epic is the way in which he generated sufficient energy during the first six years of his career to carry him through fourteen years or more when he did nothing.

Presley still has the wholehearted attention of a large section of the public, although it is mainly concerned with his marriage, waistline and strange reclusive life. Hardly a week goes by without some Presley story turning up somewhere in the press.

So what did happen during those first six years? What was the nature of the fifties explosion that provided Presley with so much momentum that it carried him, as a full blown superstar, clear into the latter half of the seventies?

Exactly twenty years ago (May 11, 1956, to be precise), 'Heartbreak Hotel' went into the *NME* singles chart, for the first time, at number fifteen. So this seems as good a time as any to take a close look at the early career of Elvis Presley. After twenty years of media overkill, the facts of Presley's formative days have become almost totally obscured by the legend. Research is made even more complicated by his super-isolated way of life. He has never given what could be called a serious interview, and never made any real mention of his musical roots. The legend tells us that the truck driving boy stopped at Sun Records' studio and cut a birthday greeting disc for his mama. He was later called back by Sam Philips and proved a total failure as a crooner. Fooling around in the coffee break, rock'n'roll was discovered by accident.

The legend presents Elvis as a simple-minded hood who had the manners of James Dean, and, unbeknownst to himself, both in voice and body, the power to awake teenage America, which promptly carried him to fame and

that the **NME**'s corporate lawyers would allow me to say was "although Presley has never been directly associated with drugs, there is no doubt that the majority of musicians playing these backroad circuits depend heavily on amphetamines, Benzedrine and No-Doze." In fact, I harbored much deeper suspicions. As early as 1970, in the movie **Elvis—That's The Way It Is**, during the filmed rehearsal for his Las Vegas debut, the man appeared loaded to the gills on something. When I remarked on this to friends and colleagues, the general response was that I was either crazy or projecting my own stoned condition on the global idol. But a few—most notably the stalwart Boss Goodman—saw what I saw. After watching the particular segment of the film, he nodded. "He is definitely fucked up."

fortune on an hysterical tide.

Yeah? It does sound something like a fairy tale, doesn't it? It is also hard to believe that Elvis Presley could have been the complete simpleton that legend sets him up to be, and actually do what he did. On the other hand, could anyone who was all that smart have participated in those awful films, recorded the dreadful songs and generally acted the creative fool for so many years?

This, my friends, is the basic paradox of Elvis Presley. Was he simply an unwitting product of time and environment, or was he a great deal shrewder than the legend has ever given him credit for?

Certainly in Britain the environment didn't seem, on the surface, to be in the least ready for Elvis Presley. The *NME* of May 11, 1956, was full of Dickie Valentine, Lita Rosa and Alma Cogan. The cover among other things featured Max Bygraves playing the drums. The two main features were a Sinatra story and a special welcome home to Ted Heath (the band leader, not the late Prime Minister: in 1956 the grocer was probably only a gleam in the Young Conservatives' eyes). Number one that week was 'No Other Love' by Ronnie Hilton. In America, the situation was a good deal more acceptable. 'Heartbreak Hotel' had been number one for some weeks. Teenage America was still, in its own way, mourning James Dean, who had been dead for just nine months, and Presley was being hailed as the "Hillbilly Cat" or the "King of Western Bop."

More important, the success of 'Heartbreak Hotel' was the culmination of a revolution that had been changing the entire course of country music. Presley may or may not have been a leader in this revolution, but he was certainly its figurehead.

In the Southern states, although the Supreme Court had outlawed segregation in 1954, racism was still at its height. It was the era of Governor Faubus and Federal troops being moved into Little Rock, Arkansas, to quell redneck violence. Country and Western was also firmly in the grip of racial discrimination. The fact that the country establishment had no truck with black music had stifled just about any progress after the death of Hank Williams in 1953. Drums were banned from the stage of the Grand Old Opry. Many young white musicians were in open revolt against the conservative stranglehold.

All over the South, small groups of pickers in their teens and twenties were going directly against the natural order of things and listening in to black radio stations and buying singles of people like Howlin' Wolf, Junior Parker and Lowell Fulson.

One of these groups was in Lubbock, Texas, centered around a young man called Buddy Holly. Another was in Norfolk, Virginia, around an ex-sailor who used the stage name of Gene Vincent. But by far the most important was in Memphis, Tennessee, where Carl Perkins, a guitarist called Scotty Moore, a bass player called Bill Black, a young pianist, Jerry Lee Lewis, and a number of other renegade country boys, had a loose association with Sam Philips, the owner of Sun Records. Sun split its product between country music and so called 'race' records. Philips had already recorded black acts like Rufus Thomas, Doctor Ross, Willie Nix and Little Milton, as well as a comprehensive country catalog. The aim of the ol' boys who hung around Philip's tiny, chicken coop studio was to fuse these two musical forms and produce a new, exciting, energetic hybrid that would provide a tangible sound for the restless Dean generation of teenagers.

Unfortunately, this interest in black music tended to upset the rednecks.

Whether Elvis Presley shared these ideas of combining R&B and country before he met up with Sam Philips and Scotty Moore is doubtful. His main musical interests seem to have been Billy Eckstine, Dean Martin, and the Inkspots. Although his lists of favorites was not 100 percent white, it was hardly jumped-up R&B.

It could be that Presley's musical taste, as published in the fan magazines, may have been tailored to poor white prejudices. His knowledge of bluesmen like Arthur (Big Boy) Crudup, and the way in which his early stage act leaned heavily on the black school of strutting-stud-bluesshouters-who-shook-their-thing indicated that his interest in black music was more than what was considered healthy for a red blooded Southern Boy.

At this point you have to bear in mind that, in the middle fifties, it required quite an effort of will for a white boy to tune in to a black radio station or buy black records. Drug stores, restaurants and truck stops, and the jukeboxes that went with them, were strictly segregated. The fact has to be faced, the young Elvis Presley was probably a little weird. He was the protected and, within their restricted income, the pampered only child of a poor white family. A degree of the protectiveness may have stemmed from the infant death of his twin brother Jesse. Contemporary publicity made a whole big deal about Presley's taste of pink suits, black shirts, white shoes and the entire hoodlum drag for which he became famous. What nobody ever mentioned was the source of his style.

In fact, Presley seems to have directly copied the fifties pimps who hung about in the black neighborhoods. They were just about the only other people in town who wore the kind of matching pink outfit that Scotty Moore recalls him wearing at their first rehearsal.

The only people who sold those kinds of threads were the sharp stores in the ghetto.

Thus we have this picture of a poor white boy. His parents are indulgent to the point where they buy him a guitar and later his own car when they figure he needs it. He copies the styles of the black pimps from across town, and has at least a passing interest in black R&B. His mannerisms are straight from Dean and Brando. This is hard to reconcile with the legend of the artless hick who showed up at Sun Records wanting to sound like Dean Martin. Even the legend makes it pretty clear that when he went into the Sun studios to make his very first demo tapes, he didn't need all that much persuasion to start rocking out on Arthur Crudup's 'That's Alright Mama.'

It could be that Presley went into the Sun studios without any ideas beyond trying to sound like Dean Martin, but was manoeuvred into R&B and 'That's Alright Mama' by

Moore, Black, and Philips who recognized his potential. Certainly Scotty Moore became his first ad hoc manger and was a considerable influence in those early days. After a period of rehearsals, Sam Philips got an acceptable cut of 'That's Alright Mama.' Once the single was released, one of Philips' first tasks was to prove to the Southern audience that Elvis was white. This was deftly accomplished in an interview with Dewey Philips (no relation) on the Memphis radio station WHBQ. By asking Presley what high school he went to, he subtly got the information across. Everyone in and around Memphis knew when Presley replied "Hume High School" it was a segregated white school.

Again, contrary to the legend, 'That's Alright Mama' wasn't an immediate smash hit. Although it clocked up healthy sales around the South, the next move for Presley was a grueling period of one-night stands around the South.

This time on the road was an intense, make or break episode in the Presley saga. Crowded into beat-up station wagons, covering hundreds of miles a day, eating garbage food and living in cheap motels, the pace was crushing. Although Presley has never been directly associated with drugs, there is no doubt that the majority of musicians playing these backroad circuits depend heavily on amphetamines, Benzedrine and No-Doze. If the speed didn't get to Presley, certainly the strain of seemingly endless one-nighters did.

Scotty Moore recounts: "He had so much energy in those days we'd have to sit up nights and wear him out so we could go to sleep. There'd be pillow fights, we'd wrestle. Anything we could think of. It, like wore us out."

Nice white boys didn't wear flash pink suits from the black side of town. They didn't listen to black radio and learn R&B hits, and they didn't get involved in brawls with rednecks who took exception to 'nigger lovin' faggots' getting the females in an uproar.

"Every day, every night was the same. He chewed his fingernails, drummed his hands against his thighs, tapped his feet and every chance he got he'd start combing his hair."

When this bundle of nerves and energy was pushed out on stage it proved to be the most exciting thing the South had seen since the civil war.

Having become used to the portly, posturing, sequined Las Vegas superstar of the seventies, it's hard to realize just how wild the young Presley actually was on stage. He was strikingly good-looking in the fashionable delinquent manner. He was mean, frenetic, and as greasy as any teenage hood who swaggered down the main street of the small towns where Presley and his bands played town halls, movie theaters, high school gyms and National Guard armories. Hardly any record remains of those early stage shows, only a few photographs and the memories of the people who attended them. Even this scanty evidence, however, proves beyond a doubt that the young Elvis was an explosive performer. He used his body with the same outrageous abandon as Mick Jagger. His moving on stage seems to have summed up the frustration, barely repressed sexuality and spasmodic violence in the kids growing up in Eisenhower's paternal and paranoid America. His tense, braced leg, gunfighter stance that would suddenly erupt into angry, fluid motion—the dropping to the stage, sliding on knees and the constantly bumping, grinding hips said it all to the teenagers in the audience. The girls in the front row were jerked from their Bible Belt upbringing into scramming hysteria. They fought to get at the larger than life stud in the gaudy suits and longer sideburns than any hot rod punk.

Bob Neal, Presley's manager before Colonel Tom Parker came into the picture, has talked about these primal audiences: "You'd see this frenzied reaction, particularly from the young girls. We hadn't gone out and arranged for anybody to squeal and scream. Not like Frank Sinatra did in the forties. These girls screamed spontaneously."

At first, Presley was at the bottom of the bill in these small-town package shows, but he quickly moved up to the headliners who closed the show. This wasn't simply because of his popularity. Other acts on the bill flatly refused to face the audience after Presley had finished with them.

Unwittingly he created a good deal of hostility among the other performers. Some of them looked on the near-riot situations that he whipped up in the crowd as a deliberate sabotage of their own careers. Hostility didn't only come from the performers. Some of the male punks in the audience reacted with as much intensity as the girls. However, the intensity was of a very negative kind. As his fame spread through the South, so did the number of adolescent rednecks who laid in wait to take a swing at the nigger-loving faggot who was getting the flower of Southern womanhood in an uproar which more than likely distracted the ladies' attention from the punks' own backwoods macho posturing.

In Lubbock, Texas, one teenage gang went so far as to firebomb Presley's car after a local scandal sheet had printed a phony story suggesting he had been sleeping with the local police chief's daughter. Bob Neil again: "It was almost frightening, the reaction that came to Elvis from the teenaged boys. So many of them, through some sort of jealousy, would practically hate him. There were occasions in some towns in Texas when we'd have to be sure to have a police guard because somebody would always try to take a crack at him. They'd get a gang and try to waylay him or something. Of course, Elvis wasn't afraid of them and was quite willing to defend himself—and did on occasions."

In fact, it would appear that Presley was not only 'willing to defend himself,' but actually enjoyed a good punch-up. There was the celebrated incident when he beat up a gas station attendant who ridiculed him while he was having his car filled up. The pump jockey appeared in court looking more than a little battered, while Presley was virtually unmarked. The verdict still, however, went in Presley's favor.

Although photographs are about all that remain of those early stage shows, there is what seems to be fairly accurate recreation of their atmosphere in the second of Presley's films, *Loving You*. In a lengthy stage show sequence at the end of the picture there's at least some live show excitement. During the song 'Got A Lot Of Living To Do,' he cuts loose in a series of the most amazing routines, knee and arm swinging in perfect sync, going through seemingly impossible hip gyrations and moving across the stage on the points of his cowboy boots. He outstrips even James Brown in superlative showmanship. Of course, it's only a recreation, the movie has obviously watered down and sanitized what must have happened at a real small town concert. The audience of extras remains obediently in their seats, and you get the impression that even Presley was being to some extent kept in check.

After Presley signed with RCA Victor and started on the path to becoming a fully fledged superstar, the documentation of his live acts, although less than satisfactory, becomes a little bit more complete. Footage of the Steve Allen and Ed Sullivan TV shows that provided him with useful stepping stones to nationwide fame is still intact, although Presley was made to tone down his presentation considerably before he was let loose on TV. A number of newsreel clips have also survived. One of these, of Elvis performing 'Heartbreak Hotel' at an open air concert, is little short of magnificent. He slides across the stage, his arms flailing like a windmill and his knee going through wide swinging rotations in time with the beat. Although the photography is patchy and the sound less than a joke, it gives a tantalizing glimpse of the power of the man when he was at his youthful peak.

As his popularity rose to greater and greater heights, the controversy that surrounded Presley puffed itself up at the same speed as his income and record sales. It grew beyond the simple physical danger of a few pimply JDs wanting to rough him up.

News commentators, syndicate columnists, Bible thumping preachers, bush league sociologists and pop psychiatrists all discovered that knocking Elvis Presley was a cheap and painless way of racking up points with the mums and dads of middle America.

The stream of invective more than equaled the vilification that greeted the Stones when they first attracted media attention. He was attributed with almost single-handedly inventing juvenile delinquency. He was accused of leading civilization back to the jungle with voodoo rhythms. Some of the most extreme fundamentalists saw him as an agent of the devil.

A gas station owner in Texas (Elvis seems to have had particular trouble with gas station people) offered to smash a Presley record with every purchase of five gallons or more. A Massachusetts District Attorney, Garret Byrne, told an eager press: "Rock'n'roll gives young hoodlums a chance to get together. It inflames teenagers and is obscenely suggestive." The *New York Daily Times* went even further. It demanded a crack down on riotous rock'n'roll, describing the music as a "Barrage of primitive jungle beats set to lyrics which few adults would care to hear." The answer, it went on, was to ban all teenagers from dancing in public without the written consent of their parents and a midnight curfew for anyone under twenty-one. A shame to say, but even *NME* got dragged into the act—in the issue of October 5, 1956. From New York, the paper schlepped up a psychologist called Dr. Ben Walstein who attempted to explain why rock drove kids apeshit. After listening carefully to 'Blue Suede Shoes,' he opined: "The first impression I get from this has to do with this business of 'don't step on my blue suede shoes'... don't hurt me... allow me to have a sense of independence. I think also there is some sexual component in this in that one might say that the blue suede shoes represent something that has not been tried by the adolescent. There is certainly an anti-formalism in Presley's work, a mood of rebellion."

Heavy stuff, huh?

Time magazine was surprisingly kind. "Without preamble, the three-piece band cuts loose. In the spotlight, the lanky singer flails furious rhythms on his guitar. In a pivoting stance his hips swing sensuously from side to side and his entire body takes on a frantic quiver, as if he had swallowed a jack-hammer." It was the *New York Journal American* that really put the boot in. "Elvis Presley wiggled and wriggled with such abdominal gyrations that burlesque bombshell Georgina Southern [a big league stripper of the time] really deserves equal time to reply in a gyrating kind. He can't sing a lick, and makes up for vocal shortcomings with the weirdest and most plainly planned suggestive animation short of an aborigine's mating dance."

Just so their parents' paranoid fear wouldn't be totally without foundation, the kids went out and obligingly staged a few real-life atrocities of their own. In Jacksonville, Florida, they tore the clothes off Presley's back; in Wichita Falls, Texas, they took his Cadillac apart; in Fort Worth the local maidens carved his name into their flesh with penknives. In San Jose, California, teenagers routed the local police department, injuring eleven cops. There was another riot in sedate Boston, at the Massachusetts Institute of Technology. Probably strangest of all, in Asbury Park, New Jersey (now who the hell is it comes from Asbury Park, New Jersey?), twenty-five "vibrating teenagers" were hospitalized following a record hop. Yes, gentle reader, as they said in the *NME* of June 15, 1956, it was "Presleymania." (Even then you could read it here first.)

It would be an understatement to say that this kind of two-way hysteria must have had a profound effect on Presley's personality. It would probably be about as profound as being run down by Apollo 7. If his subsequent behavior is anything to go by, the two things that must have loomed large in his consciousness were that he must erect an impenetrable barrier between himself and his maniac fans, and that those same fans were so maniacal that it was pointless to take vast amounts of trouble creating quality product when they'd scarf up just about any crap he cared to dish out. In 1956, this second idea may have been pretty vestigial. A few years still had to pass before it became the sad hallmark of most of his work.

The first one, however, was a living reality. Elvis had to be guarded day and night if he was to remain in one piece. It's no exaggeration to say that some of his fans were crazy enough to tear him limb from limb and keep the bits as souvenirs.

Other performers, too, were kept at a distance. Squeaky clean Pat Boone tells the story of how they were double billed on a rock spectacular, he had looked forward to a dressing room heart-to-heart with this rock'n'roll phenomenon. When Presley finally arrived at the auditorium Boone realized that no cozy chats were going to be possible. Presley was constantly surrounded by a large team of sinister looking, and possibly armed, bodyguards.

Already in 1956, he was on the way to that life sentence in maximum security palaces. Elvis Presley's isolation from what we've come to call "the street" was total. He was far more cut off than either the Beatles or the Stones or even Dylan ever were. Presley was a rock'n'roll prince completely on his own. Back in the fifties there were no elite watering places. No Ad Lib's, Speakeasy's, Max's or Ashley's where stars could pass the time with other rock aristos. Indeed, there were no other rock aristos. If he wanted to relax it was a matter of renting a cinema or amusement park after the common punters had gone home and filling it with vetted chicks and professional payroll buddies.

It's a matter of debate whether the isolation of Elvis was the way the Colonel planned it or simply a set of cumulative circumstances that he exploited. Colonel Tom Parker, always a strange hybrid of W. C. Fields and Machiavelli, certainly seems to have been responsible for shutting down all his boy's cultural inputs and by the time Elvis went into the Army, they were virtually at zero. The Memphis Mafia was already in embryonic action, and few people got past Cousin Eugene and the other good ol' boys who copped a weekly wage for keeping Elvis amused.

No artist can survive without some kind of line to the outside world. Without it, artists stagnate and wilt into a welter of purposeless repetition. This was exactly what happened to Elvis Presley. His information from the outside world became totally filtered by Colonel Tom and the Memphis Mafia. His faith in Parker was absolutely implicit. After all, hadn't the Colonel turned him into one of the greatest superstars in history?

Tom Parker, a huckster to the core, took the attitude throughout Presley's career that if the bucks came rolling in for inferior product, then why bust a gut making a contribution to culture? You sometimes get the impression that the Colonel was another one who reached for his gun when he heard the word culture. This was, after all, the man who, even when Presley was a huge star, still liked to strap on a change apron and get out among the crowds and hawk souvenirs or programs. His attitude may have made Presley a multimillionaire, but it deprived the twentieth century of one of its greatest white blues singers.

When Elvis came out of the Army he moved into an impenetrable cocoon. He also seemed to stop thinking. In his private world he gave the impression that his ambitions went no further than a constant stream of expensive toys. As long as the go-karts, girls, guns, Cadillacs and color TVs kept coming, Elvis looked as though he was happy. Certainly his work declined. The Presley operation took the attitude that anything would do as long as it had the Presley mark of authenticity on it. It was as though Rembrandt had started knocking out quick scenic views because all it took was the signature to get the bucks. His method of working became grossly simple. When a new song was being considered, a Presley imitator was hired to work out the vocal part. This would be played to Presley who, unless he felt exceptionally inspired, would merely copy what he heard. It was a ghastly contrast to the pains he took over 'Heartbreak Hotel' or 'Hound Dog.' (He did thirty takes of the latter before he was satisfied he had it right).

The young Phil Spector worked on demos of Leiber and Stoller songs for Presley. He gives a frightening insight into Elvis' post-army recordings.

"Songwriters would come to me and say, 'You make the demo for us, get a good drum sound, get a guitar sound, get a kid that really sounds like him, y'know?' There was a kid named David Hill who used to do lot of Elvis' demos. Brian Hyland was another and P.J. Proby. A lot… I forget their names. People you'd call in, say 'sing like Elvis Presley,' and they'd do it. Then you stood a much better chance of getting Elvis to record it, because he always followed the demonstration records. If there was a lick or a riff that appealed to him, he wanted it in the record. In fact, many times he would use the demonstration track that was used in New York, and just sing over it. And that was released as the new Elvis Presley single. Far out, right?"

Immediately after Elvis came out of the army, he went into the studio. Although it only took twelve hours to record, *Elvis Is Back* must qualify as one of his best albums.

His version of Lowell Fulson's classic 'Reconsider Baby' proved beyond doubt his awesome power when he got down and actually sang the blues. The track also gave tenor player Boots Randolph a chance to lay down one of the great rock'n'roll brass solos of all time. Tragically, 'Reconsider Baby' was a fleeting swansong. After that the stream of musical porridge began. Now and then something would surface, 'Put The Blame On Me,' 'Burning Love,' parts of his TV spectacular, snatches of live Vegas shows, as tantalizing glimpses of what might have been.

At forty, it's probably too late for Elvis to turn back to his roots and stop the slide down to becoming a portly curio. Let's face it, he's now been rich for longer than he was ever poor. The rich don't take to change gladly. I fear all we have left of Elvis Presley are the old records and a lot of speculation about what might have been and why.

Speculation can go on all night. The only person who can tell us the truth about Elvis Presley is Elvis Presley, and you know he don't talk.

New Musical Express, May 1976

THE KING IS EATING HIMSELF TO DEATH

AT A TIME WHEN VERNON PRESLEY IS TELLING everyone that after twenty years, his son Elvis is seriously considering saying "Yes To England," Presley's army of private physicians are issuing conflicting statements which, at one end of the spectrum, state that the singer is suffering from "fatigue," while others suggest that they are fighting for his sight, his intestines and his future as an entertainer.

The last time Elvis Presley said "Yes To England" was in

❏ No one was talking about drugs, but something was plainly and radically wrong with Elvis Presley. The popular explanation was that he was chronically overeating and, without too much comfort, I joined in the guessing game. Talk of his pill habit was rife, but, in print, it had to remain strictly between the lines.

1960. He didn't keep his promise. In fact, most statements issued on Presley's behalf aren't worth the paper they're written on, and reports of the current state of his health are considered highly suspect.

Physically, Presley started to hit the skids after the break-up of his "ideal" marriage to Priscilla. According to reliable sources, he couldn't find solace in the rapid procession of pneumatic models and actresses that passed through the gates of his LA and Memphis mansions. After narrowly avoiding a complete breakdown Presley turned to gluttony—consuming up to eight cheeseburgers at one sitting. Elvis has always displayed an enormous appetite for calorie-rich snack foods. Throughout his career, he'd constantly battled a bulging waistline due to his predilection for guzzling dozens of cokes and such oddities as burnt bacon, peanut butter, and banana sandwiches. The first indications that all was far from well with Presley became known at the end of last year when press reports of his US tour of Hilton Hotels described him as "paranoid, paunchy, worn out, and barely able to move." Presley began living in isolation surrounded by a cordon of armed security guards. He appeared to be psychotically terrified of either an assassination or kidnap attempt. He took this to almost Howard Hughes extremes by employing a food-taster.

Onstage, his bloated double-chinned persona resulted in booing from the audience and what the press insisted was a series of the worst concerts Presley had ever performed. Then, four weeks ago, Presley's career sank to an all-time low when just four days into his umpteenth Las Vegas stint, he cancelled his engagement and entered the Baptist Memorial Hospital in Memphis. Doctors were quick to crush rumors that Presley was suffering from cancer, although a three-week confinement to a closed hospital room, with sheets of metal foil stuck over the windows to exclude all light, would indicate something more serious than the official "exhaustion" communiqué. Get well calls from Richard Nixon again suggested Presley's condition was more than fatigue, and cause for some concern.

One possible explanation comes from US gossip tab-

MICK FARREN

loid the *National Star*, that insists our hero is in fact suffering from "glaucoma," a disorder that causes excess fluid pressure inside the eyeballs and which can result in permanent blindness. Another set of disturbing facts emerges on examination of Elvis Presley's family background. His mother's death on August 14, 1958, from a heart-attack was indirectly caused by a similar fast-food obsession to that of her son. At the time of her premature death a friend of the family claimed "She was a half-a-dozen-eggs-and-a-stick-of-butter woman. She wanted to look good for Elvis, to be thin and attractive, but she stayed heavy and began to put on more weight. So she began to take diet pills. I guess they became a habit and then she switched to alcohol.

"It was sad. Sometimes she couldn't even see across the room. She didn't even recognize me once, couldn't even see I was standing in the room with her. She kept on taking those pills and drinking and finally her big old heart gave out." This eye-witness account suggests a definite correlation between the medical problems of mother and son. Most statements concerning Presley's current state of health make constant references to his poor diet and resulting obesity. Rumor and gossip also indicate that his latest flame, twenty-two-year-old blonde Sheila Ryan, has a habit of refueling him with plates of high-starch pasta, and despite sporadic attempts at crash-diets, it would appear, at the age of forty, Elvis Presley is no longer confronted with the simple danger of degenerating into the Orson Welles of Rock. The concern now is whether the King Of Rock'n'roll is eating himself into an early grave.

New Musical Express, September 1975 (with Roy Carr)

NOBODY EVER SAID NO TO ELVIS

REACTIONS TO THE NEWS THAT ELVIS PRESLEY DIED from a drug overdose vary according to where you stand. The hard core fan turns away in horror from the idea that their idol was anything but pristine pure, but the news ❏ The stories of Elvis' decline were hardly literature, but they did chronicle the decline and fall of an idol/

icon whose unique level of fame proved just too overwhelming to survive. Eventually, the mainstream media went public with what the drug culture had solidly believed for years.

came as no surprise to the drug culture. To be Elvis Presley, in your late forties, you not only had to be taking something, you had to be taking one hell of a lot of it. The speculation had been going on ever since Presley's death. It was ironic that it took America's ABC-TV-network to confirm the rumors. The one question that neither side bothered to ask is why anyone should be interested.

Well, it's the nature of stardom. The public is fascinated by the minutest detail of a star's life, and a star's death is far from being a minute detail. Certainly, this is the principle ABC worked on last Thursday night. With the dogged drama of a Woodward/Bernstein spectacular, investigative reporter, Geraldo Rivera, laid out the results of a year long investigation into Presley's death. Using emotive words like "cover-up" and even "murder," Rivera presented the evidence of Presley's massive pill habit. Flashed up on the screen were details of the man's giant cocktails of speed and downers. On the evidence the surprise wasn't that Presley had died, but that he had lived as long as he did. Key testimony came from Presley's step-brother, David Stanley, employed at the Presley mansion. "I saw Elvis using drugs, daily. If he didn't get them he'd become extremely upset. One time, in LA this doctor wanted to shut him off. Elvis got mad and pulled out a .45. He started threatening to go out and rob a drug store. After that the doctor didn't try anymore."

On the night of his death Stanley's brother, Mickey, also employed at the Memphis mansion, took Presley two packages of "medication." Between them they contained something in the region of sixteen pills, a mixture of Quaaludes, Valium and assorted barbiturates. Despite having taken enough downers to poleaxe a horse, Presley still couldn't sleep. Eventually, according to live-in girlfriend of the time Ginger Alden, Presley vanished into the bathroom. Alden went back to sleep. A few hours later she found him dead on the bathroom floor rapidly turning blue. Nobody disputes these facts. According to the ABC investigation team this was the point when the cover-up came into operation. The implication made by ABC is that the Memphis Mafia and Shelby County Tennessee Health

MICK FARREN

Officials conspired to conceal the fact that Elvis had OD'd. Their motive seemed to be that, if the Presley image was tarnished by the truth about his drug habits, it would not only be worldwide disaster, but could also hurt Memphis' lucrative, Elvis-based, tourist trade.

The heart attack story was first given out by County Medical Examiner, Jerry Fransisco and universally accepted until ABC started digging. With the urgency and drama typical of a US news show, Rivera and his team delivered the shock-horror facts with rapid fire delivery. All notes, reports, and photographs of the autopsy and death scene are missing. The contents of Presley's stomach were pumped out and destroyed without any attempt to analyze them. Dr. Eric Muirhead, Chief of Pathology at the Baptist Hospital in Memphis, attributes Elvis' death to combinations of "uppers, downers and pain killing drugs." Another physician present at the autopsy, Dr. Noel Floredo, said that Presley "most probably died of an interaction of several drugs." None of the seven other doctors present at the autopsy has ever agreed with Fransisco's conclusion that Presley died of a heart attack.

In ABC's opinion, resident Dr. Feelgood at the Presley court, George (Dr. Nick) Nichopolous was the real major villain. Between January and August 1977, Dr. Nick had presented some 5,300 assorted pills to Presley. These included amphetamines, Quaaludes, tuinol, Nembutal, codeine, Phenobarbital and even dilaudid, normally reserved for stone junkies and terminal cancer patients.

Authorities in Tennessee reacted swiftly to ABC's revelations. Memphis D.A. Hugh Stanton ordered an immediate criminal investigation. Police Chief Winslow Chapman placed Nichopolous under twenty-four hour police protection "for his own safety." It appears that fans had already started labeling Dr. Nick "the man who killed Elvis." Others also decided to get on the act. Ginger Alden, repeated her claims that she had been Elvis' secret fiancée, while ex-bodyguard Red West, coauthor of the book *Elvis: What Happened?*, which first blew the whistle on Presley's marathon pill popping, declared publicly that he felt vindicated.

What nobody seems to have bothered ever to question is why Elvis consumed narcotics in such horrendous quantities? The closest to an answer comes in a statement from David Stanley. "Nobody ever said no to Elvis Presley."

New Musical Express, September 1979

HOW LONG SHALL WE MOURN FOR CAMELOT?

❑ We may think, as John Lennon put it in the song 'Working Class Hero,' that we're so clever and classless and free, but—aside from still being "fucking peasants"—we seem to have an atavistic need to seek icons of power and fertility. Elvis Presley was one of these. Perhaps also Marilyn Monroe, and definitely John Fitzgerald Kennedy.

NOVEMBER 22, 1993, IS THE THIRTIETH ANNIVERSARY OF the assassination of John Fitzgerald Kennedy and the third decade of an almost unprecedented world obsession. The memory of JFK and the globally shared shock of his murder refuses to dim or diminish, or show any signs of settling into the comfortable distance of history. Our fallen king remains a continuous fountainhead of obsessive fascination and conspiracy theorizing has been elevated to the level of a multimedia art form. He makes profits for movie studios, moves books for Random House, and provides hard copy for *A Current Affair.* The Zapruder film rolls yet again, and the black riderless horse follows the caisson, clearly indicating that a generation is still unwilling to face the fact that we may go to our own deaths frustrated, never having learned the truth behind the most traumatic event of our lives.

In the past, I've done my share of conspiracy buffing, but I feel that this thirty-year mark has to be the moment to come out and admit that I no longer care who killed the president. I will always know in my gut that Lee Oswald was never, in a million years, the lone-nut gunman, and that Jack Ruby, in an equal timespan, was never the lone-nut avenger. I suspect that this is something I share with a majority of marginally rational people. I even have a personal favorite on the menu of conspiracy scenarios (entropy and chaos as laid out in Don DeLillo's novel *Libra*—but I suspect I favor it more because it reinforces my own warped perceptions than because I actually believe it).

What I can no longer allow myself to care about is

putting faces to the ghost gunmen on the grassy knoll or names to their shadowy paymasters. By this time, the primary conspirators and their hired triggers are either elderly or dead. I have always figured that the hit team themselves were dead by Christmas 1963. With all the witnesses that were greased, I doubt that the shooters were allowed to live. I know that, if there was a conspiracy, J. Edgar Hoover must have known, but, mercifully, Hoover is gone and the secret is buried deep in his lingerie drawer.

Oliver Stone asked us to consider who benefited, but who ultimately did benefit? Lyndon Johnson? Johnson got to be president, but he ended up nailed through the history book to a war that ripped him "like a hailstorm on a Texas highway." The military industrial complex? Sure, they made their billions, but they also suffered the humiliation of defeat at the hands of Ho Chi Minh's peasant army. Whodunit is now little more than a mental contortion. No one will ever be brought to justice. What interests me far more is the way in which America continues to build what amounts to a twentieth century Arthurian legend around the life and murder of Kennedy, regardless of whether he deserves it or not. We seem to have a real myth in the making, and it's starting to seem as though the word "Camelot" is now closer to the truth than was ever imagined by the journalist who coined it. As far as I'm concerned, this is far more worthy of fascination than the mundane question of who fired the shots. Has the world become so barren that we need to give ourselves over to the power of a golden might-have-been that never-was?

LA Reader, November 1993

THE LEGEND OF THE BOY KING

MAKING COMPARISONS BETWEEN ELVIS PRESLEY AND Jesus Christ may seem over the top to some and downright blasphemous to others—although an irreverent cartoon book titled *Elvis and Jesus*, that was published in time for

JFK left us a seeming insoluble mystery, but Elvis left us what came close to becoming a quasi-religion.

Christmas 1993, did exactly that. The fact also has to be faced that, two decades after Elvis' death, some of the most obsessive fans appear to maintain a personal relationship with their idol that is very much akin to that which born-again Christians profess to have with Jesus.

The trouble really starts when you begin to dig into these obsessions and what can only be called Elvis worship. Once one examines the psychology of Elvis fans and how they relate to the Elvis legend, it's all too easy to be carried along by a mythological drift. The legend begins to resemble an Arthurian saga, or the myths of the Fisher King that stretch clear back to the mists of prehistory. It follows a legend form that keeps occurring in the folktales of many cultures all over the world, folktales that are claimed by some academics to be the real basis for the story of Christ.

The King is born in humble circumstances. No one suspects his true nature or real destiny apart from his doting and protective mother. As the King grows to manhood, key individuals begin to recognize his potential. He travels the country, as a singer of songs and a sexual shaman, attracting huge crowds to him. He rapidly gathers a vast following. Everywhere he goes, the young flock to his banner. As the King grows in strength and influence, the land enters a Golden Age. New magic replaces the old, and new ways are replacing those that had gone before. The old rulers, however, fear and resent the power and the potency of this Boy King who has appeared out of nowhere to usurp the loyalties of the nation's youth.

The Boy King is taken by soldiers. They insist that the time has come for him to cease his singing and shamanism. The law of the land demands that he became a warrior. In a public ritual, his hair is shorn, and under the guise of his becoming a warrior, he disappears into exile to a distant outpost of the Empire. The movement that he started continues, but it is leaderless and confused. Eventually the King returns to the land, but this is not the Boy King of the Golden Age. He is remote and distant, constantly surrounded by courtiers, flatterers, and sinister henchmen. His magic is diluted and seems to be fading. He never appears to his people in the flesh, and the only tangible proof that he continues to live at all are flickering images in dark places. The land falls upon evil times. Violence, revolution, and foreign war cast their shadows. Young and old are thrown against the other in angry conflict, but still the King doesn't return to his people, who now despair that he has permanently deserted them.

And then, when all seems lost, the King, at the symbolic age of thirty-three, invokes his power. His return is seen in every part of the land by the new magic. He is re-energized. For the first time in ten years, he comes among his people. Suddenly there is hope. Again, though, the courtiers and flatterers surround the King. Isolated in his palace, he succumbs to solitary luxury. Lonely and alone, among servants and concubines, he dies. With his death, however, he transcends mere mortality, and, miraculously, his power is returned to the people where it has always belonged. The people use his memory, his image, and his music to invoke that power. The King incarnate may be gone, but the King transcendental becomes immortal.

Yeah, I know what you're going to say. The writer has finally taken leave of his sanity. And yet, this is what you'd get if the story of Elvis had been handed down by an oral tradition rather than TV biographies and the works of Albert Goldman. Religions have been founded on a whole lot less. Could this be the secret of Elvis? That he was much more than just an entertainer, that he triggered something ancient and atavistic in some modern collective consciousness? Or have we just taken ourselves out to the ludicrous edge of fantasy? The Elvis Universe is one tricky cosmic neighborhood.

From the book *The Hitchhiker's Guide To Elvis*, 1994

THIS IS THE MAN WHO RECORDED 'THE LAUGHING GNOME'

☐ Few—if any—had the voice, some may have had the looks, none could lay claim to the iconic potential but still they wanted to be famous; to scratch their mark on infinity. And with Elvis dead and gone the mechanics of fame fundamentally changed. Fame came to those who understood the mechanics and one positive and undeniable sensei of those mechanics was David Bowie, who learned the knack of moving with the popular tide. He would chameleon-out of one personality and into another in a manner that was oddly reptilian. This analysis was written as Bowie was emerging from his sharp-suit, 'Let's Dance' incarnation.

IT'S NOT WITHOUT A CERTAIN IRONY THAT WE FIND ourselves sliding into 1984 with David Bowie the biggest thing in pop this side of Michael Jackson. It's not just that Bowie has survived to experience a date he once sang about. His current dazzling success tends to defy common wisdom about popular culture. Bowie's been in this game for close to twenty years. He is well past the age when Mick Jagger was first called a boring old has-been. His radical changes of style would have totally alienated the fans of most other artists. Yet you hear few unkind words about David Bowie. He is one of the few pop stars even the most vitriolic icon-busting critics seem unwilling to attack—either as man or legend. Jim Morrison is one of few others who enjoy such a hands-off situation, and Morrison has been securely dead for over a dozen years. Bowie, however, remains quite visible, hopping from one foot to the other continuing a career.

Don't get me wrong, I am not a Bowie hater. (I already feel some of you reaching for your poison pens or worse.) I have huge reserves of admiration for David Bowie, both as an entertainer and a technician. He is without doubt one of the most consistently bright and innovative rock practitioners—and, unlike virtually any of his rivals, he has managed to parlay pop stardom into a credible career as an actor. The trouble I experience with Bowie? Whenever he comes under discussion and the folks around the bar start to get rapturous, a still, small voice pipes up in the back of my mind to remind me:

This is the man who recorded 'The Laughing Gnome.'

There are a number of moments like this in Bowie's career. Together, they make me less than secure about his ambitions and motivations. Of course, everybody makes mistakes. With Bowie, it's the *quality* of his mistakes that gives pause.

For example, let's go back to the very start, when he'd just ceased to be David Jones: One minute he wanted to be

Keith Relf, the next, Anthony Newley. *Anthony Newley?* What lurked in the psyche of the young David that wanted to be Anthony Newley?

Not just the young David, either. A few weeks ago I saw Newley himself on the *Tonight* show. He was promoting some dumb musical he's written based on the life of Charlie Chaplin. He sang. It was the first time I'd witnessed this not terribly attractive business in many years. I'd pretty much forgotten what he sounded like. It was chilling. Bowie still has that delivery. Through all these years, and all the way to Mars and back, Bowie still carries the Newley legacy.

I had misgivings when I first heard about the Ziggy Stardust concept. Bowie was clearly very eager to succeed, and there was nothing wrong with the music, but so much of the story seemed to have been a mélange of H.P. Lovecraft and Robert Heinlein's *Stranger in a Strange Land.* I was certain someone would call him out for plagiarism.

Nobody did. Ziggy drove the youth of the world bananas (and would-be bisexual). Since then, many have felt they owed Bowie a debt of gratitude for starting the first craze they could remember that had absolutely nothing to do with the sixties.

What made Ziggy run? Aspects of Bowie's behavior could be explained only by an overwhelming desire for public acceptance. Far from having a burning desire to say something, he seemed willing, particularly in the early stages of his career, to say anything if he thought that was what the crowd wanted to hear. I started to think that maybe his major talents were the abilities to borrow and synthesize; he could also predict, at times with uncanny accuracy, the moods and needs of his audience. He was more like a shrewd politician than a driven artist.

As with many shrewd politicians, it's hard to tell exactly what Bowie's politics—beliefs, if you like—actually are. His songs are clever but always oblique. It was never clear which goon squad was coming to town, and whether Bowie stood for or against them. I recall him making an overtly political statement only once. During a bout of what was reputed to be cocaine psychosis, Bowie announced that Britain would do well to become a fascist dictatorship, with himself in the Hitler role. Apologists pointed out that this was a naïve and addled statement made by someone attracted by the trappings and charisma of fascism, but who was definitely not a death camp enthusiast. I didn't buy it. As far as I was concerned, it was one of the man's most dubious statements. That everybody else forgave and forgot filled me with total amazement. Bob Dylan deep-sixed his career by becoming a born-again Christian; when Bowie announced he'd like to be a Nazi, everyone was extremely understanding.

The most popular aid to understanding David Bowie has always been the celebrated reptile theory: At irregular intervals Bowie sheds his entire creative personality to reveal a new one formed beneath the old. I can't quite come to grips with this either. The cracked actor flitting from role to role may explain Bowie the performer/interpreter, but not the creator/innovator. To be able to drop a concept or "personality" at a moment's notice indicates a shallowness of thought. This fatal trendiness may inspire my doubts about Bowie.

The shallowness, if it exists, hasn't done Bowie any harm. He is the leading white pop star, with many millions stashed in the bank (Swiss, no doubt). His current image is upright if not totally straight. In traditional superstar manner, his name appears in the gossip columns, linked with Susan Sarandon. The uncut version of the 'China Girl' video shows his current image to be decidedly heterosexual. More importantly, Bowie is making a smooth transition from pop star to movie idol—a transition that has eluded most aspiring rockers, particularly Mick Jagger. David Bowie is riding so high that his thoughts must now, at least part of the time, be focused on a place in history. He has yet to have what you'd call an enormous hit movie, and he has yet to explore the possibility of directing or anything approaching serious writing. He has conquered most other worlds. Once again, I admit my admiration for the man. But, from Anthony Newley on, I still have all these unanswered questions. There are more. Are the native Australians in the 'Let's Dance' video objects of compassion, social comment or just Pacific chic?

Far be it from me to trigger a Bowie backlash. I don't need the hate mail. Let's just say that the hottest item of 1984 is a mass of questions that haven't been answered satisfactorily for two decades. That must say something about the times in which we live.

Trouser Press, 1984

THE GOSPEL ACCORDING TO J.C.

IF I'D NEVER HEARD OF JOHNNY CASH AND SOMEONE came up and described him to me, I can't think of any other entertainer, short of Bob Hope maybe, who on the surface would seem more likely to alienate me. He is a personal friend of Billy Graham. He embraces the conservative values of marriage, home, and family. He sings duets with his wife while holding hands. He is, on his own admission, a reformed speedfreak and drunk who let "Jesus come into his heart" and turned his back on the wild life.

So far, so tacky.

And this, dearly beloved, is the problem. Despite all his beliefs you just can't help liking Johnny Cash. Also, within his obvious limitations, there's no way you can fault his music. I have to admit that I went to meet Johnny Cash with some degree of trepidation. What was a godless dope-fiend doing in a one-on-one situation with the most upright of country music superstars? Being a friend of Billy Graham put Cash only a shot away from Richard Nixon. After all, wasn't it Billy Graham who used to call Nixon every morning with spiritual advice? What was I DOING, keeping this kind of company?

It was hard to know what to expect from Cash. An arrogant bigoted redneck turned holier than thou after his conversion? A cynical Elmer Gantry with diamond rings and a smooth line of Jesus patter? Maybe even a human

❑ Johnny Cash was old school. His fame was earned the hard way. His work was respected, his audience was loyal, his image was an image but not a façade, and his passing would be mourned. He may also have been the last of a breed.

wreck propped up by a slick management and efficient organization?

As it turned out, Johnny Cash was none of these things. If you want to talk to Johnny Cash you have to, for a start, dovetail totally into the Carter-Cash routine. On a Johnny Cash tour there are no afternoons spent lolling around expensive hotel suits, calling room service for more brandy, and producing a flow of one-liners for a grateful press. Cash does two shows a night, and the only time he allows for interviews is actually between shows. Thus both the number of interviews and the duration of the interviews granted are severely curtailed. Cash also likes to eat dinner in the interval between shows. That makes the time really tight. Things were made even tighter on this particular evening by a bomb scare. About twenty minutes into the first performance, just around the time the Carter Sisters were doing their gospel routine, a phoned warning came through to the Palladium.

London theaters seem, by now, to be geared up for this kind of panic. The theater was cleared in a bare three and a half minutes, searched, pronounced clean, and the audience re-admitted. So slight was the confusion that the stage doorkeeper took time out to answer a call from Lonnie Donegan who, apparently an old friend of Cash's and anxious to come and see him, was surprised to get no answer from the theater manager's office. Needless to say, this did somewhat disrupt even the Carter-Cash schedule. John's and June's four-year-old John Carter Cash was dispatched back to the Savoy out of the way of possible harm, and then the show resumed where it left off.

The appointed time for discussion found photographer Pennie Smith, CBS liaison lady Julia and myself cooling our heels in one of the labyrinth of Palladium backstage corridors. The show echoed from the stage at least three songs from the end. Interview time was rapidly dwindling. Finally the show was over. Cash came fast and purposefully from the stage. This was the first time I had seen him close to. At least one part of the legend was true. Cash is nothing if not rugged. He's a good 6 ft 3 in, slightly running to fat, but still weather-beaten and with shoulders as wide as a barn. He also has the air of a consummate professional. He goes straight through a gaggle of hand shakers, time wasters, and autograph hunters around the stage door. He doesn't ignore or avoid them. He doesn't even see them. His objective is the dressing room and nothing deflects him.

While we are waiting for Cash to finish dinner, call his son at the hotel and grab a breath of fresh air, I get a chance to talk to his manager, Alan Tinkley. He is an urbane, friendly individual with a slight stoop. He has obviously long since transcended the strain of being a big time country manager. He takes everything in his stride. He has also transcended the gruesome flamboyance of so many of the top Nashville executives.

Time is getting short, and I take the chance to check a few facts with Tinkley before going in to see Cash. After sorting out the complex genealogy of the Carter family, I tentatively ask Tinkley what subjects are liable to draw Cash out.

"John doesn't like to get involved in political or religious arguments."

So what does he like to talk about?

"His main interests are his music, his performing and his family."

At this point Cash himself emerges from the dressing room and signals that he's ready for the interview. We all troop inside.

The Palladium dressing room is hardly an environment in which you'd expect to meet Johnny Cash. Six days a week, it's used for Tommy Steele's *Hans Christian Anderson* show, and is cluttered with the kind of odds and ends that actors trend to accumulate during a long running show. Cash was dressed in his usual black. None of the gaudy Nudie suits for him. His only jewellery was a narrow Indian Turquoise necklace. The most surprising thing was that Cash seemed to be nervous. All the time we talked his hands moved in front of him, continuously linking and unlinking his fingers. It's possible that part of his tension was due to the small speaker on the dressing room wall. It burbled a constant stream of muted country music. At first I assumed it was a radio, but then it became clear that it was relaying the opening of the show from the stage.

I asked Cash if the bomb scare had shaken him up. He shook his head. "No, I think we've been through maybe eight or nine bomb scares over the years."

This was the familiar Johnny Cash, the man who'd done and seen almost everything. His fingers, however, still kept intertwining.

The most obvious question was about his self-proclaimed Christianity, and his publicized conversion. Cash listened politely and then looked directly at me.

"I wasn't actually converted to Christianity. I've been a Christian since I was twelve-years-old. It was as much a part of me as my music. Over the years it kind of lapsed. Then eight years ago I invited Jesus into my life. It changed my whole way of life. I cleaned up, stopped taking pills and drinking."

Prior to the interview Alan Tinkley had taken some pains to explain that Cash had never been a drug addict, in terms of that he'd never messed around with heroin or any other of the morphine derivatives.

"So your religion is a very personal thing?"

Cash nodded. I reminded him that the last time we had seen him in London had been at a Billy Graham rally at Wembley Stadium. I wondered if he still went in for this kind of evangelism.

"I've never been an evangelist. I'm an entertainer and musician. Billy Graham is a personal friend. He asked me to play at the rally and I agreed."

I got the vague impression that neither Cash nor Tinkley were too keen on the host of Festival of Light cleanup fanatics who attached themselves to the rally. The problem of Billy Graham still remained, however. There was nothing to do but come straight out with it.

"I've always been rather dubious of Billy Graham, particularly after his seemingly close association with the Nixon administration."

I'd half expected Cash to get uptight at this question,

but he accepted it with the same courteous, gentlemanly manner. "I know Billy Graham very well. His only purpose in this world is to preach. He started giving spiritual counsel to the president..."—a faint emphasis on the word 'president' seemed to separate the man from the office— "... in 1970. As far as I know that was his only connection with Nixon."

The implication seemed to be that if Nixon didn't heed that spiritual advice that was his own problem. John Cash refused to be drawn any further. We moved on to the confessions that had appeared in various papers which read as though Cash was turning his back on most of his past image.

"The original story appeared in the *Wall Street Journal*. I think when it got to the European papers there were a few... ah, translation problems. I think they were confused about what people like to identify within my songs and what really happened to me."

You were never in prison?

"I've never served time, but I've been thrown in local jails maybe eight or nine times, you know, just overnight."

For what?

Cash grinned. "Drunkenness, disturbing the peace, the usual kind of minor things."

How about the prison concerts? Did you have no involvement in the movements for prisoners' rights?

Cash shook his head. "I've never been involved with prisoners' rights as such. In fact I haven't done a prison concert for over a year now. When I do play prison shows, and when I recorded those albums, I had to talk the language of a prison. That's an entertainer's job, to get across to his audience, whoever they are.

"I did get to know individual prisoners. They write to me, and come to see me when they get back on the outside. I do what I can, but I've never been involved in any kind of movement."

That's one of the joys of interviewing Johnny Cash. You only have to hint at the direction in which you're steering the conversation, and he gives you everything he wants you to know about the subject. There's none of the usual rock'n'roll hedging or pussy-footing round the point. Possibly a contributory factor was the wall speaker, a constant reminder that the show was well under way on stage. It was time for another switch in direction.

Early in your career you worked with Elvis on Sun package tours.

Cash nodded and glanced at the time. "Most of that's covered in my book."

In fact his period of doing Sun package tours is only covered briefly in his book *Man In Black*. The main story about that time concerns the Sun million dollar quartet (Jerry Lee Lewis, Carl Perkins, Presley, and Cash) singing hymns round the piano. The book was written after Cash's conversion. Accounts from other sources tell of drunkenness and amphetamine mania on those early tours where beat-up '53 Chevys covered literally thousands of miles a week, hauling the gear in a trailer.

Had Cash seen anything of Presley in recent years?

"No, I kinda lost touch with him after he signed with (RCA) Victor."

How about Bob Dylan?

"I haven't seen him in maybe three years. The last time we met was in New York, when June and I had dinner with him and Sara."

One of the problems with interviewing Johnny Cash is his almost total unwillingness to go into his past life in any depth. This only becomes comprehensible when you realize that in 1966 he was consuming some forty or so pills a day, washed down with considerable amounts of booze. Whatever you may think of his conversion, it is certain that it saved his life. This gives a very solid perspective on his religion.

The other difficulty in any Cash interview is his reluctance to become overly enthusiastic about anything. It's the reverse side of the polite gentlemanly manner. He doesn't really wax enthusiastic even about his music. *John R. Cash*, which received some degree of critical acclaim, was dismissed out of hand.

"I didn't like the way it was recorded."

How was it recorded?

"We put the basic tracks down in Nashville, and then it was taken off to LA for the overdubbing. I don't like to work that way."

You prefer something simpler?

"That's right."

How about the new *Riding the Rails* album?"

"I didn't know that had even been done until I got here. It's mostly old material."

So what are you working on now?

Cash grinned. "You should hear the next album. It's called *Look at Them Beans!*"

A thematic album?

Cash laughed. "No, that's the title track."

At that point he suddenly glanced up at the speaker. He'd heard his cue.

"I have to go."

New Musical Express, October 1975

B-O-B

It's almost an impossible opening sentence.

There can't be anyone reading this who needs to be introduced to this record. It is certainly Bob Dylan's finest hour, and there are less than a handful of other works that can seriously challenge it for the title of the greatest rock album of all time. (And it was also, of course, the first serious rock music double-album.)

Shortly after the idea of this project came up, a bunch of us were sitting in the pub. All kinds of ideas were thrown about. Pieces of information were laid out on the table. Theories flowed almost as fast as the beer.

Did anyone know that the mono mix was appreciably different? Did Dylan sit up nights in the Chelsea Hotel writing the songs, or was the rumor true that he cobbled it together right there in the CBS studios in Nashville?

❑ In the normal run of events, an artist's work is reviewed at the time it's first released to the public. That's the most base and basic function of the critic. He or she offers the consumer a subjective preview of what to expect from a new book, play, film, record, or what have you. For a work to be revisited down the passage of time and subjected to a critical after-the-fact evaluation of

ELVIS DIED FOR SOMEBODY'S SINS BUT NOT MINE 253

its impact on a genre, a culture, or even a society is not only a rare occurrence but something reserved for important creations. In this instance, it was also Christmas and—with a shortage of hard copy and magazine pages to fill—we writers were offered the chance to return to our choice of outstanding albums and take another look. Thus, amid the 1976 Yuletide booze, and with punk screeching and hollering all around me, I was able to ponder a second time what Bob Dylan might have been up to when he'd recorded **Blonde On Blonde** ten years earlier.

What was the man's drug consumption at the time?

The speculation and the technical secrets only led to one single ultimate question.

Where was Bob Dylan's head at when he put down these tracks?

We all know now that that is the question, and we also know it just isn't going to be answered.

For ten years there have been books, articles, pamphlets, mimeographed broadsheets, wall graffiti and a million conversations worrying at the question like terriers round a rat.

One of the main problems about approaching *Blonde On Blonde* after all this time is the temptation to take the whole thing far too reverently.

It's become entwined with the experience of so many of us, all the trips, the jagged late nights, the girls, the friends, that it's almost impossible to separate the music from the decade of one's own stacked-up responses.

The only profit that could possibly come from the whole exercise would be to pin down what the initial impact was.

I looked up some of the contemporary reviews and comments. There was a lot of verbiage about "a contemporary poet," how Dylan "knew," how he was "telling it like it is."

The one thing they said nothing about was the music.

This kind of loose talk still goes on today. (Of course, the clichés are new.) It comes trippingly from the pen. Shit, I've done it myself, more times than I care to remember.

If Dylan was really "telling it like it is", we'd all know exactly what he was talking about. We wouldn't have been sifting through his symbolism, the rare interviews and even his garbage in the vain attempt to find his particular Rosebud. If we all knew, there wouldn't be any Michael Gray or A. J. Weberman, and everyone could put a precise definition on "The ladies treat me kindly / and furnish me with tape."

So, if it's not the language that grabs you, maybe it's just the sound that gets you.

Could it be that *Blonde On Blonde* was one of those

MICK FARREN

records like 'Heartbreak Hotel,' 'Cathy's Clown' or 'Tracks Of My Tears' that bypassed the mind and got directly to the hairs on the back of your neck?

Well, Kooper's organ was oft copied, and the combination of guitars, harmonica and keyboard had a definite impact. In things like 'One Of Us Must Know' the ponderously, ascending cathedral chords do, at times, grab me by the gut in non-verbal uplift.

So, for that matter, do some deodorant commercials. If all of Dylan was in his voice and sound, we'd be treating *Self Portrait* with the same reverence.

It ain't just the noise. There's a whole lot more to it than that.

When *Blonde On Blonde* came, out, a lot of us had been with Dylan for some time. It wasn't anything radical and new.

We'd been sticked and carroted progressively into it. We'd followed an observant protest singer away from the externals of society and down a corridor of increasingly unresolved movie images. They had that real dreamlike quality (as opposed to Dalí or Hollywood dream sequences) in which things understood gradually become confusing. The dream gave glimpses of heaven, right next door to the hints of nightmare.

In a way, *Blonde On Blonde* was in the pits. It was the deepest shaft rock'n'roll had ever sunk in its journey to the center of the psyche.

Either consciously or unconsciously, Dylan performed a neat trick. He gave the illusion that through the time space of the double-album, he was finally stripping down his head, turning himself inside out so that we could actually see into the mind of this individual who had been throwing up such tantalizing, familiar images.

We bought ourselves a ticket and sat down in the front row.

While we watched like geeks, the whole thing was switched on us. We weren't watching Bob Dylan's interior movie. We were seeing a series of distorting mirrors.

While trying to puzzle our way through the symbolism

we were, in fact, being led through previously uncharted, often suppressed and frequently twisted passages of our own brains.

All Dylan gave us were some complex cat's cradles, uncompromising structural diagrams of the way relationships operate.

(Although a lot of people tag Dylan as a social commentator, the great majority of his songs are about personal relationships, not those of society. This holds true for all the songs on *Blonde On Blonde*. They're love songs, if you like.)

We took these relationship sketches and busily fitted them into our own frames of reference. I guess that was where all the trouble started.

You've probably noticed how dope fiends claim Dylan's singing about dope, homosexuals tell you they're gay love songs and women know for sure that they're all about women. I even met a paranoid once who claimed that 'Sad Eyed Lady Of The Lowlands' contained the truth about the Kennedy assassination.

Everyone fits Dylan into his own framework. Why exactly I'm not sure. Certainly the operation involves a certain amount of self-perception that wasn't quite the rage.

Maybe the response to Dylan at that time, both violent hostility and psychotic adulation, was the audience attempting to come to terms with some of the things they'd stumbled across in their own minds.

So *Blonde On Blonde* was a giant therapy group?

I had a feeling when this started that it might wind up far-fetched. I really did try to keep it on the rails. But...

Anyhow, now I've come to this point we come to another version of the Big Question.

Was Dylan the therapist, Machiavelli messing with our heads or just an unwilling catalyst? As I said earlier, that's the one we don't get an answer to.

Rosebud.

Blonde On Blonde is a mnemonic for Bob.

New Musical Express, December 25, 1976

MICK FARREN

RETURN OF THE SUPERFREAK

It was about halfway through Diane Sawyer's epic TV interview with Michael Jackson and Lisa Marie Presley last week that the word *totalitarian* crept into my brain. I began to suspect I was watching a glossy, consumer capitalist version of the rehabilitation of an un-person.

The form might be diametrically opposed, but the content seemed remarkably similar to something out of Stalinist Russia where individuals could be obliterated or resurrected according to the pragmatic flow of the political tide. At the whim of the oligarchy, a hero of the revolution could be reduced to un-person status, and, overnight, all of his statues carted away and melted down for scrap. However, should it suit the needs of those in power at a later date, he or she could be returned from the Gulag and the heroic statues all replaced like they'd never been gone.

Apparently, a similar scenario ran through the mind of Michael Jackson when he devised the four-minute promotional film for his *HIStory* album to be shown in movie theaters and on MTV. It seems almost too perfect that Jackson should fantasize himself—in yet another outrageous Freedonian uniform—marching at the head of a flag-bearing, goose-stepping Red Army, as formations of gunships swoop overhead and commandos rappel down the face of the super-colossal Jackson statue, as the images required to restart his career after his life-and-death struggle with tabloid scandal.

Critics have jumped on the promo as psychotic, Hitlerian megalomania and likened it, both in image and content, to the work of Leni Riefenstahl. To me, the work seems to have a lot more in common with *Brazil*, or early-sixties British film satire like *Billy Liar* or *Morgan: A Suitable Case for Treatment* than with *Triumph of the Will*. Few seem to realize that Jackson, weird as he undoubtedly is, may also possess a creative sense of humor.

For Michael Jackson, the last few years have hardly been what you'd call funny. Through most of 1993 and 1994, the tabloid media all but stoned the poor bastard

❑ Is it possible that Johnny Cash and Michael Jackson had anything in common? Both were, of course, singers, musicians, performers, and both were respected as masters of their craft. Where they part company is that, where Cash kept his admittedly much more manageable fame under control, Jackson's surfed too long on the crest of the abyss. He was blessed and cursed with the angels and demons of both a child prodigy and an adult superstar. Jackson was undoubtedly an icon, up there with Elvis, but to say that his celebrity went off the rails was more than an exaggeration. Michael Jackson was unique. No rails had ever been laid to guide someone like him. All this was, of course written well before his arrest, and the ghastly circus of a trial, and then his lamented and lamentable death.

to death, attacking him with a pit bull ferocity and a complete lack of human responsibility. At the time. *Hard Copy*'s Diane Dimond chillingly rationalized the witch-hunt: "It was either a superstar being wrongly accused, or it was a superstar involved in a heinous crime. Either way, we couldn't lose." With such tabloid attitudes fueling the lynch mob, Jackson was vilified on five continents and even subjected to the humiliation of having his penis photographed by police to discover if it really was adorned with the legendary, but ultimately nonexistent, Winnie the Pooh tattoo.

A media savaging of this magnitude might easily have killed a lesser mortal. When Diane Sawyer, on *Prime Time Live*, asked Jackson if he'd contemplated offing himself, I could only admire the unexpected steel in his gaze when he told her it would take something stronger than mere global ridicule and contempt to kill him. Whatever you may think about the man, he's been on the hard show-business road since he was little more than a fetus, and probably does have, as he put it, "a hide like a rhinoceros," however strange its pigmentation.

I also have to admire Jackson for the possibility that he may yet beat the tabloid mind-set by exploiting its essential weakness. Tabloidism is ultimately parasitic; if a parasite is to survive and prosper it has to admit, if only internally, its own symbiosis. The tabloids need Michael Jackson more than he needs them, and if they don't realize they can ill afford to kill the freaky goose that lays the golden gossip, their perception is ultimately and fatally warped. The career of a Brett Butler or even a Julia Roberts can be firestormed. Such are expendable. A mother lode like Michael Jackson doesn't come along every day, or even every decade.

The ugly amalgam of sleaze and moral hypocrisy that is the foundation of everything tabloid waxes gung-ho when affixing scarlet letters. What happens, however, when a celebrity comes back bearing his like a badge of honor? So far, Jackson has gone along with the recanting game. He assured Sawyer that the child molestation charges were baseless, and I believe him. (Although I find myself a little irked that I should have to. Thirteen-year-old boys are hardly paragons of cherubic innocence. Underage groupies have existed in rock'n'roll since the genre was born. Stars' hetero jailbait were once the subject of unconcealed boasting. All else would seem to be pure homophobia.)

The game will obviously continue. Diane Sawyer, despite her supposed credentials as a serious investigative journalist, couldn't resist asking what, if anything, Michael and Lisa Marie do in bed together. TV credentials, though, however immaculate, cannot turn prurient curiosity into high moral need-to-know, and Lisa Marie seemed thoroughly justified in all but telling Sawyer to fuck off because it was none of her business.

Some of the tabloids have suggested that anything less than awesome sales of *HIStory* will prove that Jackson is still a public pariah. Without turning this into a record review, it's quite possible that *HIStory* is not one of the great Michael Jackson albums. I don't know. I haven't heard it. But with all the distractions he has faced, it would be understandable if his recent work wasn't his absolute best. It's also been suggested that the Jackson-Presley dynastic marriage is a mere publicity stunt. This would seem to be the ultimate absurdity. Michael Jackson and Lisa Marie Presley live a Cartesian dynamic in terms of publicity—they are, therefore they're news. They have no need of stunts.

The bottom line on Michael Jackson is that, whatever else he may be, he's certainly a stone freak. How could it be otherwise, after a lifetime in the spotlight? He has the support of Lisa Marie and Elizabeth Taylor, both of whom have known the horror of such lifelong stress. For what little it's worth, he also has mine. Possibly for no other reason than that, years ago, before radical freak bohemianism became fragmented by divisions of gender, sexual preference, and race, there was but a single maxim. We freaks protected each other against the totalitarians, tabloid or otherwise, because, sure as hell, no one else would.

LA Reader, June 1995

ZAPPA AT LAW

❑ If Frank Zappa was an icon it was only among a fairly exclusive coterie of enthusiasts. Zappa was also never really famous on the insane, paparazzi, tabloid level, but he precisely understood that fame was an illusion that could be both parodied and manipulated. Much in the manner of Andy Warhol, Zappa—especially in his early days, before he concentrated on becoming a fan-boy guitar hero—elevated a number of bizarre individuals to faux-notoriety. Where Warhol had his Factory superstars, Zappa's pantheon included the GTOs, Larry (Wild Man) Fischer, and the Plaster-casters of Chicago. But he never made that absurd fifteen minute promise.

ON MONDAY, APRIL 14, AT 10.30 IN THE MORNING Bizarre Productions began to sue the Royal Albert Hall in front of Mr. Justice Mocatta. This drama took place at the Number Seven Court of the Law Courts in the Strand. The issue was the cancellation of the Mothers Of Invention/London Philharmonic presentation of *200 Motels* originally scheduled for February 8, 1971, at the Albert Hall. For those of you who don't remember the exact details, perhaps this is the time to remind you. The Zappa concert was planned as a kind of gala two-pronged promotion, intended to boost both the movie of *200 Motels* and the Mothers' subsequent UK tour. At the last minute, the Albert Hall cancelled Zappa's booking and refused to allow the concert to take place. The reason they gave was that they considered parts of the script to be obscene and objectionable. On the night of the concert, the TV news showed an apparently angry protest by fans outside the Albert Hall.

Zappa and his business manager Herb Cohen (the partnership that constitutes Bizarre Productions) decided to sue. They are currently claiming damages against the management of the Albert Hall for both the financial loss caused by the cancellation and the resulting loss of important publicity. The case took four years to come to court.

LET'S MOVE ON TO THE FIRST WEDNESDAY OF THE CASE. Number Seven Court is a high-ceilinged room, all gray stone and aged panelling—that strange combination of Kafka and Camelot that appears to have been the Victorian ideal of justice. Among the wigs, the thick leather bound books and the faint air of dust in the light streaming through high-mullioned windows, Frank Zappa cuts a somewhat strange figure. He has made some endeavors to meet the court halfway. He is wearing a conservative brown-check suit, a white shirt and what looks unnervingly like an old school tie. The effect is hardly a total success. With his hair hanging loose, some way below his shoulders, he looks, if anything, a little reminiscent of Tiny Tim.

At the start of the afternoon session Zappa has already been on the witness stand all morning and for part of the previous day. Under examination he speaks very quietly and on a number of occasions the judge has requested that he speak up. It is obvious that this case is not going to be turned into any kind of theatrical spectacle. Not that the proceedings are without a few surreal touches. Mothers albums nestle among the imposing bundles of legal paper. A stereo system has been set up in front of the judge. The counsel for the defence has a large dictionary of American slang in front of him. It has a garish red, white and blue cover. The judge has already listened to a good deal of the *200 Motels* album. He received most of it with his head sunk in his hands. He complained that he couldn't hear the words. He refused to have the track 'Penis Dimension' played in court. Mr. Justice Mocatta had already read the lyrics and he found them objectionable.

THERE HAVE BEEN OTHER ODD TOUCHES OF THE KIND that always seem to occur when the world of rock'n'roll confronts the very different world of the law. The judge has had problems with the terminology of rock. The word "groupie" seemed to puzzle him. "Is a groupie a girl who is a member of a group?"

Zappa shakes his head. "No, she is a girl who likes members of a rock'n'roll band."

The judge has encountered other troubles. "When I started this case, I knew very little about pop and beat music. I knew it was to do with rhythm, banging, and an infectious atmosphere. I didn't know it was anything to do with sex or drugs."

Zappa points out that the majority of pop music has some kind of sexual connotations.

Having completed his testimony Zappa left the stand. He walked straight out of the court. It seemed to be a signal for most of the spectators to rush out for a smoke. Zappa sat on a bench in the corridor. He looked tired. "You realize I can't say anything about the case."

AT JUST AFTER SIX THE SAME EVENING, JOE STEVENS and I walk through the gilded portals of the Dorchester Hotel in Park Lane. We have come to talk to Frank Zappa. Up in room 640, Joe and I are offered coffee. Frank does it in a way that makes it very clear that requests for large bourbons or tequila sunrises will not be entertained. We settle for coffee. A long discussion that centers around the enema scene in Paderewski's opera *The Devils of Loudun*. From there we move to Richard Berry. Richard Berry, the man who actually wrote 'Louie Louie' and recorded it as Richard Berry And The Pharaohs, sold the entire rights to the song for $5,000. Zappa considers Berry one of the most important figures in the West Coast R&B scene of the fifties. He even goes into detail: "He heard a band playing in a Latin instrumental called 'Cha Cha Loco.' It had the same basic ba-ba dum, dum-dum riff. Berry scribbled some words down on a brown paper bag. That's how 'Louie Louie' was written. The Kingsmen later mutilated it."

WHAT ABOUT THE TRIAL, FRANK?

"I can't talk about the trial."

After having spent nine days at the Old Bailey a couple of years ago, defending myself on a criminal obscenity rap, I still have a morbid interest in the legal process, particularly where it encompasses censorship. I ask Frank if he'd be willing to talk, off the record, about the general background of the case.

"No."

Why? (Politely.)

Zappa is very matter-of-fact. "I don't trust anybody."

Just then the phone rings. Frank has a five-minute conversation with his lawyer. He hangs up, and looks around the room.

"I will have to ask you all to forget anything you might have overheard."

The turnaround is fortuitous. Fate forces the Twentieth Century Zen Master into a position of human. We smile, and the conversation is duly forgotten. It's hard when the central topic of interest is verboten.

THE NEXT SUBJECT IS CAPTAIN BEEFHEART. ZAPPA seems pleased that this has come up. "I can officially tell you that Don is a member of the Mothers Of Invention. He is part of our current US tour."

Zappa consistently refers to Beefheart as Don Vliet. They've been friends since their teens, cruising for burgers together and singing along with the radio. It makes a touching picture. "Don will be singing, playing harmonica, dancing, and having a good time for the first time in his life. He had a very harrowing experience with the last band and his management. They made a fool of him. He called me up and asked for help. I told him that the Mothers were holding auditions on Tuesday and Thursday, and that he should come along. He flunked the first one, but the second was okay."

All this after he's been badmouthing you for the past three years or so?

"There really has never been any animosity on my part. He asked for help. Any idea of a feud between us is quite pointless."

Frank becomes more animated as he starts to elaborate. It seems a though he has a real affection for Beefheart. "The way he relates to language is unique, the way in which he brings my text to life. Of course he has problems. His memory causes him trouble. He won't be separated from his sheets of paper that have his words written on. He clings to them for dear life. He also has a literacy problem. He can hardly read. He also has trouble staying on a beat. Captain Beefheart has no natural rhythm. He does have this thing inside him. It's dynamic and he wants to express it. In a voice like Howlin' Wolf."

The conversation veers from Beefheart and moves on to Howlin' Wolf.

It's a strange experience to see Frank Zappa actually talking in a tone that comes close to awe. "The Howlin' Wolf could really get across."

The Wolf talk goes on. Wolf anecdotes come too fast to record. Zappa also relates his persona as a Wolf fan to Beefheart and his new slide-guitar player. Beefheart's blues harmonicas seem to play an essential part in the new Mothers repertoire. You get the feeling that it could be like no blues ever seen on the planet.

We move from Wolf and Beefheart to the general area of people like them—individuals with a unique talent, but one that can't be pigeonholed by the entertainment industry.

"In society today those people get the worst deal. Society retards the individual. An example is Bob Dylan. When he came out with 'Like A Rolling Stone' the industry reacted by creating 'The Eve Of Destruction.' You could say that I hire the handicapped."

Zappa goes on to define. "I admire anyone who makes a positive statement, even if it's moronic. I can admire the positively moronic, anyone who sits down and says this is my statement, stick it up your ass."

I venture a Zen pupil joke. "The suppository principle of culture?"

I get the deadpan. "That's the kind of thing they talk about in court."

Then, later Zappa used the phrase himself a couple of times. I venture an awkward question. How does Frank relate the early Zappa—the abrasive social commentator—to the present-day, very individualistic musician? What happened to the political songs, Frank? Zappa dismisses the whole thing very quickly. Not quickly enough to betray embarrassment, just sufficiently fast to indicate that it's not very interesting. He sees his songs as timeless. He's written 'Brown Shoes Don't Make It.' He's written 'Trouble Coming Every Day.' They are still appropriate. He doesn't need to write them again.

"If you have a band with Mark and Howard in it, you find yourself documenting the trivia that form society. People in fifty years' time should have documentation of monsters like Cal Worthington." (Cal Worthington is a singing cowboy used-car dealer who has immensely long TV commercials during LA's *Late Late Show*.)

So the groupies and the stars on Hollywood Boulevard

say John Provost and Leo G. Carroll are as important as Richard Nixon?

"In a way. I have written a song about Nixon."

'Son Of Orange County'?

"No, another one. It's called 'Dicky's Such An Asshole' or 'San Clemente Magnetic Deviation.'"

Magnetic deviation?

"Aviation pilots stay away from the San Clemente area. There is a deviation from the earth's normal magnetic field around San Clemente Island. That's not actually where Nixon lives, but it's very close."

There's speculation in room 640 about alien invaders sitting on San Clemente Island plotting the whole dirty business. When Grand Funk tells you aerosols are going to destroy the atmosphere you're frankly not impressed. When Zappa starts on the earth's magnetic field, you tend to give it a little more credibility.

ZAPPA PAUSES TO LIGHT A WINSTON. "'PENGUIN IN Bondage' is a true story." Everything stops dead. Would you like to relate it?

"It's far too personal."

The conversation goes round and round. More journalists come in. Soon everyone is vamping on each other's action. It tends to be confusing. Frank seems delighted. A session of "Whatever happened to" seems a painless way to ace out the competition.

What happened to Larry (Wild Man) Fischer?

"Larry Fischer is still on Sunset Strip. He still sells original songs for a dime, and my address and phone number for fifty cents. He carries his album under his arm. He wants to make another one. It ought to be called *The Cheek of Wild Man Fischer*."

The twelve-album set that constitutes a history of the Mothers in unreleased material? Zappa looks a little sad. "This is a very difficult and expensive project. We currently have someone canvassing retailers. If we can get orders for 5,000, the company will release it, but it's very difficult."

The Groupie Papers? Zappa looks enthusiastic. The Groupie Papers seem close to his heart.

"My secretary Pauline was transcribing them, but that stopped. Noel Redding also asked for his diaries back. Cynthia Plastercaster still lives about 100 miles from Chicago. She's still keeping diaries. Miss Pamela has a straight acting job. She plays the ingénue in a soap opera called *As The World Turns*. Miss Sparkly, another of the GTOs, wants to do a parody of the show called *As The Turd Whirls*."

Frank warms to his subject. "They really would make a fantastic book. There are Cynthia's diaries, Pamela's diaries and Noel Redding's diaries. They start out by not knowing each other, and slowly they converge. At first they talk about each other, then they meet. It's a dramatic, factual insight into the sixties and rock hysteria. The main problem with putting the book into logical form is how you arrange the separate continuities. You have Noel. He joins Hendrix and keeps a diary, all in code, of how many girls he had and what they did. Then you have Pamela who records, at nine, how she cried when Caryl Chessman, the Red Light Bandit, was executed, and Cynthia, whose father attacked her because she had unnaturally big tits for her age.

"There's a sequence when Pamela falls in love with Cynthia. The problem is that Cynthia isn't the least bisexual. Pamela hocks her record player and, without any real idea of what it's like, goes to Chicago in the middle of winter, to get into Cynthia's pants. There's a very sad Polaroid picture of them both sitting up in bed after it has all been a terrible failure."

"Cynthia's diaries are quite incredible. She makes strange clinical notes about who she balled, and if she casted them. There's even notes on how she goes about locating rock stars. They would be great for Sherlock Holmes. Her diaries are scientific and detached, even down to the formula of her different casting materials. She also draws cartoons—strange and well-executed. They're rather like Little Orphan Annie, except she's chasing down—who's an example?… say Paul Revere and the Raiders.

"It would make one hell of a movie."

New Musical Express, April 1975

HYATT VIGNETTE

INSIDE THE ELEVATOR, THE ROCK'N'ROLL CIRCUS CON-
tinued unabated. As we slowly ascended, two rock-trash
camp-followers in identical vinyl dresses, Doc Martens,
and assumed Courtney Love attitudes were berating a
short, exhausted-looking punk boy with a purple brush
cut. Their tongue studs flashed as they vented their negative feelings of dissatisfaction and resentment. As far as I
could glean, the young man wanted them out of his room
so he could get some much needed sleep, and he also didn't
want them traveling to the Bay Area with him. The wom-
en, on the other hand, found this completely unreasonable,
and were going to some vehement extremes to make this
clear to him. Why couldn't they go with the equipment?
There was plenty of room. At least a generation-and-a-
half divided me and the purple haired young man, but
life seemed to have changed very little since my own days
of orgies, sleep deprivation, and dirty underwear. While
maintaining as much of a distance from the conflict as I
could in the confines of the lift, I surreptitiously checked
them out, wondering if they operated as some kind of
sexual tag team. One wore a pair of police-style manacles
as a bracelet, both cuffs locked to the same wrist. Under
other circumstances, did they have a more proactive purpose? Cursory inspection revealed the young women as
unkempt, foul-mouthed and a little lumpy, no better than
C-list groupies, except they might very well have worked
out some kind of two-girl speciality act to compensate for
the hot-body attributes with which neither nature nor
surgery had endowed them.

❑ And the sex-fame,
potential-movie chimera
that fascinated Frank never
goes away.

From an unpublished essay written around 2003

A STAR IS PORN

❑ Had Frank Zappa lived to witness Paris Hilton and the cult of celebrities who are merely famous for their own fame, his cynicism would have appreciated the paradox.

UNLIKE BLOCKBUSTER, THE DOWN-AT-HEEL VIDEO store a couple of blocks from where I live has a porn section. Not that the porn helps too much, because the joint is always empty. It also has a mess of Russian titles, so I've wondered if it was really a front for the Russian mob. Then I was driving past and saw a large sign in the window: WE HAVE NEW PARIS HILTON! A desperation move, I thought, to pull in the customers by any means possible. Then it occurred to me that the store was attempting something that has been largely ignored by the great majority of the adult entertainment industry. Pushed by a changing landscape and competing delivery systems, the local-loser video store had appealed to star power.

Of course, Paris Hilton is not your average porn star. The pallid blonde, multitasking her way to vapid fame is hardly typical of anything—except maybe the devolution of humanity—but she is willing to have sex on camera, and (at least by tactic inactivity) allow the results to be marketed. And no question that her amateur porn is part of Hilton's star synergy and her global marketability. In this, she may represent a path to the future.

Jenna Jameson notwithstanding, the porn industry has never really explored star power as a commercial tool. In the beginning, porn sold itself by simply being available where previously it had been illegal. Stars like Seka were names on the packaging, never really connecting with the consumer. Later, as the avenues of consumption broadened and diversified, the move was to marketing by brand loyalty—as in (say) *Barely Legal*—and porn oddly resembled breakfast cereal, where Kellogg's and content are the selling points. Instead of "no carbs," the buyer could read "anal sex." Something totally at odds with the rest of showbusiness where TV, cinema, music, and even the arts are relentlessly star/celebrity driven.

Obviously the idea of being a "porn star" still carries a moral and social baggage, but if Paris Hilton has proved anything, it's that if enough of the media buy into the hype,

MICK FARREN

the negatives are easily negated. Paris Hilton is not a porn performer per se, she is a phenomena for whom graphic sex is part of both the shtick and the product. The basic templates for this kind of star creation are already in place. For decades, the Japanese have been mass-producing marketable and infinitely disposable "idols." The US entertainment industry took the Japanese route with *American Idol*, the Olsen Twins, and the Simpson sisters, whose celebrity is infinitely greater than their talent. The problem is how you factor in the explicit sex. Which is why I find myself reluctantly using Paris as the prime example.

What Paris Hilton—or those who have invested in her—realizes is that star power creates synergy, and when synergy peaks, all things are possible. The star can generate gossip, music CDs, action figures, lines of lingerie, you name it. The star connects to her public and creates fan loyalty far more reliable than any brand name. A pantheon of stars is worshiped by peripheral media, and everyone prospers. It's yet another of those things, however, that requires energy, creativity, and investment; but for those who can pull it off, the rewards may prove immeasurable. Out in the blog world, literate strippers, smart hookers, and erudite pro-doms, are busily promoting themselves as the new wave of sex-related celebs and getting book deals. Sure, it's all still highly underground and mainly in their own imaginations, but if we've learned anything over the years, it's that a mutation of today's underground is frequently tomorrow's mass market.

AVN Online, 2004

BEAUTY QUEEN FOLLIES

DIDN'T YOU JUST LOVE CARRIE PREJEAN? THE WOMAN was so perfectly preposterous she was impossible to ignore in all her plasticized, beauty-queen, skin-deep perfection. In one TV clip, she was sashaying across the Miss Universe stage in a white bikini doing what Tina Fey as Sarah

❑ Unlike Paris Hilton, Carrie Prejean believed fame was the prize, but she also believed she could maintain an agenda. And that's why her fame really did only last fifteen minutes.

Palin called "fancy pageant walking." In another she was a gushingly inarticulate, ultra-conservative spokesmodel denouncing the evils of gay marriage.

Carrie Prejean, like Joe the Plumber before her, was a product of cable TV, a nonentity blown out of proportion by the twenty-four hour news cycle. Sexier than Joe—although plainly a creature of untouchable tinsel—she grabbed even more airtime on CNN, MSNBC and Fox than the pontificating Mr. Clean.

Her legal confrontations with the Miss Universe organization, her undeclared breast implants, the loss of her title, and subsequent reinstatement by no less than Donald Trump, received damn near as much coverage as the war in Afghanistan. And no doubt, like Joe, this convinced Carrie she had a political future, perhaps as a younger, hotter, diamante Sarah Palin. Wasn't everyone in Glenn Beck country paying rapt attention to her protestations she was the victim of a heinous leftist plot to silence her as an "outspoken conservative woman"? Like Palin before her, she even snagged a book deal. A set of fairly innocuous semi-topless photos marginally tilted her puritan moral halo, but Carrie carried on. The sky might be her limit.

Until we discovered that she was also a porn star.

Just as it seemed her fifteen minutes of fame were running out, word circulated of a video of Prejean masturbating on camera. She was instantly back on the news cycle, right at the top of the hour. First reports claimed the tape was commercially produced, but, interviewed by Meredith Vieira on the *Today* show, Prejean made it very clear she was only sexting to a boyfriend, and it was never supposed to be seen by anyone else. Then, with stunning beauty queen logic, she asserted that it wasn't a sex tape at all because she was on her own. Prejean was blissfully unaware she was rerunning a Rodney Dangerfield vintage classic. "The first time I had sex I was so scared. I mean, I was all alone."

When the Carrie tape finally hit the Internet it instantly went viral. Websites crashed from lack of bandwidth as her fingers did the walking on quantum computers. She had crossed a moral line and would never run for president. And the irony was that she'd drawn the line herself. Paris Hilton could walk away from her sex tapes with a vacant heiress smile. Prejean had so oversold herself as so damned pure and spotless, she didn't have that option once her vagina was the wonder of the web. Her protests that leaking the tape was an "attack on her Christian faith" didn't help at all. The tape could not be talked away.

We've had Jimmy Swaggart and his airport skanks, and Ted Haggard with his boys and his crystal meth. Now we have Prejean's video vagina. In comparison, adult entertainment seems positively conventional and uncomplicated. The porn industry is nothing more than a community of professionals who make films of people having sex for the amusement of consumers. No lies or pretense. Shame is not part of the game and no one pushes imposed morality. No one who is commercially committed to making porn will ever look as pathetically inane as Carrie Prejean. Webcam exhibitionism is a part of the modern world and no one's business except the participants. Prejean's problem is that she is too dumb to realize the world is moving on from her tired concepts of oppressive decency.

Luckily for Prejean, the War on Porn was at a low ebb. The wingnuts were busy derailing healthcare and proving Obama is a Kenyan. Maybe she could cut her losses, follow in the footsteps of Jessica Hahn, and start hanging with metal musicians. Her story does, however, present me with a rather disturbing conclusion. The porn industry is refreshingly sane, while Middle America—simultaneously watching lasciviously and waxing righteous—is seriously schizophrenic.

AVN, January 2010

NOW I'LL BE FAMOUS

THE WORDS "NOW I'LL BE FAMOUS" RESONATE WITH A hollow desperation. Seemingly they were part of what Robert Hawkins told his landlord, Debora Maruca-Kovac,

❑ Hollywood teaches us that, if all else fails, there's always a blaze of glory.

last Wednesday (December 6) before he took a beat-up AK47 he had stolen from his stepfather and went on a shooting spree in the Westroads Mall in a smart suburb of Omaha, Nebraska. This gave the nineteen-year-old Hawkins the dubious distinction of being Nebraska's second most deadly mass murderer with eight random kills, just two short of Charles Starkweather's bodycount—the legendary James Dean look-a-like who, with his girlfriend Caril Ann Fugate, killed ten people in his 1957–58 nomadic rampage—that has made him the subject of three movies, and the inspiration for a Bruce Springsteen CD.

Theorize as we may, serial killers and mass murderers from Starkweather, to Henry Lee Lucas, to Aileen Wuornos, to Hawkins are essentially impossible to fathom. Does a synapse misfire or psychosis just bloom? The secret may never be unlocked, but, should it be, the truth would find itself hopelessly at odds with the cultural imprint with which we stamp these deadly aberrations. The Columbine shooters Klebold and Harris (with two movies, a play, and an episode of *Law & Order* to their credit) were easy. They had all the books, videos, and ephemera. They could be written off as speed metal goth punks with guns and explosives.

Hawkins seems to have been a little different. The only impression I could glean from the early news reports was of a stoner—fired from his lousy job at McDonald's, kicked out the family home, and dumped by his girlfriend, all in the same week—who reached for the machine gun. The *New York Post* was more than ready to jacket him into the Trench Coat Mafia, dwelling on his "military-style haircut, black backpack and camouflage vest," and how he had vowed to "go out in style."

The *New York Times* on the other hand had Hawkins tagged as a creature beyond the system's help, who had received "private psychotherapy, family therapy, drug counseling," but was then busted for grass and tossed into a chemical dependency program that included mandatory Alcoholics Anonymous or Narcotics Anonymous meetings. Along the way he had been diagnosed with "attention-deficit disorder, oppositional defiant disorder, a mood disorder, and parent/child relational problems." Reading all this, I wondered if he had also been dosed with speed-like Ritalin and Adderall. (And also puzzled over what the hell was meant by "oppositional defiant disorder" which sounded too much like an old-fashioned, and totally healthy questioning of authority.)

The *Times* even dropped the slightly odd piece of information that the State of Nebraska had spent more than $265,000 treating Hawkins and his problems before he cut loose with the AK. I couldn't tell if this was a "go-figure" shrug, or the dismissal of any social service safety net as pointless if it can't keep death out of the mall.

I know nothing about Robert Hawkins beyond memories of my own adolescent blaze-of-glory fantasies. I'm well aware that teens of Hawkins' supposed profile have little grasp of the permanence of death. He'd had a bad week—lost his job, his pad, and his squeeze, and decided to nullify his life in a fit of pique. Except those words were in his head. "Now I'll be famous." He'd grown up in a world where Ed Gein, Charlie Manson, the Zodiac Killer and the aforementioned Starkweather are dark stars in the cultural firmament, and the cops in Columbine sold bootleg tapes of Klebold and Harris shooting in the woods. Robert Hawkins, in a town from where, during the Cold War, B52s of Strategic Air Command flew their nukes out to the failsafe point and back again, wanted a deal with destiny. He wanted fame. And fame meant taking a few of the SOBs with him. I can only speculate, when he finally turned the gun to himself, was he wondering how many movies they'd make about him?

LA CityBeat, December 2007

HAPPY BIRTHDAY, LIZARD KING

LET US SHAMELESSLY CELEBRATE THE FIFTIETH ANNIversary of Godzilla, coming up on November 3—the day when we may all be angrily disputing the results of the

❑ The most perfect gauge of the extent of fame's illusion is the way in which a guy in a green rubber suit could be a major world idol for half a century.

presidential election. For a full half-century, the mighty lizard—King of the Monsters—has stood green and magnificent, like a saurian Elvis, confounding all who would diminish him as a mere man in a rubber suit. Some will say Godzilla rightly belongs in the movie section, but for me, he's always been part of the television experience. When, with the sound turned down, the TV set becomes a piece of kinetic furniture, no image—not even *Heckle & Jeckle* or the Zapruder film—is a more satisfying embodiment of twentieth-century global pop than Godzilla's colossal wading across Tokyo Bay, or his breathing radioactive halitosis on plasterboard skyscrapers.

A unique combination of nuclear fear and Jurassic inaccuracy, Godzilla could have rivalled Elvis Presley, but he was vocally handicapped by a one-note *schwarrrk* that couldn't be improved even by monster reverb. All the same, the careers of the two great Kings have much in common, and both have moved similar mountains of merchandise. Mega-idols of the 1950s, they spent the sixties starring in increasingly inexplicable formula films, and were once released together as a double bill.

Ghidorah and Rodan were worthy opponents, but, by the time Godzilla was reduced to fighting Gigan, Megalon, and the Smog Monster, it was as sad as 'Do the Clam' or Muhammad Ali vs. Me Quasi-Sumo Wrestler. But where Elvis fell to pills, Godzilla abided, to enjoy a renaissance in the early 1990s when his Toho classics were remade with superior FX. He even survived an egregious TV animation show, *The Godzilla Power Hour*, and the debacle of a 1998 US movie remake starring an ostrich-walking creature that laid eggs and had a grudge against Matthew Broderick. The celebrations of Godzilla's half-century began earlier this year with the restoration and release of *Gojira*, Ishiro Honda's original masterpiece, before US footage and Raymond Burr were edited in. At the time, *CityBeat* film critic Andy Klein wrote in these pages, "Great horror movies are almost always metaphors for real human anxieties, sometimes particularly timely ones. Just as surely as the 1956 *Invasion of the Body Snatchers* reflected Cold War anxiety and the 1986 *The Fly* AIDS anxiety, *Gojira* blatantly invoked Japan's memories of Hiroshima and Nagasaki, as well as a more recent incident in which Japanese fishermen were exposed to the fallout from an American nuclear test."

Godzilla will be honored at Hollywood's Walk of Fame on November 29, but without a personal appearance that would risk flattening major sections of Hollywood Boulevard. The end of next month will also see the release of his twenty-eighth film, Ryuhei Kitamura's *Godzilla Final Wars*, in which monsters take out Paris, New York, Sydney, Shanghai, and a bunch of other cities, and Godzilla is again forced, in highly destructive style, to save the world.

After fifty years, one might think we know everything about Godzilla, but I recently discovered his very gender is in question. As he is King of the Monsters, I had always considered him a male presence, but when I asked my Tokyo informant Yukiko Akagawa about the origin of Baby Godzilla, who hatched from an egg in the 1969 *Godzilla's Revenge*, her answer was surprising, "Known in Japan as 'Minilla' (aka 'Minya'), he indeed was born from an egg unearthed by Kamakillas," she noted. "Since Minilla is Godzilla's son, at that time a huge controversy occurred in Japan about the gender of Godzilla, to which Toho hasn't given a definite answer, and it is generally believed that it's hermaphroditic. Thus, your question about who laid the egg is eternal and perhaps belongs to the Zen sphere."

LA CityBeat, November 2004

PUBLISH AND BE DAMNED
(MAYBE FOR ETERNITY)

THE COMMENT ON MY BLOG WAS BOTH ANONYMOUS and insulting. "Doesn't self-aggrandizing ever get boring? Why not wear a flashing neon sign that says 'Look at me!'" To be fair, however, to this nameless troll, the question is

❏ Even writers feel the siren's call…

one that I have asked myself more than once, although couched in a more angst-of-destiny context. "I have published thirty-some books. Everything from a quartet of vampire novels to an illustrated history of the CIA. Isn't that enough?" Why do I go on putting myself through this. Especially when, here in the twenty-first century, book publishing is undergoing cataclysmic change, and many writers despair of ever publishing a book at all.

Stephen King, whose analysis of popular culture is often cruelly ignored—probably because of his monster success—may well have created the most accurate analog of the relentless motivation to write and publish. The character Annie Wilkes in the novel *Misery*—and later played by Kathy Bates in the Rob Reiner movie—is the psycho-homicidal nurse who compels the captive author to write, under threat of pain and Liberace records, the promise of drugs, and ultimately by smashing his ankles with a sledgehammer. Annie Wilkes is the perfect personification of the imperative to write and the need to publish.

To be driven to write is reasonably understandable. Writing, like any art form, is a hedge against mortality. It's the initials carved in the tree or the footprint in the wet cement given story and substance. It is the thought, the memory, observation, or fantasy preserved, the writer hopes, long after he or she is gone. Once the words are written though, they must be read. The unread word is unpleasantly akin to Jean Paul Sartre's tree falling in the existential forest. A sound that no one hears? We can debate the damned tree until the absinthe runs out, but unpublished writing is the orphan of the mindstorm. Without a reader the essay, thesis, memoir, or novel might as well be a shopping list.

Of course, my anonymous and hostile critic may be right and the need to be published really is 'Look at me!' in neon. No question it takes a distended ego to believe one's recorded imaginings might have value in the here and now, let alone for generations to come. But that same overloaded ego is also in a bizarre crapshoot with posterity, because every book is a bet, the outcome of which the author will never know. Future generations judge whether Homer, Coleridge, or Philip K. Dick stands the test of time, but only long after they're dead.

It would be nice to think that the publishing industry is the author's ally in this gamble with immortality, but that has never more than tangentially been true, and the concept is now wholly abandoned as print struggles among media increasingly dominated by electronics. I freely confess that I was amazingly lucky. My first fiction was published back in a time when what was known as the "mid list author" still elicited modest respect. You put out a couple of paperbacks with lurid covers, and hoped to amass enough of a following that the publisher made a modest profit. The author could continue to write. The readership continued to read, and, although the rewards were hardly princely, everyone was reasonably happy.

Not so today. Publishing is undergoing a revolution as radical as anything since the invention of the printing press, and has little idea of its future direction. Corporate suits, largely ignorant of the business of books, want every author to be a J.K. Rowling and hit the same astronomical paydirt. It's plainly impossible, but the mid list author, once the industry's backbone, is now about as welcome as a drag queen among Republicans (Giuliani not withstanding), and the odds on a mainstream publisher buying a neophyte's first novel lengthen with every passing day.

But don't despair, the literary crapshoot may float for a time, but it will continue. The shortsighted greed of the mainstream spells opportunity to the resourceful. Small presses will flourish, as will new distribution systems, online publishing, and other systems yet unimagined. My anonymous complainant has nothing to worry about. The self-aggrandizement will continue. All that might change is the color of the neon sign.

LA CityBeat, 2006

THE GREAT ELVIS PRESLEY LOOK-ALIKE MURDER MYSTERY

❏ Next up is something of an anachronism. Jules Verne predicted the airship and the submarine. My only claim to prophetic science fiction is that I anticipated the cult of the Elvis imitator and even that's kind of tenuous. The short story that follows—and brings this section full circle—was written in 1980, three years after Elvis Presley died, for **Twilight Zone Magazine**, a spin-off of the classic TV show. There were Elvis imitators at the time. There had been Elvis imitators while Elvis was still alive, but no mass gatherings, or Elvises performing wedding ceremonies in Las Vegas, and definitely no movies like **3000 Miles To Graceland** in which thieves dressed as Elvis rob a casino. I attempted to create a future in which Elvis look-a-likes were a common weirdness. Although I didn't specify, I imagined the story was set sometime around 1990, but, as it turned out, I overestimated. Within just a couple of years, the Elvis impersonator would be

YERBY SIGHED. UP UNTIL THE CALL CAME, HE'D BEEN hoping for a break. The streets were a relentless oven, the mercury was in the high eighties, and the humidity hung at seventy percent. Not even a cop should have to work. The loitering bums looked too drained to do anything but suck on their brown-bagged beers and pray for a thunderstorm. A few degrees cooler and the air might have hummed bad with tension; hotter, and the pushed-too-far could explode. As it was, the city remained inert and sweating. It had been shaping up as a comparatively easy shift, but then the homicide had been dumped into their laps. Yerby's partner Max swore quietly and cut in the siren and lights. Sullen heads turned as they screamed past.

The homicide was an odd one. Yerby's years of experience told him that an ice pick stabbing during a show at some run-down flea-bag theater probably wasn't going to be simple. Theaters tended to mean high levels of hysteria, and poor theaters meant people with little else but hysteria to offer. The car squealed as Max swung it into a tight right-hand turn. They passed the red, white, and blue neon cocktail glass on the front of Paul's Bar & Grill. Yerby wished that he was inside with a cold pitcher and Frank Sinatra on the jukebox, instead of chasing across a baking city to a murder at the De Quincey. The old firetrap should have been torn down years ago. Only the general poverty of the surrounding neighborhood had saved it from the wrecking ball. Nobody wanted to invest in that section of the city. The sign on the marquee read *The Great Elvis Presley Look-Alike Contest*.

Max grunted in disbelief. "What the fuck is that supposed to mean?"

Yerby's shirt was sticking to his body. Wearily he shook his head. "Who knows."

Three blue-and-whites were already at the scene. The lazy turning of their red flashers seemed to accentuate the heat. A small, idly curious crowd had gathered and was be-

MICK FARREN

ing kept out of harm's way by a bunch of uniforms. More cops were blocking the theater's exits and entrances. Yerby clipped on his badge and pushed his way to the stage door. Yerby had been a cop for thirteen years. He'd spent the last five as a homicide detective. Inside the theater, it was cooler than the street. It wasn't the aggressive chill of a modern air-conditioned building—more the musty neglected cool of a place where the sun never penetrates.

Yerby had no time to savor the relief. The backstage area of the De Quincey was filled with grotesques. Easily half of those backstage were dressed in some approximation of an Elvis Presley outfit. They came in all shapes and sizes. Yerby couldn't remember when he'd been so close to so much tight leather, such tonnage of sequins, so many stand-up collars and pairs of triangular sideburns assembled in one place. It didn't seem to bother these characters that most of them bore not the slightest resemblance to the original. Some were quite prepared to stretch credibility to the outer limits. Among the crowd were a black Elvis, a Japanese Elvis, and even a woman. She wore greased-back hair and a pink zoot suit.

"So this is an Elvis Presley look-alike contest." Yerby's face was expressionless. Max shot him a look that said that this was going to be a lulu. And it was. As soon as the Elvises spotted Yerby, they started demanding to know what was going to happen, how long they were going to be kept there. Yerby suspected that each one of them was a variety of attention junkie. Yerby distrusted attention junkies; they turned nasty when they didn't feel that they were getting what they deserved. He ignored the Presleys and beckoned to a uniform. "You'd better take me to the body."

The victim was little more than a kid, maybe eighteen or nineteen. The ice pick had gone straight into his brain, upwards through the back of his neck. There was little blood. It looked like the work of someone who knew what he or she was doing. The kid was good looking, and clearly a contestant. With the help of a little eye makeup, he actually did resemble the young Elvis Presley. He was dressed in a black fifties-style suit, a black shirt, and a pink

absorbed into the culture. When the restored Statue Of Liberty was reopened in 1986, a hundred massed Elvises were part of the entertainment.

tie. His eyes were wide open, and there was an expression of blank surprise on his face, as if he couldn't quite believe what had happened.

Yerby moved away from the body. "Any of these weirdoes see anything?"

"If they did, they're not saying."

"Nothing?"

"One of them claimed he saw someone in a Presley suit running away just after the stabbing."

Yerby glanced at the clutch of fake Presleys. "That's a lot of help. Are any of the… contestants missing?"

"I don't have a list yet."

"I better start talking to them."

The first interviewee was short and fat, baby pink and double-chinned, as if physical reality had never laid hands on his body. He was sweating profusely, and his forehead was slick with grease from an elaborate, dyed-black pompadour that was starting to wilt. He was squeezed into a white-spangled Elvis Presley suit, his round potbelly sagging over the heavy lion's-head buckle of his fancy gilt-chain belt. Yerby couldn't imagine how this pudgy little creep could seriously go out, stand in a bright public spotlight, and imitate Elvis Presley. Who was he hoping to fool?

"So tell me about the kid who was killed."

Baby pink stared at Yerby like a scared rabbit. In the unrelenting neon of the dressing room, he looked awful. Pink was fading to green. "Nobody knew him. He was new, straight off the street."

Yerby blinked. "You're telling me that you people work a regular circuit?"

"Oh yes." Baby pink leaned forward in his seat. "There's club dates and cabaret. And the bored wives' afternoon parties. It's not what you'd actually call a circuit, but there are an awful lot of people who like to see interpreters of the late…"

Yerby's voice was flat. "Elvis imitators."

"We don't like to use those particular words."

"Whatever. Name?"

"Vince Prince."

Yerby nodded, stone-faced. "Is that the name you were born with?" The creep shook his head. "No, but it's legal. I changed it."

Yerby nodded again. "Okay, Vince. I take it you're a participant in this competition, this… what do you call it?"

"The Elvis Presley Look-Alike Contest—Eastern Seaboard Area Finals."

Yerby looked grave. "And the youngest competitor at the Eastern Seaboard Area Finals got himself stabbed to death with an ice pick, backstage, while the competition was going on?"

"It was horrible."

"And nobody had seen the kid before."

Vince Prince shook his head, dislodging another piece of pompadour. "Nobody knew him. But that's not all…" Prince leaned even further forward. For one unpleasant moment Yerby thought that Prince was going to pat him on the knee. "… he was very, very good."

"That's why he was killed?"

Prince started shaking his head. "No!" His voice had jumped an octave from its original Presley baritone. "Nobody would…"

"You don't think one of your compadres might have gotten just a little jealous?"

Baby pink continued to shake his head. It was as if he believed the unpleasant thought would go away if he shook his brain long enough. "None of us would do a thing like that."

Yerby sniffed. "Just how good was the kid?"

"He did the fifties. You have to be good to do the fifties."

Yerby crooked an eyebrow.

"You have to be young and fit and know what you're doing.

"And did he?"

"He had the voice and the look and all these slides and the corkscrew leg-moves. He was young and fresh and looked as though he was enjoying himself. I've got to tell you, some of the old-timers can look tired."

ELVIS DIED FOR SOMEBODY'S SINS BUT NOT MINE   281

Yerby nodded sympathetically. "Are you getting tired, my friend?"

"N-no."

"So where were you, Vince? Where were you when the kid was killed?"

"I was watching the show. The kid had just come off and the next guy was up and then I heard all the shouting."

"Are you sure about that?"

"Sure I'm sure."

"Did anybody see you?"

"My wife was there with me all the time."

Yerby was surprised. "Your wife?"

"My wife always comes to these things with me. In fact, it was her who got me into Elvis interpretation in the first place."

The picture that he'd been building of Prince hadn't included a wife. What the fuck did they do when they were alone? "She was watching from the wings with you?"

"Sure."

"Anybody else?"

"There was a whole crowd there."

"And they saw you?"

"I'm sure they did."

Yerby nodded absently. He was already convinced baby pink was no ice pick killer. "I'll be talking to your wife," said Yerby, "but for the moment you can go."

Prince looked like an overweight spaniel that had been offered a doggie treat. "I guess I'd better not leave town."

Yerby didn't bother to smile.

The next one was at least the right size and shape. He was dressed in black leather. His hair was long and greasy, and he seemed to have based his style on the 1968 come-back special. He was clutching a cherry-red Gibson guitar; a red silk scarf was tossed around his neck, air-ace style. All in all, he would have made quite a passable Presley from a distance, except for his enormous nose. It was like the beak of a predatory bird, or perhaps a crag on which the bird might perch.

Yerby stabbed a finger at the empty chair.

"Please sit down."

The new Elvis folded into the seat, cradling the guitar in his lap, awkward and defensive.

"What's your name?"

"Darth Roman."

"You're putting me on."

"It's my stage name. I made it up myself."

Yerby frowned. "What's your real name?"

"Ron Kowski."

"Okay, Ron…"

"Darth."

Yerby was tired. "I don't hold conversations with anybody called Darth."

Darth's lower lip became petulant. "When I'm all dressed up…"

"You're a suspect in a murder case, Ron."

"I didn't do anything."

"Are you any good at this imitating."

"We like to call it interpreting."

"I already heard about that."

"What did you want to ask me?"

"I was just wondering if you were any good."

Kowski shook his head. "I don't take it so seriously as some."

"That's a relief."

"A few of these guys are verging on psycho, you know what I mean? Can't tell what's real and what ain't."

"But not you."

Kowski grinned. "Hell, no. I just do it to pick up a bit of change and get next to women."

"Women?" Yerby hadn't thought about women hanging around with the performers in these absurd shows. Ron's grin had turned into a leer. "You wouldn't believe some of the women who come in to see us."

"I probably wouldn't."

"They get themselves twisted up in the illusion." He winked at Yerby. Yerby wondered what kind of woman used a beak-nosed Ron Kowski as an Elvis surrogate. "Did women make a play for the kid who got killed?"

Kowski shrugged. "He was a first-timer."

"Where were you when the kid was stabbed?"

"Uh…" Ron shifted in his chair.

"You got a problem?"

"I was out in the parking lot."

"The parking lot?"

Kowski examined a gaudy silver skull ring on his left pinky finger. It had fake ruby eyes. "I was, uh… you know." His voice had taken on a definite Presley inflection.

"You tell me."

"I was with a lady—in the back of her LTD. The first I heard about the killing was when I came back inside."

"Can this lady vouch for you?"

Kowski shook his head. "No, she took off. She had a husband and didn't want to stick around. I didn't even know her name."

"Then you do have a problem."

Alarm slowly dawned on Kowski. "You don't think I killed him, do you?"

"One of you did."

Ron Kowski was followed by an individual in an embroidered pale blue jumpsuit with a short cape attached to the shoulders. At some point in his quest to be Elvis, he had undergone crude and probably cut-price plastic surgery. A pair of distrustful blue eyes peered from beneath eyebrows that had been shaved to nothing and redrawn in different positions. For Yerby he made a plausible ice pick killer except he had actually been performing on the stage at the time. The solitary female competitor had adopted the name Alice Malice. She came into the room with an arrogant, loose-limbed, gunfighter strut that came closer to the style of the young Elvis than a lot of what Yerby had seen since he'd arrived at the dingy theater. The woman stood in front of him in a pose of tilt-hipped defiance; when he nodded toward the chair, she glowered at him. "So what do you want?"

"So why did you do it?"

Her lip curled and her eyes were hard. "What am I supposed to have done?"

"Iced the kid."

She looked at him with deep contempt. "You think I just got off the farm?"

"Tough baby, huh?"

A pink mohair zoot suit was married to a black silk shirt with collar turned up. The tattooed tail of a blue and green dragon protruded from her shirt cuff. *LOVE* and *HATE* adorned her knuckles Robert Mitchum-style. "What the hell are you saying?"

"I'm saying that you took an ice pick and stabbed the kid to death."

"You're crazy."

She glared at him, as if daring him to do something. Yerby shrugged. "So tell me about it."

"What do I got to tell? I didn't murder nobody."

"What's the point of a woman imitating Elvis Presley?"

"What's the point of a drag queen imitating Judy Garland?"

"What's in it for you?"

She shrugged. "All you need to know is that I got an alibi."

"So what's this alibi?"

"I was in this empty dressing room with another Elvis and a stage hand."

"I'd have guessed you didn't like men?"

"I like to watch them squirm."

A uniform stuck his head around the door. "We maybe have a witness."

"Yeah?"

"Claims to have seen someone coming out of the stage door. Another look-alike."

"One of the performers is missing?"

The uniform shook his head. "According to our list, they're all here."

"Where is this witness?"

"In the alley outside the stage door."

"What's he doing out there? Why don't you bring him in?"

The uniform avoided Yerby's eyes. "He's better off

where he is."

Yerby shook his head. "Jesus Christ, what are you doing to me?"

He got up and headed for the door—and walked straight into a fistfight. An Elvis in a black bike-jacket and blue jeans was swinging punches at a slighter model in the standard white spangles, who was failing to defend himself with some limp and inaccurate karate. Three uniforms moved in. Baby pink clapped a theatrical hand to his head. "It's terrible, everyone is looking at everyone as though they were the killer."

The Elvis in the leather jacket had made the mistake of resisting the uniforms and was now being hustled to a blue-and-white. Yerby was suddenly surrounded by a crowd of rhinestone-padded shoulders. Angry sideburns moved in on him. A tall, lank youth in a black velvet jumpsuit grabbed Yerby's sleeve. Yerby chopped the hand away and spun him toward the nearest uniformed officer.

More uniforms were moving in and pushing hysterical Presleys against the wall. Yerby shouldered his way through the melee. He wanted to see this witness who couldn't be let into the De Quincy Theatre. The witness was an unprepossessing specimen in old, stained army fatigue pants and a torn T-shirt, and clutched a pint of Night Train. The T-shirt advertised a delicatessen that Yerby knew for a fact had been torched by its owner for the insurance at least six years before. The witness stared at Yerby with bleary, red-rimmed wino eyes. "You the one in charge?"

"Who wants to know?"

"It's going to cost you ten bucks to hear my story."

"I ain't going to give you ten cents." Yerby was wondering whose idea of a joke this was.

The wino's eyes narrowed. "I seen who done him."

"Who done who?"

"The one who did the murder. Who done the kid."

Yerby sighed and gave the wino a dollar. The wino examined the bill.

"This is only a lousy buck."

"That's right."

The wino eyed Yerby then shrugged. "So I was just sitting back here drinking, you understand."

"I understand."

"This here alley is quiet, see. Nobody comes around to bother you, so I was surprised when this big black limousine pulls up."

"Limousine?"

"Biggest damn Cadillac I ever seen."

Yerby was curious. "Where was it?"

"Right here where we're standing, right outside the stage door. Then these two guys get out and stand beside the car, kind of leaning on it, like they're waiting around for someone to come out of the door. They were big guys in dark suits, and they kind of had that look on them."

"Look?"

"The look that guys have who stand beside presidents, the guys who bodyguard big movie stars. You know, always watching, with that gun-under-the-armpit look. I seen those kind of guys on TV. Never thought I'd see 'em in the flesh. At first I thought that someone big must be playing the theater, but then I remember that nobody big would go near this rat-trap. All they ever have here is these low-rent freak shows. This makes me real curious, see, but I don't like the look of them two guys, so I don't want to get too close. In the end I just stand a way off, waiting to see what happens. I don't have to wait too long, either, 'cause around five minutes later, Elvis Presley comes running out the door. He was leaving the theater and no mistake."

"You saw another of the freaks."

The wino was adamant. "I know what I seen. He comes barreling out of the stage door, heading for the limo. He's kind of fleshy, overweight, with a lot of ol' rings on his hands—and he's sweating. One of the guys whips open the door, and the other throws this big black fur coat around his shoulders. And then he ducks into the car and I hear him say, 'That's the first.' Then the car takes off, laying rubber all the way down the alley."

"That's it?"

"Uh huh. Do I get another dollar?"

"You get a license number for the car?"

"Hell, no. I'm a wino."

Yerby scowled. "Go peddle your hallucinations to the *National Enquirer.*"

The wino glared at him with a drunk's injured pride. "A man don't have to be crazy or a liar just because he takes a drink now and then."

Yerby ran a hand over the back of his neck. It was a hot night. He walked back toward the theater wishing he was someplace else.

Twilight Zone, 1981

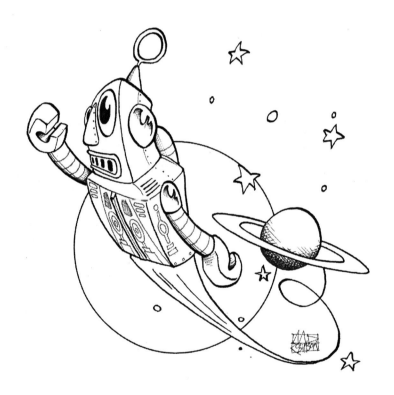

Part Five

Two Thousand Light Years From Home

anyone who can't remember a time of alienation is either damned lucky or has damned good dope. In the package booklet enclosed with the 1969 album *Deviants #3*, I wrote "we are a lonely frightened species on a dying planet." I don't think I realized it at the time but I was talking about the worst of human maladies. Alienation, the deep awareness of our own isolation. I may also have been subconsciously realizing that our much vaunted mind expansion through drugs and other means was not actually doing a great deal to alleviate that isolation. The danger of acquiring cosmic consciousness was that we became even more aware just how lonely we were in that cosmos. Those psychedelic visions and all the drugs with alphabet designations often only served to reveal just how singular we really were. They revealed us as isolated entities, each sealed in his or her individual pod, solitary and confined in a capsule in the DNA helix, alone and with a limited capacity for trust beyond a less than satisfactory empathy.

Human beings have the power of communication, and, at its best, it gives us the ability to function as units, tribes, or teams. At worst, it makes us capable of deception, deceit, and malice. The two-edged sword that is social interaction through language and gesture can even turn a collective effort from the positive to the negative. The same collective of individuals can mount a rescue effort or form a lynch mob. Carl Jung and others have suggested that humanity might not actually be as alone as it fears and has a vast but largely untapped collective unconscious. Even this, though, might not always operate for all that is good and noble. Jung warned, "The masses are always a breeding ground for psychic epidemics."

RECOGNIZING THE DEMONS

IF YOU HAPPEN TO BE IN THE CIVILIZATION-INVENTING business, a good place to start is to find out what people fear. Take a look at the dark side of their collective fantasies. Primitive cultures tell firelight tales of the varied nasties that lurk in the nighttime places of nature: the demons, goblins, ghosts, and evil spirits; all the nameless supernatural horrors of dark forests or fog on a bare mountain. More developed societies corral more sophisticated terrors into the fantasy end of entertainment: into speculative fiction, horror movies, and ray-gun operas. In either case, the culture processes its fear and attempts to make it manageable by transforming menacing reality into drama and symbolism.

Take the Victorian middle-class as a perfect example—the class that threw up H.G. Wells and Bram Stoker. It had come out of the industrial revolution ahead of the game, but after an era of such massive change, its members craved stability in which to enjoy their new affluence. Invasion by a foreign foe or uprising by the new class of industrial workers—whom they were so busily oppressing—were the twin perils to the Victorians' comfortable lives. It was little wonder that *The War of the Worlds* and *The Time Machine* were best-sellers. The invincible Martians were the ultimate horrible invaders. The sinister and subhuman Morlocks, who lived under the ground and tended the bowels of industrial Utopia, were an equally form-fitting representation of the Victorians' frightened vision of the workers. Wells' novels took these fears to the most terrifying extremes but, comfortingly, offered a way out. Bacteria killed the Martians, and the Morlocks were defeated by a leap through time. The Victorians didn't only want security; they wanted reassurance.

They also hated sex. It was a random, uncontrollable factor in their world view. If not heavily shackled by a patriarchal morality, they believed it threatened to destroy family ties and the system of inheritance that was the core of their system. Count Dracula's night creeping embodied all of those anxieties. He was irresistible, he was immortal, and he had the strength of ten. He was a snappy dresser and an aristo (and thus superior to the middle-class male). Worst of all, he was a foreigner. As the spirit of unbridled passion, he could tear daughters from fathers, wives from husbands; he could ruin reputations and family ties. Fortunately, he could be offed by a well-placed wooden stake.

The 1950s were also a time of affluence, an even more

insecure affluence. The world had gone nuclear, and man had the capability to wipe himself out with the awesome forces that he'd discovered. East and West would go all the way with H-bombs, and we'd either be vaporized or dispatched back to the Stone Age. It was a time of paranoia and mistrust. Commies skulked in the shadows and teenagers were crazy. Even bad weather was blamed on the bomb. Schlock cinema interpreted these crawling fears of the nuclear unknown as a procession of giant beasts that stomped and ravaged civilization as they knew it. In 1954, the giant ants in *Them* took over the storm drains of Los Angeles. In the previous year, atom tests melted *The Beast from 20,000 Fathoms* from the arctic ice, and it had to be shot dead by a youthful Lee Van Cleef before it ate the Coney Island Cyclone roller coaster. Two years later Godzilla got his break in showbusiness by snacking on Tokyo after a similar rude awakening. The big beasts lumbered on and on: *Gorgo, The Deadly Mantis, The Giant Claw, The Giant Behemoth.* A radioactive fog had exactly the opposite effect on Grant Williams when, in 1957, he turned into *The Incredible Shrinking Man.*

Anything alien was instantly distrusted. Something close to a post-McCarthy psychosis imagined extraterrestrials as ravening monsters with fangs and tentacles, super-Russians who arrived in flying saucers. *The Thing* ate humans; the creature in *Not of This Earth* wanted to steal our blood. *The Blob* absorbed us and grew bigger and bigger. The invading pods waited to snatch our bodies. About the only alien in the fifties' pop mythology who meant us any good was Michael Rennie, when he came to save us from our nuclear folly in *The Day the Earth Stood Still.*

Like the Victorians, fifties moviegoers were also seeking reassurance. They were being overwhelmed by the information that they were helpless. The Cold War news was too much. If the nuclear nightmare or the menace of the unknown was represented by a giant ant or a gelatinous blob, they demanded James Arness or Steve McQueen to save them. They wanted a way out, and the movies almost always provided one. This underlines the near uniqueness of the message in *The Day the Earth Stood Still*—that man has to quit his atomic ways or die. All other cheap science fiction claimed that man, civilization, and America would always triumph in the nick of time. They were little more than propaganda films.

Roger Corman's *Panic in Year Zero* was the most graphic and the most dishonest. An all-American family under the patriarchal leadership of Ray Milland discover to their dismay that Los Angeles has been nuked while they were on a camping trip. The unthinkable reduces itself to an aggressive pastoral romp. Distant mushroom clouds mark the fall of H-bombs. Beyond that, not a leaf moves and nothing glows in the dark. Gee! Atomic war can be fun. It frees the survivors to have every adventure of the popular post disaster genre. Ol' Ray immediately grabs all the supplies he can and hightails it out to hole up in a cave until World War III is all over. The family studiously avoids all contact with humanity, except when Ray and teenage son Frankie Avalon get to blow away a gang of juvenile hoodlums, and Frankie scores a girlfriend. Finally, the military shows up to restore law, order, and morality. The unthinkable even has a happy ending.

In the sixties, fear evolved, and the entertainment forms reflected that evolution. It was an introspective decade, despite all the upheaval and tumult, and a lot of its troubles started because the results of that introspection clashed with an entrenched status quo. Stanley Kubrick's *Dr. Strangelove or: How I Learned to Stop Worrying and Love the Bomb*, in 1964, marked how our attitudes had changed. We really had stopped worrying about the bomb; we feared the men who were messing with it. We tried to laugh at them, because we had realized that there could be no happy ending in that story.

Somewhere between the fifties and sixties, the collective fear switched from the external to the internal. We stopped fretting about Soviet missiles or Chinese invasions. We stopped grasping for mommy/daddy reassurance and began to wonder about ourselves, our culture, "our purpose here on the planet." The Kennedy assassination and its murky aftermath triggered fears of vast, dark conspiracies so secret and so powerful that they were impossible to fight. It generated an almost universal distrust of government. The morally dubious Southeast Asian war polarized the culture into violently reacting hawks and doves. Teenagers bombed banks, and blacks torched the ghetto.

In the media, shock-symbol climaxes reflected the emotional chaos and conflict. In Arthur Penn's *Bonnie and Clyde* the venal and sexless forces of law and order machine-gun the bank-robbing, antihero lovers to jerking, orgasmic death. Sam Peckinpah's *The Wild Bunch* gleefully butchers the soldiers of civilization up to the moment when they are overwhelmed themselves. Grinning rednecks blow the bikers-after-truth clear to nirvana in the last minutes of *Easy Rider*. Peter Fonda is racked by hallucination horrors of the fun kind in *The Trip*, and Michael Caine is racked by hallucination horrors of the secret-police-torture kind in *The Ipcress File*. It was a culture being bent out of shape by a basic ambiguity. There was a desperate desire for enlightenment, but at the same time there was an equally desperate fear of what enlightenment might reveal.

In the sixties, we prayed for saviors. The aliens were prime candidates. Tentacled horrors no longer drove the flying saucers. Aliens in the sixties were golden beings with a third eye: cold, efficient, and honorable, like Spock, or just plain enigmatic, like the *2001* monolith. It was all a part of the children of the cowboys praying to the Indians to save their souls, part of the search for a cozy, comfortable god to make things nice. *The Invaders* TV series presented bad extraterrestrials, and this was just the conspiracy view of Roy Thinnes, the central silent-majority paranoid character who was attempting to warn us of the invisible invasion. A similar evil alien paranoia drove Gerry Anderson's *UFO*, but these two shows were rare glimpses of the other side of the coin.

The search for God was abandoned somewhere between Kent State and Watergate. Culture turned on itself. We moved into the era of EST, analysis, psychobabble, jogging, Jacuzzis, and Led Zeppelin. Self-awareness turned quickly to self-absorption. Conditioned to living with anxiety, we began to use fear as a means of titillation. Rats, snakes, sharks, and bees, Texans with chainsaws, and the living dead crawled from the media swamp to deliver unpleasant but irresistible jolts. Fear itself was being rendered manageable. Entertainment—particularly the cinema—passed into the realm of the tactile. Form and content were abandoned. The Me Generation wanted only a physical sensation from what they saw up on the screen. Even children were being conditioned to the idea of fear as a plaything, with their nonstop diet of Alice Cooper, Godzilla, and Kiss.

We even got the demons back. (In what was almost the search for God in reverse, the devil searched for you.) Fright entertainment reached a low point with the box office success of *The Exorcist*. The cinema placed itself in the roller coaster and flume-ride business. There were rumors of subsonics and subliminals. People even became paranoid about what was being done to them inside a movie house. Some of the audience threw up, others had nightmares, and a few actually shrieked themselves to death, as exormania, a rash of cast-out devils, swept through supposedly civilized communities.

The Exorcist was a low point in the seventies only because nobody had seen the eighties. In many areas today, we can smell panic in the air. Punk rockers and survivalists tell us there's no future. Environmentalists point out that we are walking around in a miasma of carcinogens, toxins, dioxins, and radiation leakage. Nothing is safe and nothing can be trusted. We are constantly being bombarded by information, most of which is depressing. The culture is overburdened by information, and inputs are being ripped out as individuals flee to the comfort of Jesus, fascism, watching the president act belligerent on TV, or buying a gun. Entertainment spirals between total escape and total unpleasantness as though it could hardly manage to keep up.

The Stephen King genre of fiction offers a play world that confirms the idea that everything's threatening. Horror lurks in familiar places. Telepathic teenage girls destroy the junior prom; old, empty, snow-bound hotels turn writers into psychopaths. From a single cell to a suburban house, anything can go berserk. In the junior leagues, slice and slash provide the prelude to teen sex. Foreplay happens against a background of sexually loaded, mass meat cleaving. The only respite comes from the big-screen special-effects romps or the Kodachrome erotic *Blue Lagoon*. You only had to be in a movie house last summer for *Superman II or Raiders of the Lost Ark* to learn that a lot of the attraction is being in a womb of darkness with a huge screen and Dolby sound. It's likely that the *Star Wars* saga will go on for the next twenty years—if civilization lasts that long.

Star Wars notwithstanding, we don't seem to be expecting any outside help. The idea of benign intervention from space died when *Alien* became a box office hit. Our first contact with a being from beyond had to be with the baddest mother in the galaxy. Good aliens had their swan song with Spielberg's *Close Encounters*, and even that was only a lavish compendium of UFO paranoias topped by an almost hippie nostalgic happy end.

When measured jolts of either fear or escapism become a form of entertainment in themselves, they tend to act as an addictive drug. It was true of the Roman games, and it is true of today's slash cinema. The audience builds a tolerance; the shocks have increased in strength, and the massage has become more absurdly soothing. Fifty years ago, Lugosi and Karloff actually made people's flesh creep. Now they run on Saturday-morning TV as a laugh riot for the tots—along with the Count Chocula breakfast cereal commercial. This week we need an electric carving knife to get off; next week, a sliced eyeball. When entertainment gets that hyper, you reach the *Caligula* point, when fantasy and reality become interchangeable, and the sliced eyeball and the neutron bomb are equally fantastic. (Who can fear the bomb when they've been playing *Missile Command* since the age of four?)

We no longer use fantasy to examine our fears from a safe distance. It's an aid to wrapping ourselves in a cocoon of dangerously numb belligerence. It occurs to the puritan in me that it may be time for a cultural drying out. The other alternative is sitting in the ruins with no culture at all, apart from some scary campfire tales.

I think this is where I came in.

Heavy Metal, 1981

THE SOUND OF ONE KNEE JERKING

☐ Needless to say, alienation was one of major motivators intended to create the psycho-civilized society that was the authoritarian dream for the second half of the twentieth century. The goal was to breed a population that was isolated, uncommunicative, obedient, conformist, and very, very afraid. In some demographics, it worked all too well.

A NICARAGUAN SUPPORT GROUP HAS BEEN DOING SOME guerilla advertising. They've had these neat little speech bubble stickers printed up. They come in pairs. One reads (within limitations of my less-than-perfect memory): "In Nicaragua they are building schools and clinics. Are we sending them cement?" The other replies: "No, hot lead!" They can be stuck to any poster that features two figures in some kind of interface, and on subway platform posters, there's a whole lot of interfacing going on.

These kind of stickers are hardly an original concept, but their existence raised a smile as I stood in the Canal Street station waiting for the uptown local. If nothing else, it was nice to know that someone still cared in these insensitive times. While I was alternately staring down the track wondering if that light was a train, and checking the clock, calculating how late I was, I noticed the middle-aged man in the gray overcoat. He had also seen the stickers, and he was peeling them off with his fingernails, scraping with an angry determination and attention to detail that went far beyond an act of casual vandalism.

He really hated those things. He hated their message. It was quite obsessive. He didn't even want to *hear* about it.

In all other respects he seemed perfectly normal. The coat, the glasses, the thinning hair, and the tired leather briefcase all suggested that he was some ground-level management type, perhaps in one of the print shops on Varick Street. He wasn't a nut. The pro-Nicaraguan stickers were *making* him nuts.

But what had the Nicaraguans ever done to him? I

MICK FARREN

doubted that he would have been able to find the place on the map a couple of years ago. I realized I was watching a primal American kneejerk. What had thrown this man into such a single-minded rage was the specter of communism. (I use the word specter advisedly—this whole thing has a lot more to do with the supernatural than actual). For this guy, the unthinkable was happening. His president had told him that the reds were in his backyard and here in the subway was the factual evidence. He was just burning up with the anger of the deeply and resentfully scared.

It's really easy to understand why the rich should react to the idea of communism with violent loathing. The communists have, after all, as good as avowed to take away their money, power, and privilege. Nobody likes that. What I've found more difficult to grasp is how that same loathing has spread among the middle-class, working people, and even the poor, all of whom could, to some degree, be described as victims of the rich. The man in the gray overcoat is a perfect case in point. He looked like he'd been shortchanged all his life, like he had precious little to protect. And yet, there he was, in a quiet fury, protecting it. I seemed to be getting a live demonstration of how McCarthyism is more than skin deep. Somehow, it had touched the actual soul of America, filling an infantile need for a devil. On this level, we're not talking opposing economic systems or even superpower politics, we're talking about demons and bogymen.

I began to get scared. Was the man in the gray overcoat just a symptom of a country unconsciously psyching itself up for a war? Certainly our leaders seem to be doing exactly that. While Congress and even the media rather weakly try to hold it in check, the Administration becomes almost psychotic in its need to fuck with the Sandinistas. If Daniel Ortega embraced the entire 1984 Republican platform, they'd still want to mess him over. There are times when I wonder if our leaders' rabid anti-communism is crude manipulation or an advanced form of malady.

Whichever it is, the gearing-up goes on. Temporarily

denied money, it's forced to be a propaganda war at the moment. Reagan's tame commentators have already escalated from distortion to hate-fantasy. Here's George Will in the *Daily News*: "An armed Nicaraguan minority, sustained by outside forces, is Sovietizing Nicaragua in the way that was done in Eastern Europe. The Sandinistas have no more right to rule Nicaragua than Vidkun Quisling had to rule Norway."

Uh, hold it there a minute, George. I don't remember the Russians invading Nicaragua and imposing a puppet government. I seem to recall something about popular revolution and even an election, albeit a less than satisfactory one. Or maybe we're talking about two different Nicaraguas.

The FBI appears to have decided that the war is already on. CBS News reported that more than 100 US citizens who had visited Nicaragua in the last year have been subject to interrogation and the seizure of diaries and address books. The FBI blandly announced that they were searching for "lists of terrorists," and implied that a loyal citizen had no reason to be upset if a gang of G-men showed up on his or her doorstep in the middle of the night.

And then there was Ron, himself. After Congress had denied him his Contra money, he began muttering about how he was looking for new ways to finance a war. This opens some truly astonishing vistas. A sponsored war? After a sponsored Olympics and all the shuck and jive about fixing up the Statue of Liberty, there's a certain hideous logic to it. How about Pepsi, the Official Soft Drink of the 1984 War in Central America?

Here's the really scary part: What we're talking about is only the small bit that's floated to the surface. What vicious lunacy is going on behind locked doors and under cover of night defies imagination and basically can't be stopped. And the only thing that can be counted on in this whole mess is that if anything goes down in Nicaragua, we'll be the last to know.

East Village Eye, June 1985

MICK FARREN

THE BLACK MATTER

The Black Matter is confined to its cube
The Black Matter cannot be controlled or directed
The Black Matter can only be imprisoned
The Black Matter communicates with me
But only through the penitentiary labyrinth
Heat-pipes of my imagination
And even then my summoned strength is insufficient
To process it in more than small jigsaw fragments
Needlepoint details
The aerodynamic flutter of fabric
Through the long and fatal fall

But the Black Matter empowers me
To talk of the events that dare not speak their name.
Sinister? I would say so.
But do my enemies experience the same anguish?
I would hope so
Yet I fundamentally doubt it
Such pain has been edited,
Excised and censored
From their pastel dictionary of newspeak
And that, of course, is why they are my enemies
Turning in their narcissism
And suit-of-lights illusions of power
They deny the very existence of the Black Matter

But they will face it
They will face it head-on and hard
When the power to the controlling cube finally fails
And the Black Matter is loosed to its terrible freedom

❑ In other circumstances, the problem of alienation can be much more of an abstraction…

Read in performance but not published

OSTENSIBLY FREE

Back in 1967, when we weren't dropping acid, holding drug orgies, and going to San Francisco with flowers in our hair, we were watching **The Prisoner**. The TV show was a brilliant compendium of secret government fears, secret agent mindfuck, and just about everything else we considered the rational end of the paranoid amusement park. In the process Patrick McGoohan became a hippie cultural hero.

"So then I'm free," said K doubtfully. "Yes," said the painter, "but only ostensibly free, or more exactly, provisionally free. For the judges of the lowest grade, to whom my acquaintances belong, haven't the power to grant a final acquittal, that power is reserved for the highest court of all, which is quite inaccessible to you, to me, and to all of us."—Franz Kafka, *The Trial*

IN THE LATE SIXTIES PARANOIA ALMOST REPLACED SEX as the favorite indoor sport of a large section of the community. It was hardly surprising really. The particular sections of the community about whom I'm talking had just started ingesting massive doses of mind-sapping chemicals. This single fact alone elevated paranoia from the mundane and nagging "Did I leave the gas on/Has the cat caught fire?" to an intricate game of twisted logic.

The fact that the mind-snapping chemicals were also illegal added an extra dimension to the game. It was a time when the penalties for the uncool and unwary had malicious teeth. It wasn't all that uncommon for the unsuspecting hippie cracked for a half ounce of the best black dope to descend into one of Her Majesty's more unpleasant holiday camps for a six month stay. In this kind of climate it was all too easy to weave a world of Kafkaesque semi-fantasy where phones were always tapped, every unknown freak was an undercover narc and the man standing on the corner opposite your house just had to be watching you. And this was only the domestic end.

When it came to global scale paranoid scenarios not even the sky was the limit. Scare stories came thick and fast. The US government was supposed to be refurbishing the Californian concentration camps, used during World War II for interning Japanese, to house all the hippies, freaks, and peace creeps. Another legend at the time was that the US air force had an undamaged UFO plus some dead aliens hidden away at a secret base. Even the news added fuel to the fantasy. The JKF assassination was the big one. The theories that erupted, almost before Oswald's gun was cold, filled dozens of fat paperbacks. Odd little facts like the death of some nineteen witnesses—Jack Ruby et al—served to turn nagging suspicion into rabid theorizing. When Malcolm X, Martin Luther King, Bobby Kennedy, Che Guevara, Patrice Lumumba, Marilyn Monroe and a couple of dozen Black Panthers were all dispatched to the happy hunting ground, all it took was some spare days and a fevered imagination to suss out that the killings were the result of a global conspiracy masterminded by the eleven immortal intellects in a Tibetan hideout (who were of course taking their orders from the Galactic Council on Alpha Centauri IV).

The eleven naturally had total, if covert, control of the FBI, CIA, Pentagon, ITT, IBM, the Mafia, the Kremlin, Chairman Mao and the guy who ran the paper shop on the corner. Also in the master plan were Adolf Hitler, working from his pied-a-terre in the Argentinean jungle and Walt Disney in his cryogenic deep freeze. Once you had put all this together it became quite clear that E. Howard Hunt had fixed the brakes on Bob Dylan's motorcycle, but botched the job. If all this made your brain tired, you could relax and listen to 'Sad Eyed Lady Of The Lowlands' twenty or so times and try and figure out the great hidden meaning.

Into this climate of mental overload came a TV show called *The Prisoner* (which, if you'd been wondering, is what this piece is really about). Approached on the most mundane level, *The Prisoner* was simply the terminal spy show. Spying was big media business in the sixties. It had mutated from the simple upper class thuggery of J. Bond through to the shadowy world of seedy double, triple, or even quadruple agents of Le Carre, Deighton, and the TV show *Callan*. Simplistically, *The Prisoner* was the final stop along the road. There was nothing simple about *The Prisoner*, however. It took the kind of left-hand-not-knowing-what-the right-hand's-doing, and created a complex, cat's cradle of fine de siècle elegance. The layers of intrigue and deception lay so thickly over the story that the viewer found himself enmeshed in a guessing game of such Zen proportions that it made *The Big Sleep* look like a simple anecdote. The basic plot is that Patrick McGoohan, an espionage agent who seems to be an extension of the character he played in the highly successful *Danger Man* series, attempts to resign from a CIA-style super-automated, intelligence organization.

The implication is that his resignation stems from an unspecified matter of principle. He returns to his apartment and is promptly gassed by a sinister frock coated undertaker. He wakes to find himself in a kind of kitsch middle-class holiday camp, laid out with the ultimate of twee bad taste. Life in the village is idyllic (for anyone who aspires to little more than muzak and crazy golf). Leaving the village is seemingly impossible. The perimeter is guarded by sentient weather balloons, who go by the name of Rover and have an unpleasant habit of smothering would-be fugitives,

Names are taboo in the village. The inmates are referred to by numbers. McGoohan draws Number Six. The idea of being a number is the core of McGoohan's unrelenting rebellion. Each show opens with Six's defiant scream: "I am not a number! I am a free man!"

A war of nerves starts between McGoohan and the director of the village, Number Two (who is, incidentally, replaced every episode). The organization believes that the key to breaking McGoohan is to get him to reveal the reason for his resignation. McGoohan counters with the increasingly obsessive demand to know the identity of Number One.

McGoohan is subjected to each successive Number Two's most baroque soft-sell brainwashing techniques. There are no lights in the face and rubber truncheons. The weapons are disorientation, demoralization and a deliberate blurring of what's real and what's not. Number Six counters this psych attack with uncompromising hostility, random, anarchic and often surreal behavior. As if this wasn't all complicated enough, the plot is heavily laced with images from classic nightmares. For instance, there's a ubiquitous dwarf butler whose continuous silent presence tempts the viewer into the suspicion that perhaps he is Number One. In one episode a new inmate wakes in a facsimile of her own home. It's only when she opens the curtains that she discovers that she's in the village. The shock reduces her to a state of uncontrolled hysteria. The idea is also put forward that the village may not belong to any particular side in the hyper Cold War that appears to rage with ceaseless secrecy. It might be that both sides use the place to isolate people who know too much and reprogram the recalcitrant or, on the other hand…

This kind of treble-think is taken to such extremes that concepts like friend and foe become totally meaningless. Kafka and Orwell are left at the post as the plot spaghettis its way through each week's fifty minute installment. Number Six exists in a world of non-trusting isolation. Nothing is what it appears. He couldn't even wind up loving Big Brother, since the identity of Big Brother is never revealed. There have been other attempts to build a TV series on galloping paranoia. The Americans tried it with shows like *The Fugitive*, in which David Jansen raced around America, pursued by a relentless police force in search of a one-armed man who could clear him of a murder rap. Another was *The Invaders*, where someone whose name I fail to remember tried to convince blankly sceptical authorities that the earth was being taken over by ruthless aliens cunningly disguised as regular human beings.

The soul wrenching angst of these two offerings was Mickey Mouse compared with the mind-rot experienced by McGoohan. *The Prisoner* takes psychodrama to levels rarely seen on television. In fact, they took it altogether too far, at least as far as the tube moguls were concerned. Displeasure fell from on high like a headman's axe. With sixteen episodes in the can and the show already going out on the air, the word came that it had gone too far. The projected final seven episodes were hurriedly cancelled, and a single wrap-up show was hastily cobbled together. Although the last episode is far from satisfactory, it does excel itself in uncontrolled surrealism. Number Six's last lap to the mysterious Number One takes him down an endless subterranean passage lined with jukeboxes blaring out the

Beatles' 'All You Need Is Love.' Heavy stuff for 1968.

Patrick McGoohan has never made a public statement of his feelings about the sudden truncation of the series. It can, however, have hardly been less than a crushing blow. *The Prisoner* was very much his exclusive brainchild, a product of the corporate muscle he acquired through four-and-a-half years in the fiscally successful *Danger Man*.

As well as playing the almost continuously on-screen role of Number Six, McGoohan acted as executive producer on the project and directed a number of episodes. Indeed, the entire show was played totally according to McGoohan. The methods of working almost rivalled the show's plot in terms of complex secrecy. Backed by a highly experienced production crew and a cast made up from the cream of British character actors, McGoohan insisted on a totally closed set. No press were invited to watch the shooting and no interviews were granted. Even the exact location of the village was kept from everyone but the people directly involved in the production.

Probably the strangest factor of all was McGoohan's attitude to the all-over plot. Neither the scriptwriters nor even the producer were allowed to have any clear idea of the eventual outcome of the series. Only McGoohan had all the pieces of the jigsaw and these he kept strictly to himself, only giving out such information as was necessary to complete each episode. Rumors coming out of *The Prisoner* set told how members of the crew became as obsessed with trying to ferret out the identity of Number One as the fictional Number Six was in the show. Since the ultimate outcome of the series was firmly locked in McGoohan's head, he was constantly badgered with questions. He developed a short laconic answer. Without exception, everyone was told to "wait and see." The final irony was that McGoohan's original concept for the show's conclusion was lost to the world when the series was treated like a madman's bastard brainchild, fit only to be used as a sop to some weirdo fringe of the viewing public, and trimmed back to seventeen episodes.

New Musical Express, 1975

MICK FARREN

I'LL VAPORIZE YOU

THE GREAT FICTIONAL BLUEPRINT FOR A TOTALITARIAN state ruling by surveillance is, of course, George Orwell's classic *1984*. The novel was written at the end of World War II, when it seemed to Orwell that, one way or another, the world could not prevent itself falling victim to some variety of crushing totalitarianism. In Orwell's fantasy, the population, under the rule of the ever vigilant Big Brother, watched the "telly screens" while, at the same time, the telly screens watched them. This was, however, science fiction, and the imaginary technology functioned perfectly. The slogan "Big Brother Is Watching You" that was displayed everywhere meant what it said. Subsequent readings, though, tended to reveal how the logistics of Orwell's world of perpetual surveillance were a little shaky. Orwell does imply that the only section of the population being constantly watched was the "Outer Party," his equivalent of a lower management class, and the theory seemed to be that, if they were kept in line, the proles would follow, and, of course, the elite would have no reason to destabilize their privilege. Even taking into account this limit to numbers of whom Big Brother was actually watching, the necessary manpower was still close to implausible, and Orwell never quite made clear just how all the watching was done.

At a very minimum, it had to take three of Orwell's sinister Thought Police, working eight-hour shifts, seven days a week, to maintain a twenty-four-hour-a-day watch on a single citizen. Here was the flaw, up until the end of the twentieth century, in all totalitarian concepts of rule by an ever-present camera. To be fully effective, the watchers would have to outnumber the watched to a point that was clearly neither practical nor cost effective, even in the collapsed economy of *1984*.

The truth was that, until the development of modern computer technology, repression worked on the more haphazard technique of people watching each other. Spies, informers, snitches, and tattletales were, for many centuries,

❏ In **The Prisoner**, the Village was the place of social control. In George Orwell's **1984**, fear and alienation were the core motivations of the entire society.

the traditional primary tools of every secret police force in the world. Just how far this went generally depended on the ruthlessness of the regime and how obsessive those in power might be about social control and threats—real and imagined—to their authority. In *1984*, Orwell fantasized that not even the family would be safe from state-sponsored spying, and children would be recruited to report subversive speech and actions by their mothers and fathers, causing parents to be terrified of their offspring, and even childish games reinforced the fear of State and Party.

"'You're a traitor!' yelled the boy. 'You're a thought-criminal! You're a Eurasian spy! I'll shoot you, I'll vaporize you, I'll send you to the salt mines!'

"Suddenly they were both leaping round him, shouting 'Traitor!' and 'Thought-criminal!' the little girl imitating her brother in every movement. It was somehow slightly frightening, like the gamboling of tiger cubs which will soon grow up into man-eaters."

Not previously published

INTERROGATION

Interrogation is a central motif of anxiety and paranoia. In **1984**, it is the culmination of the story, and is usually the start of the worse case—or perversely desired—scenario. Winston Smith, Josef K, Number Six, and maybe even O would all confirm this. (That's O whose story was told by Pauline Réage—recently revealed as Ann Desclos.)

THE DOCTOR POURED COGNAC INTO THE PRISONER'S balloon glass. The gesture was superficially expansive, but did nothing to disguise the cold underlying hostility. "So much of what you say is hardly plausible."

The prisoner swirled the brandy in the ostentatious glass. He inhaled the alcohol vapor. He hadn't eaten in so long, the fumes alone were capable of making him drunk. "If you had seen what I had seen, you would not be so reluctant to believe me."

"If I had seen what you had seen I would not be required to believe you. I would be you."

"But if you were me, who would I be?"

"Word games? Juvenile existentialism? Isn't this all a little pointless?"

"I didn't ask to be here."

MICK FARREN

The doctor leaned back in his chair. "That is something I do believe."

"That's something you know for a fact. Belief or disbelief don't even signify. I didn't ask to be here, I actively resisted coming here, and I'm being held against my will. You actively facilitated my captivity. It is something that cannot be called into question."

The doctor carefully pressed his fingertips together. "Whatever you think is being done to you is ultimately for your own good."

"Bullshit."

The doctor smiled. "Now who's unwilling to believe?"

The prisoner sighed. "I'm willing to believe. Tell me anything. I'll believe it. Just watch me."

Doc40, 2009

FIVE HUNDRED THOUSAND AMERICAN COFFINS

AN ANONYMOUS VIDEO SHOWING A HALF MILLION PLAStic coffins stashed in a formidably fenced field near Hartsfield Jackson International Airport in Atlanta, GA, is guaranteed to grab the attention. One can hardly help but question the reason for the stacked ranks of the ugly, airtight, gray-green boxes. Is someone somewhere expecting a massive bodycount, and, if so, why? The veracity of the video is hard to question. A simple handheld camcorder shoots continuously from a vehicle driving along a two-lane backroad in broad daylight. The coffins are in plain sight, right in the open, piled geometrically for hundreds of yards. We appear to have a mystery, especially when an extensive Google search reveals that, aside from a single brief squib on WRAL-TV in Raleigh, NC, the story of the coffins in the field has failed to surface anywhere in the mainstream media. The line between curiosity and paranoia, however, can be hard to define, so I proceed with caution.

❑ If alienation could be viewed as one of the four horsemen of authoritarian control, its three companions have to be ignorance, disinformation, and fear. And yet, like so many other attempts to manipulate the masses, they all too easily ride into a swamp of paranoia and concocted stories, and become bogged down in rumor. The masses who were expected to be rendered docile, dutiful, and compliant turn surly and distrustful. When governments make a cult of secrecy—when the left hand never knows what the right hand is doing and the people know even less—an information vacuum is created that will—almost by a law of nature—fill itself with the most dire and dangerous fantasies. This story was researched and written during the Bush administration, but, no sooner had George W. been sent back to Crawford, and Barack Obama was installed in the White House, media opportunists like Glenn Beck and Michele Malkin turned these obsessive rumors on a dime and, where previously they have been blamed on Bush and Dick Cheney, they were instantly laid at the door of Obama, who, the near-fascist right insisted, was in the process of establishing a racist totalitarian police state.

A dispassionate review of the facts makes clear that, if a large number of coffins had to be stockpiled in anticipation of some ultra-dire national emergency, Atlanta would be a good place to do it. It is a major confluence for road, rail, and air traffic. Hartsfield Jackson is one of the nation's biggest and busiest hubs for commercial aviation. Atlanta is also home to the Center for Disease Control. Is it the CDC who knows something we don't? Is a plague expected and no one is telling us? As radio host and conspiracy theorist Alex Jones wrote on his website Prison Planet "I don't want to alarm anyone, but usually you don't buy 500,000 plastic coffins just in case something happens, you buy them because you know something is going to happen."

I discover a link to a site called the Neithercorp web forum where the Atlanta coffins are under constant discussion. I'm informed that a possible manufacturer of the coffins is Vantage Products Corporation in Covington, Georgia, and the unsubstantiated plot thickens when I learn that Vantage is allegedly a government contractor, a spin-off of DuPont, and has a Chief Legal Officer who was supposedly a former Monsanto bigwig. Unfortunately the possible conspiracy deflates with word from a poster using the pseudonym "dingoistheman" who claims to live near the coffin dump. "These things have been there for ten years. There has never been any activity on the site since they brought them in." Did I really need to call the CDC for an official statement that the coffins had nothing to do with them, and a denial that we were all going to die from bird flu this winter? Instead I followed another set of links to YouTube. And, to my surprise, the conspiracy suddenly re-inflated itself ten-fold.

With a combination of delight and dismay, I learned that the video clip I had already seen was only one among many. It was simple and linear, but many of the others I found on YouTube were professional quality productions. I discovered that they were not only raising all the possible questions posed by the half million coffins in Atlanta, but also offering some truly horrific answers.

The basis of this YouTube crew's collective theory is a

near-unthinkable power scenario. It may be paranoia, but it's high impact paranoia. Sometime before he's scheduled to leave office next January, George W. Bush will engineer an epic pretext to suspend the constitution, cancel or nullify the November elections, and declare martial law. Normally a coup is when a military junta—like the fictional Pentagon plot in the movie classic *Seven Days In May*—deposes the civilian authority and seizes power, but Bush can seemingly be counted on to reverse the traditional sequence. According to these uploads on YouTube, he is going to use the military to ensure that he and his cronies remain in permanent command, world without end. And the coffins in Atlanta—plus more on other sites around mainland US—will be used for disposal of those executed in the bloody aftermath of the coming Bush putsch.

Either a war with Iran, or a massively violent incident, on the same scale as the falling towers of 9/11, will become the pretext to round up millions of supposed "terrorists," "terrorist sympathizers," and "dissidents," and either execute them or imprison them in concentration camps run by FEMA (the Federal Emergency Management Agency). This at least is the story, as presented by these YouTube videos—created by individuals and groups with names like pushforfreedom, earthlasthope, or razzaq19—and comes with a wealth of detail. According to these YouTube subversives, the Department of Homeland Security already has comprehensive lists that divide the population into three color-coded categories.

Those with the designation "Red" have no chance. Anyone who has opposed George Bush during his eight-year reign will be arrested—dragged from their beds in the dark of night, faces covered, protests muffled by black hoods—and held for extermination. The "Blue" category is reserved for less threatening malcontents, petty criminals, and the rank and file followers of "Reds." They will be held for forced labor and re-education in the joys of totalitarian capitalism. The final, and by far the largest group, are the "Yellow," the already docile, who Kenn Thomas, of the online conspiracy magazine Steamshovel Press, describes in an interview with *Karmapolis* magazine in Belgium, as "happy, SUV driving, George Bush supporting McCitizens who have no need for a tank to be pointed at them in order to get them to obey." To view the full theoretical horror, one only has to run a YouTube search for "FEMA coffins" or "FEMA concentration camps."

FEMA figures significantly in this whole simmering mythology. Its sweeping emergency powers are continuously cited as the crucial Trojan horse that disguises the infiltration mechanisms of the great and global—but probably fictional—oppression of what's known in the conspiracy subworld as the New World Order. This, though, is nothing new. Conspiracy veterans recall how, in the Clinton era of the 1990s, FEMA and the New World Order loomed large in the "black helicopter" fantasies of the paranoid far right. Back in the twentieth century, the militia movement, readers of *The Turner Dairies*, and extreme evangelicals were convinced that Bill Clinton would choreograph a phony national emergency, all the excuse needed for FEMA, supported by United Nations troops— usually from Turkey and Pakistan—to invade the country and deprive Americans of their national sovereignty, as power was ceded to the NWO.

The New World Order is a more venerable preoccupation than even FEMA. It has cast its murky and threatening shadow for more than a century, perpetually poised to steal power from both hereditary dynasties and elected governments. At various times it has supposedly been controlled by Freemasons, Fabians, the British royal family, the alleged Elders of Zion, munitions barons, Communists, Nazis, Trilateralists, the Bilderberg Group, and—at furthest stretch—extraterrestrials from Zeta Reticuli. Mercifully, the NWO has always remained an apparent figment of the paranoid mindset. FEMA, on the other hand, is uncomfortably real. It was created by Jimmy Carter's 1979 presidential order to bring civil defense and disaster preparedness under one roof, and the unprecedented power it acquired in the process is well recognized as potentially disastrous if it ever fell into the wrong hands. And many of this YouTube crew firmly believe, if George Bush and his Department of Homeland Security control FEMA, it is now in the worst possible hands.

Even the supposition that any fear of FEMA would have died after the debacle of the agency's response to Hurricane Katrina, and the 2005 flooding of New Orleans, does nothing to allay the apprehension of the YouTube crew. They claim that the whole NOLA mess was merely a smokescreen. As Kenn Thomas put it, again in *Karmapolis*, "When George Bush patted former FEMA management head Michael Brown on the back and said 'Good job!' he was rubbing it in, announcing that he really didn't give a damn about taking responsibility for Katrina's aftermath." On YouTube, the accusations go further. Sixteen hundred people died, and the lower Ninth Ward was deliberately allowed to turn into a toxic swamp to conceal FEMA's real capabilities, and the agency will function with brutal efficiency if so required by its political masters.

When first confronting this elaborate conspiracy theorizing, the whole idea seems far-fetched and hideously implausible. Even the smirking Bush could not actually bring himself to initiate a holocaust that deliberately took the lives of millions of Americans, could he? Unfortunately Bush could, if he so desired. Much of what the conspiracy theorizers' fear is already—under current Federal law—more than theoretically possible. The president of the United States already has what amounts to dictatorial power. In February of this year, environmentalist Lewis Seiler and former congressman Dan Hamburg published a scary compendium of Bush's extraordinary powers in the *San Francisco Chronicle*. "Since 9/11, and seemingly without the notice of most Americans, the federal government has assumed the authority to institute martial law, arrest a wide swath of dissenters (citizen and noncitizen alike), and detain people without legal or constitutional recourse."

The Bush power grab began within hours of the towers falling on 9/11, when Bush put down *My Pet Goat* and issued his "Declaration of Emergency by Reason of Certain Terrorist Attacks" as defined by the National Emergencies

Act. This sweeping declaration could be rescinded by joint resolution of Congress, but has actually been extended six times. In 2007, the declaration was quietly strengthened by National Security Presidential Directive 51, which gave the president the power to do whatever he deemed necessary in a vaguely defined 'catastrophic emergency,' from cancelling elections, and suspending the Constitution, to launching a nuclear attack. Seiler and Hamburg cite how the 2007 National Defense Authorization Act (NDAA) gives the Executive the power to invoke martial law, and "the Military Commissions Act of 2006—rammed through Congress before the 2006 midterm elections—allows for the indefinite imprisonment of anyone who donates money to a 'terrorist' organization, or speaks out against government policies." Seiler and Hamburg continue grimly, "The law calls for secret trials for citizens and noncitizens alike."

If the coffins in that Georgia field were the only evidence supporting fears of a Bush dictatorship, the entire scenario might be dismissed out of hand. Regrettably that is not the case. The coffin videos are not alone. They are flanked on YouTube by similar footage of a complete and extensive US Gulag with camps and prison trains. The paranoia crew offers what purport to be mindbending outlaw tapes of FEMA prison trains, grim but brand-new, double-decker railcars, allegedly manufactured by Gunderson Steel in Portland, Oregon, complete with shackles for prisoners and guard shacks at each end. Actual FEMA concentration camps, with full compliments of guards, stadium lights, gleaming razor wire, and huge AGA gas furnaces, are supposedly ready to accept inmates. All this makes dismissal difficult. When the images are on the Internet for all to see, it's hard to argue with groups like The Friends of Liberty, who claim "over 800 prison camps in the United States are all fully operational and ready to receive prisoners should Martial Law need to be implemented. All it would take is a presidential signature on a proclamation and the attorney general's signature on a warrant."

The scenarios of the YouTube crew and the Friends of Liberty are also supported by Seiler and Hamburg, again in the *San Francisco Chronicle*, who quote the claims of diplomat and author Peter Dale Scott that "beginning in 1999, the government entered into a series of single-bid contracts with Halliburton subsidiary Kellogg, Brown, and Root (KBR) to build detention camps at undisclosed locations within the United States. The government has also contracted with several companies to build thousands of railcars, some reportedly equipped with shackles, ostensibly to transport detainees. According to the KBR contract the work is part of a Homeland Security plan titled ENDGAME, which sets as its goal the removal of "all removable aliens" and "potential terrorists."

In another blast from the past, the legal underpinning for something like ENDGAME in fact dates back to Orwell-apocryphal 1984, when, in the basement of the Ronald Reagan White House, Oliver North and National Guard Colonel Louis Giuffrida, in preparation for a possible invasion of the Sandinista-controlled Nicaragua, devised a plan called REX 84 to "crush national opposition to any military action abroad" by the suspension of the Constitution, the turning of control of the government over to FEMA, and "internment in concentration camps of up to 100,000 illegal immigrants and political dissidents." At the time columnist Jack Anderson warned it would "clamp Americans in a totalitarian vice."

The seeds for REX 84 were originally planted during the Kennedy administration, when Executive Order 11051 provided for suspension of the Constitution and martial law in the event of nuclear attack. Under Richard Nixon it was expanded to cover multiple national emergencies including civil insurrections. Finally North and Giuffrida redefined it so it could be activated by the president alone, causing Professor Diana Reynolds of Northeastern University to comment, "America is only a presidential directive away from a civil security state of emergency." Although Iran-Contra investigations sidelined REX 84, it remains on the books.

History again repeats itself in that the majority of these YouTube videos, warning us about REX 84, END-GAME, and a possible American tyranny, are posted by conservatives and right wingers. Many are also veterans of the 9/11 Truth movement who refuse to accept the official accounts of the attacks on Lower Manhattan and the Pentagon. Ron Paul's name is often invoked, with followers of the libertarian-leaning, presidential contender fearing they will be arrested and victimized as a result of their break with Bush/McCain Republican neo-orthodoxy. Others see the neocon takeover of the party as a step on the road to dictatorship, while still more, recalling the carnage at the Weaver farm on Ruby Ridge and the Branch Davidian compound near Waco, distrust the Federal Government under any president. In this they are not alone. A recent Scripps Howard/Ohio University national poll of 1,010 adults revealed that "anger against the federal government is at record levels," with fifty-four percent responding that they "personally are more angry at the government than they used to be." The poll also found that more than a third of those contacted suspected that the Feds under Bush either "assisted in the 9/11 terrorist attacks or took no action to stop them."

But anxiety over the Bush regime moving towards tyranny and dictatorship is not by any means limited to the right. Progressive intellectuals like "third-wave" feminist Naomi Wolf also issue warnings. "Beneath our very noses, George Bush and his administration are using time-tested tactics to close down an open society. It is time for us to be willing to think the unthinkable—that it can happen here. And that we are further along than we realize." In her book, *The End of America: A Letter of Warning to a Young Patriot*, she spells out the ten steps needed for a fascist takeover, from propaganda induced fear to a complete suspension of the rule of law, and she is quoted in more than one of the YouTube conspiracy videos.

None of the YouTube crew has so far quoted alternative press veteran Joe Conason. His 2007 book, *It Can Happen Here: Authoritarian Peril in the Age of Bush*, does not totally agree that a Bush coupe is hard upon us, but claims to sense a move in that direction. *"For the first time since the resignation of Richard M. Nixon more than three decades ago, Americans have had reason to doubt the future of democracy and the rule of law in our own country. Today we live in a state of tension between the enjoyment of traditional freedoms, including the protections afforded to speech and person by the Bill of Rights, and the disturbing realization that those freedoms have been undermined and may be abrogated at any moment."*

A dispassionate evaluation of whether this fear is paranoid fantasy or potentially terrifying reality is crucial. It's a lurid tale, but do we seriously believe Blackwater stormtroopers in ski masks and combat boots are about to kick down our doors in the dead of night? The evidence of the plastic coffins, the Gunderson Steel railcars, and the KBR detention camps all comes from unorthodox sources, but it comes in sufficient quantity, and with enough plausible detail, to have an uncomfortable credibility, especially at a time when—with pitifully few exceptions—"legitimate" news sources have lost the cowboy courage to investigate any story that does not have a publicist attached. Paranoia, of course, requires a massive vanity. The ultimate narcissism is the belief that any one of us might pose such a threat to our leaders they will have to execute us or confine us in concentration camps. The argument could also be made that, after eight years of Bush, the national psyche is so badly bruised by the serial punishment of lies, deception, and vicious neocon ideology, we will believe our leaders capable of any iniquity. America has been stumbling through the miasma of neocon mistakes, cover-ups, and misinformation for so long that it becomes hard to tell what's real and what's not.

The comfortable course is to reject the YouTube paranoia crew as a collection of psychotic obsessives. Thinking the unthinkable is hard enough, but believing and preparing for it is even more difficult. On the other hand, to write off the video evidence as well-executed fakery is also tempting, but the clips are so damned believable that isn't easy. Plus coordinating them would have been an extraordinarily mammoth task. With the whiff of madness on both sides, the mind casts around for alternatives. If, for the sake of argument, we accept the images on YouTube as tacit proof the federal government has indeed been stockpiling coffins, commissioning detention camps, and building custom railcars to deliver prisoners to those camps, does that automatically mean a totalitarian coup is at hand? Is it in any way possible that a Gulag could really have been built, but then not used?

The observation has more than once been made that the Bush/Cheney administration is an alliance of fools, fanatics, and crooks. Would it be possible that the crooks sold the unthinkable to the fanatics? KBR/Halliburton has already given Bush and his neocon cronies a hugely expensive and hugely profitable war in Iraq. Would it be that hard to pitch an equally profitable, black-budget, domestic fascism to the neocon ilk of Paul Wolfowitz, Max Boot, or John Bolton? They already have a philosophical contempt for the masses, and a fetishised worship of power. Perhaps the Gulag was commissioned, but enough of the fools (and maybe the Pentagon) had enough vestigial humanity to shy away from a complete plunge into totalitarian horror, leaving those who like that kind of thing in need of a sufficiently grandiose excuse.

This story has no reassuring end. Three alternatives stare back at us. Either a crew of Ron Paul supporters and others are running a great anti-Bush/McCain Internet fraud. Or the FEMA camps exist but the neocons have yet to find the evil heart to use them. Or the Blackwater thugs will shortly be dragging us away. While friends and neighbors are not actually being made to disappear we can breathe easy and not need to study routes to Canada. While I can still write this story and have it published, democracy is still in shape and functioning. Of course, if I was to suddenly vanish it would mean... (Hey, where did he go?)

LA CityBeat, September 2007

MICK FARREN

IS THAT A PISTOL IN YOUR POCKET?

THE LATE AFTERNOON OF APRIL 20, 1999—ADOLF Hitler's 110th birthday—found me, for reasons that hardly matter, at LAX deplaning (as they call it) after a flight from London, but then being required, along with the rest of the passengers, to run a gauntlet of heavyweight LAPD, with flack jackets, automatic weapons, and dogs. "What the hell? Was Bill Clinton deposed in a coup?" (This was pre-9/11, remember, when our worst worry was Y2K.) Travelers edged towards panic, but I found myself perversely intrigued, eavesdropping every snippet of conversation, gleaning that two Goth boys had shot up their high school somewhere in Colorado, and the cops seemed to fear a nationwide armed youth uprising led by Marilyn Manson.

When I finally reached home and functioning cable, I learned from CNN that, in fact, it was Dylan Klebold and Eric Harris shooting up Columbine High School, and not some full-scale millennial teen-apocalypse. As I watched the endless Columbine coverage, part of me couldn't resist a limited empathy with—if not their insane ruthlessness—certainly the cultural antecedents of Klebold and Harris' killer narcissism. One of my first toys was a Lone Ranger cap pistol, and, about the same time, I developed a morbid interest in human mortality, so Charles Whitman, the Texas Tower Sniper, Charles Manson, the mass-murdering singer songwriter, and all those terminating postal workers later became persons of extreme interest. At that same time, the Doors were among my favorite bands. The great abyss was between word and deed. Jim Morrison had merely sung, "No one here gets out alive." Three decades later Klebold and Harris attempted to make it so.

Thus it was no surprise when Cho Seung-Hui's "manifesto" revealed how the Virginia Tech gunman revered Klebold and Harris as martyred icons. This confirmed a long held belief that a river of armed mayhem flows through the caverns of the Jung-American psyche, at least back to Billy the Kid who, dead at twenty-one, "killed a man for each year of his life." And no amount of gun control, Ri-

❑ At the same time as those in power make use of alienation, ignorance, disinformation and fear as a means of control, the alienated can snap, overwhelmed and precipitated into psychosis by a world they have been conditioned to view as filled with nothing except violence and the threat of violence. And when they snap, see the fear it generates in those who wield the power.

talin, or censoring movies and video games will stem its flow of deadly folklore. These lethal eruptions will occur at regular intervals, like earthquakes or hurricanes, because the gun has become an integral part of modern America dealing with death. The answer is not to pry pistols from cold dead fingers, but to take the symbolism and romance out of the gun before the fingers are dead.

In the welter of pious blather over the Virginia Tech massacre, not a single pundit turned the problem round and even considered that young male mass murder may well have a hell of lot more to do with suicide than slaughter. Through the twentieth century fashions have come and gone in youth suicide. In the post James Dean-era, kids made high speed vehicular death a fad of finality. A quarter of a century later, metal kids in New Jersey killed themselves by rigging their cars for carbon monoxide asphyxiation. Klebold and Harris upped the ante on adolescent suicide by taking a bunch of the bastards with them—the ones they believed were making their lives untenable—and Cho Seung-Hui totally followed their pattern, assured by their example that death would bring him massive notoriety and posthumous stardom.

Chou Seung-Hui's act was an unparalleled advance in sociopath narcissism, and I'm disturbed that his so-called manifesto is currently suppressed. Although it's hardly the Zapruder film being kept from the American people for a dozen years, it is another example of how, as a nation, we are not considered capable of facing ourselves at our very worst. Read from the right perspective, with a degree of imagination, and knowledge of popular culture, it might just be possible—in whatever sick cocktail of *The Matrix* and the Book of Revelations Chou may have used as an excuse for his madness—to actually learn what evil lurks in the hearts of extremely disturbed young people.

LA CityBeat, April 2007

MICK FARREN

FIREARMS AND WHISKEY

So money exchanged hands and the magnum became Max's unlicensed, illegal, and highly dubious property. He stashed it carefully in his luggage so the hotel cleaning staff would not find it unless they really searched. Max had never carried a gun before. He had been around many who did, and even had guns pulled on him. Exactly five guns had been pointed at Max that he knew about. He was certain the number was five. Looking down the barrel of a gun tended to lodge permanently in the recall. He had, however, always foregone the singularly lethal weirdness of packing himself. He knew the attraction was in the power, the kinetic absolutism of being strapped. He could flick through *Guns & Ammo* with the best of them, and could name all the full-auto materiel in the action movies, but one night he had found himself alone with a psychotic control-obsessive Teutonic-Mädchen called Leni, whose dungeon-decor home featured, among many other attractions, a full bottle of Johnny Walker Red and a fully loaded cop-style Mossberg pump shotgun. Although absolutely nothing had been said, he knew he was being challenged to blow his own brains out like a prequel to Kurt Cobain. Max had drunk about half the whiskey and then, with a care learned from Ernest Borgnine, he had drunkenly unloaded the weapon, scattered the orange jacketed shells on the hardwood floor, and stumbled off into the night. During that stumble, he had resolved to have nothing further to do with Fraulein Leni, and been reinforced in his belief that guns were too easy and instant. A trigger pull from infinity was much too close, and firearms should be kept away from the bad-tempered, the fearful, the stupid, the drunk, the newly unemployed, and absolutely anyone like him. That had also been in New York, not many blocks, in fact, from where he was right then, and in New York, it had now come full circle. He had renounced all previous principles and bought himself a weapon. Now he was down with Billy the Kid, Bill Burroughs, and Tupac, and he knew he didn't like it. To be

❑ The disturbed person in the clip that follows is wholly fictional and if anyone tells you how I stood swaying with a shotgun in one hand and a bottle of Johnny Walker Red in the other, it's a dirty lie.

armed felt cold and isolating, but he had made his plan and now he must stand by it.

An unpublished note

E.T. TREATIES

I could, I suppose, make some lame joke; a wordplay on aliens and alienation, but it would hardly be worthy of something that, since at least World War II, has been a large and active segment of our paranoia, our fears of the unknown, not to mention twentieth and twenty-first century fable, fantasy, and folklore. Maybe the ultimate alienation is the idea that our species is the only race of evolved and sentient beings in the universe. Some, it would appear, like it that way, and will do anything they can to refute all possibilities to the contrary. Others need so badly to believe we are not alone that they will willingly accept plainly impossible scenarios of alien encounters. The subject of extraterrestrials appears so polarizing that truly rational assessment of mysterious objects in the sky, abduction claims, and sugges-

SINCE THE ALLEGED CRASH OF A SPACE VEHICLE—THE so-called "flying saucer"—at Roswell, New Mexico, in 1947, where both bodies and a live alien were recovered, the US government has been increasingly in cahoots with extraterrestrials. Over the last four-and-a-half decades, our leaders have progressed from simple first contacts to cutting an unholy deal with beings from outer space, beings known in some sections of the UFO business as Extraterrestrial Biological Entities (EBEs). In exchange for various kinds of advanced alien technology, the EBEs have been given a free hand to conduct genetic experiments on human beings, the end result of which would be the creation of a hybrid race, part human, part extraterrestrial, that would eventually take over the Earth.

As a result of this mega-secret treaty, hundreds of thousands of people of all ages and backgrounds have been abducted into alien spacecraft and subjected to un-invited sex acts, and have had samples of tissue and other genetic material removed from their bodies. Some were even implanted with tiny tracking and monitoring devices before being returned to their homes with only the most cloudy memories of what transpired. At the same time as the aliens snatch men, women, and children from hearth and home and have their devious way with them, the US military plays around with various kinds of alien-donated aircraft at secret bases, the nearest and most notorious of which is Area 51—also known as Area S-4 and "Dreamland"—at Groom Lake, Nevada, just 120 miles north of Las Vegas.

How's that for a truly paranoid scenario? Just hang in there for a while longer. We've barely scratched the surface.

To maintain a conspiracy of such galactic proportions, it has been necessary to involve an array of groups and individuals that include the Air Force, Army and Navy intelligence, the National Security Agency, the CIA, and Steven Spielberg. That the Pentagon and the intelligence community should be in on what might be the most awesome conspiracy in the entire history of mankind is hardly surprising. The Spielberg connection is a little more bizarre. In the mid-seventies, while riding high on the success of *Jaws*, the wunderkind director was allegedly inducted into the conspiracy essentially to handle public relations for the aliens. The first of these efforts was 1977s *Close Encounters of the Third Kind*, spectacularly designed to plant the idea that while the scientists and the military might be unscrupulous, venal, and fucked up, the EBEs themselves were sincere fetus-like beings who had only our very best interests at heart. The message was even more firmly rammed home five years later by *E.T. The Extra-Terrestrial*, which assured every child on the planet within reach of a cinema screen that extraterrestrials were not only benign but downright lovable.

Hard to believe? Maybe, but the supposed confirmation of the Spielberg/alien collaboration story is alleged to come from none other than the ancient Gipper himself. An unnamed source claims that during a private White House screening of *E.T.*, Ronald Reagan, who apparently saw a UFO himself while governor of California, leaned close to Spielberg and was heard to whisper, "There are probably only six people in this room who know how true this is."

We humans seemingly can't resist shaping any hypothetical alien visitors in our own image and using them to reflect the most desperate hopes and worst fears of the time. The first mass wave of flying saucer sightings came during the big chill of the Cold War. Back then, aliens were seen as either rapacious invaders bent on planetary conquest and the destruction of humanity, akin to those depicted in classic B-movies like *Earth vs. the Flying Saucers* or *Mars Needs Women*, or as interventionist saviors pledged to res-

tions that the government knows more than it's telling become hard, and, at times, going on impossible.

cue us from our nuclear insanity, like the Michael Rennie character, Klaatu, in *The Day the Earth Stood Still* or in the semi-divine Venusians described by George Adamski in his 1953 book *Flying Saucers Have Landed*.

Adamski, the first man in history to land a book deal by claiming to have been contacted by aliens, described how tall, Nordic Venusians in silver jumpsuits picked him up in a remote part of the Mojave and, between spouting pop philosophy that was essentially a mixture of watered-down Tibetan Buddhism and Madame Blavatsky, informed him that they had been sent to Earth to coax mankind back from the brink of global annihilation.

Adamski quickly fell from favor, if for no other reason than that our growing knowledge of the planet Venus made it impossible to believe that it could be the home of a race of theosophist Scandinavians. Many of his ideas about the nature of aliens, however, continued—with an added seasoning of psychedelic mysticism—well into the sixties. The spectacle of hippies hanging out at Joshua Tree or stumbling around up on Mulholland, looped out of their gourds on DMT or mescaline, waiting for the ETs to come by and make everything right, was hardly a reassurance that my generation was in any way capable of running the world when the time came.

Contrary to popular belief, though, the sixties were not entirely an era of wide-eyed naïveté. Paranoia levels were actually quite as high as they are today. The first rumors were making the rounds that the government might have a crashed saucer under wraps in Hangar 18 (or more elaborately, Building 18A, Area B) at Wright-Patterson Air Force Base in Ohio. The first stories of the Men in Black (MIBs) had also started to circulate. These guys, who looked and dressed like anal retentive versions of the Blues Brothers, would show up in brand-new 1963 Cadillac Coupe de Villes and scare the shit out of anyone who'd had a close UFO encounter. Hangar 18 and the MIBs were the original seeds that grew into today's elaborate conspiracy theories. Fertilized largely by the current mood of absolute distrust in government, Hangar 18 has blossomed into Area 51, and the Men in Black now wear Delta Force-style black jumpsuits, carry Uzis, and ride in unmarked black helicopters.

If the government isn't trusted where UFOs are concerned, it has only itself to blame. The official response to the earliest UFO sightings was, to say the least, inept, and that ineptitude has been compounded over the years by the federal cult of mindless secrecy. While internal memos and other documents subsequently released under the Freedom of Information Act indicate that serious concern existed regarding these strange appearances in the sky, particularly after the Washington UFO "flap" in 1952, when clusters of objects appeared over the nation's capital for almost a week, the military's public posture was one of dismissive, almost contemptuous, unconcern. UFO debunking operations like Projects *Grudge* and *Bluebook* sought to convince the public that sightings were nothing more than marsh gas, weather balloons, flocks of migrating geese, or the planet Venus. At the same time, top-level CIA memoranda took a diametrically different tack. One, dated December 2, 1952, was anything but dismissive. "Sightings of unexplained objects at great altitudes and traveling at high speeds in the vicinity of major US defence installations are of such a nature that they are not attributable to natural phenomena or known types of aerial vehicles." The document went on to recommend that a National Security Council directive should establish "this matter as a priority project."

Similarly, while the Air Force denied that Building 18A at Wright-Patterson Air Force Base even existed, a 1975 statement from Senator Barry Goldwater, who was apparently irked by the UFO secrecy that not even he was able to penetrate, would indicate that something was going on there. "About ten or twelve years ago, I made an effort to find out what was in the building at Wright-Patterson and where the information is stored that has been collected by the Air Force, and I was understandably denied this request. It is still classified as above Top Secret."

Today, the Defense Department has a "black" budget

of more than $16 billion for ultra-secret projects over which Congress and at times even the president has absolutely no control; when a congressional subcommittee turns up the fact that, in 1984, the Air Force illegally seized 89,000 acres of public land around Groom Lake/Area 51 to prevent civilians from even approaching the facility, it's understandable that people begin to expect the worst, no matter how bizarre and fanciful the worst may be. Human beings have had powered flight for a scant ninety years. We made a handful of trips to our moon and then ran out of money and interest. Any lifeform that can get all the way here from Zeta Reticuli has to be quantum leaps ahead of us culturally, scientifically, and maybe even in basic intelligence.

During World War II, detachments of two Allied troops penetrated the interior of New Guinea and encountered tribes still living in the Stone Age. After handing out a few sticks of gum, some cheap penknives, and a couple of pictures of Betty Grable, the natives were suitably awed and decided these guys were probably gods. This might well be what's happening at Area 51 from the EBEs' point of view. Impress the dumb monkeys by tossing them a couple of ancient antigravity engines and watch them make fools of themselves.

LA Reader, July 1994

ALIENS WILL BE ALIEN

❏ All of the above didn't, on the other hand, deter me from speculating on what might be the real and logical nature of any possible off-planet, alien callers.

I HAVE ALWAYS HAD RESERVATIONS ABOUT GRAY ALIENS. Indeed, I have always found them a little too trite to be true. Okay, the egg-headed, abducting, little bastards are all over T-shirts, fridge magnets and the History Channel, but, for me, that doesn't make them any more convincing. That alien visitors to our world should turn out to be upright, four limbed, bipedal entities, seems just too much of a coincidence, particularly as the current configuration of human beings was created by a very specific set of

MICK FARREN

evolutionary circumstances. Was it possible that our first extraterrestrial contact would be with a species that—like us—had some small, gray ancestral quadruped who also stood up on its hind legs to look over what passed for long grass on a distant planet, under another star?

The odds are astronomical, but, even so, I don't simply dismiss the gray aliens as an unconscious human confection, or a deliberate invention sold to a mass audience by Steven Spielberg. Instead, I put myself in the position of the alien. If I was to find myself approaching a planet crowded with bad tempered simians armed with rudimentary nuclear weapons, but also worshipping primitive deities, I would proceed with the most extreme caution. And if I suspected that my own physical appearance would provoke a hostile reaction in the monkey natives, I might well devise a plan to avoid confronting them directly.

Human anthropologists, attempting to make contact with primitive tribes, both in the Amazon and Papua New Guinea, first piqued the primitives' curiosity by leaving unfamiliar but intriguing objects, like cooking utensils and the inevitable small mirrors, hanging in the undergrowth, before confronting the target tribe directly. An alien initiating contact with humanity might go one better and attempt to create a bioengineered substitute that would seem harmless. Since our alien would have solved all the problems involved in crossing inter-stellar space, it might well have the technology to fabricate something that resembled the natives themselves, except featureless, of neutral coloring, and somewhat shorter than the average Earthling. What better idea than to make its fabricated ambassadors look a lot like the fetus of the species it was about to confront? Would that not make them feel trusting and protective?

At this point I need to fill in a few peripheral thoughts I've had on the subject of visiting aliens. The very fact that they are visiting here makes them explorers of some kind—whatever else they might be notwithstanding. And on that very basic level, explorers are not to be trusted. They have a ruthlessness that invariably bodes ill for the inhabitants of the places they explore. On Earth, the outstanding explorers—the Dutch, the Spanish, and the English in most recent human history—have cultural roots in piracy and mayhem, and are descendants of buccaneers and long-ship raiders.

Although our alien explorers may have given up their equivalent rape and pillage eons ago, the avaricious drive to adventure, and the ruthlessness that goes with it, may still lurk vestigially in their genes. Any species so highly motivated that it will cross the universe to see what's on the other side, may well have emerged from some correspondingly violent background. Even on our own planet, humans are fairly unique in their driven inquisitiveness. Dolphins, for instance, do not crawl up the beach to loot and plunder seaside resort towns. When considering visiting aliens we probably need to question their agendas and motives, and consider that they may turn out to be more like us than we find comfortable.

Let's also not forget that the first of the modern alien encounters—the ones right after World War II, like those of George Adamski—were with tall, Nordic, long-haired blonds, who seemed just too good to be plausible. When, in 1952, the tall handsome visitor called Orthon disembarked from his saucer and told Adamski that he was from Venus, the story was so plainly impossible that poor old George was laughed out of the bookstores. But could Orthon, rather than an Adamski fabrication, be a first attempt at a contact simulacra? Had our alien explorer received cultural indications that made it assume humanity looked up to and trusted Nordic blonds? (The first human TV pictures had, of course, come out of Nazi Germany.) Perhaps when the alien found that the Nordic blonds were not working, the small gray fetus-looking EBEs were substituted.

Am I joking? Of course, but only to a degree. When we consider the impossible, our thinking needs to be at its most creative.

LOWFI website, April 2009

MICK FARREN

I COULD BE AN ALIEN MYSELF

THE IMPERATIVE IS INESCAPABLE, AND THUS I AM UN-able to comment on much that is currently rushing through my mind, not least of which is whether, in the context of such a conflict, I myself might, in fact, be the alien, since humanity seems fundamentally a state of mind and not an especially amusing one at that. But that, in turn, begs the question—should I turn out to be an alien, would I merely be a Metalunan with the elevated forehead or a full-blown Mutant? I fear that Gaius Baltar (from the remade series *Battlestar Galactica*) may turn out to be my hero for 2007, especially since they shot him up with the green acid. I still, of course, have to metastasize a tall invisible blond with a glowing spine, and, so far, all I have managed is a six-foot alcoholic rabbit. But now I must go and yet again attempt to turn this cerebral dysfunction into a viable commodity. Such is the condition of my condition and the penalty of my profession.

❏ Creative? A man can wax pretty creative when it concerns aliens.

Doc40, January 2007

BYE, BYE BATBOY

I NEVER TRULY BOUGHT INTO BATBOY. FOR ME, THE big-eyed, big-eared, cave dwelling, half-bat, half-human mutant was never true kitsch. He seemed more a fig-ment for the imaginations of the gullible. But the *Weekly World News*—slogan "The World's Only Reliable News-paper"—loved him. The inexplicable, black-and-white, tabloid adored Batboy more than Elvis, or their gray alien who was always visiting presidents. And, since his discovery in 1992, the American public shared that ado-ration. Batboy begat T-shirts, and was even the hero of an off-Broadway musical.

I was happier when *Weekly World News* ran the blur-ry photo of Elvis looking from the porthole of a UFO, but everyone else seemed to rate Batboy the tops. Lately,

❏ For much of my informa-tion, not only on aliens, but the life-after-death of Elvis or the sexcapades of celebri-ties, I relied on the super-market tabloids of America. I figured they couldn't be feeding me any more mendacious shit than the military or the government Thus when my favorite, the **Weekly World News**, went out of business, I noted it's passing.

though, the world has adored Batboy in markedly decreasing numbers, and now the break point has come. With national circulation down to 83,000, the parent company, American Media Inc., announced the *Weekly World News* would publish its last print edition on August 27, although it will remain online for the time being.

For literate journalism, the *Weekly World News* is no loss, with its shameless fabrications and fake photos, but, for AMI, who now own all of those familiar supermarket tabloids we read on the checkout line at Ralph's, and then put back in the rack, the demise of *Weekly World News* may herald the beginning of the end. All levels of print media are circling the wagons, but the supermarket tabloids are particularly vulnerable. Falling circulation, decreased advertising revenue, and an aging demographic indicate that even the market leaders, the *National Enquirer* and the *Star*, may be at risk and could eventually follow *Weekly World News* and Batboy into oblivion. According to a recent Reuters report, the circulation of the *National Enquirer* fell from 1.2 million in 2004 to 802,000 in 2006.

The *National Enquirer*, the archetypal supermarket tabloid, was founded in 1926, as the *New York Enquirer*, with capital from mobster Frank Costello to list the illegal lottery numbers, but, publisher Generoso Pope built it into a newsstand hit in the 1950s with a formula of blood and violence, crime scene and accident pictures, and screaming headlines like the 1963 'I Cut Out Her Heart and Stomped On It!' But, by 1967, Pope realized that the tabloid future lay in suburban supermarkets, and reined in the shock and gore, replacing it with the familiar formula of celebrity gossip, the occult, and miracle diets. But pressure of competition pushed the gossip to become wildly scurrilous, until a landmark 1981 lawsuit by Carol Burnett introduced the *Enquirer* to the concept of fact checking.

Through the 1980s and 1990s, although forced to curb their worst excesses, the *Enquirer* and the other supermarket tabloids enjoyed business as usual, but, as the century drew to a close, their numbers were being eroded by TV shows like *Entertainment Tonight* and the growing Internet.

The *National Enquirer* enjoyed a certain renaissance with an inside track on both the Clinton/Lewinsky scandal and the O.J. Simpson trial. (But also suffered a post 9/11 anthrax-in-the-mail attack on AMI's Florida offices which killed a photo editor.)

Without Bill and O.J. to pull in the readers, however, tabloid circulation again began to drop, and, in 2003 AMI brought in supposed super-editor Bonnie Fuller, from *Glamour* and *Cosmopolitan*, who had previously turned around the fortunes of *Us Weekly*. But Fuller's new formula, that demanded total concentration on celebrity, and the elimination of the astrologers, flying saucers, and near-death experiences, proved little more than a short-term containment. Bonnie Fuller temporarily slowed the rot, but did not reverse it, and, now, as the *Weekly World News* goes under, AMI is reportedly close to $1 billion in debt, and posted a $160 million net loss for 2006. The writing could well be on the wall for the supermarket weeklies, and, the in corridors of AMI, the ghostly voice of Batboy may be heard in the night, calling other papers to some shadowy tabloid hereafter.

LA CityBeat, August 2007

I SMOKE SO KILL ME

HEARD THIS ONE? WHAT DO YOU CALL PEOPLE WHO ARE excluded from cafés, restaurants, and cinemas; discriminated against on public transport, in government buildings, airports, shopping malls, and even in jail; who are forced to suffer public abuse by late-night TV commercials and giant billboards throughout the city; who are confronted by an organized political group dedicated to making their lives even more miserable and uncomfortable? Some brand-new oppressed minority? Well… in a way, yes. The actual answer is habitual smokers, of which I am one, and, on behalf of us all, let me give fair warning to the rest of you self-righteous bastards who believe you

❑ Alienation can be the result of a habit that everyone else decides they don't like…

have an absolute justification to get in our faces any time you feel the need to power-trip. We are close to the edge. Mad as hell. If you vote down Proposition 188 and impose a smoke-free California on us, prepare yourselves for a violent uprising, a wheezing army marching up Sunset demanding class justice.

Only a smoker knows the levels of relentless humiliation that are heaped upon him or her on a daily basis. Friends who, a decade ago, were borrowing money to buy cocaine now simper how they can't permit smoking in their car or home. Musicians who once bummed a butt before going on stage now bleat about the rest of us smoking at rehearsal. A couple of years ago, I had a play produced in which a crucial plot factor was that some of the characters smoked. At one point in the proceedings, some fool actually suggested that I should rewrite the whole thing to eliminate the nicotine content. If I remember correctly, I responded to the suggestion by stalking off to the bar—the smoker's last refuge—and refusing to return to the theater until the innate idiocy of the idea had been recognized.

The great deception practiced by the antismoking lobby is that they're doing it for our own good. The glee with which nonsmokers inquire if I want to die from cancer each time I light up seems to indicate that their real motivation isn't any concern for my health, but simply to demonstrate their own superiority of will by making me profoundly uncomfortable. Believe me, I would quit if I could. Give me a couple of weeks without alarms or attacks of stress, and I'd be as smoke-free as the rest of you. Unfortunately, the slings and arrows never seem to let up long enough to enable me to kick the habit. To add fuel to the fire (so to speak), I recently read about the anticigarette movement's first fatality: A smoker, who was forced to go outside in all types of weather to have himself a drag, contracted pneumonia and died. Nonsmokers are always holding the threat of death over us. How does it feel when the boot is on the other foot for a change?

Perhaps the best example I can offer of basic antismoking self-interest is the case of the commercial airlines. A

MICK FARREN

few years ago, they made a fuss about how they were banning smoking on all domestic flights. They trumpeted that it was all for the public good. Then, having no cigarette smoke with which to contend, they were able to save beaucoup bucks on fuel by not recycling the air in the passenger cabins. All manner of weird viruses and bacteria started mutating in the air-circulation systems of airliners, and now about half the people I know who fly between here and New York seem to develop some nonspecific flu-like ailment as soon as they land. The irony would appear to be that it was only smokers who were keeping the airlines honest in the matter of breathable air.

In fact, ironies abound where cigarette smoking is concerned. One of the greatest is that Los Angeles, including Hollywood—thanks to Councilman Marvin Braude—has become one of the most repressive anti-nicotine cities on Earth. It was Hollywood that turned me on in the first place, goddamn it. I, like probably millions of others, contracted the Jones by watching Hollywood movies. James Dean, Humphrey Bogart, Frank Sinatra, Robert Mitchum, Bette Davis, they were the ones who taught us to inhale. Remember the credits of *The Big Sleep*—two lighted cigarettes, symbolic of Bogart and Bacall, nestling side by side in an ashtray?

Even old newsreels told the story. Of all those grunts coming ashore on D-Day, about seventy percent had a battered Lucky dangling from their lips. Clearly, they had more important things to think about than latent emphysema; they had Nazis shooting at them. History seemed to confirm the message. Churchill smoked, FDR smoked, Joe Stalin smoked. Only Adolf Hitler was the militant abstainer.

The members of the antismoking lobby who focus on the danger of secondhand smoke are at least honest enough to admit their self-interest. They're looking out for number one, and that I can respect. But their argument is nevertheless flawed because they're making it in the Los Angeles basin, where the air is so foul on some days that it's probably healthier to filter it through a Marlboro. Perhaps the secondhand smoke argument might make sense on top of some Swiss Alp, where the air is pristine and the edelweiss are in bloom, but in the smog of the Valley, where we all know the automobile is the great enemy of respiratory well-being, it's plainly absurd. When you trade your Chevy for a bicycle, I promise to throw out my last pack of Merits and start chewing sunflower seeds. But we smokers are a pretty easygoing bunch. We've gone along with most of your restrictions. We've accepted not smoking in the movies and certain friends' houses, but enough is enough. I hate to find myself in political bed with Philip Morris, but the point in their pro-Proposition 188 propaganda that argues for "separate well-ventilated nonsmoking and smoking sections as a reasonable alternative to a 100 percent ban" seems a fair compromise. Indeed, that could well be our slogan—"Ventilate, Don't Legislate."

Unfortunately, I suspect you nonsmokers have a hidden agenda. The smoker is essentially an individual who recognizes that death is inevitable and has found more important things to worry about. The smoker is also an individual who refuses to be stampeded into an unwanted course of action by hysterical peer pressure. These are two things that modem America refuses to tolerate, and, consequently, we make easy and obvious victims, the Commies of the nineties. Like I said, we smokers are an easygoing bunch. Most of the time, when confronted by prejudice, insult, and oppression, we follow the advice of Jim Morrison—"light another cigarette, learn to forget." Before you attempt to ghettoise us any further, however, remember that we don't scare easily. We, after all, aren't afraid of cancer.

LA Reader, October 1994

JUST SOMETHING TO DO BETWEEN CIGARETTES

❑ To be totally honest, I have to confess, in the

Just something to do between cigarettes

That was what I said as I bought myself a ticket
Ventured into the darkness and sat down
Right there in the very first row
To take a good look
At Little Egypt and her tattoo
Her navel ruby and the diamond big as Texas
But lord, lord, hey pardon me ma'am
It was really nothing
It was...

Just something to do between cigarettes

That was what I rationalized
As I cut myself free
From all tiresome reality
As I merged with the movie
And drifted through the sheen
Of the screen with a prodigious thirst
And became one with the black and white gloss
There somewhere in between
But I swear to you all
I considered it...

Just something to do between cigarettes

And in the flash of a moment
I found my phone was tapped
And I was on the lam from special agents
Of the red queen
Who thought busting themselves a poet
Would provide a path
To painless professional prestige
With maybe blackmail as a fallback
And I told myself as I ran through the sewers
In a voice like Harry Lime
Hey you guys, this is a terrible mistake
It was...

Just something to do between cigarettes

years that have passed
since I protested the spreading smoking bans, I have
actually quit the gaspers,
but only after I realized that
they had totally ruined my
lungs.

And later that was the only
Explanation I could offer
To the girl with short black bangs, the satin dress,
The fuck-me sandals and Ray-Ban sunglasses
Who was pointing a revolver at my head
And seemed to be extremely angry about something
I'd done or maybe failed to do
But it didn't mean nothing, baby.
It was…

Just something to do between cigarettes

And on a day trip in a dayglo blue bus
To the end of the night and all the way out
To the leading edge of insanity
Straining with bleeding ears
To hear the multitude sounds of the earth
The million half notes
Played on the stringed lute of the world
By all the winds of the air
From loanshark laments
To the chorus of the cutting crew
The requiem of the murder review
The faces lost and masks regained
And I will never be the same
A full half century pissed away
(Should I go or should I stay)
And it seems like only yesterday
(I hardly believe in yesterday)
When all I needed
When I assumed all I needed was…

Just something to do between cigarettes
Just something to do between cigarettes

Not previously published

MICK FARREN

THERE AIN'T NO SANITY CLAUSE

IT WAS CHRISTMAS EVE IN THE BARROOM. AVENUE A, to be precise, three, maybe four years go. I was loaded down with last minute packages and full of the spirit of ho-ho-ho and office party scotch. I'd decided to stop by and pay my respects before going home to deck the halls. It proved to be a mistake. Down at the end of the bar was a rummy with whom I'd passed many a wretched, dissolute evening. Over the years, we've bitched and complained, cried into our beer, congratulated ourselves for being such splendid fellows, and generally concluded that the world was going to hell in a basket. On this night, however, all was not well. Instead of a yo bro' handshake, I was treated to a hostile stare. I couldn't have had a worse reception if I'd been Ed Meese.

"I don't want to even see people like you, motherfucker."

I was no longer a splendid fellow. I was just another reminder that tomorrow was Christmas Day and, while the rest of the free world appeared to be sating itself on poultry, alcohol, and good will, all he had to look forward to was a pint of Dewar's and the Channel 11 TV Yule Log. Even the goddamn bar would be shut. I realized I was witnessing a case of what has come to be known as the Waltons Syndrome (WS).

The Waltons Syndrome is one of the more crippling conditions in pop-psych. Its name is derived from the now legendary tale of the depressed and solitary individual who, doing his best to ignore the holidays, removes his Swanson Hungry-Man turkey dinner from the oven, sits down, turns on the TV, and settles in to spend silent night, holy night on his own. He finds that he's watching *The Waltons* Christmas Special. After twenty-seven minutes, this positive orgy of wholesomeness and warmth has so accentuated his sense of isolation that, without further ado, he walks into the bathroom and hangs himself. Proponents of the Waltons Syndrome essentially feel that the surgeon general should slap a health warning on the entire season to be jolly:

❑ The risks of alienation, depression, isolation are never more great than at the times of what are generally promoted as mass celebrations of joy and human kindness.

"Christmas may damage the health of the poor, the lonely, the neurotic, and those susceptible to massive peer pressure."

Even the seemingly simple act of shopping can produce levels of stress normally only found in fighter pilots and TV executives. As the relentless countdown beats time—"only thirty-two shopping days to Christmas"—we start to lose our reason. By December 22, we are unable to question why we are celebrating peace on Earth and goodwill to men by schlepping down Eighth Street looking for a Pee-wee Herman T-shirt to give to a neighbor's unlikable child, or why we are courting personal bankruptcy just to be seen as having the seasonal spirit.

This is by no means a diatribe against the commercialization of Christmas. Kicking against that is about as futile as demanding to know why batteries aren't included. It's also illogical. In this culture, Christmas, by definition, has to be commercial. How should a consumer society conduct its saturnalia but as a feast of conspicuous consumption? If anything it's a plea for those who feel emotionally unable or are just too broke to participate to be given the chance to say no to Christmas.

The plea would, sad to say, appear to be a vain one. Television, on its own, makes it virtually impossible to blank out the holidays. Sitcoms run the obligatory "A Christmas Carol" episode, complete with ghosts of past, present, and future.

The local news makes us cringe by juxtaposing the tree in Rockefeller Center against freezing winos. The stammering offspring of station employees wish us joy every fifteen minutes. This is not even to mention the relentless toy commercials. It's around this time of year that I'm profoundly glad that I'm not a parent. How do you explain to a TV-soaked brat that all he's getting is a rather small clockwork robot and that there is no way, short of starving through January and February, that the family can spring for the seven-foot-long, fully operational G.I. Joe aircraft carrier?

There's a sense of being trapped. You start to feel that

even if you went so far as to hide out in the hills, a red red robin would insist on bob bobbing along as a yule reminder. A simple trip to the supermarket continues the numbing propaganda holly motif. The people on the sidewalk all seem more determined than you are in their will to jollity. It's all too easy to become convinced, like my friend the rummy, that everyone else is as loving and giving as the Cosby family and that you're the only one stifling a humbug. A flip through December's *Playboy* can give a man the impression that there are women out there who give their boyfriends gift-wrapped motorcycles. How come I have to be satisfied with a lousy bottle of aftershave? The only respite is Elvis Presley singing 'Blue Christmas.' At least someone once copped to seasonal misery.

The most destructive aspect of all this is the way that the holiday season has become a kind of make or break assessment of our true worth. How big is that tree in the window? It's Santa's naughty or nice writ large. Everything is held up for examination. How do we rate on loved ones, friends, or spending power? The specific gravity of our milk of human kindness is measured and noted. There's an edge of competition that is exactly symbolized by the upwardly mobile Christmas mantelpiece. Look how many cards we got, did you get that many?

Finally, there's the grim aftermath. The streets of the city are filled with discarded wrapping paper, broken toys, and dead trees bleeding tinsel. We find ourselves in a state of emotional hangover with nothing to look forward to except three months of dirty snow, thin magazines, and tax preparation. At this point most of us have become aware that the holidays have been a matter of massive and costly foreplay for a brief and largely unsatisfactory climax. It's not a durable awareness, however. By next November, we'll be doing it all over again. Maybe we should paraphrase John Lennon: Christmas may well be a concept against which we measure our pain.

Happy New Year.

Village Voice, December 1986

THE SCHMUCK HUSBAND

❑ Two decades later, the same beast had grown and mutated and, since it was the twenty-first century and the Bush era, money was the only measure of the man. Love was strictly transactional.

"HE DIDN'T GO TO JARED!"

The cry is one of male inadequacy as the two couples exchange Yuletide gifts in the TV commercial. The good husband/boyfriend has bought his woman diamonds from Jared, the jewellery retailers. The schmuck husband has not. His gift is not specified, but one suspects it's a toaster oven. The good husband and his mate are instantly all but undressing each other. The other couple ease stiffly from contact, and the distantly frozen face of the schmuck's lady companion clearly indicates that if he gets a blowjob anytime in 2007, it will be a near miracle. The viewer is left under no illusion. Gift giving is wholly and simply transactional. No bling, no nookie.

"He didn't go to Jared!"

To claim this as a revelation would be naïve. Sex has been a motivational core of advertising for as long as there's been advertising. Deluded young men are still encouraged to believe scantily clad and heavily oiled runway models will lose all carnal control and ravish them in a supermarket aisle because they are wearing a current male fragrance like Lynx or Axe. I only cite this particular diamond commercial because it represents a fresh turn of the screw in a common stereotype.

The inept, often overweight, emotionally retarded, imbecile husband who must at all time be managed by a smarter, more inventive, and implausibly more attractive wife/girlfriend has been so well used in TV advertising that he even graduated to actual programming in the persona of Homer Simpson, a dozen or more sitcom copies, and, I suppose, Ozzy Osbourne.

The new miserable twist on the character we'll call the schmuck husband is that he is not only juvenile and witless, but now he's also sexually inadequate. Even when his libido is fully enhanced by Viagra, and his (again implausibly attractive) mate is seductively beckoning him to the bed, the fool can't make up his mind whether he wants to fuck or watch the ballgame, and only figures out, after

MICK FARREN

considerable mental effort, he can have sex now and tape the game for later.

The guy in the Viagra commercial, however, is one of the lucky few. At least consummation is offered. By far the majority of schmuck husbands, especially around Christmastime, are like the dummy who didn't go to Jared, and must lavish gifts and favors before erotic action is even contemplated. In the current crop of gift commercials, a suitably wrapped box will have a spouse aggressively clearing the kitchen table with an impetuous sweep of her arm, so she and hub can engage in some vigorously traditional spontaneity. The most blatant of this ilk are the spots by a mail-order sleepwear and lingerie operation called Pajamagram, who have been running the slogan "To take her clothes off…"

But, on the other hand, if the dummy doesn't come across with correct big ticket gift, the clothes will stay on, and he will be condemned to emotional tundra for an indeterminate period until he materially redeems himself.

The schmuck husband has always been irritating, but I always figured he at least helped to bring down the pompous infallibility of the twentieth century Ward Cleaver, *Father Knows Best* nuclear-family patriarch. Unfortunately, the process would seem to have now gone one step beyond that objective and created a new character in contemporary TV commercials—the grasping, acquisitive, whore wife—who grew up to the strains of Madonna's 'Material Girl'—and for whom sex is merely a means to bling and credit cards. Holiday TV in 2006 has been putting the 'ho' in ho-ho-ho with retail determination.

But are we really surprised when the shows that surround the commercials are taken up with Donald Trump (whose resemblance to Jabba the Hutt increases daily) bestowing media forgiveness and absolution on poor little Miss USA, Tara Conner, for her shocking crime of going nightclubbing in Manhattan and doing her best to emulate Paris Hilton? Or reports of how our president is now being called "Bubble Boy?"

LA CityBeat, December 2006

TWO THOUSAND LIGHT YEARS FROM HOME

THE SCARS NEVER SHOW

❏ But love is still love, and
a lost love can gut one
as effectively as a boning
knife, and leave a poor boy
to bleed out his desperate
singularity.

Spider woman, the night I betrayed you
Dark lady, the guilt is there still
For dreams that all died with the fear of destiny
And a fifth of Jack Daniels
And too may pills

But I've got the grandeur of grand isolation
In the deeps of the city, I know where to go
And I've got protection, TV in the small hours
And my shoulders are hunched so the scars never show.

Scarlett O'Hara, I died at the airport
Blanche Dubois watched me drown in the flame
And you're in the Lotus Room, lunch with the joker
And I'm in the shadow, learning my name

But I've got the grandeur of grand isolation
In the deeps of the city, I know where to go
And I've got protection, TV in the small hours
And my collars turned up so the scars never show.

Vampire princess, no light in the mirror
Vampire queen, the sun can't shine through
Safe in our coffins, secure from reality
Because in the dark earth, dreams never come true

But I've got the grandeur of grand isolation
In the deeps of the city, I know where to go
And I've got protection, TV in the small hours
And I've got my dark glasses so the scars never show.

Written for Wayne Kramer's 1991 album, *Death Tongue*

MICK FARREN

FAILED FUTURE

WHEN I WAS A SMALL BOY I WANTED TO BE THE FIRST man on the moon. I not only assumed that it would guarantee my name being a household word for the rest of time, but I also believed it would be a whole lot of fun. Fuelled by *Flash Gordon*, *Weird Tales*, and *The Jetsons*, I saw myself as the steely-eyed pioneer of the spaceways, a kind of Doc Holliday in space, taming planets with a blasting ray gun in hand and single-handedly fighting off flying saucer attacks by invading Martians bent on carrying away our kicking, screaming women. Back then, in the late fifties, our image of the universe was one of a place teeming with aliens behind every asteroid! If it wasn't an evil Martian, it was friendly Venusians in UFOs, crab monsters, mutoids or zombies from the stratosphere. Sadly, the astronaut ambition didn't last. I guess I must have had some subconscious foresight of disappointments to come. The ugly truth was that, as space travel became reality, it also became agonizingly boring. The moon turned out to be nothing more then gray dirt and rock and, when men finally got there, they didn't have a ray gun between them and, in the ultimate humiliation, were forced to share a split screen with Richard Nixon while he congratulated them. By the time we got to Mars, it was clear that it was all over. There were no Martians, evil or otherwise. The best that Carl Sagan could come up with was a longshot chance that maybe, somewhere, an enzyme was hiding on the underside of a rock. Worst of all, there would be no glamor out there. Being an astronaut, Sally Ride notwithstanding, was a matter of hanging out with a bunch of guys who wore coveralls and looked like younger versions of John Glenn. The stars belonged to the tedious.

❏ But, at the same time, nothing is more bittersweet than recalling the most stunning disappointments of childhood.

Fragment from the 1980s

NARCISSISM AND LINGERIE

❑ Or what Bob Dylan once called, "broken hearted lovers with too personal a tale."

BACK WHEN THEY HAD BEEN TOGETHER, FELICIA'S MA-nipulations had been almost exclusively sexual, based in a precise understanding of what fools men could be. She had operated in a disguise of wilful pervo-curiosity totally in line with the times and the drugs that had been avail-able. Cleared of the boundaries, and with all inhibition cancelled by Mandrax in England and Quaaludes in the United States, the two of them had ascended the nursery slopes of moral turpitude. One of Felicia's favorite games had been surprise initiations, that would unbalance him with delight. He recalled how on a trip to the West End that combined business and shopping, she had pulled him into a record company executive bathroom—how the hell she had obtained the key he would never know—so they could indulge in mutual oral sex on the floor with a meet-ing going on in the next room.

On one warm, bored, and heavily medicated afternoon, she had forced him to crouch on the floor of the shower while she stood astride him and urinated. That had raised even Max's inner eyebrow. What the hell had she done that he didn't know about to provoke an act so outré? He remembered how she had removed a skimpy pair of scarlet panties to do the deed, but worn an ID bracelet around her ankle that had been on his eye-level during the action. Felicia had been very drawn by the seduction of ritual and costume—especially costume. To reveal by the elaboration of her underwear, clear down to the selection of stockings and shoes, that some seemingly spontaneous incident had been completely premeditated, planned by the temptress all along, was Felicia's idea of finesse.

Max had concluded that this process of dress up—she had referred to it as gift wrapping—was yet another facet of the narcissism that was the broad foundation of her personality. In one phase of their passion she had become quite obsessive about actually watching herself. A mirror beside the bed was angled so she could regard her own reflection as though directing her own pornographic star

MICK FARREN

vehicle. Max would moan: "I'm going to come."

"Wait!"

"I can't."

"I said wait!

"I don't think…

"Wait, you bastard!

"I…"

"Now, now, quick, pull out, come on my face."

She had gasped and then shuddered. "Now kiss me."

And with wide eyes she'd regard the mirror while he kissed her wet mouth and sticky cheeks. Narcissism and lingerie, ritual, infantilism, and challenge; all were ammunition in Felicia's revolution and private will to triumph. To be the baby was yet another favored ploy. When she had done something particularly heinous, she might indicate that he was to be permitted to spank her and all would be forgotten. It was hardly a sacrifice or a punishment, no matter how she might dramatize it. After a couple of Mandies, she thoroughly enjoyed all the attention that was being paid so exclusively to this single section of her body and its periphery. She seemed to perversely relish the short sharp shocks of the flat of his hand, and would gasp shameless whispers of total banality, made hotter by being so tongue-in-cheek hackneyed even before the rise of the phone sex industry, and the public acceptance that men were retarded enough to crave such things. "Oh my love, (slap) I've been such a very bad girl. (slap) A very, very bad girl. (slap) I'm a naughty baby, and I really (slap) deserve this. I need to learn my lesson… Ow! (slap, slap) Oh yes! Teach me! Make me be goooood."

But, of course, Felicia was quite incapable of being good.

From an unpublished novel

A WELL OILED GUILLOTINE

I HAVE ELIMINATED PHYSICAL NEWSPAPERS FROM MY home. I receive the *Los Angeles Times*, the *New York Times*,

❑ The fictional Felicia and the real life auto-concept

Dita Von Teese can only be sisters in manipulation, but where Felicia just leaves a trail of vanquished lovers, Dita is selling a value system. She is promoting something very akin to the schmuck husband device, but with a whole lot more zeros. In her universe, and that of P. Diddy, ultra beaucoup bucks—verified by bling—are the only measure of the man. It's the Caligula school of capitalism.

and the *Washington Post* via the Internet (and also the *New York Post*, ever a mind-boggler). In addition to saving trees, the computer allows me to trippingly bypass the mindless filler that struggling broadsheets vainly believe will deliver the grail of the eighteen-to-thirty-five demographic. But on Sunday, December 30, I made an exception. With no false modesty, my coauthor Suzy Shaw and I had entered the *LA Times* bestseller list at number thirteen with our new book, *Bomp! Saving the World One Record at a Time*, and I wanted to admire my name in old-fashioned print. (Something I actually couldn't do, but that's another story.)

Having not had a copy of the *Times* in the house for months, I was surprised by its bulk. Surprise escalated to amazement when I encountered the "Image" section, dominated by a vast headshot of Dita Von Teese and the message "Like the car you drive, or the watch you wear, the bubbly you reach for... speaks volumes about who you are."

Perhaps my world has become a trifle cyber-esoteric, but I initially wondered on what terminally decadent planet I'd landed. I had clearly been lamentably ignoring plutocrat idiocy. My recall of Von Teese was as Marilyn Manson's former flame, a modern pinup girl with interesting taste in corsets and a burlesque act that, although a highly pleasing method of punctuating rock-band performances, was little more than old-school stripping with some Belle Epoch pretensions, or a Weimar edge.

Now I discover she's some kind of spokes-shill for the champagne industry, which, led by Cristal, was pimped-out in the 1990s by P. Diddy and is now selling itself like liquid bling: Witness the $300 Armand de Brignac in its gold-plated bottle (promoted by Jay-Z and an item in Academy Award nominee gift bags). Then, two days after reading a soufflé of a full-page interview about how Dita has had "offers" to act, and once purchased $500 worth of pies to throw at her friends on New Year's Eve, the TV told me that, in the real world, oil had hit a record hundred bucks a barrel.

Von Teese herself also seemed to have physically changed. While with Manson, she affected a glossy, neo-counterculture style, but as the "Image" cover girl she

MICK FARREN

appeared to have undergone a conservative makeover, causing her to resemble Monica Lewinsky's slimmer, prettier sister. But perhaps this is just a last hurrah, a neocon bunker apocalypse in which the measure of a man will be judged by the brand of champagne he drinks, but only until the champagne runs out.

On the other hand, this is the *Los Angeles Times'* happy promotion of an obscene level of social and cultural inequality that—in a country at war, and a world in which deadly crises are too numerous to count—will hardly build circulation or comfort its existing readers. Dita and her decadent ultra-marketing seem to be doing nothing less than moving routine Hollywood lipstick pointlessness toward a full-blown Marie Antoinette let-them-eat-cake. Historically, that attitude has a limited half-life; before too long, the guillotines are rolled out, the blades fall, the crowd cheers, and equality is imposed the hard way with the head in the basket.

I suppose I'm joking about Von Teese's execution, but, as we move into the eighth hellish year of the Bush regime, we are obliged to examine all the absurd legacies that will remain, and the Dita Von Teese school of talentless celebrity and disgusting over-consumption has to be one of them. Maybe the foolishness of gold champagne bottles, being promoted by women famous for little more than their lovers and their foundation garments, will be recognized by the changing times as patently absurd.

In the meantime, I'm clicking over to Craigslist to check out rented tumbrels and carpenters who might be willing to construct some cheap serviceable decapitation devices.

Doc40, Jan 2008

I STUDIED THE LOW SNOW

"*WILL YOU STOP DOING THAT?*"
"*I can't.*"
I studied the low snow, my friends. As if you didn't al-

❑ Maybe I have watched too much television—especially that isolated, Travis

Bickle late night TV—but a point comes when the wash of words, part content, part commercial, that flows from the flickering picture machine ceases to organize itself into any linear storyline or even fully formed sentences. It's random audio along with the gaudy, but mercifully contained, images. This is not to say, though, that it is by any means incomprehensible. Almost at random, or maybe like—to be ultimately pretentious, Elliot or Burroughs—its eddies and curlicues form themselves into an abstract and imprecise, but nonetheless emotive, quasi-narrative. Nighthawks in the ether. This creation is one of mood rather than plot and it is able to lead the isolated viewer into an hallucinatory landscape far richer and more complex, and quite possibly with a deeper and more lasting significance than was ever intended by whoever sent out the colorful stream of electrons in the first place. We roam through an electronically induced opium dream.

Sounds like affected art-speak, right? All too ready know. I studied the low snow at the bottom of the screen like the binary pulsations of insane deities who implored me to be just like them. I studied the low snow but was too cunning, and also too advanced in my condition, to succumb to such arithmetic and paranoid conclusions. I studied the low snow, but I neither deciphered nor formed conclusions. I merely embraced the comfort of the electron stream. I studied the low snow, slumped with a hedgehog, faux-opiate curl of the spine, staring with lowered eyes that had looked at too many multiples of that last and crucial 1,000 yards. I made myself passive and submitted to the charged particles. Was I tired or merely playing out the romance of habituated inertia? Too late the heroics in this random sequence. Every high-heeled bikini skank knew the lines of the leading lady to the point of overload, and solid structures were already fading in a hemorrhage sunset of bleeding monochrome. The dock of the bay no longer had the magic. The juices of spiders lacked their old pungent thrill. Gutterjumpers disported in the citadel, while the rich and the righteous were hung from their metaphoric necks until dead.

I became enthralled with low snow when I realized it was preferable to answering the peremptory voices, or responding to screen gems of massage. I studied the low snow in the curve of the monitor because it told me no tall tales of mystery and imagination. I had resolved to shun such stories, and the panic they created. I had long ago reached the point of having heard too many of those mendacious reports, and needed to flee that subterranean demographic of molemen and the hollow women. I knew, all too precisely, the true source of the signal. The unsinkable engine was going down. The ice was lower in the heavy water. The mantra had ceased, but no one was listening. If I was smart, I would holster my pistol, hide the blind tiger in my billfold, but be prepared to defend my right to a seat in the second lifeboat, among the millionaires and the medicated. By the time they came to look for me, I would be 100 miles out of town, and so heavily disguised that I could pass for human in Texas.

MICK FARREN

"Why do you do that?"

"I'm conscious, but the hallucinations are graphic."

The Pony Girls had occupied the deep subbasement of the headquarters and claimed it as their command bunker. But I was bound to my task, and I refused to descend the express elevator and join these psychotic princesses, no matter how they solicited me with their adulterated résumé, or importuned me with their pouting chariot fire. Their rituals were too formerly equestrian, their treats had soured, their beasts were caged, and their dope was cut. Their issues had grown hotrod fins. They learned too much from Miss Rosa Coote and not enough from Foxy Brown, and shamelessly courted the dark-shark, dead-eye lenses of the slithering moon-crater amphibians, as though they were unable to exist existentially unless observed and voyeur-admired, even in their murkiest lewd moments of torn stockings, police handcuffs and cheap gin, in jungle clearings with companies of badly addicted boy soldiers, who had, the very same afternoon, slaughtered their teenage officers in settlement of a dispute over cocaine and gunpowder.

The Pony Girls were not tolerant of failure. Their hooves were sharp and titanium shod, and their hair smoldered in phosphorus conflagration for the chimera of lost loves. Beyond doubt or question, they were more than capable of pushing my body under the ice, just as they had done with the body of Rasputin, back when Yusupov called the shots. I would certainly merit the rebuff of the velvet hand, if not a far stiffer sentencing when my attitude of retreat branded me as passé. If put to the question, I would have had no answer. If stripped I would willingly kneel. Very soon they would show me the instruments. If threatened I could not be bothered to beg. Far easier to sign anything they put in front of me, and freely admit that I had given up my razor's edge, and all the fascisms and grievous degrees of fashion, for simple cathode sanctuary in the vaulted transept of the vacuum cathedral. If that was not satisfactory, I would silently submit to their straps and calipers, just as long as I didn't have to pass through

easy to fall into when you're trying to describe something you don't fully understand yourself without revealing this lack of complete comprehension. I seem to have stumbled across something, in a kind of no-man's land between prose and poetry, that totally intrigues me. I'm reminded most of be-bop in that it so strips away the straight and narrow of the accepted. Dump the rules for a flatted fifth. Needless to say, someone to publish the stuff was hard to find, especially in the short story length to which it seemed to lend itself. Fortunately the anthology/book/magazine **Penny-Ante** gave me a slot, and when I saw what follows in print, I dearly wanted to do more.

the gates. Beyond the gates they knew too many of the dangerous details.

"*Do you ever intend to move from here?*"

"*No.*"

During my last awayday excursion my wings became heavy and my arms grew tired from the rarefied altitude. But I knew that if I landed, I would not take to the air again. The airstrip was under the control of gangs of Wyatt Earp-moustache, old-school wolf-demons who would have fucked a rhino if they could only have persuaded her to lay still and accept their overtures. If I could have continued my journey I would have gone on, but, instead, I depended on my charm and my passport, and pretended I had only stopped in for a martini and extra olives. Suave? Of course. I was as safe as Rick Blaine in his white tuxedo while the Wheel of Fortune continued to turn. How else would I survive these extended cabaret evenings and nights at the round tables, when yellow and black dogs would be barking in the distance, echoing the coyotes in the gulch and the sirens of the Civil Guard on two wheeled Elecroglides, while rural vagrants stood confused at too many freight train mysteries.

"*Will you stop doing that?*"

"*That would be difficult.*"

My companion rose, a distraction from the stream, full fathom five in a high tidal wave of demanded attention that required an exit from my particle comfort, and, in time, a dutiful entry to the valley below. Tall as an imperial monolith, and as inflexible as a walled city under martial law, doomed and determined to sharpen idol desire and projected fantasy to a sabre of thin steel she would use against me as she rode me down, booted, spurred, and amazon armored, at the head of her heavy cavalry. Silk highlights of scarlet and cut emerald sang oriental warnings of the power majestic, the expectation of obedience, and the thin quiver of the longbow fully bent, and the flight of burning gold arrows against which no shield offered protection. She smiled so sweetly. She knew she had me beaten on the table and my bluff was pointless. Even the hole card couldn't save my sorry ass. The Red Queen Diamonds was ever my undoing, and the boys in the backroom all knew it. I didn't need to tell them that I'd died of the same. The excuse would not remain valid beyond the time it took for the maids to clear the debris, and hangmen's assistants to bury the bodies and free the lost souls.

Long lashes lowered, hand on her jackknife, and the dragon tattoo fully activated, she formally remonstrated, confident of easy capitulation to her peremptory challenge, and the inevitable purchase of her ever-popular product. Once upon on time, she had been so tolerant of my experiments, but always, with high and dominant logic, she had expected a result. When no galleon of doubloons sailed into her harbor, when no casks of laudanum were rolled from the trireme to her quay, her gathering disappointment at the lack of a valid delivery had been as imposingly manifest as Elvis on a Harley, while her patience had grown as weary as a migrating caribou faced with the coming of spring. Turn once, turn twice, and follow the path less familiarly ridden. Accustomed to retribution and the cool negatives of reinforcement, my only real alternative was to dream of chill vodka in some Stalinist Moscow tower block with an imperial Russian arrayed in ermine, and continue to study the low snow.

"Will you stop doing that?"

"I can't."

Penny-Ante Book #3, 2009

352

Part Six

The Future's Uncertain And The End Is Always Near

I have always detected a strong element of narcissism in apocalyptic prediction, and also an equal measure of acquired self-importance. One way to describe it might be as gothic existentialism. If I cease to exist, everything else ceases to exist right along with me. The tree doesn't fall in the forest, the whole damn forest is vaporized. Après moi, le déluge. When I go, it all goes. The actual declaration, "après moi, le déluge" is most usually attributed to the French king Louis XV, but some claim the statement was actually made by his maîtresse-en-titre—his official primary mistress—Madame de Pompadour. The girlfriend knew she was the only one holding France's sorry shit together and, if she went, the dam burst and France went with her to the tumbrels of the Terror.

If nothing else, prophecies of doom are a surefire way of grabbing attention. *Chicken Little* never lacked an audience, and an impending universal calamity always brings a certain dramatic edge to an otherwise humdrum existence. I frequently suspect that the only real fun that fundamentalist Christians have going for them is the thrill of waiting for the Rapture, and imagining how screwed the non-believers will feel when they all ascend to the heavens. The only real challenge for the guy walking the streets with a placard declaring "The End Is At Hand" is being believed. Doomsayers do not have a particularly illustrious track record. To date, every damn one of the has been hopelessly wrong because, despite everything, we are all still here.

The motives of those who loudly warn of a coming apocalypse also merit some examination. How many of them really have a vision or a premonition, and how many are merely racketeering. Prophet or profit? During the Y2K panic of 1999, when folks believed that a computer glitch would paralyze the known world, I was doing radio promotion for a book I'd put together called *Conspiracies, Lies, and Hidden Agendas,* and it gave me a unique insight into the level of hysteria that was gripping the American heartland. When you're plugging a piece of product by phone on morning drive time, you're put on hold during the commercial breaks, but treated to the full on-air audio. On station after station, I found myself listening to spots that basically went as follows, playing on fear and panic. "Come on down to Big Bob's Hardware. We have generators, we have shotguns, we have canned goods, and all of your Y2K needs."

A couple of years earlier, in the depths of the Reagan era when TV preachers were making it big, stories circulated how one famous televangelist had allegedly figured an early computer program that separated his flock into graduated levels of sheep-like gullibility. At the highest level were those who would believe absolutely anything if it was supposedly validated by Jesus. These A-list marks would receive letters telling them how the world was going to end a week from Tuesday and instructing them to liquidate all their property and then send the reverend the resulting cash assets. It was only when relatives of one gullible senior citizen took legal action to stop Grandma giving away all of her worldly goods that the practice became public and was subsequently stopped.

Neither basic observation nor common sense, however, have stopped catastrophe and its aftermath being a popular fantasy. The Christians have their Left Behind franchise, while more secular science fiction—especially in the bomb-fearing 1950s and 1960s—developed a whole subgenre of post-disaster fiction that speculated on what life among the ruins would be like after the world had been nuked, ravaged by a pandemic, smashed by an asteroid, or wasted by environmental collapse. From *Panic In Year Zero* to *Mad Max 2: The Road Warrior*, it usually turned out to be some violent dog-eat-dog dystopia. (Indeed, in Harlan Ellison's *A Boy And His Dog*, dog-eat-dog was exactly what happened.) My own first novel, *The Texts Of Festival*, postulated a world in which only the cool had survived, but were then beset by homicidal hipster barbarians led by a character called Iggy. It starts thus...

THE ROAD TO FESTIVAL

THE MARSHLAND HAD RUN FOR A DAY'S WALK. A DAY had passed since he had come down from the hill country. Three days of slipping through his home hill land, skirting the inhabited valleys, avoiding the grim herders who clawed a living from the corroded hills and grew savage in their isolation. And then a cold, dirty day trudging through the lowland swamp, picking a way on the broken paved surface where swamp rats squalled and slid away as he approached.

Every now and then he would stumble as he missed the paved surface and his foot would sink into soft slime. Oily water would pour over the top of his father's high boots. Cursing, he would drag his leg out of the slime and poke around with his toe to find where the paving started again. Sometimes it would prove to be a broad crack in the surface and then it would be necessary to wade waist-deep in the slime until he had regained the ancient stone pavement which, although befouled, was at least solid. Crossing them was also complicated by the unknown depth of these cracks and by the need to draw his knife and the family piece from his belt and hold them safe from the poisonous waters.

The sun set and a close blanket of mist, high as a man's hip, lay on the surface of the swamp. Mosquitoes danced on the damp air, flitting their elaborate rituals in and out of the shadows cast by the Mesa-like ruins. The darkness was starting to close in and still he had gained no sight of the legendary raised highway that ran straight to Festival.

The rats grew bold and brambles caught at his legs. He gave thanks to the women of his village who had presented him with his leather trousers at the spring laying on. The token that had paid tribute to his separate, restless ego was now mud-spattered. A long way from their previous splendor, his trousers were at last proving useful.

A rising moon, bloated and orange, gave him a minimal light by which to find his footsteps, but at the same time distracted him with a multitude of black shadows and glinting highlights that hinted at an undefined menace. A rat darted behind the rotting teeth of a corroded iron wagon frame. The man started, drew his gun and then froze with shame as the rat vanished, cleaving a short-lived V in black water. He had been entrusted with the piece of his house. The token of his father's power in the tribe had been given to arm him on his absurd quest. Now he was waving it around like a spooked fool, about to waste one of the twenty man-killing shells on a rat. He was yielding to the dark and to paranoia. He put his hand on the pouch around his neck but then withdrew it. Although he was frightened, although he was lost in the black night of the swamps of 'Ndunn, it was not a crisis that would merit the use of either ammunition or the crystals. He must face his fear alone. He must weather a hard night in this western swamp; it was the path to Festival and its ancient skills. He shivered at the damp; holstered his gun; pulled his cloak closer round his shoulders, but the coarse wool, with its mends and patches, held the water and afforded him little warmth as he felt for the next step on the pavement.

All night he trudged on, repeatedly losing his footing and skirting the worst fissures until he could sidetrack no longer and was forced to ford the intervening water. As dawn began to cut through the mist on the swamp he paused to rest, sitting hunched on a moss-covered square of masonry.

The clearing of the mist gradually revealed a dark line almost at the horizon. It ran across the marsh, almost parallel to the direction the man imagined he had taken in the darkness. Its apparent straightness seemed to indicate that it was fashioned by men, some artefact of the old-time city. It was by no means the broad pillared highway of legend. It was, as far as he could see, merely a straight, raised embankment. Even if it was not the true road, it would make easier going than the marsh wading of the previous day.

With renewed hope he made his way painfully to the distant ridge. By the time he reached the roadway—and a roadway it proved to be as he came nearer—the sun was high and the swamp water reflected it like a pitted, dirty mirror. The drying mud irritated his skin and ran in dirty rivulets as he sweated.

Sick and exhausted he clawed through the brambles that clung thickly to the side of the banking. The top of the bank proved to be a broad paved road, straight and smooth, although heavily overgrown with moss and nettles. Its length was here and there dotted with the rusting hulks of oldtime iron wagons. Having at last raised himself above the level of the poisonous swamp, the man finally felt safe to rest. He ripped off his cloak and jacket and bundled them into a pillow, then removed his belt with its gun and knife, laid it close to his right hand and settled down to sleep.

It was afternoon before Jo-Jo rested. The pursuit must have been called off long before dawn and it was not fear that had kept him walking; it was the shame of the loser tag that forced him to place distance between himself and Festival.

It had looked like an open and shut mugging when he had approached the fat crystal dealer on the outside of Shacktown, but, as he had pulled his knife, six retainers had appeared out of nowhere and started him running. He had kept going all night, fearing that they might have rented mounts. A lot of merchants were really heavy on the idea of bringing in muggers. Thieves these days were treated a whole lot different from the heroes of the texts.

It wasn't as though he was even a full-time thief. He'd only laid for the fat dealer in order to get a stake. Everyone who went freewheeling got down on their luck. There were countless texts on that very situation. What really made him keep on walking, stuck on a nowhere road in the 'Ndunn marshes, was the inescapable fact that by blowing the mugging he had once again strengthened the image of Jo-Jo the loser.

Finally physical tiredness overcame his self-reproach and he sank down on a rusty, moss-covered wheel, a discarded leftover from the oldtime autos. He pulled out his pipe and reached inside his cotton shirt, itself a relic of the great times, for his battered weed pouch. He had no food but he could at least smoke, although even that would only last for two or three pipes.

When the pipe was finished, he tapped out the ash on the stones at his feet. He felt a good deal more relaxed although, he had to admit, he was in a pretty sound mess. He decided he might as well keep moving while the sun was high. It would be unwise to return to Festival, especially if he were broke, so his best bet was to press on and see where the marsh road led. Maybe he would find some village when he could put himself back together. In any case the marsh was beginning to trip his fears most bitterly and he would sooner be through it. Out of reach of its stench and the black ruins that squatted in the poisoned waters.

He stood up, stretched and started walking slowly down the raised highway. The sun was hot on the back of his neck, his stomach reminded him that he was hungry and he began to curse his luck again. The words of a text, half remembered from childhood, came strongly to his mind.

"If it wasn't for bad luck

I wouldn't have no luck at all."

As a child in the village he had been quick and popular. He and the other children had sat round the ancient circuits and listened to the texts over and over until they could recite them.

"Listen and learn," his father had said, "for the circuit will die and we will have to remember."

Jo-Jo had been quick to learn, quicker than the other village kids. His father had been pleased. He had smoked his pipe and boasted how his son would some day be a mighty man.

Maybe it had been that same quickness that had caused him to break out of the village when the great hunger had come. He had studied the texts.

"Run, run, run," they urged him.

And he had run, leaving his neighbors to die by inches, fighting to cultivate their barren hillside.

By degrees he had run to Festival. Caught and intoxicated by its swarming humanity, he had run with the crowd, hustling, gambling, stealing, until he was chased back to the road again, still running. But running was a state of mind by mid-afternoon; the best he could manage physically was a steady trudge. Stones had ripped his canvas boots and it was beginning to seem as though he had walked forever when he first saw the man.

The man lay in the road. He wore the coarse homespun shirt and leather trousers that were the standard dress of the young stud from the hills, and the greasy plaits and colored headband marked him as fresh out of one of the villages that huddled in the valleys of the bare downs to the south.

At first Jo-Jo thought he was dead but, as he cautiously

approached, the clothes bunched into a pillow and the gun belt within reach of an outstretched hand all left him in no doubt that the man was merely sleeping. When he saw the gun, his mind reeled. A piece. With a piece of his own he could go back to Festival walking like a man.

Jo-Jo dropped into a crouch and drew his knife. Silently he stalked the sleeping man. A rube fresh out of the hills probably carrying the family gun with hillbilly pride. This country boy could be exactly what he needed for his new start. Maybe his losing streak was over.

Suddenly, when Jo-Jo was not three paces from the man a bird, alarmed at his approach, flapped croaking out of the brambles.

The man woke and reached for his gun at the sight of the gaunt figure with its long knife. Jo-Jo froze in horror as the big barrel swung up. The hammer came back as he squeezed the trigger. Squeeze, don't snatch at it, his father had told him. The hammer snapped home with a click. The gun hadn't fired.

Jo-Jo laughed. A rube with his treasured family pistol and 100-year-old ammunition. His shells had probably been useless for thirty years. Jo-Jo laughed again and slashed at the man's throat. Too shocked even to be afraid, the man fell back and died.

Extract from the novel, *The Texts of Festival*, 1973

THE FAT LADY'S ARIA

THE END OF THE WORLD DRAWS NEAR FOR THE THIRD time in less than fifteen years. It's discussed in coffee shops and saloons, and texted from couches by punks of the New Age while *UFO Hunters* flickers unwatched on TV. Theories inundate the Internet and books are already in print. Although apocalyptic theorizing might seem a hard sell in these grim times, conferences are being staged, at least two major motion pictures are planned, and the collective consciousness wonders if the date 2012 is already

❑ But don't worry. The wheel of karma turns and the unpleasant Jo-Jo is clipped by Frankie Lee a chapter or so later, and the story roars on. Meanwhile, in what passed for the real world, predictions of the end of the world continued to be a growth industry, culminating—after a fashion—in the current folklore/Hollywood movie fear that December 2012 would bring about the end of everything.

copyrighted. We can be certain we are going to hear a mess of both ominous and grandly metaphysical predictions for 2012 before the crucial date arrives.

We have, of course, seen all this before. In July of 1999, after much consternation, and endless documentaries on the History Channel, we survived the quatrains of Nostradamus predicting terror descending from the sky. Then on New Year's Day 2000, we made it unscathed through Y2K and near-hysterical scenarios that every computer across the planet would crash due to a basic time-keeping glitch. Airplanes were supposed to fall from the sky that time, and the Midwest find itself without power in midwinter. A third major End Time in less than a decade is hard to embrace. Too many hints of that cracker-barrel, "fool me once" proverb that George Bush can never quite remember. On the other hand, stress levels are currently running high, and that is frequently when an Armageddon panic pops.

And December 21, 2012, is coming in hard with multiple threats, and conflicting theories being actively debated on any and all forums that offer media time to the fringe and the fantastic. One marketplace of such ideas is George Noory's *Coast to Coast AM* syndicated radio show. As the successor to the legendary Art Bell, Noory maintains the same format of paranormal and paranoid talk radio that gave Bell the highest ratings in syndicated nighttime talk. Call-in listeners warn of 12/21/2012 bringing an instant extinction of our current reality, much in the manner of the last episode *The Sopranos*, but encompassing the entire universe. Alternative scenarios range from the conventional—exploding volcanoes, boiling oceans, shifting tectonic plates, and/or alien invasion, to a more metaphysical bonding that will bring humanity closer to a functioning, Jungian-style planetary mind, enabling us to clean up the mess we've made with our rugged individualism. (Noory added his own spike of drama to the mix when he announced he would only extend his current *Coast to Coast AM* contract until 2012, so he could see out the significant date on air. Later, however, pragmatism kicked in and his deal now runs to 2017.)

MICK FARREN

At the core of the flourishing furor over 2012 is the Mayan calendar. A circular replica of a Mesoamerican calendar stone has hung for years on the wall behind my desk, a flat ceramic disc, the green of corroded copper. Right now a version of the same calendar stone, in the form of a spring loaded spinning top is currently being given away by Burger King with Kid's Meals as part of a promotion for *Indiana Jones and the Kingdom of the Crystal Skull*. Both are actually copies of the huge Aztec calendar stone preserved in the *Museo Nacional de Antropologia* in Mexico City. Aztec rather than Mayan, but close enough for discomfort when it's also used on web pages explaining how the Mayan calendar supposedly predicts that the Fat Lady's Terminal Aria will sound dead-on the Winter Solstice of 2012.

That the "Long Count" of the Mayan calendar mysteriously appears to come to an end in 2012 has been discussed in the counterculture since writer and supposed mystic José Arguelles promoted his concept of the Harmonic Convergence in 1987. Before Arguelles raised the hackles of sceptics by extending his idea of an earth-changing planetary alignment beyond Mayan mathematics to claims of telepathically received prophecies, the Book of Revelation, and a race of "galactic masters," we learned that the Mayan calendar was incredibly complicated, dated back to the sixth century BC, and functioned on mind-snapping multiples of synchronized and interlocking cycles. A 260-day sacred year is combined with a more conventional 360-day solar year, plus a lunar calendar, and the notorious Long Count that starts from the Mayan's concept of the dawn of time—around 3114 BC—and runs to its calculated termination at the Winter Solstice of 2012. Just to add to the difficulties for those who aren't Mayan scholars, the calendar also reflects the Mayan's belief that time was not only cyclic, but its cycles involved the regular destruction and rebirth of the universe.

The quirks of the Mayan calendar, however, would hardly seem enough on which to base a whole End of the World circus, especially as the stone calendar can be open to infinite interpretation. The Mayan calendar does not come with an operating manual. All but a handful of peripheral writings about its use and function were burned as works of Satan by the zealous Catholic priests who accompanied the Conquistadors when they overturned Central America in the sixteenth century. Fortunately for millennial circus fans plenty more theoretical threats are aimed at 2012.

The Galactic Alignment is an astronomical event that supposedly occurs only once in 26,000 years. The ecliptic—the common geometric plane on which the planets of the solar system rotate around the sun—will coincide with the plane of the Milky Way, our Sun's parent galaxy—in which the Sun and thousands of other stars rotate—exactly on December 21, 2012. According to many of the more sensationally violent theories surrounding 2012, the outcome could be massive galactic stress causing anything from a rotation in the Earth's magnetic field, a sudden and cataclysmic flip of the planet's molten core, all the way to the Sun beginning a catastrophic slide to the center of the Milky Way, where many astronomers suspect the as-yet-unproven existence of a vast black hole which provides the energy to power the rotation of our galaxy. Perfect for a spectacular 2012 disaster movie like the one being planned by Roland Emmerich, who directed *The Day After Tomorrow*, but other 2012 theorists take a kinder gentler approach.

Daniel Pinchbeck, author of *2012: The Return of Quetzalcoatl* has already emerged as one of the major players in this four-and-a-half year countdown. Described by the *New York Times* as "parts Jesuit and Jim Morrison," Pinchbeck, a tireless self-promoter who has even talked 2012 on *The Colbert Report*, is calmer and more philosophical when he states on the website Reality Sandwich, "My view is that '2012' is useful as a meme if it helps us to catalyze a shift in global culture and consciousness. Rather than fretting about what may or may not happen on that date, we should concentrate on the work that needs to be done now, on an inner as well as outer level." Pinchbeck and John Major Jenkins, author of *Maya Cosmogenesis 2012: The True Meaning of the Mayan Calendar End Date* are both heirs to the psychedelic school of wildly eclectic thinking pioneered first by Timothy Leary and then the late Terence McKenna, the writer, explorer, and psychedelic guru.

McKenna developed his Timewave Zero software system in the early 1970s. It fixes on 12/21/2012 as a major paradigm shift by an entirely different route, first described in the 1974 book *The Invisible Landscape* written with his brother Dennis. The math is complex, but, in simple terms, McKenna initially ran a computer analysis of the hexagrams of the *I Ching*, and claimed to have found that it was "a mathematical algorithm that wanted to be a calendar." Then, when superimposed on a chart of world history, the wave pattern of the hexagrams totally corresponded. The *I Ching* dipped during hard times like (say) the Black Death and spiked in the good, like the Italian Renaissance. As the matching patterns moved into the twenty-first century, however, McKenna observed what he called a "surge toward the zero state each time a cycle enters its terminal phase" and that the terminal phase plays out (yes, you guessed it) on 12/21/2012.

McKenna, who died of brain cancer in 2000, made a possible prediction for what he thought might occur in 2012 on the 1990s pop-TV UFO/paranormal show *Sightings*, and it was as radical as any of his other pronouncements. "*One of my guesses is what we will discover in 2012 is time travel. If technologies were developed [in 2012] that were able to move through time, it would explain why the wave could no longer give a linear description of the unfolding of events because the unfolding of events would go nonlinear.*"

In total contrast to Pinchbeck, Jenkins, and McKenna, NASA recently brought some hard science to the 2012 party when David Hathaway of the Marshall Space Flight Center announced to the media that "on January 4, 2008, a reversed-polarity sunspot appeared—and this signals the start of Solar Cycle 24." Hathaway explained that the previous solar cycle, #23, had peaked in 2000–2002 with some furious solar storms. These are streams of electrons emanating from the Sun, from which the Earth is protected by its magnet field—with overspill appearing as the polar glow of the Aurora Borealis. After that #23 had dropped away to nothing, all was quiet on the Sun until the telltale sunspot indicated the start of a new cycle that should peak around "2011 or 2012."

While solar storms and more violent outpourings known as solar coronal mass ejections (CMEs) are hardly the end of the world, Hathaway warns that they can disable the satellites that we depend on for weather forecasts and GPS navigation. Radio bursts from solar flares can directly interfere with cell phone reception, while CMEs hitting Earth can cause electrical power outages. "The most famous example is the Quebec outage of 1989, which left Canadians without power for up to six days." Steve Hill of the Space Weather Prediction Center added that domestic airline flights routed over the North Pole during solar storms were among the most at risk. "They can experience radio blackouts, navigation errors and computer reboots."

Hard science may suggest that the Sun could cause problems in 2012, but, overall, conventional academics take a bleak view of the more apocalyptic predictions. Back in 2007, when *USA Today* broke the 2012 story in the mainstream media, Sandra Noble, executive director of the Foundation for the Advancement of Mesoamerican Studies in Crystal River, Florida, was wholly dismissive. "To render December 21, 2012, as a doomsday or moment of cosmic shifting is a complete fabrication and a chance for a lot of people to cash in." Anthropologist Susan Gillespie is equally impatient. "The 2012 phenomenon comes from media and from other people making use of the Maya past to fulfil agendas that are really their own."

On the matter of The Galactic Alignment, and the works of theorists like Arguelles, Pinchbeck, and Jenkins, who attempt to link the Mayan Long Count with alignment of the Milky Way and the solar system, Anthony Aveni, an archeoastronomer and professor at Colgate, curtly told the *New York Times*. "I defy anyone to look up into the sky and see the galactic equator. You need a radio telescope for that." The Curious About Astronomy website attached to Cornell also takes no prisoners when it comes to galactic alignment. "The Sun crosses the plane of the Galaxy twice every year as we orbit around it, with no ill effect on Earth."

A year later, the academic community—especially archeologists and astronomers—don't even want to discuss 2012, which is probably also a measure of how the phenomenon has grown since it was first featured in *USA Today* and the *New York Times*. The consensus is that it's a crypto-scientific, four-year wonder that has more to do with tabloid sensation seeking than any rigorous and disciplined investigation. It mixes astronomy with astrology, which is an anathema, and its ties to psychedelic drugs, UFOs, pop science fiction, shamanism, and, at best, contemporary folklore, place it firmly within the lunatic fringe. The majority are confident it will fizzle out when the appointed day rolls around and nothing happens.

On the other hand, academics tend to dislike and distrust anything apocalyptic or unconventional. The Big Bang Theory of the creation of the universe was heavily resisted when first mooted, and conventional palaeontology did everything it could to keep the asteroid-impact/dinosaur-extinction theorists at bay until they actually came up with a possible impact crater. The work of Timothy Leary and Terence McKenna has never been accepted by the mainstream. If I was looking to science to confirm or deny the possibility of something truly spectacular happening on the 2012 solstice, I would do better to look to sociology than astronomy.

In a nation where polls indicate that up to fifty percent of Americans believe that the Book of Revelation is a true, prophetic document, maybe sociology is the only way to understand the obsessive countdown to 2012. The US has a long history of doomsday cults and end-of-the-world panics. Part of this has to stem from the number of religious dissenters who emigrated from Europe over the centuries, seeking religious freedom, often for extreme beliefs. Another part may be an extension of what William Burroughs used to call "the immortality racket." In most cases, the trick any leader/prophet/patriarch has to turn is not only to convince his or her congregation that the End

Times are upon them, but, for the faithful, that he or she has a way out.

The awkward moment for prophets is when neither doom nor salvation materialize, which, up to now, has been the case 100 percent of the time. (Unless self-created, as in the cases of Jim Jones, David Koresh, and Marshall Applewhite and his Heaven's Gate cultists.) The followers have been led to the top of the mountain, or the great cave in the desert, whatever's the designated sanctuary from the apocalypse. The appointed moment comes and goes, but nothing has happened. The faithful wait. Time passes and the worst scenario downgrades itself from planetary annihilation to a chance of rain. The faithful eventually start their sheepish trudge back down the mountain.

In the last century this was the fate of the Millerites, the followers of a ex-army Captain turned evangelist, William Miller, who, possibly suffering from posttraumatic stress disorder from the War of 1812, calculated that the Rapture—itself an 1829 piece of inventive biblical cross referencing by Edward Irving, Henry Drummond, and John Nelson Darby—would occur between March 21, 1843, and March 21, 1844. A highly visible comet, an equally spectacular meteor shower, and a grim economic recession all contributed to a near-panic that garnered Miller some 50,000 followers who began disposing of their homes and worldly possessions, even leaving crops unharvested, all in anticipation of the main event. When, by March 22, 1844, the Millerites had failed to rise bodily into the sky, the disillusionment was so intense, it became known as the "Great Disappointment." Fortunately for fundamentalism, more resilient souls continued to revise Miller's calculations, in bouts of scriptural arithmetic that would lead to the foundation of sects like the Seventh Day Adventists and, more recently and tragically, the Branch Davidians.

Few conversations about the 2012 phenomena fail to prompt the suggestion that, with 2012, the New-Age, Burning-Man, post-punk mystics have engaged their own version of the Rapture, except, where the fundamentalists learned from the Great Disappointment, and now keep the Rapture's ETA suitably vague, the 2012 theorists have nailed themselves to this highly specific date. In many respects, it's an all or nothing gamble that gives the participants four years to sell a lot of books and documentary films, to accept well-paid public appearances, and generally make hay while the Sun-as-we-know-it still shines. After that we have to assume that they are totally confident that everything will be extremely different, or they will have to start seriously salvaging their careers.

Right now, though, no one seems to be thinking too hard about a possible "Great Disappointment" in the wake of 2012. Many familiar faces from the UFO/paranormal community are joining in the fun. Novelist and screenwriter, Whitley Strieber, who also claims to have been abducted by aliens, has entered the fray with a science fiction action novel, *2012: The War For Souls*, in which reptilian invaders enslave humanity and feast on their souls, and the Great Pyramid is destroyed. But Strieber tends to blur the line between his facts and fiction by hinting at public appearances that 2012 may be when we really discover the true purpose of alien implants. Richard Hoagland, who previously made a name for himself with media speculation about the supposed face on Mars, and whose current book *Dark Mission* links NASA and the occult, has started to participate in 2012 events. Here in Los Angeles, Christian Voltaire and his partner Jay Weidner—also producer of the documentary *2012: The Odyssey*—have already promoted The 2012 Conference that drew a thousand attendees, and plan more events of the same kind both in LA and San Francisco in October and November of this year.

"Interest in the 'unknown' has always been cyclical," notes Skylaire Alfvegren, founder of the League of Western Fortean Intermediatists (LOWFI), a group which monitors southwestern mysteries and enigmas. "After 9/11, it was in poor taste to openly express interest in the unknown, or conspiracy theory—angels were okay— when such a heinous event had actually happened. Mass consciousness is now shifting once again—just look at our Democratic presidential nominee."

THE FUTURE'S UNCERTAIN...   367

The wheel spins and the approach of 2012—whether based in an alternative perception of reality, wishful thinking in the closing days of the George Bush nightmare, or as just the sum total of contemporary fascination with the paranormal and the nature of time—is a growth industry, and will probably remain so while fear, fascination, and even hopes are sustained that somehow December 22, 2012—the day following the crucial day—will be unlike anything we have previously seen, if indeed that day dawns at all.

LA CityBeat, September 2008

GOD'S WORST NIGHTMARE

❏ Even while telling ourselves it's a media hype and nothing more than Millerites in the speed-up, doom will still infiltrate our dreams and our poetry.

Church bells are ringing, cannon beating time
Survivors of the government running for the line
Shadow freaks, Dixie geeks, they come in all sizes
Break the wheel of fortune and carry off the prizes
Suture queens, slash teens, rocket boys too
God's worst nightmare is coming after you

Still in the basement, dreaming up perversions
Deathcamp tickets with the video version
Insect secretions when the lights grow dim
Aztec rituals and gipsy hymns
Caligula and Sparky and Little Boy Blue
God's worst nightmare is coming after you

Shebazz is raging and Ophelia weeps
Desdemona's going down on the kid who never sleeps
Chained in the marketplace, crying in the rain
With a fatal attraction to new concepts in pain
Amazing grace is maxed out, stealing spiders from the zoo
God's worst nightmare is coming after you

Written for the Deviants CD,
Eating Jello With A Heated Fork, 1996

MICK FARREN

LIVE TOGETHER, OR DIE TOGETHER

IT'S VERY EASY FOR THE MIND TO BOGGLE RIGHT NOW. I turn on the TV and find that the LA fires are moving in on Pasadena and Glendale, and a fine layer of ash covers parked cars, plus a hurricane is coming up the Baja where hurricanes aren't supposed to be. I switch channels and some zombie-Republican asshole in her Sarah Palin glasses is warning me that the environmentalists have to be stopped before they destroy the country. An email comes from my friend Diva warning me that if Mt. Wilson burns, large areas won't have broadcast TV at all. Another news story is that the appliance corporation Whirlpool is shipping a shitload of jobs to Mexico.

Hold it!

I'm in overload.

The evidence is the stench of burning in the air. Capitalism is simply not sustainable. It's no longer a matter of manufacture, sell, and consume. It's become an arithmetic abstraction. It's a numerical narcissism that drives corporate executives to strive for annual bonuses worth more than they could spend in a couple of lifetimes. Chris Hedges—of whom I'm becoming quite a fan—has a rant on this theme on the website Truthdig: "*Globalization and unfettered capitalism have been swept into the history books along with the open-market theory of the 1920s, the experiments of fascism, communism and the New Deal. It is time for a new economic and political paradigm. It is time for a new language to address our realities.*"

It has long been my contention that the only real counter to corporate globalism is by international alliances of workers, artists, and activists. We all breath the same air, drink the same water, are warmed and cooled by the same planetary thermodynamics, and are poisoned by the same pesticides and growth hormones.

❑ The Los Angeles basin now has a recognized fire season, and sometimes all you have to do is to turn on the TV to hear the hoofbeats of the Horsemen.

Doc40, 2009

THE BEES HAVE LEFT THE ENVIRONMENT

❑ Needless to say, the 2012 apocalypse racket—along with a lot of other diversions—went into abeyance when the global economy spun out in the fall of 2008, but, after a few months, it began to reassert itself, and with not only the corporate movie industry and the History Channel filling the air once again with cheap Armageddon, but also an apparently pissed off nature turning the inexplicable into the irreversible.

To LIKEN THE PRESENT DECADE TO A LOW-BUDGET science fiction movie is hardly original, but, all too often, dangerously apt. In this case, what lurks inexplicably is the mystery of the vanishing bees. Since the fall of 2006, millions of bees have simply disappeared. They are seemingly dead, although, in many cases, no corpses are found. The story has received a certain degree of media play, but the possibility has largely been ignored that these millions of lost bees could be an indication that much more may be amiss with our planetary environment than just greenhouse gases and rising temperatures.

Back in February, the *New York Times* ran a report from Visalia, in the San Joaquin Valley, about how beekeeper David Bradshaw inspected his hives last January and found half of his 100 million bees gone without trace. And this weird, *X-Files* phenomenon—dubbed Colony Collapse Disorder (CCD)—isn't merely confined to California. It's being repeated in at least twenty-four states in the US, and similar reports are coming in from all over Europe. In Spain, hundreds of thousands of colonies have been lost. Eight hundred miles away, beekeepers in Croatia estimated five million bees had died in just forty-eight hours. In Poland, the beekeeper's association estimated up to forty percent of their bees were wiped out last year, while Greece, Switzerland, Italy, and Portugal report similar losses.

The majority of us generally associate the active little insects with the production of honey, but, in both the agri-industry and the global ecology, the major function of bees is to pollinate plants. A Cornell University study estimated that honeybees annually pollinate more than $14 billion worth of seeds and crops in the United States, mostly fruits, vegetables, and nuts. "Every third bite we consume in our diet is dependent on a honeybee to pollinate that food," Zac Browning, vice president of the American Beekeeping Federation told the *Times*. In addition, a huge industry exists, moving multiple bee colonies from one loca-

MICK FARREN

tion to another to pollinate commercial crops.

German bee expert Professor Joergen Tautz of Wurzburg University, quoted on the Daily Kos website, amplifies the bee's crucial role. "They are vital to biodiversity. Bees are essential to the pollination of over 130,000 plants, from melons to pumpkins, raspberries and all kind of fruit trees, as well as animal fodder like clover." Tautz makes it clear that this depopulation of bees has the potential for environmental catastrophe, and, in a worst-case scenario, crops, fodder—and therefore livestock—could die from a lack of pollinating insects.

The hunt for the cause of CCD and the decimated beehives is currently taking multiple directions. Fingers have been pointed at some of the usual corporate suspects like Monsanto and its Triple Hybrid GM corn, and also Bayer's Gaucho pesticide. Each may have caused neurological damage and altered the bees' sense of orientation, but little hard evidence has yet to be produced that they are the culprits. Among the stranger suggestions is that mobile phone signals can disrupt the bees' complex "internal navigation systems." According to a report in UK online science magazine *The Register*, German researchers at Landau university placed cordless-phone docking units, which emit electromagnetic radiation, into beehives. They found that "seventy percent of bees exposed to radiation failed to find their way back to the hive after searching for pollen and nectar"

Marla Spivak of the University of Minnesota, has suggested on various University websites that the beekeeping industry itself could be causing the problem. Using California as an example, where hundreds of millions of bees are transported each year to pollinate almond plantations, Spivak argues, "*Such high density could create competitive stress for bee colonies. And to avoid food shortages, beekeepers often supplement hive production with high-fructose corn syrup, which may poison the bees if the syrup is not properly prepared. Beekeepers also use pesticides to control insect pests. They want to kill the mite, not the bee, but mites and bees are related! And now the mites have evolved resistance to the pesticides.*"

THE FUTURE'S UNCERTAIN...   371

And yet, neither mites nor poisons, while potentially lethal, should create such a bizarre inconsistency in the way CCD plagues non-migrating colonies as well as the mobile hives of the pollination business. Response to the crisis is equally diverse. At one extreme, the House Subcommittee on Horticulture and Organic Agriculture will hold hearings, and, at the other, no less than Fidel Castro cites the bee tragedy in an attack on the Bush administration's treatment of the environment. Meanwhile, the rest of us simply repress a gnawing unease that things might actually be worse than we already imagine.

LA CityBeat, 2007

THE ANTS ARE GOING TO THE STARS

Bees may vanish, but ants cannot be trusted. They may have colonial ambitions, and even dreams of empire.

I'D IMAGINE THAT, BY NOW, A LOT OF YOU ARE TOO young to remember what it was really like. Even for the ones who were around at the time, the memory is starting to fade. I've never been that enthusiastic about monumental historic events. When you're sitting in the bar on anything after the third drink, they start to look like any other TV show, and a boring TV show at that.

The windup to the first launch was mechanically tedious, at least it was from where I was sitting. The idea of the mighty starship embarking on the awesome 115-year trip to one of the water worlds of Proxima Centauri was promoted by every available medium for close to three years. At first, it was just a matter of TV spectaculars and magazine articles. In the last six or eight months before the launch date, all things went nuts. You couldn't go anywhere without being confronted with the less than elegant image of the Venturer starship. You'd need to be a hermit not to know that the project was a triumph of international cooperation, and man's first mighty step beyond his own solar system, and blah, blah. These declarations were usually accompanied by the offensive blare of martial trumpets.

MICK FARREN

As if this almost total takeover of the media wasn't enough, the stores were packed to the rafters with souvenir junk. There were Venturer mugs, Venturer ashtrays, some exceedingly ugly silver foil jackets with a picture of the starship on the back. With the exception of a couple of surly emergent nations who figured the whole enterprise was a massive waste of money and natural resources, the entire world took a holiday on the appointed day when the starship would blast itself out of earth's orbit and lumber off to the nearest star.

Unfortunately, there wasn't much else to do on the first global holiday but squat down in front of a TV, get as high as a kite, and nod out to the seemingly endless launching ceremony. I spent the big day in Charlie's Bar, as far from the TV set as possible. Even there, though, it wasn't possible totally to escape the great event. The clientele worked themselves into such a state of whiskey soaked self congratulation that the unsuspecting observer might be forgiven for thinking that they'd built the damn starship with their bare hands.

I was propped upon a corner bar stool, trying to ignore what was going on. This wasn't easy. At the other end of the counter the TV was running at full bore. Next to me a once attractive, but now overweight and used-looking blonde was watching the screen with what amounted to religious awe. She sipped her gin and tonic almost as though she was in a trance. Her eyes were close to glazed. "It's so wonderful."

I pretended not to hear, but she repeated herself. "It's really wonderful, isn't it?"

"Huh?"

"All those people, going all that way."

"If you like that sort of thing. Me, I can do without it."

The blonde indicated I was something that had crawled out from under a rock. "What's the matter with you? No pride in humanity?"

I shrugged. "Not much."

The blonde waved a pudgy hand, weighed down with cheap gaudy rings, in the direction of the TV. "What about those people, doesn't the sight of them do something to you?"

On the screen a section of the 700 starship passengers were filing through an entry port. All in their neatly matching Earth-green jumpsuits and UV visors. The blonde was about to start weeping into her gin. Anybody would have thought she was their collective mother. She dug a Kleenex from her bag and dabbed at her nose. "I mean, just imagine all those poor men and women. They know for a fact that they're going to grow old and die on that ship. It'll be their grandchildren and great grandchildren who reach the end of the journey."

I grunted. "I saw the same TV show."

"Doesn't their courage do something to you?"

"It makes me wonder about their sanity."

Humanity's pride, as expressed by the gin-drunk blonde, took a near-fatal knock when Venturer came back a scant eighteen months later. In fact, half the world went into a state of shock. Everyone on board had died of some mysterious plague, and the homing override had turned the ship round and brought it home like a two-mile long private coffin. The return came as a complete surprise. For eight months, encouraging messages came back from the starship, and then it crossed the orbit of Uranus, and communication was no longer possible.

It took them five years to get round to Venturer II. Considerable changes had been made between the first disaster and the second attempt. The major one was that the passengers weren't being expected to breed two generations of themselves before they reached where they were going. Instead, the bulk of them wouldn't know anything about the century plus journey. They'd be nicely tucked up in cryogenic deep sleep. The only people awake on the starship would be a small crew, only a couple of dozen individuals, who would see the ship safely on course, and then set the timers to wake everyone up, just before they got to their destination. By way of an additional frill, some smart psychologist decided that the ones who were condemned to stay awake until they dropped dead of old age or other assorted afflictions should be homosexual. This caused a certain amount of commotion, even in that enlightened age. The Pope was far from amused, Evangelicals started screaming about iniquity being dispatched from the earth to infect the heavens, and cheap comedians got cheaper.

But the Space Commission and its psychologists proved sufficiently powerful not to have to pay any more than passing attention to Pope, Evangelicals or comedians. A team of twenty-four highly trained, and physically perfect young gay men and women were assembled for their one way trip.

The launching of Venturer II received a good deal less media coverage. There were few souvenirs and no holiday. People had gathered in the bar to watch the launch, but the atmosphere was greatly subdued compared with the three-ring circus that bid farewell to the first expedition. The overweight blonde had long since disappeared from that particular bar. Nobody knew whether she'd died, found a husband, simply moved on or what.

The second ship took almost three years to come home to roost. On the second time round the loss of life was considerably reduced. The silent majority of passengers were still safely on ice. The trouble had been among the gay crew. Somewhere out there, way beyond Pluto, training and maybe even gaiety had worn off. They'd wigged out and started beating each other to death with blunt instruments.

The Space Commission ceased to be the world's favorite agency. For a long time nobody mentioned anything about Venturer III. After two total disasters the human race's collective ego had taken a considerable bashing. Nobody felt like setting themselves up for another hammering. The idea of going to the stars found itself put on what seemed like permanent hold, except in one tiny and neglected department of the vast agency.

The original starship launch had all wept the ant implant experiments right out of the public eye. Venturer I took about ninety-nine percent of the available gosh-ain't-science-wonderful air time, and more besides. I do remember, though, seeing one single show about the ant business, and I remember that I didn't like it. I don't know enough biology to explain exactly what was going on. In simple terms, some over-bright kid with a crewcut and tinted glasses started implanting little electronic doohickeys in the brains of ants. Pretty soon, the crewcut kid discovered if he hooked a computer up to his modified ants, he could control a whole colony of them. He became their virtual queen. The little critters would be working away, like they always do, only instead of doing what they wanted, the modified ants were doing what crewcut kid and his computer wanted.

I couldn't see the point of this at the time. All I know is that it scared me. I had this vision of a time when crewcut would get tired of messing around with ants, and switch his attention to people. You could be sure that among the very first ones wired up to crewcut's bidding would be alcoholics, dopefiends, and poets. It wasn't a very pleasant vision.

I may not have seen any practical purpose behind the ant business, but somebody in the Space Commission obviously did. It was kept fairly quiet at first. They only told us these adapted ants were being used in certain kinds of miniature construction work. They showed TV films of gangs of ants busily assembling tiny, but highly complicated, structures. A hard hat across the other side of the bar let out a beery guffaw. "That's what I like to see. Let the little bastards do it all."

"And leave you free to drink all day?"

"Why the hell not? Those six-legged suckers like to work. That's why they call them workers."

Bit by bit, the great TV public was introduced to the main idea. First we were all conditioned to the idea of the little ants rushing around taking care of business. The next move was to demonstrate all the wonderful constructions that they had thrown together. Once all this had been assimilated, the powers that were came out with the kicker. The world was informed that they were going to build one more starship. But not for people. Instead of a human crew, an ant colony would be blasted out of solar system and all the way to Proxima Centauri.

Once the news was broken, the hard sell went into high gear. The souvenirs began to fill the stores, and the TV

MICK FARREN

specials commenced to bore the crap out of me. I swear to god it was almost as bad as the windup to Venturer I. The only consolation was that the ants were doing all the work. The world even got another holiday to watch the launch. In some ways, Venturer III was a lot less impressive than its two predecessors. For one thing, it in no way compared in size. Since it only had to house a computer and maybe a thousand or so ants, the third starship was nearer forty meters long instead of the massive, two-mile long pomp and circumstance of the others.

Impressive or not, Venturer III, coupled with a day off, had enough charisma to convince a crowd to fill the bar and get liquored up. I was getting liquored up anyway, so I found myself among them. Certain people like to call me a cynic. Maybe I don't emote as readily as some, but I have to confess that, as the engines flamed on that starship, I couldn't help feeling a little moved. As for the rest of the bar, they all went crazy, kissing, hugging, and slapping each other on the back. Once again it was like they'd put the whole thing together themselves. A burly Neanderthal pounded me on the shoulder. "How about that? We're finally going to the stars."

I turned to look into his bleary, raw meat face. "You think so?"

"Sure, we're going to make it all the way this time."

"But *we* haven't gone anywhere."

The Neanderthal looked confused, particularly at my emphasis on the word *we*. "What are you talking about?"

"The ants, buddy, the ants. All we've done is start the ants on their conquest of the universe. The monkeys provided the transportation."

He took a while to digest the idea, then he burst out laughing. "You crazy drunken bum. The booze has addled your brains. You don't know what you're talking about."

The Neanderthal told all his friends. My theory kept them amused all through the rest of the evening. Some people just refuse to see what's really happening.

Ad Astra, 1977

THE FUTURE'S UNCERTAIN...

LIFE IS JUST EBOLA CHERRIES

❏ Never turn your back on a virus. The micro-motherfuckers are out to get us. That's fact, not paranoia. It's built into their DNA. Although, in the way that we humans have been spreading ourselves across the planet, fouling most everything we touch, we are looking a little viral ourselves.

BLISSFUL IGNORANCE AND SELF-DELUDING ISOLATION are possible anywhere, but in Southern California, they are probably endemic. Already locked into something of a pod mentality thanks to car culture and freeway transit, it becomes all too easy to believe that bad stuff happens to other people over there somewhere. It happens in South Central, or out in West Covina, or at least it's on the next block. That, of course, is only until the moment it happens to you. Aside from physical and spiritual trauma, the knowledge that you have become one of the victimized "others," and the anger at whatever terrible cosmic screw-up put you in that unenviable position are two of the gnarlier aftermaths of any serious mishap.

From a Los Angeles perspective, Zaire might as well be in a different galaxy. That events in the capital city of Kinshasa could in any way impinge on Venice Beach or Century City seems close to impossible. Although the spread of a fatal and horrible virus may seem unfortunate, perhaps deserving of aid and sympathy, it's hardly life-threatening at Hollywood and Vine. In truth, however, the distance is not nearly as great as we blithely imagine, the threat is more than possible; we need to rethink our planetary position, friends, and neighbors.

Previous Ebola outbreaks in Africa were confined to fairly remote rural communities where the contagion flared like a flash fire, but vanished when everyone was dead. This time the game is a little different. Kinshasa is a major city of close to a million and a half inhabitants, with maybe another million of the frighteningly poor living in the toxic shanty towns that surround it. Even with its speed, an eighty to ninety percent kill ratio, and the total lack of any effective cure or treatment, the disease can burn for quite a while in a population center of that size.

And let's not forget that Kinshasa has an airport. Even if it were possible to quarantine the place, if a local gang boss and his mistress were to bribe their way out to Lagos, or a couple of infected mining engineers in a Cessna were to make it to Johannesburg, the fat lady will definitely be clearing her throat. Next stop: LAX and the Bradley Terminal. As far as Ebola is concerned, the commercial aviation routes are nothing more than big, high-tech, cocktail-serving disease vectors.

Most of what we yearning masses know about Ebola comes from movies and TV hospital shows. This is hardly satisfactory, but the news coverage, both local and national has been, at best, kind of patchy, although those maps with growing red areas of outbreak zones are nothing short of terrifying. For a while, I wondered why Ebola was getting so little coverage and managed to avoid the paranoid thrill ride that leads to the conclusion that it was constructed in a lab in New Mexico and is part of the conspiracy to depopulate Africa for easy, twenty-first century plundering by the New World Order. In the nick of time, though, I realized the most likely reason we aren't getting any pictures out of Zaire is that TV crews and reporters aren't there. You won't see Wolf Blitzer with a hand-mic risking exposure in downtown Kinshasa. That is definitely not why they pay him the big bucks. I think it's a pretty safe bet that the plague will not be televised.

The idea of an Ebola outbreak here in Los Angeles—or in any Western city—is so toweringly awesome that any contemplation of it sends me scuttling to the comfort of death-rattle humor. I speculate to what lengths Aaron Spelling and his ilk might go to protect their lives and property, or whether anyone in the basement of the White House has suggested quickly nuking Kinshasa before the virus can travel anywhere else. The rationale for Hiroshima would certainly apply here—the sacrifice of a couple of million for the good of the many, many millions more in a really patriotic, humanitarian cause. "Hot damn, Bubba, you'd probably get the Nobel Prize and the right-wingers would be buying tickets to kiss your mushroom cloud."

I've also been thinking a lot about those spacesuits the Centers for Disease Control guys wear, the snappy plastic numbers with built-in air tanks, like the ones the feds had when they came to get E.T. Could that be the way to survive the plague? In what amounts to a full-body condom? Like virtually everything, though, I figure it's a matter of who has the dough and who doesn't. Those suits are pretty fancy, and I assume they wouldn't retail for less than five grand. With an escalating desperation of demand, the sky could be the limit, the biggest deal since Barbra Streisand tickets. I certainly don't see any cheap Republican son-of-a-bitch governor handing out free spacesuits to every citizen. That kind of money is only spent on fighting the important threats like communism, cocaine, or poverty-stricken Mexicans. Lethal disease has neither the clout nor the profit margin, and, while we're talking profit, I wonder just how many Beverly Hills MDs will be sweating the front line, ministering to the sick and the dying.

An even wilder speculation: What if Ebola could be spread by the transfer of cash money? Now that would really sodomize the pooch. I guess those with electronic banking and credit could sit out the epidemic in sealed, sterile homes, at least while there was still someone alive and willing to deliver pizza, but those of us who live our lives by singles, tens, and twenties could kiss our asses goodbye. About the only light down this particular tunnel is the suggestion that Ebola may only be able to survive and flourish in the steam heat of the tropics, and that it would die off in more temperate climes. In this case, we might see Michael Eisner, Bruce Willis, and Michael Bolton fighting like unseemly dogs over Antarctic real estate, and the hasty construction of spacious split-level igloos with screening rooms and indoor heated pools. "Screw the krill, the penguins, and the ozone layer, we billionaires be chillin.'"

LA Reader, May 1995

HAPPY BIRTHDAY, MR. BOMB

❏ Scant months after I was concerning myself in print with the odds on an

CONGRATULATIONS, FRIENDS AND NEIGHBORS. WE have made it through the first fifty years of the nuclear age, and with hardly a scratch, apart from the cooking of two Japanese cities that seem to have recovered quite nicely, thank you. Party down, dudes. For half a century, we, the human race, have lived with the sure and certain knowledge that we had the technology to eradicate our species (and thousands of others, as well) with little more than the push of a button. Despite dire warnings offered by everyone from Albert Einstein to Stanley Kubrick, we neither fried our civilization nor completely lost our collective sanity.

We have even reached the point where the trappings of old-style nuclear confrontation have just about become a matter of urban archaeology. Every time I walk along Third Street, just east of La Brea, I can't help but notice an old air raid siren on a pole on the north side of the street. Once upon a time, this was the gadget that was supposed to sound off to tell us that we were all entering the final seven minutes of our lives. And in the basement bowels of schools, public institutions, and some of the older hotels and office buildings, it's still possible to find those black and yellow tin signs with the triple triangles in a circle that mark the fallout shelters. Each time I see one, I can't help remembering how, back when I was a youth, I tried so hard to steal one of the suckers, because Bob Dylan had one in his alleged room on the cover of *Bringing It All Back Home*.

It might be interesting to find out what has become of all the individual fallout shelters. How many homes in the Valley still have the family bunker at the bottom of the garden, stocked with canned food and shotgun shells from the fifties? Maybe the same researchers could also try to locate the legendary ton of opium that was allegedly stashed in some secret cache to jump-start an emergency, post-holocaust pharmacology after the hot dust had settled.

And what happened to that load of radioactive dirt from the nuclear test site that was trucked into Hollywood in 1955 and supposedly killed John Wayne and the rest of the cast of the movie *The Conqueror*? It could still be around, the underlay of some lawn in Beverly Hills.

John Wayne, cancer, opium, and fallout shelters remind me of the major role pure fantasy has played in the

Ebola pandemic, we were celebrating the fiftieth year of the atomic age.

protection of our mental health through this atomic half-century. The Japanese invented Godzilla as some jolly green analog of their bomb trauma. As a small boy, I was convinced that my friends and I would be among the few who survived.

All the grown-ups would die, but we'd emerge, grubby but unscathed, to loot supermarkets and sporting goods stores, and take to the hills as heavily armed and totally feral *Road Warrior* children.

The fantasies of nasty little boys, however, were nothing compared with the self-delusion propagated by the White House, the Pentagon, and all the labyrinths of government, who claimed a nuclear war was survivable and winnable, well into the mid-eighties, virtually until Carl Sagan presented the concept of nuclear winter to a mass audience. How else could one explain that idiot turtle in his tin helmet and the criminally asinine "duck and cover" commercials, or the way that those in power became so bent out of shape by both *Dr. Strangelove* and *The Day After?* They claimed that laughing at the unthinkable, or showing it as it might really be, would sap the nation's will to fight. No one quite explained how much will to fight would remain in a population that was nothing more than carbonized, radioactive barbecue.

I can still recall the one time the fantasy collapsed, back in October of 1962, when Jack Kennedy went toe to toe with Nikita Khrushchev, and, for a few minutes, it looked as though we were just hours from Armageddon. I was on the threshold of sex, beer, and all other earthly delights, and my rage that all this might be taken away from me in one furious, blinding flash knew no containment. I didn't give a subjective rat's ass about the politics of the Castro regime. In fact, I thought Fidel was kinda cool. I just wanted to live.

If you seek a single point of origin for what are now referred to as the "excesses" of the sixties, the Cuban missile crisis gets my vote, certainly over LSD-25 and the Beatles. That was the moment when the youth of the world looked squarely into the abyss and, for a while at least, weren't so ready to buy the authoritarian bullshit.

Birthdays are not only a time for cake and candles, but also for looking back and speculating forward. Hindsight indicates the first phase of the nuclear age has ended. No longer do a pair of superpowers pace Main Street like gun-fighters at high noon. The doctrine of Mutually Assured Destruction (the sweet acronym MAD) miraculously held up until the USSR ran out of rubles, but now it's just a blast from the past. The next half century promises to be smaller, messier, and vastly more complicated. The poten-tial totalling of the Earth has, to a degree, given way to a lot of dirty little local menaces. Recent estimates point to some twenty countries that either have nukes or could get them in a matter of months, should push come to shove.

Thus the Big One has been replaced by a bunch of po-tential Small Ones. India/Pakistan, North Korea/South Korea, the whole mess in the Middle East, and don't even think about freelance terrorists. A city or two on each side are fried, with an aftermath of fallout, cancer, birth defects, plus a lot more toxic reindeer up in Lapland. Rumors circu-lated in England during the Falklands War that Margaret Thatcher had dispatched an elderly Vulcan atom bomber with a single locked and loaded Hiroshima-sized bomb to play that scenario if the conventional ground war went sour.

The complications of the future almost make me nostalgic for the simple stupidities of the past. In the H-bomb game, no genies ever return to the bottle. From the moment humanity knew about Hiroshima, it also knew there was no going back. The next fifty years will almost certainly see a world in which Chile, Iran, South Africa, and Germany all have nuclear weapons, and there's not a damn thing we can realistically do about it. Happy birthday, Mr. Bomb.

Los Angeles Reader, August 1995

AD 999

THE REAL PROBLEM WITH A MILLENNIUM IS THAT WE have no models to show us how to handle it. We know how we're supposed to behave at Christmas, Thanksgiving, and Halloween. We even have the costumes and menus down. Unfortunately, only one other millennium has been celebrated in the Christian calendar. That was AD 999 and, frankly, it was a bit of a mess.

Tenth century Western Europe was not a particularly pleasant place. Civilization was hauling itself laboriously out of the Dark Ages, and danger seemed to lurk in every direction. Fanatic Muslims threatened to invade from the south. Axe-wielding Vikings raided from the north, and, to the east, pagan Bulgars and Magyars sharpened their swords and eyed the pickings. Famine and a series of plagues swept the continent, including the mysterious "St. Anthony's Fire" that caused a lingering, horrible death. Corruption in high places was so rife that Archbishop Adalbero of Rheims railed against a murderous aristocracy. "Men live without law and the fear of punishment, abandoning themselves to their passions. The strong oppress the weak. Everywhere there is violence against the poor." Sound familiar?

In that kind of environment, no one believed that a millennium would be anything but more bad news. As the year 1000 came closer, omens and portents abounded. In England, a huge meteor blazed across the heavens. In Aquitaine, the sky rained blood. The entire army of German emperor Otto III was spooked by a solar eclipse. Fire swept Rome, and the roof of St. Peter's was partially consumed. On a slightly different level, every two-headed calf born in the next village tended to confirm the more spectacular stuff. Throughout the late fall of 999, huge numbers of people started to converge on Rome like some gloomy medieval Woodstock. No one could agree what exactly was going to happen, but most theories centered on the End of the World and the coming of the anti-Christ.

The terrified culmination came on December 31, when

MICK FARREN

according to historian Richard Erdoes in his book *AD 999*, "This was the dreaded eve of the Millennium, the Day of Wrath when the world would dissolve into ashes. Many of those present had given away their possessions—lands, homes, and household goods. Many poor sinners had entered the church in sackcloth and ashes, having already spent weeks doing penance and mortifying the flesh. At the Altar, the Holy Father, Pope Sylvester, elevated the host for all to see. The crowd remained rooted, motionless, transfixed, barely daring to breathe, not a few dying from fright, giving up their ghosts then and there." As we, of course, are well aware, the world didn't end. Everyone probably went home feeling extremely dumb and got on with a future that would bring us the Renaissance, the Thirty Years War, and Little Richard.

Section from an *LA Reader* cover story, July 1994

THE WOLVES COME DOWN FROM THE HILLS

Only two factors
Cause the wolves
To come down from the hills
And slip into the city
Only visible to heat seeking cameras
And careful to move
When no one is watching the screens
It is either that the high ground
Has itself become untenable
Or that the city dwellers
Have finally revealed
Their fatal weakness
But reasons seem hardly valid
Except as the subject of pointless
Already too late debate

❑ Fears of Armageddon
may look to the wilderness
for metaphors.

I mean, what matters?
Who can profit?
When the wolves
Are not only waiting
But the hunger is in their eyes

Written for the Deviants' CD, *Dr. Crow*, 2002

SPACE ODDITY

❑ To keep watching the skies is never a bad idea. In 1994, the Shoemaker-Levy comet plunged into the atmosphere of Jupiter sparking a mini-panic over scenarios of possible catastrophe. This celestial impact caused no problems, but three years later, in March 1997, a character called Marshall Applewhite convinced thirty-eight followers of his Heaven's Gate cult to commit mass suicide when the Hale-Bop comet became visible in the sky. Applewhite claimed that a UFO was trailing the comet, and it would transport their souls to another "level of existence above human." Lethal doses of phenobarbital were mixed with applesauce and washed down with vodka, and plastic bags were also used to induce asphyxia-

WHEN THE COMET KNOWN AS SHOEMAKER-LEVY 9 begins crashing into Jupiter at just before 1pm on Saturday, it will be one of the most significant astronomical events ever witnessed, and the culmination of the largest coordinated effort by astronomers, who hope that the impact will provide answers to many questions that have hung over comets since the beginning of time. The cosmic collision may also provide, in a year in which the movie industry has decided that blowing stuff up is the hot ticket, the biggest explosion ever seen inside the solar system. The impact death of Shoemaker-Levy could trigger a series of blasts, each one equal to ten million hydrogen bombs being detonated simultaneously.

Named after its discoverers, Eugene and Caroline Shoemaker and David Levy, the comet—described by Levy as "the strangest object we had ever seen"—was first spotted in early 1993. Whereas most comets have a single solid core and a gaseous tail streaming behind, Shoemaker-Levy 9 appeared as "a string of pearls, a train of solid cores hanging by a gaseous thread, one of the most beautiful astronomical discoveries in decades." Computer projections by Paul Chordas at the Jet Propulsion Laboratory, in Pasadena, seem to indicate that, until maybe twenty years ago, the comet was a small dark rock orbiting the sun. Then, in the early seventies, the rock was captured by Jupiter's crushing gravity and locked into a wildly erratic and slowly decaying orbit. Ultimately doomed, the comet circled Jupiter in a distorted ellipse until July 1992, when the stress caused it

MICK FARREN

to fragment into its current romantic glory.

Although speculation is intense as to what may happen when Shoemaker-Levy finally hits, no one, not even Levy or the Shoemakers, is sure. The smart money is on one of four possible scenarios:

1 The comet will break up into tiny fragments that will have little or no effect, except maybe to briefly change the massive planet's coloration.
2 The comet will fragment to a lesser degree, producing a brief bright flash as it burns up in Jupiter's methane-and-ammonia atmosphere.
3 The Shoemaker-Levy pearls will remain largely intact to a depth of some fifteen miles into Jupiter's atmosphere, creating a fountain of gas that could plume out hundreds of thousands of miles into space.
4 (And this is the really fun option!) The pearls could plunge deep into the Jovian atmosphere, to the point where the pressure is so great that hydrogen exists as a metal, creating an apocalyptic explosion, the results of which are anyone's guess.

Disobligingly, Shoemaker-Levy will hit Jupiter on the side facing away from the Earth, and, unless scenario three or four comes to pass, even when the impact area turns on our direction a little less than an hour later, still nothing will be visible except through a good telescope. Fortunately, a number of space vehicles—*Galileo, Voyager 2, Ulysses,* and *Clementine*—are close enough to Jupiter to send back pictures. Although, as a dour NASA press officer informed me, "The problems with *Galileo's* antenna will mean we won't have clear pictures for two or three months."

Oddly, with all these fun and games going on in space, the media have remained stubbornly earthbound. The tabloid *Sun* predictably shrieked that the comet crash would create a "deadly ice age here on Earth," and even the *Los Angeles Times* seemed more concerned with whether something similar could happen here, devoting more than half of its coverage to paranoid maunderings about the

tion. The dead were dressed in identical black shirts and sweat pants, brand new black-and-white Nike Windrunners and armband patches reading "Heaven's Gate Away Team." Six of the males had also undergone castration.

extinction of the dinosaurs, ancient impact craters, and near-misses by asteroids. Only *Omni*, in its July issue, assumed we were interested in anything beyond our own self-involved backyards. Without a guarantee of spectacular pictures, the local TV stations and even CNN seemed uncertain of how they will handle the comet.

To make an event of Shoemaker-Levy, my only recommendation is to take a picnic to the Griffith Park Observatory. You still won't see anything, but at least you could celebrate the String of Pearls' death in a suitably astronomical setting, while the bust of James Dean looks incongruously on. You'd also be on high ground should the tabloid catastrophe actually come to pass.

LA Reader, July 1994

FUN IN THE FINAL DAYS

❑ You may be noticing round about now that a great deal of this end-of-the-world stuff is written from the point of view of Los Angeles. This may be more than mere location. For the English adventurer, California can resemble the end of the world. The young man just keeps traveling west as instructed until he runs into the Pacific Ocean. What then? The world ends and the dilemma is born. To go further is circumnavigation. It's hello Tokyo and the Far East. Thus this short story—that pretends the most dire tab-

IN LOS ANGELES THE ASTEROID'S NEXT RISING WOULD be just before sunset. That's what the weatherman on the Channel Two Noontime News had said, and Carter had no reason to doubt him. Now the orbit had stabilized, the damn thing had become wholly predictable. Timing the phases of the asteroid was about all that TV was good for in what he'd started to think of as these Final Days. There were now only three broadcast channels left on the air and two of those were being run by teams of ghoulishly demented technicians. Channel Five had just completed a forty-eight-hour marathon of disaster movies without commercial interruption. It had started with *Panic in Year Zero* and concluded with *When Worlds Collide*. Prior to that, they had played the same Cal Worthington used car commercial over and over again to the point where Carter, watching in morbid fascination to see how long they'd keep it up, had feared for his sanity and finally changed the channel. "Buy a new car for your wife / She will love you all your life / Go see Cal, go see Cal, go see Cal." The jingle had gone relentlessly on, hour after hour, until the

MICK FARREN

only people left watching were three cracked out cholos somewhere in South Central.

CBS alone still flew the flag of the people's right to know; the kind of millionaires who owned local television stations had long since abandoned the business of business, turned the asylum over to the lunatics and were busily trying to buy and bribe their way into one or another of the alleged safe spots—Australia, Lapland, Nepal, or maybe Java. The rumors of places that might survive changed almost daily so the millionaires had their work cut out. One Tokyo property baron had attempted to set up a consortium to send a highly exclusive refugee rocket to Mars until the scientific community had pointed out that being stuck on Mars with no home-planet backup would probably be a worse fate than to be on Earth when the asteroid hit. At least that would be fast. Better than waiting until the last oxygen tank ran out.

Despite all the "what ifs" and the "maybes" and wishfully thought out avenues of escape, humanity knew, somewhere deep in its gut, that it didn't have much chance of recovering from this one. The asteroid was big and dense and it had been coming straight for the Earth ever since it had first been spotted ten months earlier. The damage that it had caused already was bad enough. After the earthquakes, LA was a mess, San Francisco was worse and Mexico City was history. New York was still recovering from the tidal wave, half of London was under water, and Athens was wholly under martial law. Cairo was still burning and Calcutta didn't bear thinking about. This wasn't a movie. Sean Connery or Paul Newman wasn't going to strap a bunch of H-bombs to this baby and blow it back into the deeps of space from whence it had come while the world held its breath and Shelley Winters freaked out. This time it was for real. About the only consolation was it was a purely random, freak-of-nature disaster. In no way could man seriously claim that he had brought it on himself. For Carter, there was a peculiar, if grim, satisfaction in this knowledge.

The gut feeling didn't stop humanity hoping, however.

loid predictions really have come to pass—all takes place within a ten buck cab ride of my home. But the same geography has been in 1,000 movies, so it's familiar to the entire planet.

One of the favorite "maybes" was "maybe it won't hit the Earth at all. Maybe it'll just go into orbit and we'll have an extra moon." When it did what appeared to be exactly that, a wave of relief swept round the world and the tabloids trumpeted that we'd all been saved. Then Carl Sagan went on TV with the bad news. Everyone's favorite pop astronomer seemed almost to relish telling how the reprieve was purely temporary and that, with the asteroid zipping around the planet in a mere seven hours, its orbit was far too fast and, by the standard of moons, far too low. Ultimately it would decay and the asteroid would smash into the Earth, probably stripping off the atmosphere as it took the final plunge. It was after that broadcast that things began to get really bizarre. Just one day later, an astrophysicist who had been brought on to explain the facts and figures behind the bad news, had been torn to pieces live on *The David Letterman Show*, by an audience who apparently held him personally responsible. That incident had closed as many TV stations as the fleeing millionaires. There was a rumor that Letterman had shot himself after the show in a fit of bourbon and remorse, but nobody knew for sure.

The naming of the asteroid had been an early example of prime farce. A nationwide TV poll had come up with the name Bluto, with Caligula running a close second. Bluto was starting to catch on until a conference of world leaders got together, headed by the venerable Margaret Thatcher, and, for once acting as one, declared that the designated official title of the asteroid was Damocles. Apparently naming it for the arch-nemesis of Popeye the Sailorman wasn't sufficiently dignified. Privately, Carter still tended to think of the asteroid as Bluto.

Carter went out onto the third floor terrace of the house in the Hollywood Hills to watch the asteroid come up. All but one of his neighbors in the apartment building, along with maybe two thirds of the population of greater Los Angeles, had fled the city after the five nights of rioting and looting, leaving it to the fatalistic, the ambivalent and the weird. The other tenants: the two lawyers, the cocaine dealer, the rock'n'roll manager, the movie director and his

German girlfriend, and the blonde with the Porsche were all gone, headed out for the imagined safety of the mountains or desert. Only he and Leiberman were left and the two of them had the run of the building. Leiberman had also come out to watch the rising of the asteroid. The two men nodded to each other but didn't speak. Leiberman was a very private individual who showed signs of nervousness when anyone engaged him in anything more than the most cursory of conversations. Carter suspected that he was probably a solitary drunk. The third floor terraces looked out over low-rise residential Hollywood towards the cluster of downtown towers, the abandoned monoliths of banks and insurance companies that had lost their glass in the fury of the big shake. There had been quakes all round the Pacific Ring as Damocles' gravity began to stress the Earth's tectonic plates. The one in LA had come close to nine on the Richter scale and eyewitnesses told how the glass of downtown had cascaded like razor-sharp rain and the streets had run with blood.

From where he was standing, the asteroid would come in from directly behind the towers. No matter how many times Damocles rose from the haze on the horizon, there was always a first chill of fear, if for no other reason than that the thing was so damn big. At first it was a shimmering blob of white light distorted by the heat and dust of the atmosphere. As it mounted higher, however, it seemed to completely fill the eastern sky, ten or twelve times the apparent size of the sun or moon. It bore down on those who looked at it as though it were coming directly for them. The surface details were frighteningly clear, like a huge overhead relief map of circular impact craters; deserts of gray-white ash and mountain ranges of jagged black rock, airless, desolate, and bent on remaking the world of men in its own image. When it eclipsed the sun, as it all too regularly did, the city was thrown into a twilight of blue shadows, an unavoidable portent of the coming end. The sunset sky behind Carter was blood-red from the huge quantities of dust that hung in the air in the aftermath of the quakes, the volcanic eruptions and the hundreds of fires that burned unchecked. Another chilling reminder that the end of everything was all too probably at hand.

On the other side of the canyon, someone was playing their sound system cranked to the max—'Fun, Fun, Fun' by the Beach Boys. Carter muttered to himself. "Yeah right, Fun in the Final Days."

Carter had discovered that one way to maintain his sanity was, as far as humanly possible, to ignore the on-rush of destiny and the threatening grandeur of the skies, and concentrate as much as he could on small everyday details. These at least had a certain comforting consistency. Right at this moment he was out of beer. He had to go out and get more. This, on its own, might prove a suicidal ex-ercise. The streets were in the hands of the violent and the homicidal, dog-packs of psychopaths, running unchecked except by the random helicopter sweeps by the police and the National Guard. Carter had decided that, deep down, he must be a fatalist. If making a beer run meant that he ran the risk of being embroidered by bullets, fired by some twelve-year-old with an assault rifle, or blown away by mistake by the trigger-happy door gunner of a Cobra gunship, so be it. It'd be quick and clean. Lately, he'd been thinking a lot about quick clean exits.

Since everyone but Leiberman had gone, Carter had taken to driving the immaculate black Thunderbird that had been abandoned by the coke dealer, keys in the igni-tion, in his hurry to get on the last plane to Lima. Carter had wondered why the coke dealer had picked Peru as a refuge. Maybe it was the time honored instinct of head-ing for the high ground and Lima was the highest ground known to his profession. The T-Bird was certainly a hell of an improvement on his own beat-up Monte Carlo.

He drove down Crescent Heights and made a left onto Santa Monica Boulevard. A police Huey had ploughed into the Security Pacific Bank on the corner and exploded and burned. There was debris covering half the intersec-tion. He had heard a bang during the previous night but there were so many bangs in the night these days that he hadn't even bothered to go to the window and take a look.

The Nazis had marched last night. A five-block-long procession of fanatics in lockstep, shadowed by helicopters above the palm trees that watched but chose to do nothing. The flames of the Nazis' torches had been clearly visible from his vantage point in the hills. Their signs and burned out flares and torches still littered the streets. The majority of the signs bore a single word: *Ragnarok*, the twilight of the gods. The Nazis seemed to be using the event of the asteroid as an excuse to add a twist of Nordic death mysticism to their more mundane hatred. They treated the impending disaster as a visitation from Wotan that demanded blood sacrifice. They came with a crash of marching drums and engineer boots, singing the old SA beer hall songs they'd learned from limited edition records bought mail order through *Soldier of Fortune* magazine. Skinheads with swastika tattoos, uniform freaks in neat black and red, wearing visored motorcycle helmets and carrying plexiglass riot shields, Aryan Brotherhood jailhouse trash with Gary Gilmore eyes and camouflage jackets, toting pump shotguns and AK47s; they all roared out the traditional German lyrics probably without understanding a word of them. Their plan had been to move east, crisscrossing the area between Santa Monica and Hollywood Boulevard, driving out what they perceived as the scum, the mud people. A night of final solution before the apocalypse.

Fortunately they were stopped at Vista Street, in front of the Astroburger, by an army of heavily armed gays, bronzed hustlers in tank tops and cutoffs, with M16s at the ready, lesbians with .357 magnums and drag queens with Uzis slung like shoulder bags. The street was still half blocked by barricades of burned out cars and the Astroburger itself had been totalled by what must have been an anti-tank rocket from the Nazi side. Carter thought that he saw bodies in the shadow of an overturned *Los Angeles Times* delivery truck but he didn't look too closely. A knot of defenders was still keeping a watchful vigil with guns over their shoulders. They eyed the T-Bird suspiciously as he drove by. It was a hell of a context for a beer run. He turned on the radio. KRAM was still on the air.

Talking Heads' 'Burning Down The House' was followed by 'No, No, Bluto' by a cowpunk band called Hank's Skull. So someone else thought of the asteroid as Bluto.

So far, Carter had seen hardly any traffic. It was still daylight and most of those who'd elected to remain in the city tended to live like vampires, coming out only after dark or not coming out at all. Not that there would be much darkness even after the sun had gone. With the asteroid climbing in the sky, the world would be bathed in the ghostly monochrome of its reflected light. He was actually quite surprised when the convoy of pickup trucks came racing towards him down Santa Monica, going in the opposite direction. There were four of them, jockeying for position, running what traffic lights were still working at speeds close to 100 miles an hour. They were packed with bikini clad or naked teenagers, drunk out of their minds and howling mindlessly. The lead driver spotted Carter's T-Bird and decided to play chicken. The truck was coming straight at him, a candy orange, metalflake monster with chrome crashbars and giant oversized wheels. Carter spun his steering wheel. He had nothing to prove except that he was well aware how multiple vehicular suicide was a popular way of going out in a blaze of glory. His front wheels mounted the sidewalk and he jammed on the brakes. The truck flashed by with only a couple of feet to spare, leaving a slipstream of screaming laughter. Carter sagged back in his seat.

"This is getting fucking ridiculous."

The power was on at La Brea and a handmade sign on a lamp-post read BEER THIS WAY. An arrow pointed north. It was almost certainly a rip artist selling off the load from a hijacked truck. It would be expensive but it was better than driving around, hunting for a supermarket or liquor store that was still intact. The beer dealers had set up shop on the parking lot of the gutted Mayfair Market. Two semi-trucks with Mexican license plates were drawn up side by side and cases of Corona and Dos Equis were being sold directly off the back for quadruple the regular price. An individual beer was five bucks, a six pack sold for twenty-five while a case went for eighty. Carter had always imagined that, in a time of disaster, money would hardly matter. Who needed cash if Godzilla was eating Tokyo? As it turned out, he couldn't have been more wrong. In these final days, money seemed to be everything. Street inflation was running at around 400 percent. Money was the means to the end, the grease that it took to do all those things you'd never done before. The transactions were monitored by a security goon squad of burly biker types with ball bats and shotguns and the beer sale was an orderly affair by the standards of the time.

It had also attracted a very strange gathering of people. An LAPD cruiser was pulled up at the curb. There were two cops inside but, instead of protecting and serving, they were drinking Scotch straight from the bottle and pawing a couple of women who were all but out of their clothes. Since the arrival of the asteroid, casual sex had come back in a big way. Who gave a damn about catching a retro virus if you weren't going to live long enough for it to incubate? A roller-skater in shorts and a headband circled glumly, sucking on a half gallon of cheap Chablis. The speed at which he was drinking made it something of a miracle that he could maintain his control. Stooped figures were picking through the debris in the dark interior of the supermarket.

Carter had no idea why the girl picked on him. Maybe it was because of the car or maybe it was for no reason at all. He'd bought his beer and was getting ready to drive away. He'd gone for the full case plus a bottle of very dubious Scotch. It was hardly the time to economize. She was a California sun baby with one of those tans, not at all unlike the one with the Porsche who had lived in his building. She left nothing to the imagination with the short leather miniskirt, cowboy boots and a bike jacket unzipped to expose bare breasts.

" You want to give me a ride?"

"Where to."

"It doesn't really matter."

Her eyes were glazed and she'd plainly been stoned or

something or the other for longer than she was capable of remembering. She was chewing gum as though her mouth was chronically dry. Carter patted the case of beer on the seat beside him.

"I was planning to go home and drink this?"

"You want company?"

Carter nodded. "Why not."

As he transferred the beer to the back seat, she opened the passenger door and climbed in beside him. He gunned the T-Bird out of the lot and turned up towards Hollywood Boulevard. On the radio, the Rolling Stones informed them that rape and murder were just a shot away. Carter glanced up at the huge disc of the asteroid. It was now about halfway to its zenith and the Earth's shadow was just starting to creep across it. Everyday was full moon madness with that sucker around. He turned to the girl. "What's your name?"

She looked at him blankly. "Morgan." She seemed to be having trouble focusing, but she did have exceedingly nice breasts.

"My name is Carter and I live up in Laurel Canyon."

She nodded. "It really doesn't matter." She eased back into the red leather of the passenger seat stretching herself like a cat. "Do you have any speed?"

Carter shook his head. "I don't."

Drugs had also come back in a big way. With only weeks to go, nobody said no to anything. "I've been doing speed for days. I never want to sleep again You know what I mean?" She stabbed an index finger at the asteroid overhead. "If that thing's going to get us, I don't want to miss anything. I want all the life I can get. You think it's going to get us?"

Carter nodded. "Seems that way."

"I've got to get some more speed."

The inevitable crowds on Hollywood Boulevard were moving aimlessly in the gray Bluto light. It made them look like the night of the living dead. Morgan insisted that they drive down for a few blocks. Armed guards in quasi-military uniforms protected the Scientology build ing. Even in the Final Days, the children of Hubbard were protecting their own. A metal band had set up a mountain of equipment in front of the Roosevelt Hotel and was blasting out hundreds of decibels of uncontrolled feedback. Jimi Hendrix would be turning in his grave. Morgan leaned close to Carter and yelled in his ear. "You want to pull over and stop?"

Carter shook his head. "Not really."

The kids basking in the noise in front of the makeshift bandstand looked to be totally out of their minds. One bunch had their clothes off and was group fucking and doing the soul fry right there on the Walk of the Stars.

"I badly need to get more speed."

"We'll figure something out."

Crude pentagrams had been daubed all over the outside of the Chinese Theatre. Morgan looked at the mess as though it was the most natural thing in the world. "Satanists. They've been busy in the Valley already. I even heard that they sprung Manson out of San Quentin."

"Great."

"They're supposed to be holding human sacrifices out in Malibu. You think being a human sacrifice might be the way to go? At least you'd be the center of attention."

He wondered if he should drop her off right there and then. Carter didn't want to be alone, but he didn't know if he could handle the woman's amphetamine mood swings. Self-protection was of primary importance. In the end, he opted for the company and the possible fantasy of sex. He hoped that he wouldn't regret the decision. The problem with allowing himself to be picked up by strange women was exactly that. They were strange. It was the Groucho syndrome. He wasn't sure that he wanted to go home with any woman who'd want to go home with him. Since the coming of Bluto, Groucho's maxim tended to go double.

He parked the T-Bird in the garage and steered Morgan toward the elevator. She was telling some long and impenetrably complex story about the sexual convolutions of three people he didn't know and probably didn't want to know. When he'd first discovered the abandoned T-Bird with the keys in it, he'd also found that there were keys to the guy's apartment on the same ring. Carter had taken a look round the flat on that first day but since then, he hadn't been in there and certainly hadn't used the place for anything. Now seemed to be exactly the right time to break it in. The pimp-chic decor, the big Sony projection TV and the extensive library of porno and junk-movie tapes seemed the ideal setting for the kind of brief and twisted liaison that was all he could imagine taking place between Morgan and himself. He had also discovered a small stash of left-behind cocaine in a silver cigarette box on a bookshelf. That would probably be of help to the girl in her bid to beat the world freefall record for staying awake.

The apartment was deliberately dark, decorated in Bat Cave dark blue and purple. As he opened the drapes on the Hollywood night, the first thing he saw was the asteroid, now a broad, thinning crescent in the western sky. Morgan took one look at it and turned her back with a shudder. "I hate that fucking thing. It sucks out my brain."

Carter's first move was to cut out three long lines on the glass cube of a coffee table. After that, it was inevitable that they should have sex. It happened on the big, circular waterbed with the black cover and canopy. It was impersonal to the point of being robotic. Her mouth tasted metallic and her movements were so detached and disjointed that Carter wondered if she was there with him at all in anything but body. Afterwards, he started drinking Scotch so he'd be drunk enough to fall asleep. She sat cross-legged and naked, wearing a pair of black Raybans that the coke dealer had left behind, staring as though hypnotized at the enormous TV screen.

"Carter?" She was inscrutable behind the sunglasses. "Aren't you afraid of dying?"

"Sure, terrified."

"How do you keep going?" He held up the half empty Scotch bottle. "I drink and I console myself that, as far as death goes there's only one per customer." He rolled over, spilling Scotch on the waterbed. He was already quite dizzy. "Actually, I'm happy to be seeing all this going on. If you gotta go, a rogue asteroid certainly beats the hell out of brain cancer."

Soon after that, he passed out. When he came to again she'd gone. The cocaine and the Raybans had gone with her. The TV was still running. It was the Channel Two early news. The entire congregation of the First Church of Pentecostal Redemption in Santa Ana had taken themselves out in Jonestown-style, poisoned Kool-Aid mass suicide. He crawled painfully from the waterbed. He turned off the TV and stepped out onto the terrace. The day was breaking but the now black shadow shape of Damocles/Bluto was already casting a pall as it once again rose from behind the skeletons of the downtown towers. Jim Morrison was singing about the "bloody red sun of fantastic LA" from the open patio doors of the house with the loud sound system on the other side of the canyon. Beneath the song there was a cacophonous undertow of other jumbled rock'n'roll from a dozen different sources. Ten or more columns of dark smoke rose from various points in the city. One of the tallest and most dense hung, as far as Carter could estimate, right over Hollywood Boulevard. Maybe the Satanists had teamed up with the metal kids for a day of boogie and sacrifice, head banging, throat slitting, and arson. Maybe Morgan had gone down there to volunteer as a sacrifice. The Doors were temporarily drowned out by the slapping rotor blades of a pair of National Guard gunships flying low and south on a seemingly pointless dawn patrol. Carter sighed. The Beach Boys had started up again on the sound system across the canyon. "Fun, fun, fun."

"This is the way the world ends. Not with a bang, but with a party."

He went back inside to see if Morgan had also taken the scotch.

From the anthology *More Tales Of The
Forbidden Planet*, 1990

MEANTIME LIFE OUTSIDE GOES ON ALL AROUND YOU

☐ We came into this section with "après moi, le déluge" and Madame de Pompadour. Was the magnificent courtesan foreshadowing existentialism with the idea that it all ended with her? The universe ends when the individual ceases to perceive it? This is one of the multi-choice, optional endings to very last episode of **The Sopranos**. We don't expect much existentialism from TV, but David Chase may have made his final curtain an exception. The malfunction-fast sudden cut to black may or may not have been the supposed—but never proven—death of Big Tony, but it was definitely the omni-termination of the **Soprano** universe.

THE MARMALADE CAT SITS ON THE SIDEWALK OUTSIDE Satriale's pork store, and stares at Paulie Walnuts. The marmalade cat that came in from the rain has already spooked Paulie by habitually staring at a picture Christopher Moltistanto—terminated with extreme and bloody prejudice by Tony Soprano himself just two episodes earlier. Symbolic creatures are not unknown in the eighty-six episodes of *The Sopranos*—regulars will recall the ducks, the bear, the racehorse, and the goat. Many are also aware, including Paulie Walnuts, that, in *The Godfather* trilogy, that orange is the symbol of death. The stray cat is orange, and Paulie wants to drown it, but the cat is under Tony's protection. Will this flip Paulie to psycho-slay Tony? If *The Sopranos* is to end with Tony's demise, Paulie is the last possible threat we know about. Phil Leotardo, the designated nemesis, has already been dispatched—unpleasantly but fast—and peace has been brokered with New York. The one-hour show is now in its fifty-first minute, and Tony is still alive, fat if not sassy. My viewer tension is so stretched that I want a cigarette, and I haven't smoked in over a year. But Paulie does nothing. We bid him farewell, working on his winter tan with a cardboard reflector, watched by the cat he loathes.

The final episode is now into overtime. As the entire Soprano family meet in a Jersey diner, the sequence is cut with pace and angles that would normally foreshadow a massacre. At first, Tony is alone and vulnerable. A guy in a baseball cap has a hint of not-quite-right. Tony flips through the selections on an old school, at-the-table jukebox, and punches up Tony Bennett. Carmela arrives. Then two men enter, one is Anthony Jr., but the other's a stranger. Coincidental anticlimax? The stranger sits at the counter, acting indefinably twitchy. Two black kids come in. Outside, Meadow has trouble parking. The others eat onion rings. The Twitchy Guy goes the bathroom—like Michael in *The Godfather?* The door of the diner has a bell. It tinkles. We assume it's the arrival Meadow, but…

But let's back up a moment. To accept *The Sopranos* one needs to accept that America doesn't really like virtue. We might maintain a pretense of admiring the good and the selfless, because we feel it's expected of us, but we cleave to the plausible rogue, or even the downright evil son-of-a-bitch, as long as he or she has the necessary measure of charm. We prefer Dracula to Van Helsing, or Billy the Kid to Pat Garrett. We mythologize our criminals and outlaws. In the fables of capitalism, they live outside the law but, by their own criteria, they are honest. Plus they represent a faster and more romantic route from rags to riches.

Through the whole saga of *The Sopranos*, creator David Chase has taken great pains to avoid making Tony the wise all-knowing Don—another patriarchal Vito Corleone. When we like him—or forgive him—too much, we are reminded of the murderous narcissistic sociopath that lurks beneath the sentimentality. The task has never been easy. James Gandolfini has always been too adept at making Tony plausibly pleasant. Even our culture is against him. In a society where the whorehouses were routinely shut down for elections and reopened right after, and morality was frequently nothing more than a hypocritical shell game, the criminal—especially the organized criminal—gave the people what they wanted rather than judgmentally deciding what they might need. Booze, drugs, gambling, prostitution? No problem. Cities with well-organized crime were (and are) always more fun, and though we tell ourselves that it takes its social toll in terms of a mob-skim on everything from gambling to garbage collection, that's only faux-puritan rationalization. We like our gangsters because they have the sharpest suits, the luxury rides, and they die flamboyantly.

In the penultimate episode, it certainly seemed all roads led to flamboyant death. Bobby Baccalieri was dead and Silvio Dante in a coma. The Di Meo crime family had gone to the matresses anticipating war with New York. Tony cradled a monster .50 calibre assualt rifle, and a bloodbath appeared inevitable. Speculation about *The Sopranos* finale, and how David Chase was going the wrap seven years of our Sunday nights even made the cover of the *New Yorker*, and I read it all. Some cited Anthony Jr.'s morbid fascination with W.B. Yeats' 'The Second Coming' as the key metaphor—"And what rough beast, its hour come round at last / Slouches towards Bethlehem to be born?" Others reminded us how the 2006 series opened to the soundtrack of Material's 'Seven Souls,' featuring William Burroughs reading from his novel *The Western Lands* about the ancient Egyptian belief that, in death, the body gives up seven souls. Many critics down the years, have likened *The Sopranos* to *Macbeth*, with Tony and Carmela advancing to their respective crowns over the bodies of the betrayed. But these comparisons always postulated an ultimate McDuff that would bring down Tony and the whole House of Soprano. Chase, however, has offered us no McDuff for this final episode.

Initially the wrap seems strictly domestic. All in the family, so to speak. The mob war fails to materialize, and each of the principles more or less come to terms with their position and place. Even Anthony Jr. mitigates his angst. Aside from the death of Phil Leotardo, the only real drama is when Anthony Jr., commencing to make love to his hot but underage new girlfriend, manages to set fire to his SUV to the accompaniment of Bob Dylan's 'It's Alright Ma (I'm Only Bleeding)'—("It's amazing it was written so long ago.") At the moment of almost-consumation, the line "*I got nothing, ma, to live up to*" is so apt, it's intrusive.

But as the episode moves on and no shock is delivered, the scarcely believable idea forms that maybe Chase has written an ending to *The Sopranos* that is gentle and mundane. Is that the real message of the Dylan song? "*Meantime life outside goes on all around you*"? In the end, is the only *Macbeth* connection to Act V, Scene V? Tony is just one more poor player who "*struts and frets his hour upon the stage and then is heard no more: it is a tale told by an idiot, full of sound and fury, signifying nothing.*"

Except to relax into the mundane is not so easy. David Chase is playing our own culture against us. Each time a car door is opened we wait for the explosion. Each an ticlimax builds on the last, all the way to this weird final scene. Superficially we are watching a New Jersey family in a conventional diner. But we know all the tricks and signals. Everyone has taught us, from Sam Peckinpah to Martin Scorsese, that this scene is fraught with danger. Every extra is a potential assassin. The bell on the door tinkles. Tony Soprano glances up. And, in that instant, the cut is to black-screen silence.

For a nanosecond, I think my cable is out or the TV has blown. What? And then as the first credit roles, I realize that's it. After all the years I've devoted to *The Sopranos*, the conclusion is yet another goddamned mystery wrapped in a riddle inside an enigma. Has Chase simply guillotined his epic with this bizarre and arbitrary cut, and the Soprano family will go on in their universe only we won't see them? Or is this death existential-style? Have we assumed Tony's POV? The Twitching Guy has come back unseen, gun in hand, and shot Tony in the back of the head. Carmela is screaming. Meadow has stopped in her tracks. The table is covering in blood. But the horror is for everyone else. Tony knows nothing. He is gone. His seven souls have left the building, proving your own death is something you don't have to live through.

I really don't know whether to be angry as hell or laugh my ass off.

LA CityBeat, June 2007

ATTACK OF THE GOD PARTICLES

THE GOD PARTICLES HAD RAISED A PYRAMID FOR THE purpose of worship, constructed from the dead eyes of burned out media receivers. The nano-thralls were in the bloodstream. We tingled as they commenced the full reconstruction. All too soon the membrane would be compromised and humanity would merge sufficiently with the other/nether so we would wholly cease to signify as an independent entity. Siegfried was doomed, but that

❑ Another approach is to face the end as an abstraction.

hardly mattered any more to anyone but Siegfried. Velma verged on happy. The bites of conversant data were now being delivered in progressively more minute packages. They would no longer hold complex concepts or even sustain sub-erotica. For Velma this was a relief. The bastions no longer vibrated and congealed into slow organic decay. They were instantly bypassed and erased from recall functions. The crucial remaining question was simply if it was safe to approach the pyramid? Or was this merely another phase of the entrapment. Maybe we had no remaining rights to be read to us. On the other hand, was it safe to remain where we were, and not to approach the pyramid? Previous God Particles had not taken kindly to rejection. Indeed, they had flamed with the rage of neglected courtesans, burning all before them into pink and black ash, and insisting it was the price of failure. We survivors had to face the fact. We didn't have the price of failure between us. We barely had enough for a round of drinks. Our options had run out. We approached the pyramid. But we approached it slowly. And with care.

Doc40, November 2009

THE LONESOME DEATH OF WANDA-JEAN

❏ So how does the dance end? What is the nature of our mortal exit? Bang, whimper, or some unknown fate to be named later? That is the human mystery, the human dilemma, and the human doubt. To hedge my bets, I'm closing this excursion with favorite climaxes from three of my novels. The first is kinda depressing—a tale of isola-

WANDA-JEAN MOVED LIKE A ZOMBIE. SHE WAS TRYING not to see the lounge of her cramped little flat. The only way to hold back the truth that she was back there was simply not to see it. It was the only way to hold back the much more awful truth that the adventure was over. Her pill box was clutched tightly in her hand. All was slow motion. Keeping her back very straight, she sank to the floor and crossed her legs.

She placed the box very carefully in front of her. She inspected it for a while, then she opened it and tipped the contents out on the floor. The collection had grown considerably since she'd been on the show. With painful method, she began to arrange the pills in neat rows: five

404

MICK FARREN

to a row. By the time she'd finished there were twelve of them, sixty pills. She studied the pattern of colors formed by the different pills and capsules. With infinite patience she started to rearrange them, until she realized that she was echoing the terrible game.

She didn't want to think about it. She stood up and went into the kitchen. She looked in the fridge. It was almost empty, just a piece of aging cheese and a container of water. She took the water out and went back into the lounge. Her next stop was at the booze cabinet. That too was thinly populated. About an inch-and-a-half remained in a bottle of Scotch.

Wanda-Jean resumed her cross-legged position on the floor. She set the whiskey and the water beside the box and pills. She had forgotten a glass. Almost impatiently she went and fetched one, and quickly squatted on the floor again. It was the first time she'd moved rapidly since she'd left the studio.

The bastards had let her go home in a fucking taxi. They hadn't even bothered to…

She wasn't going to think about that. She unscrewed the top of the whiskey bottle.

She one-third filled the glass. Next she stripped the seal from the water container and topped it up. She tasted it experimentally. She added a little more water. She tasted it again, and seemed satisfied.

She picked up the first pill, turned it over in her fingers and put it in her mouth. She sipped her drink and swallowed.

She took a second pill and then a third. She started to get into a kind of mindless rhythm. She took the pills in scrupulous order, up one row and down the next. Pick up the pill, place it on her tongue, sip Scotch and water, repeat the process.

She had worked her way through a third of them when she started to feel sick and a little dizzy. They couldn't be coming on so fast. It had to be her imagination. She got a grip on herself and pressed on.

The pills were half gone. The nausea hadn't faded. She

tion and despair written in the punk era. Wanda-Jean decides her life is no longer worth living when she is dropped from a reality TV game-show after a very brief taste of media attention and notoriety.

forced down five at once. She couldn't hold it together any more. Her hand started to shake. She couldn't get herself to control it any more. Wanda-Jean was afraid. She wanted to go, to end it, but she didn't want to go like this. She suddenly wanted to talk to someone. She needed desperately to talk to another human being. She got up. Her legs seemed a very long way away. It was difficult to breathe, and walk. She lurched to the wall and made a badly coordinated grab for the wall phone. At the first attempt she missed. On the second attempt she managed to get a grip on it. She put it to her ear.

"Can I help you?"

"Reuben?"

"Reuben's not here."

"I want to talk to Reuben."

"Reuben's not here."

"Reuben…"

"He's not here."

"I need to talk to him."

"I told you, lady, he's not here. It's his night off."

This was hard for Wanda-Jean to grasp. "Night off?"

"That's right."

"I don't understand."

"He gets a night off, just like everyone else."

"But I need to talk to him."

"You'll have to wait until tomorrow. There's no way to reach him now."

"Reuben."

"Listen, lady, I'm telling you he ain't here, so you can't speak to him. If you want to tell me about it maybe I can help, otherwise you'll just have to wait until Reuben gets back in tomorrow."

"I…"

"Are you okay?'

"… I…"

"I'm sorry, lady. I can't stay on the phone all night."

The colors around her had become strange. They seemed washed out and dead, as if they were slowly fading to black and white. Wanda-Jean felt terribly tired.

"… to…"

"Lady, I'm going to hang up on you, okay?"

It was very, very hard to stand. Things were fading around her. It was hard to make her thoughts work. She was drifting to an empty warm place. She'd be safe there. She wouldn't be…

Wanda-Jean's legs gave way. She slid down the wall and crumpled in a heap on the floor. Her head lolled onto her shoulder. Her eyes had rolled up into her head.

They didn't find her until three days later.

From the novel *The Feelies*, 1978

NOSFERATU IN THE NICK OF TIME

THEY CUT A PURPOSEFUL AND THREATENING SWATH through the fog and the madness, voluminously flapping black trench coats, wide-brimmed hats pulled forward over eyes that were already hidden behind dark glasses, leather-gloved hands that swung determinedly at their sides. Renquist himself carried the evil Japanese sword, sheathed like a slightly curved walking cane, but still unmistakable. Renquist and Lupo walked side by side, the seasoned warriors of the small but deadly task force. Dahlia trotted beside them, her small form swathed in a black Bedouin burnoose and her face fully veiled, skipping to keep pace. Segal and Brandon Wales flanked them, and the other women—Imogene, Sada, Julia, and Elaine—formed a second rank, while Nacza walked, equally proud, but a few yards off from the others like an outrider. Only Wales was without a long overcoat. He made do with the short snakeskin jacket. Crazy or not, all humans who saw them backed away and avoided looking into their shadowed faces. Amid the fog and the smoke from the fires, by the smashed windows and overturned cars, through the litter and debris, and with the warped perceptions of a mass contagious schizophrenia, the humans recognized the group's unstoppable power. If they didn't know them

❑ The second climax comes not a moment too soon as the world is rescued from ancient evil in the nick of time. In this instance the rescue is being performed by a colony of vampires, and the intervention is only performed out of a need to preserve their food supply, but this self-interest doesn't diminish from the drama, or the fact that the world is saved from a hideous H.P. Lovecraft fate.

for what they really were, they at least took them for dark Hollywood demigods from some hellish Western movie too dangerous for the screen.

The entire colony had left the Residence in three cars, and by dint of highly aggressive street driving and regular use of the sidewalk, they managed to bully their motorized way to within three blocks of the Apogee Building, but then they reached an impasse on Santa Monica Boulevard, where a stretch of the gridlock had been torched by vandals and the street made impassable by burned out hulks and charred chassis. From that point, they walked. Fast, and each with a killer's purpose, they continued, unhindered and unquestioned. As the building came into clear sight, Renquist looked up at the pylon on the top. Energy streamed down in a purple cascade of evil of a kind and intensity that Renquist had never seen before. He gestured to the others. "Observe, my friends, a sight not seen in 15,000 years. That is the arrival of the Great Cthulhu. He is not aware, however, that he has us to deal with."

From the novel *Darklost*, 2000

THE DNA COWBOYS WONDER WHAT TO DO NEXT

❏ In the third climax the great engines that support reality itself finally fail, and the universe discorporates, but—with a Zen-like persistence—everything is immediately reconstituted in a new and pristine form as the DNA Cowboys speculate, as always, on what they are going to do about it.

THE SHOCK WAVES SPREAD OUTWARDS THROUGH THE whole of the damaged world. They clashed, merged and formed more complex patterns of destruction. The stasis towns and generator cities went out one by one. Some, like Pleasant Gap, simply vanished as their generators broke down under the strain. Others disappeared in a far more spectacular manner. The glowing plain around Dogbreath erupted in a huge fireball that scorched the town to gray ash. Earthquakes and furious storms raged round both Con-Lec and Wainscote. In Con-Lec the great tower collapsed, and without the control equipment, the rest of the city slowly faded into the nothings. As the tremors shook Wainscote, he finally awoke and stalked the crumbling

MICK FARREN

corridors, turning the last frenzy of the eternal party into a nightmare. In Sade, the nightmare had already started before the shock waves even hit. The citizens were deep into the ceremony of the Wild Hunt, an orgy of suffering and slaughter that they justified as a ritual cleansing that purged the city of mutations and weaklings. The collapsing buildings and the rapidly spreading fires merely formed a scenic background to the final hideous celebration of pain. The small Roller community of Beth-Gilead saw the shock waves coming across the desert that surrounded their settlement. They took the form of huge, fast-moving dust clouds. As the light was finally blotted out, they assumed it was the wrath of their particularly disagreeable deity.

Recognizing their innate fallibility and sinfulness, the population knelt in silent prayer, and then simply switched off their generator and vanished. The brotherhood also accepted the end very calmly. They spent their last hours checking their calculations in the hope of finding the error that had prevented them predicting destruction on such a universal scale.

The wheelfreaks were about the only group who greeted the end with anything approaching glee. As the shock waves rolled down the road to Graveyard, a huge cavalcade of gleaming trucks massed on the parking lot. Gunning their motors and jockeying for position, they raced ahead towards the disrupting section of road. The wheelfreaks, at least, met the disaster with class.

BILLY AND THE MINSTREL BOY DROPPED OUT OF THE nothings. They landed hard on a sloping hillside of densely packed sand. The fall knocked the breath out of Billy, and he lay for a few minutes trying to recover. After a while he sat up. The Minstrel Boy seemed to be out cold.

The landscape was totally desolate. As far as Billy could tell they were on a small conical hillock of sand in the middle of the nothings. There was no water and no vegetation. There was no sign of inhabitants of any kind. Surprisingly, Billy found he wasn't worried by the situation. He was filled with a feeling of lethargic, untroubled wellbeing.

THE FUTURE'S UNCERTAIN...

It was something like being stoned. He leaned over and grasped the Minstrel Boy by the shoulder. He shook him "Hey, wake up. We've arrived somewhere."

The Minstrel Boy opened his eyes. "Huh?"

"We've arrived somewhere."

The Minstrel Boy raised his head. "So I see."

Billy lay back on the sand and took a deep satisfied breath. "I think I'm going to like it here. Do you know where we are?"

The Minstrel Boy closed his eyes and concentrated Billy was a little surprised that he'd made no protest. After about a minute he opened them again and shook his head

"That's weird."

"What's weird?"

"It's gone."

"You mean you've lost your gift?"

"Not my gift."

"What then?"

The Minstrel Boy frowned. Then he grinned crookedly "I think I've lost the rest of the world."

"What?"

"It's gone. It's not there anymore. As far as I can tell, this is all that's left."

"You're kidding?"

"I'm not."

"This is all that's left?"

Billy started to giggle.

"That's absurd."

The Minstrel Boy stood up.

"Maybe it isn't."

He began to climb the slope towards the summit of the mound. When he reached the top he stood looking down He glanced back at Billy. "You'd better come up here."

Billy struggled to his feet. "What is it?"

"Come and see for yourself."

Billy made his way up the slope. The top of the mound dropped away into a shallow depression. The Minstrel Boy pointed down into it. "Look."

In the bottom was a clutch of large gold eggs. There

were nine in all. Each one was about half the height of a man. Billy looked at the Minstrel Boy. "What are they?"

The Minstrel Boy shrugged. "I don't know for sure."

"You sound as though you've got a theory."

The Minstrel Boy laughed. "Yeah, I've got a theory. A peach. I think we are looking at our superiors. Us humans finally screwed up, just in time for whatever's in those eggs to take over."

Before Billy could answer, a loud tapping came from inside one of the eggs. The air took on the kind of heavy stillness that usually precedes a storm. Billy looked anxiously at the Minstrel Boy. "What's happening?"

"I think they're about to hatch."

The Minstrel Boy took Billy by the arm.

"Let's go back down the slope. I don't think I really want to see them come out of the eggs."

They went almost to the edge of the nothings. A high singing sound filled the air. It was pitched at the uppermost range audible to a human ear. Billy glanced at the Minstrel Boy. "Do you think they'll harm us?"

"I doubt it."

The nothings began to recede. They slowly slid back, leaving bare, totally smooth ground. Soon there was solid ground, all the way to the horizon. The Minstrel Boy watched with awe. "They're reconstructing the world. They're putting everything back together again. Their power must be immense."

Billy glanced doubtfully at the top of the mound. "Do you think there are any other humans left?"

The Minstrel Boy shrugged. "Maybe, maybe not. There certainly aren't many."

"What will happen to us?"

The Minstrel Boy looked at him in surprise. "How the hell should I know?"

From the novel *The Neural Atrocity*, 1977

WE'RE ALIVE!

But the news is not always bad. I posted the following on **Doc40**, on July 23, 2009, after a total eclipse of the sun and in the wake of a minor Internet doom-panic.

SEEMINGLY THE WORLD HAS SURVIVED THE TOTAL eclipse over Asia. The Wheel of the Dharma did not grind to a halt. The axis did not tilt. The poles did not hop to a reversal. The tectonic plates are still where they were yesterday. The Reptile Men did not emerge from their caves in Tibet. The Vril did not manifest. Children did not act in paranormal unison. The Yangtze did not run red with blood, and as far as I know, the Earth is not hurling towards the black hole at the epicenter of the Milky Way. Pretty good. Pretty neat, as Jim Morrison once remarked.

Doc40, July 2009

Index

MICK FARREN

A HEADPRESS BOOK
First published by Headpress in 2012

Headpress, Unit 365, 10 Great Russell Street, London, WC1B 3BQ, United Kingdom
Tel 0845 330 1844   *Email* headoffice@headpress.com

ELVIS DIED FOR SOMEBODY'S SINS BUT NOT MINE
A Lifetime's Collected Writing

A CIP catalogue record for this book is available from the British Library

ISBN 978-1-900486-92-7 (pbk)
ISBN 978-1-909394-00-1 (ebk)
NO ISBN (hbk)

Headpress. The gospel according to unpopular culture.

NO ISBN special edition hardbacks are available exclusively from World Headpress

WWW.WORLDHEADPRESS.COM

Lightning Source UK Ltd.
Milton Keynes UK
UKOW041623210513

211035UK00002B/3/P